THE OCTOBER

ASAF SINIVER

(*editor*)

The October 1973 War

Politics, Diplomacy, Legacy

HURST & COMPANY, LONDON

First published in the United Kingdom in 2013 by
C. Hurst and Co. (Publishers) Ltd.,
41 Great Russell Street, London, WC1B 3PL
© Asaf Siniver and the Contributors, 2012
All rights reserved.

The right of Asaf Siniver and the Contributors to be identified as
the authors of this publication is asserted by them in accordance
with the Copyright, Designs and Patents Act, 1988.

A Cataloguing-in-Publication data record for this book
is available from the British Library.

ISBN: 978-1-84904-296-3

This book is printed using paper from registered sustainable
and managed sources.

www.hurstpublishers.com

CONTENTS

CONTENTS

LIST OF CONTRIBUTORS

Dr Philipp O. Amour is a Postdoctoral Fellow at the Department of Politics and International Relations, University of Oxford. He was a doctoral Visiting Fellow at the Center for Arab and Middle Eastern Studies, American University of Beirut and at Birzeit University in the Palestinian territories (2007–9). His research examines modern political transformation and the cultural history of the Palestinians, for which he has been awarded the Swiss National Science Foundation Fellowship for prospective PhD researcher (2009) and for prospective postdoctoral researcher (2011). He is presently a visiting Assistant Professor at the department of Political Science and International Relations, Boğaziçi University.

Ms Carly Beckerman-Boys is a Junior Research Fellow at the Global Policy Institute and a Doctoral Researcher in the Department of Political Science and International Studies, University of Birmingham. Her research focuses on the Arab–Israeli conflict, foreign policy analysis and contemporary British foreign policy.

Dr Ahron Bregman was born in Israel. After six years of army service, during which he took part in the 1982 Lebanon War he left the army to work at the Knesset as a parliamentary assistant. He studied in Jerusalem and London, completing a doctorate in War Studies at King's College London in 1994. He is the author of *The Fifty Years War* (Penguin, 1998, with Jihan el-Tahri), the companion book to a six-part BBC television documentary and its sequel *Elusive Peace* (Penguin, 2005), the companion book to a three-part BBC television documentary; also of *A History* *of Israel* (Palgrave, 2002) and *Israel's Wars* (Routledge, 2010). His book *Cursed Victory: A History of Israel and the Occupised Territories* will be published by Penguin in 2014. He teaches at the Department of War Studies King's College London.

Dr Assaf David a Jordan expert, holds a PhD in Social Science from the Hebrew University of Jerusalem. He teaches and conducts research on Jordan, civil–military relations and comparative politics of the Middle East at the Hebrew University. He is a chief analyst of Jordan affairs at the Economic Cooperation Foundation (ECF), an Israel-based NGO. He serves as a consultant on Jordan affairs for other Israeli and foreign NGO's, as well as private sector and public sector organisations.

Dr Claudia De Martino graduated *summa cum laude* from her BA in Contemporary History at Roma Tre University and in 2007 completed her MA at the University of La Sapienza in Rome. In 2008 she spent a study year at the Hebrew University of Jerusalem, thanks to an EMU2 research scholarship. She has also been a Visiting Fellow at the Van Leer Institute of Jerusalem in 2009 and 2010, and a teaching assistant at the Chair of History of Europe and the Mediterranean at the Roma Tre University. In May 2012 she obtained her PhD in Social History of the Mediterranean at the Ca' Foscari University of Venice, working on a thesis on the absorption of Mizrahi Jews in the 1950s and 1960s. She is currently a researcher on Middle Eastern Affairs at UNIMED and contributes regularly with the Aspen Institute Italy.

Dr Jacob Eriksson is a Teaching Fellow in Middle Eastern Politics at the University of York. He was awarded his PhD by the School of Oriental and African Studies (SOAS), London, in October 2011. His thesis was entitled "Swedish mediation of the Israeli–Palestinian conflict: a study of the utility of small-state mediation and Track II diplomacy." His research interests include the Israeli–Palestinian conflict and the wider Arab–Israeli conflict, conflict resolution, and Middle Eastern politics and security.

Professor Galia Golan held the Jay and Leoni Darwin Chair in Soviet and East Europe Studies in the Political Science Department of the Hebrew University and was chair of the Mayrock Center for Eurasian and East European Research at the Hebrew University, presently Professor, IDC, Herzliya. She is author of nine books, including *Yom Kippur and After: the Soviet Union and the Middle East Crisis* (Cambridge University Press, 1977); *The Soviet Union and the PLO* (Praeger, 1976); *The Soviet Union and National Liberation Movements in the Third World* (Allen & Unwin, 1988); *Soviet Policies in the Middle East from World War II to Gorbachev* (Cambridge University Press,1990); *Moscow and the Middle East* (Chatham House, 1992); *Gorbachev's 'New Thinking' on Terrorism* (Praeger, 1990).

Professor Clive Jones is Professor of Regional Security at the University of Durham. His published works include *Soviet Jewish Aliyah 1989–92* (Routledge, 1996) (with Emma Murphy); *Israel: Challenges to Identity, Democracy and the State* (Routledge, 2002), *Britain and the Yemen Civil War 1962–1965* (Sussex Academic Press, 2004/2010) (with Ami Pedahzur, co-editor); *Between Terrorism and Civil War: The al-Aqsa Intifada* (Routledge, 2005) (with Sergio Catignani, co-editor); *Israel and Hizbollah: An Asymmetric Conflict in Historical and Comparative Perspective* (Routledge,2009). He has published widely on Middle East politics, intelligence and security issues, and in March 2010 his book *Britain and the Yemen Civil War* was the subject of the BBC Radio 4 history programme, *Document*, examining British clandestine involvement in the Yemen civil war.

Professor Yoram Meital is chairman of the Chaim Herzog Center for Middle East Studies and Diplomacy, and a member of the Department of Middle East Studies, both at Ben-Gurion University of the Negev. Currently, he is a Visiting Fellow at the Islamic Legal Studies Program at Harvard Law School (2011–12). Currently, he is a member in the Working Group on Arab Transformative Movements (Center for Middle East Studies, Harvard University).

Professor Rory Miller is Director of Middle East and Mediterranean Studies at King's College London. His research and teaching deal primarily with EU and US intervention in the Middle East and the role of small states in the global economy. He is author or editor of eight books, most recently *Britain, Palestine and Empire: The Mandate Years* (Ashgate, 2010) and *Inglorious Disarray: Europe, Israel and the Palestinians since*

1967 (Columbia University Press, 2011). He has also contributed articles to, among other publications, *Foreign Affairs, Foreign Policy, The New Republic, The Wall Street Journal* and *The National* (Abu Dhabi).

Professor David S. Painter teaches international history at Georgetown University. His publications include *Oil and the American Century* (Johns Hopkins University Press, 1986), *The Cold War: An International History* (Routledge, 1999), *The Cold War*, and *Origins of the Cold War: An International History* (Routledge, 2005) (co-editor), and articles on US policy towards the Third World, US oil policies, and the Cold War. His current project is a study of oil and world power in the twentieth century.

Dr Asaf Siniver is Senior Lecturer in International Security in the Department of Political Science and International Studies at the University of Birmingham. His areas of research include conflict resolution, international mediation and the Arab-Israeli conflict, and contemporary US foreign policy. His work has appeared in various academic journals, including *Review of International Studies, Political Studies, Diplomacy and Statecraft, International Politics*, and *International Studies Perspectives*. He is author of *Nixon, Kissinger and US Foreign Policy: The Machinery of Crisis* (Cambridge University Press, 2008), and editor of *International Terrorism post 9/11: Comparative Dynamics and Responses* (Routledge, 2010). He is a Leverhulme Research Fellow (2011–13) and an Associate Editor of the journal *Civil Wars*.

Professor Kenneth W. Stein is the Founding Director of the Emory Institute for the Study of Modern Israel and Professor of Political Science, Middle Eastern History and Israeli Studies. He is author of numerous publications, articles, papers and reviews, including *Heroic Diplomacy: Sadat, Kissinger, Carter, Begin and the Quest for Arab-Israeli Peace* (Routledge, 1999); *Making Peace Among Arabs and Israelis: Lessons from Fifty Years of Negotiating Experience* (US Institute of Peace, 1991); *The Land Question in Palestine, 1917–1939* (University of North Carolina; and his most recent article, "US–Israeli Relations 1947–2010: The View from Washington" in Alfred Wittstock (ed.), *The World facing Israel—Israel facing the World:Images and Politics* (Berlin: Frank and Timme, 2011), 159–76. He heads the Atlanta based Center for Israel Education, www.israeled.org.

LIST OF CONTRIBUTORS

Professor Eyal Zisser is Dean of the faculty of Humanities at Tel Aviv University. He was Director of the Moshe Dayan Center for Middle Eastern and African Studies 2007–10, and head of the department of Middle Eastern and African History 2004–8. He has written extensively on the history and modern politics of Syria and Lebanon and the Arab–Israeli conflict, including *Assad's Syria at a Crossroads* (Tel Aviv, 1999); *Asad's Legacy—Syria in Transition* (New York, 2000); *Lebanon: the Challenge of Independence* (I. B. Tauris, 2000); *Faces of Syria* (Tel Aviv, 2003); *Commanding Syria: Bashar al-Asad and the First Years in Power* (I. B. Tauris, 2006); *The Bleeding Cedar* (Tel Aviv, 2009).

1

INTRODUCTION

Asaf Siniver

The roots of the October War of 1973 (also known as the Yom Kippur War and the Ramadan War) are directly related to the military and diplomatic outcomes of the Six Day War of June 1967. The Six Day War is commonly described as a "turning point" or a "watershed" in the history of the Arab-Israeli conflict and the modern Middle East more broadly. Israel's occupation of Arab territory at the end of the war, the rise of a Palestinian national consciousness, and the internationalisation of the conflict are often cited as enduring legacies of that war, the reverberations of which are still felt to this day.[1]

The historiography of the legacy of the October War, however, is considerably more modest in scope and intent. The vast literature on the war is mostly concerned with military-strategic questions, such as the failure of Israeli intelligence to anticipate the war, the Egyptian–Syrian surprise attack, or the American airlift to Israel during the war. Other studies are also concerned with the socio-political consequences of the war on Israeli society and the disillusionment of the Israeli public with the country's military and political leadership. Notwithstanding some notable exceptions, such as Galia Golan's and Victor Israelyan's studies of the Soviet Union during the war, the historiography is dominated by a decidedly

1

Israeli–American prism through which the origins of the war, its phases and consequences are investigated.[2] In addition, little has been done to assess the enduring legacies of the October War on the chief protagonists as well as the peripheral actors in the war, such as Europe, Jordan, the Palestinians, and the global oil economy. This skewed representation of the war in the academic literature is largely due to the disproportionate availability of primary sources. Western and Israeli archives normally operate under the thirty-year rule to declassify governmental records and release them to the public domain, whereas this practice generally does not exist in Arab countries. Compared to the substantial body of official documents about the war which can be viewed at the Israel State Archive in Jerusalem, the Richard Nixon Presidential Library in Yorba Linda, California, and the National Archives in College Park, Maryland, as well as the British National Archives in London, Arab records of the war come mostly in the form of memoirs by political and military leaders.

However notwithstanding these methodological limitations, the for-tieth anniversary of the October War provides a timely opportunity to reassess the major themes which have emerged during the war and in its aftermath. As the contributors to this volume aim to demonstrate, some of these themes have had irreparable repercussions on the international relations of the Arab–Israeli conflict and its principal actors.

Perhaps the most important international legacy of the October War was the changing nature of third-party diplomacy in the Arab–Israeli conflict and the rise of the United States as the principal and indispens-able intermediary in the ensuing peace process. The 1967 Six Day War turned the conflict into an arena of superpower competition by proxy, with the United States supporting pro-Western countries such as Israel and Jordan, whilst the "radical" regimes of Egypt and Syria were backed by the Soviet Union. Diplomatically, the United Nations maintained a visible role in the efforts to secure a lasting peace agreement between Israel and the Arabs, most notably through the mission of UN mediator Dr Gunnar Jarring, who was appointed following the adoption of UN Security Council Resolution 242 in November 1967. Jarring's mission continued until 1972, though it was often usurped by the concurrent efforts of the Big Four (US, USSR, Britain and France) to reach a Middle East settlement, and the often intransigent responses of Egypt and Israel to Jarring's proposals. The October War, however, changed irrevocably this environment of multi-party mediation where the UN played a leading role in Arab–Israeli diplomacy. By the end of the war the US emerged as the ubiquitous intermediary in the conflict, a position which it retains to this day, regardless of its record of success. This transformation is solely attributed to Henry Kissinger's grand strategy during the war, which was designed, firstly, to enable Israel to win the war whilst preventing another humiliating defeat on the battlefield for the Arabs. Kissinger's directing of American foreign policy during the war was also aimed at alleviating the threat of an Arab oil embargo by creating the conditions for Arab–Israeli negotiations after the war, and the relegating of the Soviets to the sidelines of Middle East diplomacy by making the US the only acceptable mediator to both Israelis and Arabs. The cumulative result of this grand strategy was the successful conclusion of five US-mediated limited and interim agreements between Israel, Egypt and Syria in the period of November 1973 to May 1975—the beginning of a peace process which culminated in 1978 with the successful mediation of the Camp Accords between Israel and Egypt by US President Jimmy Carter, thus further cemented the aphorism that Arab–Israeli peace can only be achieved with the help of American mediation. At the same time however, Kissinger's diplomatic success in the aftermath of 1973 has sown the seeds of criticism over the failure of successive administrations to detach the US–Israeli special relationship from America's broader interests in the Middle East.

Against the rise of the US and the decline of the USSR in the arena of Middle East diplomacy, the October War also posed a challenge to the identity of the European Economic Community (EEC). The effect of the war on the evolution of Europe's orientation towards the Arab–Israeli conflict has been relatively underexplored in the literature, despite the important consequences of the war and the subsequent oil crisis which confronted European capitals. Whereas until the war the European position on the conflict was rather fragmented and incoherent, and amounted to little more than a tepid declaration in support of a negotiated settlement based on UN Security Council Resolution 242, the October war forced the EEC to develop its own position on four interrelated issues: internally, the need to consolidate political and economic cooperation among member states; defining a distinct European policy towards the Israeli–Palestinian conflict; developing a strategic relationship with the United States; and improving Euro–Arab relations in the aftermath of the oil crisis. The consequences of this European reckoning

in the aftermath of the war were long-lasting. The EEC's Venice Declaration of 1980 in support of Palestinian self-determination presented a
distinct alternative to the decidedly pro-Israel policy espoused by the
United States, and subsequently helped to develop the EU's role as the
normative compass in the Arab–Israeli conflict, through its rhetoric on
international law, human rights and democracy promotion.

The main catalyst for change in Europe's approach to the Arab–Israeli
conflict, and to some extent the driver behind Kissinger's post-war grand
strategy, was the global oil crisis of 1973–4. Towards the end of the war
the Organisation of Arab Petroleum Exporting Countries (OAPEC), led
by Saudi Arabia, announced a cutback in oil production and an oil
embargo on the United States and the Netherlands (which was the only
European country to allow its airfields to be used for the American airlift
to Israel during the war). For the first time oil was used by the Arabs as
a weapon in the conflict, for the purpose of forcing the United States to
pressure Israel to withdraw from the Occupied Territories. Whilst serious oil shortages did not occur, the embargo and production cutback
saw oil prices quadruple. The cost of importing expensive oil had an
adverse effect on the economic growth in many Western countries,
whilst the Soviet Union actually benefited from the high oil prices due
to its large oil reserves. In the long run the asymmetrical impact of the
oil crisis on the two superpowers had altered the course of the Cold War,
as the sharp rise in oil revenues helped finance increased Soviet intervention in the Third World throughout the 1970s, which not only proved
detrimental to the spirit of détente, but also deflected from Commu-
nism's serious structural problems, which ultimately led to the collapse
of the Soviet Union and the end of the Cold War.

In assessing the impact of the October War on Israeli and Arab societies (most notably Egypt), two interrelated patterns emerge. First, the war
has been mythologised in each society in almost opposing terms to
where each side found itself militarily at the end of the war, on 24 Octo-
ber1973. Second, the boundaries of the war's mythology in both Israel
and Egypt are firmly rooted in the course of the war during the first
week of the fighting, when Egypt held the initiative, whereas the
remainder of the war, during which the military balance had changed
significantly in favour of Israel, did not form part of the war's mythology
in either society. Israelis remember the war as a "blunder" or "omission"
(*mehdal*), the most traumatic episode in the country's history; Egyptians

remember the war jubilantly, as an event which restored Arab pride and broke Israel's indefectible image. This divergence in the two countries' collective memories of the war runs counter to their military achievements at the end of October 1973. Militarily, Israel was in control of more Arab territory than during the Six Day War. On the southern front it completed a successful crossing of the Suez Canal, and for the first time Israeli troops were in Africa, only 60 miles from Cairo. The 20,000-strong Egyptian Third Army was encircled on the eastern bank of the Suez Canal and was on the verge of annihilation. On the northern front Israel conquered additional Syrian territory beyond the Golan Heights and was in control of the road leading to Damascus. Israeli loss of life during the October War was less than half of that during the first Arab–Israeli war of 1948. Moreover, Israel had no civilian casualties in the October War. As for the number of casualties as a proportion of the population, the statistics of the October War were significantly less harrowing than those of the 1948 war: in 1973 the less than 3,000 dead (all combatants) represented 0.1 per cent of a total Jewish population of more than 2,800,000; whereas the proportional loss of life in 1948 was ten times higher: more than 6,000 casualties (including more than 2,000 civilian deaths) out of a total Jewish population of only 600,000. But psychology, rather than territory, dictated the moods in Cairo and Jerusalem at the end of the war. As Henry Kissinger observed during his visit to Israel in the final days of the fighting, "Israel was exhausted, no matter what the military maps showed."[3]

The failure of Israeli intelligence to anticipate the war; the remarkable ease with which the Egyptians managed to overrun the Bar-Lev line, Israel's chain of fortified positions on the eastern bank of the Suez Canal, during the first days of the war; the long list of operational failures during the war, such as the ill-fated counter-attack in the south during the third day of the war, and the infighting between the military high command, all contributed to the creation of a collective Israeli memory of the war as the single most ominous point in the country's history. This sombre national mood was epitomised by the incongruous remark, on the third day of fighting, by a panic-stricken Moshe Dayan, Israel's Defence Minister, that this was "the end of the Third Temple"—a dim historical reference to the destruction of Jerusalem's Temple, first by the Babylonians and then by the Romans, which on both occasions was followed by the exile of the Jewish people from their homeland. The hubris and complacency which engulfed the country in the aftermath of the Six Day War gave way to a more humble look towards Israel's enemies at the end of the October War, and opened a period of introspection and self-flagellation which led to the creation of the Agranat National Committee of Inquiry in 1974. The committee recommended the dismissal of IDF (Israel Defense Forces) Chief of Staff David Elazar and other senior officers, whereas the public disenchantment with the political establishment and the government's conduct of the war led to the resignation from office of Prime Minister Golda Meir and Defence Minister Dayan. The war therefore served as an important catalyst for change in Israeli society and politics, which was most visibly manifested in the loss of power of the Labour Party in the 1977 general elections and the rise of the right-wing Likud party. The war also prompted the emergence of social and political protest movements, and led to the rise in religious zeal and settlement activity.

For most Egyptians the war is remembered as an unquestionable victory—militarily as well as politically. Whereas in Syria the war's anniversary is not celebrated with jubilation, given the fact that it failed to retrieve the occupied Golan Heights or elevate the country's regional and international standing, the date of 6 October is celebrated annually in Egypt, to mark the crossing of the Suez Canal and the defeat and the military gains during the first week of the war. These early achievements not only shattered the myth of Israeli invincibility which emerged in the aftermath of the 1967 war, but they were also translated effectively to achieve political gains in the following years, first through two disengagement agreements with Israel in 1974–5, and then the complete retrieval of the Sinai Peninsula as part of the peace treaty with Israel in 1979—the first time in the history of the conflict when an Arab country regained an Israeli-occupied territory. The fact that the war ended with Israeli troops stationed in the outskirts of Cairo and in complete encirclement of the Egyptian Third Army has not dampened the jubilant commemoration of the war in Egypt. Instead, the mythology of the Egyptian crossing of the Suez Canal during the first days of the war served as the lynchpin of a collective memory of restored national pride and the awakening of Egyptian society from the gloomy past.

Syria was undoubtedly the biggest loser of the October War. It joined forces with Egypt, but was misled by its ally about the war's aims, and despite initial success on the battlefield, within days the Syrian forces were roundly defeated by the Israelis. At the end of the war the Syrians felt betrayed once more by Egyptian President Anwar Sadat, who sacrificed Arab unity for the sake of developing very cordial relations with the United States, thus leaving Damascus in the lurch. Unsurprisingly, the Israeli–Egyptian peace treaty was viewed in Damascus as Sadat's ultimate betrayal of Arab unity, not least on the Palestinian issue. However, whilst Syria never established diplomatic relations with Israel, it refrained from launching another military campaign to retrieve the Golan Heights, and instead supported non-state proxies such as *Hezbollah* and *Hamas* in their low-intensity conflict with Israel.

This pattern of relative regional stability which emerged in the aftermath of the October War was supported by Jordan's decision not to open an eastern front against Israel. After the humiliating experience of the Six Day War in which Jordan lost the West Bank and East Jerusalem to Israel, King Hussein was mindful of the futility of another Arab–Israeli war. For the sake of Arab unity, however, and with the tacit acquiescence of Israel and the United States, Hussein agreed to place Jordan's 40th Brigade under Syrian command. Jordan's symbolic participation in the October War is more telling than the 40th Brigade's contribution would suggest. It epitomised the emerging order in the region. After a decade of clandestine meetings with Israeli officials, Hussein not only warned the Israelis of the imminent Egyptian–Syrian offensive, he also notified Jerusalem and Washington of his decision to send a token force to the Syrian front. The Israelis, on their part, did their most not to clash with this idle Jordanian unit. Whilst Israel and Jordan did not sign a peace treaty until 1994, relations between the countries in the aftermath of the October War were overall amiable. Another important dimension of this episode was the gradual acceptance by Jordan and the United States of the Palestinian people's right for self-determination in the West Bank following the war. In 1974 the Arab League summit in Rabat unanimously declared the Palestine Liberation Organisation (PLO) to be the sole representative of the Palestinian people, and in 1988 King Hussein officially relinquished all claims to the West Bank by Jordan, and recognised the PLO as the legitimate representative of this territory.

While the PLO or other Palestinian factions did not take part in the October War, and nor was the war fought over the Palestinian issue, it nevertheless served as an important catalyst for change in intra-Palestinian politics and the evolution of the Palestinian struggle for independence. The war marked a historical as well as ideological shift. Diplomacy, rather than just organised violence, joined the mainstream of *Fatah* as an acceptable means to achieve the end of Palestinian independence, whereas left-wing nationalistic groups such as the Popular Front for the Liberation of Palestine (PFLP) opposed this new direction. These "dogmatic wars" between various Palestinian factions in the 1970s were compounded by the rise of Isalmist groups such as *Hamas* in the 1980s, and internal rifts within the PLO continued into the 1990s in response to the Oslo Accords with Israel.

The regional order which emerged in the aftermath of the October 1973 War remained relatively unchallenged for nearly four decades. The Egyptian–Israeli peace treaty was the strategic anchor of a stable Middle East, which ensured that the October War was the last full-scale, conventional Arab–Israeli war (the limited Israeli–Syrian skirmishes during the 1982 Lebanon war notwithstanding). The United States, which emerged from the October War as the principal mediator and manager of the Arab–Israeli conflict, maintained its position throughout this period, despite its modest record of success. Evidence of the centrality of Washington to the peace process came in 1993, when the Norway-mediated Declaration of Principles between Israel and the PLO was ceremoniously signed on the South Lawn of the White House, despite the lack of American involvement in the secret negotiations. The post-1973 neighbourhood was also characterised by security-based agreements between political elites, rather than between peoples. The treaties between Israel and Egypt, Jordan and the PLO have been opposed by significant portions of the general public in those societies over the years. It therefore seems that the Arab Awakening, which swept the region in 2011, represents the most serious challenge yet to the post-1973 regional order. Whilst Israel signed its peace treaties with the autocratic leaders of Egypt, Jordan and the PLO, rather than with their peoples, it remains to be seen whether the recent wave towards popular democracy in the Middle East will transform Arab–Israeli relations for the better. Moreover, Washington's slow and at times hypocritical response to the recent events in the region was seen by many as evidence of the decline of American power in the region. For the "Arab street", these are times of change and hope; for the average Israeli, these are times of uncertainty and danger. It is perhaps not surprising then that, just as the October War reshaped the course of the Arab–Israeli conflict four decades ego, the recent revolutionary wave in the Middle East is destined to challenge the regional order which emerged post-1973. But as long as these events are being mythologised by Arabs and Israelis in conflicting terms, the chances that the perpetuity of the conflict will be broken remain slim.

It is not the aim of this edited volume to provide a definitive history of the October War or to deliver a revisionist account of events. Rather, it seeks to examine, collectively and as individual chapters, a broader and more comparative spectrum of the politics, diplomacies and legacies of the war than has been presented by previous accounts of this important episode in the international relations of the Middle East and the Cold War. The editor and the contributors to this volume thank the support of the Department of Political Science and International Studies, and the School of Government & Society at the University of Birmingham for supporting this project. We also thank Michael Dwyer and Daisy Leitch of Hurst Publishers for their assistance and patience throughout the process. Finally, I am also grateful for the support of the Leverhulme Trust (research fellowship #2011–222), which aided the timely completion of this volume.

2

ASSESSING THE HISTORIOGRAPHY OF THE OCTOBER WAR

Carly Beckerman-Boys

"Trauma" is a word often associated with the October War.[1] The unexpected and surprisingly successful attack of Egyptian and Syrian forces on 6 October 1973, wrenched the Israeli government, military and public from a comfortable hubris inspired by the successes of 1967. Ultimately, the conflict provided a military victory for Israel, but it is remembered as "the earthquake" or "the blunder" rather than as a successful defence of both Israel proper and the Occupied Territories. Curiously, Israeli casualties in 1973 were half the number of 1948, but while the earlier conflict is celebrated as a triumph, memories of the October War stir only a negative response.[2] The same is true of territorial losses. Although the October War and return of the Sinai represented the first stage of peace with Egypt—Israel's most dangerous rival—the conflict remains separate from conceptions of peace in the Israeli psyche; in contrast, the Suez War of 1956 also involved the return of territory, did not bring peace, yet is still remembered as successful.[3] Rather than a heroic victory or even a courageous loss, the October War has, at best, been viewed as an embarrassment; and, at worst, has been seen as a terrifying reminder of the limitations on Israel's ability to protect its citizens. This pervasive feeling of trauma associated with 1973 has had an interesting effect on the way the conflict has been studied. The widespread use of the term *mehdal*, or "blunder", implies that the traumatic circumstances of Israel's surprise and early military losses were preventable;[4] and it is somewhat predictable, therefore, that the most substantial trend within October War historiography devotes itself to understanding the enemy's element of surprise in order to prevent its reoccurrence in the future.

Since 1973, much has been written about this conflict in the fields of journalism, history and the political sciences. Several major and minor trends and debates exist within this body of scholarship. As this chapter centres quite narrowly on dominant themes within the October War historiography, it is focused primarily on Israel-centric studies published in English. It is important to note, however, that a smaller array of October War studies do exist that address the conflict with differing analyses and objectives. These include a great many military histories concerned with the conduct of the war itself. The oil dimension has also attracted important study, highlighting the connection between economics and diplomacy in the Middle East. The role played by the Soviet Union has inspired a small but rich collection of studies, and relatively minor players such as South Africa and Britain have received some attention. In terms of language, there is very little available in Hebrew that has not been translated into English—Eli Zeira's memoirs providing one significant example. Sources available in Arabic, however, unfortunately remain largely inaccessible. In terms of an Arab perspective on the October War, this lack of widespread translation increases the importance of several key works, discussed more below. Taking into account this collection of scholarship available in English on the October War, a dominant theme emerges. There is a significant line of investigation that asks: why was Israel surprised? This key trend within October War historiography then diverges into two important sub-themes that form the basis of this chapter

The first is a predominantly Israeli perspective that is targeted at understanding the element of surprise in the October War with the implicit aim of helping to prevent its reoccurrence. The second is again intended to understand and prevent surprise attacks, but it is more internationally focused and uses the October War as just one case study in a broader theoretical framework. Both of these approaches are highly practical and aimed directly at the development of better institutions, procedures and policy, predominantly in Israel and the United States. While appearing to represent two sides of the same coin, however, these sub-themes have a divergent impact on October War historiography. They actually create two extremes of analysis, from the very personal to the highly impersonal. One end of the spectrum, what this chapter calls "The Blame Game", encapsulates an acute Israeli fear following the war, and the need to identify some culpable party in order to prove that such traumatic circumstances are indeed preventable. The other extreme, which this chapter terms, "The Hunt for Historical Analogies", uses the 1973 conflict as merely one of many global examples, the relevance of which are questionable as the comparison itself exorcises the October War from its Middle East context. This *milieu* of a Middle East war in 1973 that hinged on Arab feelings towards the past—territorial losses in 1967 as well as Palestinian expulsion in 1948—is crucial to understanding how the October War is still relevant to ongoing themes in the Middle East, such as Israeli security, Palestinian statehood, oil and even Iran's nuclear programme. Otherwise, the October War is merely subsumed into Cold War historiography through issues of endangering détente or altering the balance of power. This chapter concludes, therefore, that, forty years after the October War, what is necessary and still missing from the conflict's dominant historiography is a mid-stance between the highly personal perspective solely targeted to guard against a future traumatic or even existential surprise attack on the State of Israel, and the transplantation of the October War from its Middle East setting, including its unhelpful amalgamation into a Western narrative.

The blame game

The historiographical focus on surprise is a major trend within October War scholarship, consistently asking "who was to blame?" Reflecting a focus on mistakes within intelligence, politics and the military, this type of scholarship emerged immediately after the war and has remained a feature of October War historiography throughout subsequent decades. Authors usually search for a single culpable party among the following arguments, which traverse decades and fail to fit any neat timeline or historical wave.

The intelligence failure

Israel's failure to predict the Arab attack was psychologically if not substantively crucial. Despite heavy losses, the Israel Defence Force (IDF) was able to push both Egyptian and Syrian armies back, notwithstanding their modest reinforcement by various other Arab states. As Avi Shlaim notes, however, Israel's predictive failure "enabled the Arabs to dictate the opening moves in the war and to secure their initial successes. More significantly, it radically changed the whole political and psychological balance of power in the Middle East to Israel's disadvantage."[5] The surprise itself, rather than the outcome of the war, was the source of the trauma. Following this harrowing realisation of vulnerability, a national committee of inquiry was appointed to investigate Israel's apparent lack of preparedness. Led by the Chief Justice of Israel's Supreme Court, the Agranat Commission ultimately blamed four AMAN (Israeli military intelligence) officers for failing to recognise the imminence of war, due to a dogmatic adherence to what the commission called "the Concept".[6] This concept mainly consisted of assumptions that Arab armies would not attack without first securing air superiority, and that Syria would not launch an offensive without Egypt; as Egypt's air superiority was not expected before 1975, it was, therefore, not ready for war, and no attack from either Arab nation was likely.[7] The Agranat Commission highlighted how these preconceptions prevented a realistic assessment of Egypt and Syria's intentions as the situation changed and evidence mounted of an imminent invasion. This attitude characterised the beginning of October War historiography, focused specifically on the failure to anticipate the surprise attack. Very early histories reflected a complete internalisation of these assessments, whereas slightly later scholarly investigations questioned the relative simplicity of the Agranat Commission's conclusions.

An argument based almost entirely on the Agranat Commission can be found in early histories that concentrate on a blow-by-blow account of the war, such as Nadav Safran's "Trial by Ordeal: The October War, October 1973", and more policy-driven scholarship such as Richard Betts' *Surprise Attack: Lessons for Defense Planning*.[8] Safran ultimately concludes that the "most crucial failure …consisted, of course, of the structural, conceptual and attitudinal flaws that allowed the Arabs to gain strategic surprise".[9] Similarly, Betts argues that the failure to anticipate the attacks, on both the Israeli and American sides, was due to "reliance on strategic preconceptions that degraded the perception of tactical indicators".[10] This position on intelligence failure is also echoed by Cohen and Gooch, who note that although "the Concept" was based on intelligence from a single Egyptian source—whom we now know was Ashraf Marwan—Israeli intelligence should have realised when Sadat abandoned this concept, as Sadat had specifically dismissed Egyptian War Minister Sadek precisely because he had failed to prepare Egypt for war without long-range aircraft or Scud missiles.[11] This thread of research identifies that the problem was not the concept itself, but rather intelligence leaders' dogmatic faith in it, despite evidence that Sadat had abandoned reasoning associated with air superiority.[12] The early, predominantly military histories mentioned above represent direct reflections of the Agranat Commission findings. They halt where the committee's analysis stalled also. Other scholars, however, have used this focus on intelligence and the findings of the Agranat Commission as the commencement of investigation, rather than its culmination.

Studies conducted by Uri Bar-Joseph, Ahron Bregman, Arie Kruglanski, Janice Gross Stein and Ephraim Kahana all problematise the findings of the Agranat Commission to gain a better understanding of why "the Concept" proved so rigid. The foci of their analyses vary from an investigation of the human element to the sheer cognitive difficulty in predicting surprise attacks in general. Bar-Joseph, for example, ultimately concludes that the greatest blame for Israel's intelligence failure rested on AMAN Director Eli Zeira. He highlights how Egypt's troop movements following the War of Attrition contributed to the development of "the Concept", how, as a result, warnings from King Hussein of Jordan and the CIA were ignored, as were Soviet evacuations, and alert fatigue (or cry-wolf syndrome)[13] discouraged alarm following twenty Egyptian mobilisations in 1973.[14] Rather than agreeing with the Agranat Commission's conclusion that AMAN's intelligence monopoly, a structural problem, was to blame, Bar-Joseph argues that Zeira's duplicitous actions taken to protect "the Concept" carried the most responsibility:[15] keeping knowledge of Hussein's warning from Colonel Ya'ari in AMAN's Syrian department, delaying the delivery of Mossad intelligence warning that Egyptian canal-crossing exercises were real, preventing the circulation of information regarding the Soviet evacuation and, finally, lying to his superiors regarding the activation of "special means of collection which could produce high quality warning signals". In a similar vein,

15

Ahron Bregman's theory that the Mossad source Ashraf Marwan was a double agent working for President Sadat is another argument that points to human error.[16] Specifically defending IDF intelligence, Bregman comments that the Agranat Commission did AMAN an injustice.[17] The double-agent assessment redirects blame from AMAN to Mossad, who operated Marwan, but it continues the argument that Israel's intelligence failure was actually a small, almost individual, and therefore, preventable failure.

The above studies bestow complete blame on a particular party, but others conclude that assigning blame is actually very difficult. Gross Stein's investigation raises the question of whether Israel could have deterred an attack in 1973 regardless of "the Concept".[18] Like Bar-Joseph, Gross Stein highlights how Israel's deterrence strategy in 1973 was focused on the possibility of a general attack rather than a limited war, leading to an oversimplified understanding of Egypt's preconditions for conflict. Alert fatigue caused by Cairo's constant bellicose language and frequent deployments also meant that troop concentration along cease-fire lines was no longer an indicator of imminent attack. Also, it was highly socially and economically costly as well as provocative for Israel to react to Egyptian deployments with Israeli mobilisation.[19] These more substantive concerns do not fit with "the Concept", and so an explanation of the failure to anticipate surprise must be broader than the findings of the Agranat Commission. The problem, Gross Stein posits, was one of inherent difficulty. Mobilisation was reserved for an intelligence warning that hostilities were imminent, but an unambiguous warning was not likely to be forthcoming because there are often conflicting plausible interpretations of evidence.[20] Also, overconfidence in the standing army led leaders to believe they could repel an Arab attack until reserves reached the front. This assumption gave Zeira a perceived greater margin for error in terms of warning, whereas Defence Minister Moshe Dayan and Chief of Staff David Elazar were depending on intelligence assurances of adequate warning; civilian leaders relied on both and dismissed the need for further defensive action.[21] The problem, Gross Stein concludes, was not simply "the Concept" or one man's adherence to it, but a set of interrelated strategic assumptions.[22] This point of view is reiterated by Ephraim Kahana, who notes that a "close examination of the case of the October War reveals how difficult it is to abandon a firm concept, even though it is wrong".[23] Such arguments seem to remove academics such as Gross Stein and Kahana from the category of scholars involved in "The Blame Game". However, their research is still prescriptive, their intent consistently pragmatic. The conclusion may imply that surprise is to some extent inevitable, but the investigation itself is revealing. This historiographical focus on the intelligence failure remains an omnipresent fixture in investigations of the October War, though it is most often cited in blow-by-blow accounts as an explanation rather than as a subject of inquiry. It is important to remember, however, that the Agranat Commission's mandate was relatively narrow and did not include assessing political responsibility for Israel's failures during the October War.

The political failure

Although the memoirs of censured AMAN officers Eli Zeira[24] and Israel Tal[25] are renowned for blaming the surprise of the October War on Israel's political leaders,[26] this trend actually began far earlier, almost immediately after the war had ended. Moshe Dayan and Golda Meir seem to have felt this pressure, as both devote parts of their memoirs on the October War to defending their actions before and during the conflict. "My personal feeling", Dayan writes, "was one of complete confidence that I had not failed in my duties."[27] Meir casually blames intelligence failures and the nonchalance of Dayan and Bar-Lev for the failure to anticipate attack, but she also holds the United States responsible.[28] "In the final analysis, to put it bluntly", Meir explains, "the fate of small countries always rests with the super powers, and they always have their own interests to guard."[29] If the public mood had not developed into outrage following the effective political acquittal delivered by Agranat's censure of AMAN, then neither Dayan nor Meir would have needed to redirect blame in this way. Both Dayan and Meir's books were released in the mid 1970s, and so it was far too early to expect an honest retrospective self-evaluation, which cannot be said for Tal's much later memoir. By 2000, when Tal published his own book, he censured political leaders for not authorising a pre-emptive strike and the United States for not allowing a decisive Israeli victory.[30] This is an indictment of political leaders, but in a very different way to the rest of the scholarship discussed in this section. The desire to hold politicians primarily responsible became very common in the October War historiography, but its focus has remained diplomatic rather than military. This element of academic research has manifested itself in criticism of Israel's political elite in general, towards singular Israeli politicians and also towards the United States.

Zeev Schiff's very early account of the war was written during a mood of uncertainty and gloom that pervaded the Israeli government and public following October 1973. Schiff describes how the war "exposed the full hopelessness of Israeli leadership", as the country lacked a leader with the stature of Ben-Gurion or even Moshe Dayan of 1967.[31] According to Schiff, this meant that the "main burden of directing the war fell on the shoulders of a 75-year-old grandmother".[32] As well as arrogance following the victory of 1967, sloppy discipline in the IDF, politicisation of and nepotism within bureaucracy, Schiff blames the senior command echelons rather than the intelligence service.[33] The use of vague terminology like "echelons" meant that Schiff's criticisms were directed merely in the general direction of Israel's political elite. Later investigations, however, became far more specific.

Howard Morely Sachar, for example, places blame directly on Meir for her inflexibility in negotiations prior to the war, for insisting only on direct negotiations with "the enemy", opposing outside mediation, opposing any interim settlement or withdrawal from borders before the conclusion of the peace treaty and, therefore, failing to take Sadat's overtures after 1971 seriously.[34] This argument is then echoed in Bregman's work, which makes his book, *Israel's Wars*, one of the few to assign culpability to more than one party. Bregman highlights Meir's intransigence and lack of flexibility, but also emphasises how the prime minister's frame of reference must have influenced her approach.[35] Meir was foreign minister during the Suez Crisis in 1956, after which territory was returned to Egypt and peace failed to materialise.[36] Meir is at fault in Bregman's analysis, but the flaw is an understandable one. This element of human fallibility has probably contributed to the popularity of this approach; intangible institutional problems or interrelated strategic assumptions are far less satisfying than personal culpability in the search for cognitive closure. Bregman's previously discussed double-agent theory fits with this focus on the human element. Even Bar-Joseph, whose work has consistently placed the bulk of blame on Zeira, notes that Sadat's peace overtures were wrongly ignored in Jerusalem and Washington.[37]

This stream of analysis that pinpoints politicians for blame also includes a tendency to condemn the role of United States foreign policy in failing to prevent the outbreak of war. Barry Rubin was a very early advocate of this position, and his 1973 and 1974 indictments of the Nixon and Kissinger approach to diplomacy in the Middle East were only the first of many such investigations.[38] Rubin asserts that Nixon pressed Egypt for concessions while failing to even attempt extracting any from Israel; the administration then opposed UN Security Council resolutions that criticised Israeli occupation and lack of cooperation with the Jarring Commission.[39] This investigation leads Rubin to conclude that disappointment with Nixon's inability to jumpstart negotiations must have been a factor in the Egyptian and Syrian decisions to go to war, and Kissinger's failure to offer any new proposals in his speech before the UN on 25 September 1973 was simply the last straw.[40] Also addressing the American angle, Ray Maghroori posits that the United States missed an opportunity to prevent war by failing to exploit Sadat's differences with Moscow or to understand the domestic political pressures pushing Sadat towards war, regardless of strategic military considerations.[41] This diplomatic element of the political failure has been dealt with at length in Nixon and Kissinger's own memoirs,[42] but like Meir and Dayan's autobiographies, they were released very soon after the war itself and so provide little retrospective clarity. Most recently, Boaz Vanetik and Zaki Shalom focus on the role played by Kissinger in failing to create an Israeli-Egyptian settlement in 1973.[43] The authors utilise recently declassified documents in the United States and Israel to suggest that Kissinger's activities specifically catalysed the outbreak of war. His behaviour was based on a "stalemate policy", which meant undermining any peace initiative that failed to meet Israel's requirements on a possible settlement.[44] This led Sadat to believe the United States had no real interest in promoting a peace process that involved pressuring Israel and prompted him to abandon diplomacy and attack.[45] Although similar arguments have appeared in a great deal of October War historiography, thorough academic investigations of the role played by Nixon and Kissinger in the critical pre-war period (as opposed to the cease-fire, which has received disproportionate attention for its role in destabilising détente) are only beginning to surface. It is also important to remember that there is an opposing argument to these indictments of both Israel and the US.

Mordechai Gazit, Golda Meir and the Israeli ambassador to Washington, Simcha Dinitz, have consistently argued that Sadat's overtures were ignored because they did not represent peace initiatives at all. Gazit argues that "Sadat was not yet willing in 1971–3 to make any compromise whatsoever, insisting on every detail of the collective Arab stand. The implication of this is that the diplomatic moves of the USA or Israel in 1971 had no real chance of success."[46] As supporting evidence, Gazit points to the memoirs of Sadat's foreign ministers: Mahmoud Riad, Ismail Fahmy and Mohamad Ibrahim Kamel and their assertions of integrity in the struggle against Israel.[47] Similarly, Meir blames the diplomatic failure on Egypt for refusing to reach a peace agreement with Israel,[48] and Simcha Dinitz echoes this view in his 2000 contribution to *Revisiting the October War*. Dinitz argues that Sadat's offers in 1971 and 1972 were only suggested as part of a timetable of withdrawal from all occupied territories, which was why the overtures were refused by both Israel and the United States.[49] As this would have required the Arab states to act in concert as well as insist on total Israeli withdrawal, the plan was impracticable.[50] These arguments are slightly hollow, however, as no advocate of the hypothesis that Sadat was not really seeking peace explains why the Egyptian proposals were ignored rather than used as the opening to begin negotiations. The popular historiographical thread that blames individual politicians in Israel and the United States for diplomatic failures prior to the war is only strengthened by such simplistic arguments from its opposition. The prominence of this type of scholarship has, however, arguably overshadowed a final important facet of the "The Blame Game".

The military failure

In his military history, *No Victor, No Vanquished*, Edgar O'Ballance blames the Israeli lack of preparedness in 1973 on 1967-triumphalism.[51] Just as O'Ballance declines to expand his analysis to explain what this meant specifically for the IDF in 1973, this general realm of study has remained strangely unexamined. Whereas the intelligence failure has been studied at length and investigations of the political failure are still developing, the military failure has been virtually ignored in terms of culpability. Although many books have highlighted the mistakes made during initial stages of combat, they uniformly place blame for these failings on the lack of advance warning or political hesitation to order a pre-emptive strike. The most prominent works in this category are Peter Allen's, *The October War*; Chaim Herzog's *The War of Atonement: The Inside Story of the October War*; Stuart Cohen's "Operational Limitations of Reserve Forces: The Lessons of the 1973 War" and Walter Boyne's *The October War and the Airlift that Saved Israel*.[52] None, however, reflects even a hint of IDF responsibility for the early military failures of the October War. This is particularly intriguing considering the damning report of IDF Colonel Emmanuel Wald, first released in 1987.

The Wald Report argued that military failings in 1973 were the true culprit of Israel's traumatic experience during the October War.[53] Regardless of surprise, the IDF believed it was prepared for an attack that it was in fact woefully unprepared for, on tactical and institutional levels.[54] Israeli armed forces believed they had the option of being ready whenever the enemy attacked, but the October War showed this was not really an option.[55] Wald argued that the Agranat Commission (due to its limited remit) and the press war between generals, who argued over their respective contributions to the war's outcome, led to a consensus regarding blame; the public decided that it was intelligence and political leaders who failed, leaving deep doctrinal flaws and lack of professionalism from commanders and HQs at all levels of the IDF unexamined.[56] This report makes a coherent argument that culpable elements within the IDF require exposure in order to prevent potential disasters in future. However, Wald's arguments are conspicuously absent from subsequent October War historiography. Whereas the Agranat Commission's findings have been repeated and criticised at great length, Wald's report has not even warranted a rebuttal. O'Ballance blames triumphalism for Israel's Yom Kippur trauma, and Wald argues that the institutionalisation of this triumphalism within the IDF cost lives. The lack of historical investigation into this argument, despite the continuing production of largely military histories of the October War, is almost inexplicable, especially considering the otherwise apparent need to locate blameworthy parties. The second sub-theme within the historiography under discussion takes a very different approach. Rather than searching for an accountable figure or institution, it completely removes the very idea of Israeli trauma by linking the war to other surprises.

The hunt for historical analogies

In evaluating the state of the October War historiography forty years after the event, it is also necessary to address the ongoing relevance of October War research. Within the trend of asking why Israel was surprised, the second sub-theme is a tendency to compare the October War to other surprise attacks. This has contributed to a better understanding of surprise in general, but it has had the unintended consequence of removing the October War from its Middle East context, and consequently from the arena in which it is most relevant to contemporary international affairs. Although the intention is very similar to those scholars operating in the historiography of blame, the method is quite different. Authors in this genre explore the perceptual bases for decision-making by broadening the scope of their analyses, but in the process, they, subsume the October War into a Western historical narrative only combated by the presence of a small amount of historiography from the Arab perspective.

A Western perspective

Abraham Ben-Zvi initiated the amalgamation of the October War into a more American historical narrative.[57] Subsequent studies then utilised Wohlsetter's noise barriers to understand the inherent difficulties of predicting surprise. All, however, use historical analogies to understand the October War and so incorporate the conflict of 1973 into a broader framework of essentially Western examples. Although Ben-Zvi compares the October War to many international surprise attacks, including Chinese intervention in the Korean War and the Sino–Indian border war of 1962, the comparisons to Operation Barbarossa and, even more so, to Pearl Harbour are those that have endured throughout the October War historiography.

The salient point of this research is to question: how is it possible to detect real warning signals without the benefit of hindsight? Theoretically, Ben-Zvi notes, "whenever both strategic and tactical assumptions of actualities converge, an immediate threat will be perceived, leading the observing state to take precautionary measures. However, the question still remains whether a threat will be perceived in cases where the two sets of assumptions—strategic and tactical—conflict."[58] The examples of other surprise attacks are then useful case studies of situations when this divergence occurred.[59] Although Ben-Zvi concludes that the answer is to evaluate tactical data independent of prior assumptions,[60] in practice this is impractical and perhaps even impossible. This may be why later research by Handel and Shlaim specifically refrains from advocating a tangible change in policy.

In a pamphlet and article produced in 1976 and 1977 respectively, Handel applies Wohlsetter's "noise levels" and many Second World War examples of surprise attacks to try to explain the underlying causes of Israel's surprise in 1973.[61] The specific noise barriers Handel highlights are, firstly, that "the enemy"—its fluid, secretive and deceptive preparations for war, resulting in both real and falsified intelligence being treated the same—creates only "noise" and no "signals".[62] The second barrier is "the international environment", which can divert attention or create a false sense of tranquillity.[63] A third barrier of "self-generated noise", what the Agranat Commission identified as "the Concept", can then render signals useless, due to hyper-rigidity or flexibility.[64] The very nature of surprise makes it difficult to predict. Handel also highlights the tendency to ascribe domestic intentions to the enemy, because cultural differences change perceptions of victory and defeat. Whereas the Unites States and Israel would not consider launching a war without the prospect of total military victory, Arab countries can enter conflicts to secure political ends, even in defeat. As Handel must show similarity or correlation in order to use Wohlsetter's framework in relation to the October War, roughly two-thirds of his article, "The October War and the Inevitability of Surprise", is devoted to historical analogies—elements of Pearl Harbour and Operation Barbarossa. Based on these examples, Handel concludes that "it is always safer to gear one's plans more to the capabilities of the enemy than to his intentions", as signals of the latter are very difficult to differentiate from noise without the benefit of hindsight.[65] Surprise, he decides, is inevitable.

Alternatively, Shlaim utilises a very similar theoretical framework in his 1977 study and reaches slightly different conclusions. Shlaim's article focuses on the Israeli misperception of Arab intentions in 1973, a subject of study that corresponds to the historical examples of Japanese intentions in Pearl Harbour and German aims in Operation Barbarossa. Surprise, Shlaim posits, was never due to a dearth of information or intelligence, "but to an incorrect evaluation of the available information".[66] Also using Wohlsetter's framework of "noise barriers", Shlaim provides on overview of the psychological and institutional roots of surprise, placing emphasis on successful Arab deception and alert fatigue as key reasons for the Israeli predictive failure. The end result is a defence of the intelligence services for the sheer difficulty involved in distinguishing real warning signals from "noise", and an indictment of decision-makers whose preconceptions transformed intelligence into a rubber-stamping exercise. Although Shlaim suggests institutional reforms to combat the development of a similar situation in future, he admits that no procedure is infallible.[67] The research of Ben-Zvi, Handel and Shlaim is focused primarily on understanding the nature of surprise itself in order to gain a better understanding of Israel's traumatic experience in the October War. However, as their approaches use historical analogies within a theoretical framework, the analysis of the October War becomes somewhat diluted. The result is that in Hybel's 1986 book, *The Logic of Surprise in International Conflict*,[68] the October War is integrated into studies of Pearl Harbour and Operation Barbarossa based on Wohlsetter's noise barriers, with the specific intent of developing a predictive theory of surprise rather than advancing any understanding of the 1973 conflict itself. The effect is an erosion of the October War's Middle East context and stand-alone importance.

Arab perspective

The tendency to focus on a more theoretical understanding of surprise has led to a diluting of the October War historiography that removes the conflict from its roots in and relevance to the politics of the Middle East. The only counter to this is the October War historiography with a specifically Arab focus, which, in the English language, is relatively scarce in comparison to Israeli or US-centric studies. There are several key books that dominate this genre: Mohammed Heikal's *The Road to Ramadan*,[69] Saad el-Shazly's *The Crossing of Suez: The October War 1973*[70] and Mohamed el-Gamasy's *The October War*.[71] These works are crucial to the October War historiography precisely because they are not concerned with the Israeli failure to anticipate surprise attack and are even fairly dismissive of the Egyptian and Syrian deception achievement. What they represent instead is one part of an unbroken narrative of Israeli occupation and its disruptive impact on Arab states' regional and domestic politics.

Rather than viewing the October War as a next instalment of surprise attacks following Pearl Harbour and Operation Barbarossa, the Arab view helps to maintain the war as part of the Arab–Israeli conflict, a natural progression from June 1967 to October 1973, to reclaim what had been lost to Israeli aggression.[72] This portrayal fits neither a victimised Israeli narrative of the October War, nor a disinterested comparison to surprise attacks more generally. For the purposes of this chapter, the importance of the Arab perspective lies not in its fundamental opposition to Israeli-centric historiography—though a plurality of narratives is always desirable; the Arab viewpoint is crucial simply because it maintains an understanding of the October War as neither too narrowly Israeli, nor too broad and distorted to the point of appearing "Western". The major works in this genre highlight this common theme.

First published in 1975, Heikal's *Road to Ramadan* provides a primarily Egyptian, but overall Arab view of the conflict, with a diplomatic rather than military focus. The tone is grimly resigned, and although Heikal does highlight the comprehensive nature of Egypt's deception plan—covering military, diplomatic and informational fields—his interpretation is far from triumphalist.[73] "[S]uccessful though the deception plan proved to be", Heikal notes, "a great deal was owed to that fickle ally, general Luck."[74] Critically, he highlights the likelihood of future war because the superpowers ignored the root of Arab–Israeli tensions; Kissinger orchestrated the truce, for example, primarily as an exercise in US–Soviet relations.[75] Heikal asserts that neither Israel nor Kissinger understood the importance that Arabs placed on the historical dimension.[76] Attempting to approach issues with pure pragmatism singularly failed to address the "obstinancy of the Egyptian and Arab character".[77] It is interesting, therefore, that the dominant, Israeli-centric historiography of the October War has mirrored this fundamental oversight. Heikal asks, "[h]ow did it happen that the Israelis were completely surprised, strategically as well as tactically? In my opinion the Israelis completely misunderstood history."[78]

In contrast to *The Road to Ramadan*, books by Shazly and Gamasy largely reflect the exonerative approach taken by Moshe Dayan and Eli Zeira in their memoirs. Shazly feels he was made a scapegoat for Egypt's military failure, and uses *The Crossing of Suez* to redirect blame onto Sadat for various blunders and interferences.[79] This is a book primarily concerned with championing the Egyptian military but, like Heikal,

Shazly highlights the continuity between Arab–Israeli wars. The former Armed Forces Chief of Staff makes a point of stressing the difficulties Egypt faced crossing the canal, and how the spirit of 1967 pushed them on. Similarly, Gamasy's *The October War* focuses primarily on redressing the distribution of blame; it charges that Sadat's interference led to the four-day pause after Egyptian forces crossed the canal, even though Gamasy claims that seizing the passes was the agreed-upon objective from the beginning.[80] Again, however, a substantial section of the book is devoted to June 1967 and the Arab desire to reclaim conquered territory. In terms of the October War historiography, the importance of this simplistic acknowledgement cannot be overstated. This idea, that in spirit the Arab offensive in 1973 was a response to Israeli occupation, has been largely ignored in the dominant October War historiography. Although the purpose of this chapter is not to call for numerical equality between works with differing perspectives, the Arab viewpoint is vital to note because it demonstrates this oversight within the dominant, surprise-orientated Israeli/American viewpoint, an omission that limits its usefulness to understanding contemporary Middle East politics. In this sense, the Arab perspective, though limited in terms of availability in English, performs an important function in simply reminding the reader of the October War's regional context, and therefore its ongoing relevance.

Conclusion

The major historiographical trend discussed in this chapter is one in which consistency asks, why was Israel surprised? Within this area of research, two sub-themes have emerged. "The Blame Game" is a trend within the October War historiography that searches for an answer to the question: who was to blame? In this sub-theme, scholars search for culpable parties, finding them within the intelligence community in the form of AMAN Director Eli Zeira as well as Mossad, in the political elite within both Israel and the United States, and finally in the unexamined institutional failings of the Israeli Defence Force. This stream of analysis also begins to highlight the inherent difficulty in predicting surprise due to deception, alert fatigue, or cry-wolf syndrome, human error and over-confidence, as well as potential international political ramifications.[81] The way so much scholarship focuses on preventing future surprise should indicate the overall trauma caused by the October War. What this perspective creates, however, is a highly personal account relevant only to Israel and Israeli historiography. As the presence and actions of the Jewish state continue to impact on regional and international politics, it is important that transformative events within Israel are also understood for their broader implications on issues such as, for example, Palestinian statehood and the Iranian threat. The other sub-theme has sought to expand analyses beyond the Israeli perspective, but it has resulted in a watering down of the conflict's ongoing relevance.

"The Hunt for Historical Analogies" is the second sub-theme within the October War historiography, asking, why Israel was surprised. Although its conclusions—that noise barriers prevent adequate assessment of available intelligence, making no approach infallible—come from excellent works of scholarly research, its contribution has broadened October War scholarship to the point of making it irrelevant to contemporary international affairs. The examples most often cited—Pearl Harbour and Operation Barbarossa—are flawed historical analogies, in the sense that they represent surprise attacks in which the perpetrators later surrendered. The United States and the Soviet Union achieved unconditional victories over their attackers, which is precisely what Israel failed to secure in 1973. Using the Allies' Second World War surprises in this way distorts understanding of the Israeli trauma identified in the historiography of "The Blame Game". Also, following 9/11, it must be recognised that state-orchestrated surprise attacks are far less of a concern than smaller acts of violence perpetrated by terrorist organisations. Understanding only the surprise element of the October War is, therefore, far less relevant today than it was during the Cold War. Scholarly investigations of retrospective studies are conducted because they are perceived as useful, but warning failures are always context-specific, and as such have limitations. The problem with comparisons to Pearl Harbour and Barbarossa is that, while they were relevant to the state system during the Cold War, this model is no longer applicable. The analogies employed remove the October War from its Middle East context and distort understanding of the trauma that Israel felt following the conflict and its long-term implications for politics in the region. Highlighting the hubris that followed 1967 as a negative does not make the insecurity following 1973 a positive. Peace with Egypt did not alter the Israeli view of the October War as a near-disaster and did not reverse the existential fear reborn in 1973. The Arab–Israeli conflict is still the most pertinent and potentially explosive problem the international community faces, and history has remained paramount to both sides during periods of negotiation.

In 2006, Uri Bar-Joseph addressed the historiography of the October War and declared that it had not received the academic attention it deserves.[82] This observation remains a pertinent one. While news pundits and academics speculate on how Israel will react to Iran's nuclear programme, looking back to the conflict that re-awakened an existential fear in the Jewish state might be an appropriate place to start. The October War, partly due to the intervention of the United States, threatened the central tenet of Zionism; that Israel was a safe, self-sufficient haven.[83] Numerous studies since 1973, not least the works by Heikal and Shazly, point to very limited Arab war aims, but this has not erased what Liebman describes as "the residue of fears which the War raised, the fear for the viability of the Jewish state, the realization that there are safer places in the world for the Jew than in Israel, and the knowledge that Israeli sovereignty depends on the goodwill of at least one superpower".[84] Rather than trying to reach an understanding of the October War in a way that contributes to either an overly personal or impersonal understanding of history, scholars need to question why this war is relatively ignored in the broader field of international studies. Investigations of the war remain far more relevant to Israeli history than world history, paradoxically, because the historical analogies used to understand the war— Pearl Harbour and Operation Barbarossa—are largely irrelevant to global politics today. In the final analysis, the October War historiography could provide the utility that scholars utilising historical analogies initially intended to pursue, but first it must be reinserted into a regional Middle East context that provides the salient focus for comprehending contemporary international affairs.

3

ISRAEL AND THE OCTOBER WAR

Jacob Eriksson

For most Israelis, the October War is a traumatic chapter of history which continues to provoke uncomfortable feelings. Liebman notes that the Hebrew term which quickly became associated with it is *mehdal.* The word roughly translates as "omission", "oversight" or "shortcoming": something that went wrong because of a failure to act.[1] The joint Egyptian–Syrian attack of 6 October 1973 took Israel and the rest of the world completely by surprise, and the Israel Defence Forces (IDF) were caught off guard. Following the conclusion of hostilities, many Israelis wanted to know how this could have happened, particularly at a time when the security situation was deemed excellent.

Israeli victory in the Six Day War of 1967 radically altered the Middle East and had a profound effect not only on Israel's borders but Israel's national psyche. It ushered in a new era which seemed to invert the classic Israeli David and Arab Goliath parallel and rendered Israel a self-assured occupying power. This newfound role presented the young state with a series of difficult questions regarding national identity, national goals and future relations with its enemies in the region. They were the subject of debate, disagreement and division within Israeli society, which continue to this very day.

THE OCTOBER 1973 WAR

This chapter will examine Israeli foreign policy which stemmed from this new regional configuration and Israeli mindset, analyse the failure of diplomacy aimed to forge peace between Egypt and Israel, and consider if the war could possibly have been avoided. It will look at the Israeli rationale prior to the war in order to explain how Israel was initially found wanting. Focusing primarily on protagonists such as Prime Minister Golda Meir, Defence Minister Moshe Dayan and Chief of Staff Lieutenant General David "Dado" Elazar, it will analyse the factors which informed Israeli decision-making during this traumatic time. Finally, this chapter will consider the impact of the war on Israeli politics and society, identify the salient domestic issues which emerged following the ceasefire, and reflect on the lessons to be learned.

Post-1967 Israel: an insecure David

To the religious community, the new territorial acquisitions were nothing less than a miracle. The return of all of biblical *Eretz Yisrael* to Israeli control, including the Old City of Jerusalem and the Western Wall, Judea, and Samaria, seemed to be the work of divine providence, and the settlement of these lands was considered the next phase of redemption.[2] For many secular Israelis, these territories spurred a religious fervour which had previously been muted, and evoked "nostalgia and historical romanticism" in others.[3] Many on both sides of the political spectrum argued that the territories offered an effective defence against future Arab aggression and provided the strategic depth required to ensure Israel's security. Future wars would be fought further away from Israeli population centres, attacks could be met by a relatively small number of troops and thereby be less disruptive to society, and new well-fortified borders would have a deterrent effect on Arab forces.[4]

Prime Minister Levi Eshkol presided over a National Unity Government full of divergent positions on the future of the territories, both between and within the major political blocs, which made articulation of an official position on the matter immensely difficult. Right-wing Gahal consisted of Herut, who claimed the West Bank as part of the Land of Israel, and the General Zionists or Liberals, who did not; the left-wing Alignment saw Mapai, whose leaders were mostly "pragmatic politicians who had accepted the pre-war territorial status quo", joined with Ahdut Ha'avodah, whose leaders were territorial expansionists.

When Rafi later joined the Alignment to form the new Labour party, they further strengthened those advocating an activist defence policy and expansionism in the West Bank,[5] creating "a quarrelsome organism with diverse political philosophies."[6] Retention of the occupied territories created common ground between seemingly unlikely political allies. Foreign Minister Abba Eban observed, much to his chagrin, that a number of "virulent right-wing extremists, excited advocates of annexation and veteran Likud standard-bearers appeared side by side with members of the Labour movement", coming together under the banner of the Movement for Greater Israel.[7]

In March 1969, Golda Meir was elected leader of the Labour party and thus succeeded Eshkol, who had died earlier in February, as prime minister. She was unmistakably hawkish regarding the territories, and committed to maintaining the National Unity Government. Barzilai observes that after the 1969 Israeli elections, a Labour-led government could have been formed without Gahal, but Meir opted against it. Together with Moshe Dayan and cabinet member Israel Galili, she considered Gahal's inclusion in government "a good pretext for rejecting demands by dovish Labourites (for example, Abba Eban) to initiate a peace plan based on far-reaching compromises and territorial concessions."[8] Meir avoided any divisive national or international debate on the specifics of peace for as long as possible, claiming that "the time has not yet come to draw maps."[9]

Meir had—to use one of the more diplomatic expressions offered in descriptions of her—a "penchant for inflexibility."[10] She staunchly maintained the principles that had guided Eshkol's government: first, no return to the old international borders; second, no withdrawal without direct negotiations with the Arabs and a peace treaty. Mordechai Gazit, the director of the Prime Minister's Office under Meir, notes that "in Golda Meir's eyes, these were not abstract principles but articles of faith that were absolute and unassailable," informed by Israel's previous experience with abstract "understandings" and armistice agreements.[11] In her autobiography, Meir writes that "'intransigent' was to become my middle name. But neither Eshkol nor I, nor the overwhelming majority of Israelis, could make a secret of the fact that we weren't at all interested … in a 'settlement' that would win us compliments about being reasonable and intelligent but that would endanger our lives."[12]

Dayan describes her as "a courageous, stubborn, and determined woman," who was "blessed by the Lord with the capacity to see the world in bold black and stark white, free from the range of twilight shades."[13] Popularly perceived as the hero of the Six Day War, Dayan exercised great influence both politically and publicly, and as a member of Rafi sought to maintain Israeli control of the occupied territories. As a proponent of the creeping annexation of the West Bank and "functional compromise" rather than partition, he supported Jewish settlement in a number of key hillside positions and was "the architect of a relationship of total dependence and subservience of the Palestinians to Israel and her economy" which gave the occupation a sense of permanence.[14] To him, returning to the West Bank "was a renewed experience of getting to know the familiar land of my childhood which … had become much dearer to me with time."[15] In 1971 he also famously stated, "I prefer Sharm el-Sheikh without peace to peace without Sharm el-Sheikh."

Whether or not Meir's black and white view of the world was in fact a blessing is doubtful. Shlaim observes that "she epitomised the policy of immobilism, of sitting tight on the new ceasefire lines and refusing to budge until the Arabs agreed to make peace on Israel's terms."[16] In a similar vein, Ben-Ami describes her as a "self-righteous, intransigent" woman who "turned political inaction and righteousness into a system of government", all of which "made her premiership one of almost inevitable decline towards war."[17] This view was shared and exemplified by Abba Eban. Any notion that the territorial status quo could be maintained was, he argued, a "blatant falsehood": in his eyes, no one could have "seriously believed [as the Movement for Greater Israel claimed] that 'the present boundaries of our country are a guarantee of the security of the state and of peace.' Unless they were replaced by agreed boundaries they would be a guarantee of future wars."[18]

It was immediately clear, however, that such an agreement would be a diplomatic feat of the highest order. On 19 June, 1967, Israeli Cabinet Resolution 563 approved secret guidelines for a potential future agreement with Egypt and Syria based on the pre-existing international borders between them and the security needs of Israel. No agreement could be reached regarding Jordan and the West Bank, and the Gaza Strip was deemed to fall within Israeli territory according to the international borders.[19] In his detailed analysis of this cabinet resolution, Raz argues that the formulation was carefully worded to make the possibility of border modifications implicit rather than explicit, in order to keep parts of the Sinai and the Golan Heights.[20] Shlaim observes that this had effectively become policy by July, with cabinet ministers calling for the retention and settlement of the Golan Heights.[21]

The "three no's" adopted on 1 September at the Arab summit conference held in Khartoum—no peace with Israel, no recognition of Israel, no negotiations with it, and insistence on the rights of the Palestinian people—confirmed in Israeli eyes that the Arabs were utterly unwilling to compromise. Morris argues that in part, this was a response to Israel's unwillingness to consider withdrawal from the West Bank and Gaza. These twin stands mutually reinforced each other, with Arab rejectionism in turn forming part of the rationale behind Israeli intransigence and expansionism.[22] The cabinet resolution of 19 June was then effectively rescinded in October in favour of a more explicit position that any settlement would have to be based on secure, defensible, and negotiated borders, meaning no return to the 4 June 1967 lines.[23] Although the Israeli cabinet and Morris' analysis framed this as a reaction to Khartoum, Raz and Ben-Ami argue that Resolution 563 was never intended for presentation to the Arabs as a generous peace offer, but "a diplomatic manoeuvre" to win over the United States, and was in all likelihood never presented to the Arabs.[24]

From the end of 1967, the basic diplomatic fault-lines were quite clear. Israel wanted a comprehensive peace with the Arab states in exchange for withdrawal from parts of the occupied territories to secure borders to be determined in direct negotiations. In stark contrast, the Arabs called for an unconditional withdrawal from all the occupied territories without a formal peace, and Egyptian leader Gamal Abd-el Nasser would not countenance a separate treaty with Israel. The ambiguous language of UN Security Council Resolution 242 was, in the words of Ben-Ami, "the result of the need to find a formula that would reconcile Israel's unrealistic expectation to have full peace for less than all the territories, and the Arabs' drive for a full restitution of land in exchange for a watered-down state of non-belligerency."[25] Fundamentally, each looked upon the positions of the other as a series of unacceptable circles that could not be squared with their own.

Following a lengthy period of sporadic clashes along the ceasefire line, in March 1969 Nasser stepped up what became known as the War of Attrition against Israel. Egypt had been thoroughly humiliated in the Six Day War, and some measure of Egyptian honour and pride needed to be restored. He calculated that only through military pressure could he force an Israeli withdrawal from the Sinai, and sought to exploit the Israeli sensitivity towards sustaining casualties. In order to put an end to the domestically highly unpopular war, Israel launched an in-depth bombing campaign between January and April 1970, eventually leading to a ceasefire in August.[26] Meir and the military leadership failed to notice that Israeli possession of the territories had not deterred the Egyptians, but in fact had the opposite effect.

Although the term *mehdal* commonly refers to the immediate pre-amble to war, it can arguably also apply to the years of diplomacy preceding the war. Between 1969 and 1973, a number of diplomatic initiatives were undertaken to reach an Egyptian-Israeli peace agreement, notably by UN special representative Gunnar Jarring, American Secretary of State William Rogers, and Assistant Secretary of State Joseph Sisco, but these produced scant results.[27] This was largely due to the fact that Egyptian and Israeli positions were diametrically opposed and each was guilty of obstinacy, though a lack of committed mediators with suitable bargaining power also hampered negotiations.[28]

However, of the two parties, Egypt was certainly the more proactive. Israel rejected the initial Rogers Plan of December 1969, based on Resolution 242, and reluctantly accepted a watered down ceasefire plan known as Rogers B in July 1970. This was only made possible by a set of assurances from President Nixon, including that borders were to be fixed by negotiations, and promises of economic and military assistance. The acceptance of 242 and the concept of withdrawal from territories contained in Rogers B was enough to make Gahal leave the National Unity Government, which simultaneously illustrated the limits of Israeli flexibility and the importance of the American relationship.[29]

In a speech on 4 February 1971, Egyptian President Anwar Sadat outlined an initiative to open the Suez Canal in exchange for a partial withdrawal of Israeli troops on the east bank of the canal, to be realised "as a first step in a timetable to be laid down with a view to implementing the other provisions of the Security Council Resolution [242]." In later speeches and discussions with American mediators, he emphasised that such an interim agreement was not a separate peace but linked to a comprehensive solution and implementation of 242.[30]

Michael Sterner, director of Egyptian Affairs at the US State Department at the time, found the Israeli stance following Sadat's overture to be "singularly inflexible, unresponsive, and unimaginative." True, Sadat's insistence on linkage made the proposal anathema to Meir and a majority of her cabinet, but Sterner argues that there were signs of flexibility from Sadat and that these were not adequately tested.[31] Although he primarily blames Egyptian intransigence for the lack of peace, Gazit does acknowledge that Israel should have invested more energy in probing Sadat's positions of February 1971.[32]

Dayan had in fact previously proposed a similar interim agreement towards the end of 1970—no doubt informed by his analysis immediately prior to the Six Day War that an Israeli presence on the Suez Canal would lead to continued war,[33] and his desire for a partial settlement to avoid the tough decisions a comprehensive settlement would entail— but Meir and cabinet members Yigal Allon and Israel Galili were opposed to any withdrawal. Dayan told Eban that unless Meir accepted his proposal, he would not put it up for a cabinet vote, and so he "reluctantly let the matter drop." Eban always regretted that Dayan did not show tenacity in support of his "imaginative proposal, which could have averted the Yom Kippur War."[34] In a private meeting with Sisco in May 1971, Dayan stood by the principles of his earlier proposal. Gideon Rafael, director general of the Israeli Foreign Ministry, recalls that "Golda was demonstrably irked when Simha Dinitz, the head of her private office, reported Dayan's retreat from the official government line. She sternly admonished her cabinet to stick to its guns and Dayan returned to the fold from his sortie without firing a single verbal shot in his defence."[35]

In February 1973, American National Security Adviser Henry Kissinger and his Egyptian counterpart Hafez Isma'il met for talks in New York at Sadat's request. Isma'il spoke of the possibility of an interim agreement ensuring disengagement from the Suez Canal, but only as part of an agreed comprehensive plan to be implemented over stages, with full peace and normalisation to be realised in a settlement with all other parties, including Syria and the Palestinians. Though it contained levels of flexibility on certain issues, Kissinger described it as "far-reaching but one-sided": "[t]he hint of a separate Egyptian-Israeli accord was so heavily qualified with unacceptable conditions that it was more compatible with a come-on to get us involved than with a serious offer to negotiate." He believed that more time was needed to determine what Sadat had in mind, but time was not on their side.[36]

In a meeting with President Richard Nixon on 1 March, Dinitz and Gazit argue that after being briefed, Meir expressed a readiness to enter into either a partial agreement on the Suez Canal or an overall settlement, which would include Israel's acknowledgement of complete Egyptian sovereignty over all of Sinai, but that Egypt was not interested.[37] In stark contrast, Bar-Joseph and Rafael argue that the Israeli procurement of American arms was the focus of Meir's meeting, the Egyptian proposal being only a minor issue, and that on the basis of her priorities standstill was the preferred option.[38]

Kissinger noted that Meir was happy for him to continue to explore ideas with Isma'il, but "it gave no real reason for optimism, for it kept all options open." She "proclaimed that 'we never had it so good' and insisted that a stalemate was safe because the Arabs had no military option. ... With respect to negotiations, Golda's attitude was simple. She considered Israel militarily impregnable; there was strictly speaking no need for any change."[39] Past military heroes such as Generals Yitzhak Rabin and Ariel Sharon expressed similar views, as did major Israeli newspapers.[40]

This negative and even dismissive view of Arab military capabilities and skills meant that many did not consider them capable of an effective crossing of the Suez Canal or a coordinated modern war.[41] This impression was heightened when, in July 1972, Sadat expelled Soviet military advisers and personnel from Egypt, thereby diminishing their war capabilities. Moreover, as a leader, Sadat was drastically underestimated. The year in 1971, which Sadat declared would be "a year of decision", passed without any obvious decision, and he was generally not considered a leader capable of bold military action.[42] In 1972 Deputy Chief of Staff Major General Israel Tal, echoing doves like Eban, expressed the opinion that the status quo would inexorably leave Sadat with no recourse but war.[43] However, due to the prevailing sense of military superiority, even many of the political and military establishment who agreed did not see this as an immediate cause for alarm.

"The Concept", surprise and decision-making

Following the conclusion of the October War, the Agranat Commission of inquiry was established to investigate the intelligence failure and the preparedness of the country for war. It found that a primary reason for failure was the "obdurate adherence" of intelligence officials, primarily Director of Military Intelligence General Eli Zeira, "to what was known as 'the concept'". According to the Concept, after its experience of previous wars, Egypt would not attack Israel until she had the requisite air power to hit Israeli Air Force bases in-depth and reduce their air superiority. This capability, the military estimated, would not be achieved until 1975 at the earliest. Furthermore, Syria would only launch an attack simultaneously with Egypt.[44]

The first element of the Concept was taken as an article of faith and "not adequately reconsidered in view of the pressure of the changing political circumstances" which faced Sadat, or "the build-up of enemy strength with additional armaments systems" such as surface-to-surface missiles, surface-to-air missiles and Sagger anti-tank missiles.[45] As Brigadier General Aryeh Shalev, then the deputy director of military Intelligence, has explained, Israel had excellent information regarding enemy arms, troop movements and concentrations, capabilities and overall readiness for war, but failed to appreciate enemy intentions correctly.[46] Rigid adherence to the Concept made Zeira and others around him dismissive of dissenting analysis from a number of junior officers who, from the end of September, concluded that Egyptian and Syrian activities were for war. These evaluations were omitted from the intelligence reports presented to the political leadership.[47]

On Wednesday 3 October, Dayan convened a meeting at Meir's home in Jerusalem to discuss the reported changes on the Syrian and Egyptian fronts, attended by Meir, Allon, Galili, Elazar and Shalev (since Zeira was ill). Presenting a detailed view of both fronts, Shalev described the Egyptian build-up as an exercise and the Syrian movement as an emergency deployment. Following an unexpected aerial battle on 13 September in which the Syrians lost thirteen Mig-21s and the Israelis one Mirage, Dayan had been particularly concerned about the situation on the Golan Heights, expecting some level of Syrian reprisal.[48] He had discussed the matter at length with Elazar, who acknowledged that the Syrians could attack from their deployment, but argued that "nothing can be more idiotic." The unprecedented deployment was deemed to be due to apprehension of an Israeli attack. Dayan argued that the new SAM layout, which predominantly covered the Golan Heights, was "not a normal defensive move." Still, Shalev replied that, on the basis of their material, "Egypt estimates that it still cannot go to war" and thus "the possibility of a combined war—Egyptian and Syrian—does not seem probable," since Syria would not attack on its own. Elazar concurred. The capability and readiness existed, but the probability was deemed "low."[49] Meir was satisfied with this appraisal, and noted that "nobody at the meeting thought that it was necessary to call up the reserves, and nobody thought that war was imminent."[50]

Two days later, intelligence received information that the families of Soviet advisers had been evacuated from Egypt and Syria. Additionally, aerial reconnaissance showed that Egyptian strength along the Suez Canal was unprecedented. Following meetings of the chief of staff and minister of defence's forum on the morning of Friday 5 October, Dayan, Elazar and Zeira met with Meir. Elazar had decided to activate "an extremely high state of alert" for the IDF, particularly in the Air Force and the Armour, and to reinforce both fronts with additional tanks. At a later meeting of ministers around noon, while agreeing with Zeira's evaluation that Israel did not face war, Elazar said, "I must say that we do not have sufficient proof that they are not about to attack. We don't have adequate information that they do want to attack, but I cannot say, based on the information that we have, that they are not going to attack." Mobilisation of reserves would only occur in the event of "further indications" for war, and ministers agreed that Meir and Dayan could authorise such a move without them.[51]

The concept of early warning was a pillar of the national security doctrine. In April 1973, Zeira assured Meir that "if Egypt intended to launch a massive crossing of the Suez Canal we would know about it in advance, and we would be able to give a warning, not only a tactical one but also an operational one, i.e. a number of days in advance."[52] In the early hours of 6 October, roughly ten hours prior to the outbreak of war, an attack was forecast for 18:00, when in fact the attack began at 14:00. This was significant, as this information would help inform the leadership's decision whether or not to mobilise reserves.

However, it was not decisive. A substantial element of hubris also influenced decisions. There was an inherent assumption that the regular army as deployed was strong enough to repel or at the very least contain any attack even without reserves, who could then be mobilised for a counter-offensive. As Gazit has observed, the issue of early "warning becomes almost … a negligible thing if you assume that you are ready," and Dayan had expressed satisfaction with Elazar's reinforcements.[53]

As the Arab co-ordinated attack became an impending reality, Dayan and Elazar disagreed strongly on the required response. In a meeting at 06:00, 6 October, Elazar proposed a pre-emptive air strike against the Syrian air force and air defences, and the full mobilisation of reserves. Dayan disagreed on both counts. With regard to the air strike, his primary concern was political, in that he worried about the White House's reaction to an Israeli strike when the Americans, like the Israeli estimates, had not deemed a war likely. Dayan argued in favour of a limited mobilisation for defensive purposes, rejecting the requisite forces "for a counterattack in a war that did not start." Bar-Joseph argues persuasively that their differences suggested that Dayan, unlike Elazar, was not convinced that war would break out.[54]

Their disagreement was brought to Meir, who also rejected a pre-emptive strike. In her autobiography, she recalls, "'Dado,' I said, 'I know all the arguments in favour of a pre-emptive strike, but I am against it. We don't know now, any of us, what the future will hold, but there is always the possibility that we will need help, and if we strike first, we will get nothing from anyone. ... with a heavy heart I am going to say no.'" On mobilisation, however, she sided more with Elazar and authorised a large-scale mobilisation of 100,000–120,000 troops, after Dayan had shown his relative flexibility on the matter by saying, "I won't resign if you decide against me." Even though this might give the impression that Israel had definitively opted for war and pre-emption, as Dayan feared, Meir reasoned that "if there really was a war, then we had to be in the very best position possible."[55]

Dayan's and Elazar's reluctance to mobilise earlier was also undoubtedly informed by a previous experience in May 1973 when Elazar ruled against the intelligence estimate, which predicted that the probability of war was low, and ordered partial mobilisation at a cost of $11 million in response to warnings of an attack which never materialised. Sadat had, in fact, planned his operation for May, but postponed it for political reasons. Not only did this incident increase confidence in the erroneous September/October intelligence estimate, but also heightened the costs, financial and political, of an additional unnecessary mobilisation.[56] While in the spring and summer of 1973 Dayan had thought the probability of an attack high, confidence in the Concept was entirely renewed by July, when he forecast that war was not likely to erupt in the coming decade.[57]

In turn, this also affected Meir. Of the Friday 5 October meeting, Meir later wrote that she was ill at ease on the subject of mobilisation, but ultimately sided with Dayan, the military, and the intelligence estimate because of their combined experience. "Today I know what I should have done. I should have overcome my hesitations. ... That Friday morning I should have listened to the warnings of my own heart and ordered a call-up."[58] Shlaim notes that Meir generally displayed an uncritical approach to the views offered by the IDF General Staff.[59] Clearly, she did not relish the role of arbiter between Dayan and Elazar: "'My God,' I thought, 'I have to decide which of them is right?'"[60]

With regard to both mobilisation and a pre-emptive strike, Elazar was thinking in purely military operational terms, but on the eve of war, broader politics guided decision-making. As Dayan reflected, "It is almost a tradition in the IDF for the military chiefs to urge more activity; I speak as a former chief of staff. It is for the political authority to impose limitations when necessary."[61] For the political echelon, it was necessary constantly to take into account the reaction of their American allies. Soon after refusing the pre-emptive strike, Meir summoned Kenneth Keating, the American ambassador to Israel, and asked him to communicate her decision to Washington, and requested the Americans do what they could to urge Egypt and Syria to stop the war. Meir explained to her cabinet that American assistance in terms of military supplies and diplomacy was vital, and that they would not be forthcoming if Israel was seen to have started the war. Dinitz, the recently appointed ambassador to the US, was sent back to his post with orders to secure future weapons deliveries.[62]

The eventual American airlift, which was bigger than the famed Berlin airlift of 1948/1949, began arriving on 14 October after lengthy discussion with Washington, and proved crucial on a number of counts. Militarily, it replenished Israeli losses and provided much needed ammunition. Dayan later admitted that the IDF had at one point practically run out of certain types of ammunition, an "ill-advised public admission" which shocked and disturbed Israelis.[63] It is reported that Meir decided to postpone the Israeli crossing of the Suez Canal until the airlift had begun, to be sure of supplies for a renewed offensive. Politically, it showed the Soviets that America stood firmly behind its ally and was capable of such a re-supply effort. Psychologically, it was extremely important for Israeli morale, given the pessimistic mood that prevailed at that time.[64]

In the early stages of the war, Dayan seemed to embody this pessimism. The picture painted by multiple first-hand accounts is one of a "sad and desperate" man whose anxiety was infectious and created "an atmosphere of a threat of destruction." On 7 October, he suggested that they should withdraw into the Sinai and establish a new defensive line, which could have prevented an Israeli counter-attack, made regaining lost territory difficult, and ran the risk of becoming the new border should a ceasefire be required. Bar-Joseph observes that "if Dayan's proposal was accepted, the tactical defeat of the war's first day could have become a strategic defeat in the war as a whole."[65] Meir recalls that she "listened to him in horror." Elazar, by contrast, advised against retreat and advocated going on the offensive the next day, and the cabinet agreed. Later that day, Dayan offered his resignation to Meir but she declined it, a decision she "never regretted."[66] The resignation of a minister of defence—and a national hero, no less—in wartime would have been an alarmist signal with a debilitating effect on morale. His decision-making was further called into question on the northern front where he recommended a withdrawal from the Golan Heights, a position that was overruled on the advice of former Chief of Staff Chaim Bar-Lev, who Meir had asked to evaluate Dayan's plans.[67]

After initial bitter and desperate fighting on the northern front—which was accorded priority in the early phase, to the point of diverting the air force from south to north and thereby suffering heavy losses—by 11 October the Golan Heights were recaptured and the Syrians were largely on the defensive, though the Israeli offensive was turning into a battle of attrition.[68] In the Sinai, the Israeli counter-offensive on 8 October failed, though the tide later swung in Israel's favour following a failed Egyptian offensive and the arrival of reserve forces. On the night of 15 October, after the airlift had begun, Sharon's forces crossed the Suez Canal and the Israelis continued to mount forces successfully on the western Egyptian bank.[69] The decision to cross the canal was subject to extensive debate. Elazar, Tal and Bar-Lev were in favour of crossing once Egyptian forces had been diminished, while Dayan was sceptical about the operation, though adding that he was not prepared to "wage a jihad against it." Elazar, frustrated by Dayan's indecision, insisted on a decision and the matter was left to the cabinet.[70] Herzog is highly critical of Dayan's indecisiveness at such key junctures during the war and notes that Dayan was in the habit of sharing responsibility for decisions, evidenced by his habit of regularly bringing Elazar and Zeira to cabinet meetings, something which Ben-Gurion would never have dreamed of.[71]

On 12 October, Meir had agreed to a renewed Soviet proposal to put a ceasefire in place. Whereas the notion had earlier been rejected due to the highly unfavourable location of the front lines, this decision was motivated by "starkly realistic" reasons: the delay of American arms supplies, the Soviet re-supply of the Arab states, and the ongoing war on two fronts.[72] After Sadat rejected a ceasefire on 13 October and the military situation changed in Israel's favour, Eban communicated to Kissinger that a ceasefire in place would not be welcomed. As the situation continued to worsen for Egypt, America and the Soviet Union heightened their negotiations. When a draft Security Council resolution was presented to the Israeli cabinet by Kissinger on 21 October, due for discussion at the UN that evening, they were not pleased about the fact that the US had failed to co-ordinate it with them and presented it in a "take it or leave it" manner. Still, Eban noted that the proposed Resolution 338 was a "staggering victory" for Israel, which saw Arab acceptance of negotiations, and the cabinet accepted it.[73]

Yet, war continued beyond the agreed ceasefire after Israeli claims of Egyptian violations, which Kissinger treats with scepticism in his memoirs, and Israel took the opportunity to encircle the Egyptian Third Army. As the superpower conflict came to the fore with the infamous DefCon 3 alert and an intense flurry of diplomacy, which involved substantial American coercion of their ally, Israel eventually accepted a renewed ceasefire. The Americans "had supported Israel throughout the war" and "had just run the risk of war with the Soviet Union," but, as Kissinger argues, 'our shared interests did not embrace the elimination of the Third Army.'[74] Eban concurred, reflecting that "it was hard to believe that the destruction of the Egyptian Third Army was an aim sufficiently vital to justify military confrontation with the Soviet Union with no parallel support from the United States."[75] Having strengthened their relationship considerably, America signalled that the time for diplomacy had come and that they expected responsiveness from Israel in return, as they embarked upon a negotiating process which ultimately led to the signing of the Egyptian-Israeli peace agreement in 1979.[76]

ISRAEL AND THE OCTOBER WAR

The aftermath and the Agranat Commission

Following the announcement of the ceasefire acrimonious debate began surrounding responsibility for failures in the early stages of the war, resulting in an unprecedented political crisis. Meir notes that "the general mood in Israel was very black. ... It was not just my resignation or Dayan's that was being called for in that storm of protest: it was a call to eliminate from the scene everyone who could possibly be held responsible for what had happened and to start all over again with ... people who were not tainted by the charge of having led the nation astray."[77] Labour leaders resolutely rejected calls for the government's resignation amid accusations of complacency and failure, but with public pressure mounting, the president of the Supreme Court, Shimon Agranat, was eventually asked to lead a commission of inquiry.

Across the political spectrum and among the wider public, criticism and dissent were widespread. Demobilised soldiers formed protest groups, expressing disillusionment with the government and calling for reforms to increase political accountability. Conceptions of territory and security were questioned anew. Dovish parties on the left such as Mapam, Moked and Meri, in addition to certain factions within the Labour party and extra-parliamentary groups such as Shinui, questioned the concept of "secure borders" and called for a peace plan based on significant territorial withdrawal in exchange for peace and security. Uri Avneri told the Knesset, "if we are relinquishing a chance at peace because of a wish to annex territories—then we are creating a bloody paradox, one which will condemn us to fight a war every few years."[78]

Convinced that the war was another attempt to eradicate the Jewish state rather than a limited war to recapture lost Arab territories, Meir rebutted such arguments by asking people to imagine the catastrophe that could have befallen them had Israel withdrawn to the 4 June 1967 lines, thus looking to justify her stance prior to the war.[79] The right-wing Likud party, formed prior to the 1973 elections, had been against acceptance of the two ceasefires, favouring the complete military defeat of Egypt and Syria. They remained staunchly opposed to any territorial withdrawal, together with voices from the religious right.[80]

Ha'aretz noted that "the Israeli public is engulfed in much confusion with regard to its stand vis-à-vis the political leadership." Although a poll showed that about half the population did not approve of Meir's conduct of state affairs, 39.9 percent were unable to select an alternative candidate for the position.[81] As a corollary, polls showed a large number of undecided voters, most of them disappointed Labour supporters. Labour's campaign focused on conveying an image of a "responsible, peace-seeking" leadership, as opposed to the extreme and even "trigger-happy" Likud, who they accused of lacking a coherent peace policy, an accusation which equally applied to a very divided Labour party. Aware of their shortcomings, one apologetic advertisement read, "Even a responsible government can err, but to elect an irresponsible government would be a grave error," and another, 'In spite of everything, the [Labour] Alignment!'[82] This seemed to sum up the feelings of a number of undecided voters, many of whom came back into the fold. Labour retained power, although the Alignment lost six seats and Likud gained eight, winning fifty-one and thirty-nine respectively.[83]

The Agranat Commission, whose initial report was published in April 1974, was scathing towards the Intelligence Branch and the military leadership, while exonerating the political leadership. Zeira and Shalev, together with two subordinates, were called to resign for their personal failures, and a number of recommendations were made to alter the military monopoly on analysis which "prevented independent political, strategic, operational and tactical intelligence evaluations." These included the strengthening of intelligence analysis within the Foreign Ministry and Mossad, and the appointment of a special adviser to the prime minister on intelligence to collate information from different branches, in effect creating a kind of National Security Council.[84]

Despite Elazar's widely commended conduct during the war itself, this did "not suffice to erase the imprint of the initial mistakes" and the Commission called for his dismissal. He was particularly admonished for not ordering a partial mobilisation on 1 October and by 5 October at the latest, and further held responsible for the inadequate deployment at the time of the attack and a lack of planning to deal with such an event.[85] Elazar dutifully resigned. Dayan, however, was spared substantial criticism in the initial report, despite Kissinger's observation that "every criticism of the chief of staff applied as well to his immediate superior."[86] Herzog too observes that "it would seem inconceivable … that any minister of defence—however able, however brilliant and however effective—could avoid ministerial responsibility for what occurred."[87]

The Commission argued that Dayan had been operating on misleading evaluations from his subordinates, and had shown great concern for the situation on the Syrian front prior to war. The political motivation behind Dayan's argument not to mobilise fully on the morning of 6 October "certainly cannot be dismissed as not being legitimate."[88] This seems decidedly unjust towards Elazar, as his call for full mobilisation was denied by Dayan and the ensuing argument delayed mobilisation by a number of hours. The Commission acknowledged the lack of clear division of authority and responsibilities between the government and the prime minister, the minister of defence, and the chief of staff on security matters, a highly significant problem immediately prior to and during the war, but merely pointed out the need for the government and the Knesset to consider the problem.[89]

Aside from a few minor criticisms, Meir was similarly cleared and even complimented by the Agranat Commission: "It is greatly to the Prime Minister's credit that, under the circumstances, during the emergency of Saturday morning, she made proper use of the authority vested in her to make decisions. She decided wisely, with common sense and speedily in favour of the full mobilisation of the reserves, despite weighty political considerations, thereby performing a most important service for the defence of the State."[90] Her determined, inflexible approach which contributed to the failure of diplomacy appeared to have been an asset during the days of crisis.[91] With ministerial responsibility still absent, the report caused a public outrage and prompted mass demonstrations calling for Dayan and Meir to resign.[92] Meir resigned on 10 April, 1974, replaced by Yitzhak Rabin, and Shimon Peres was appointed defence minister in Rabin's government, thus completing the removal of the old Labour elite directly associated with the war.

Although it ended in Israeli victory, the October War was nonetheless a national trauma with immense political ramifications. Myths of deterrence, security, and Israeli superiority were shattered, and the comfort found in the territorial status quo had proved illusory.[93] Having dominated Israeli politics since the inception of the state, the war accelerated the decline of the Labour party, undermining confidence in it and its leadership. Barzilai observes that "time honoured myths, including Labour's unique responsibility over national security, were dismissed by a large part of the public as unfounded."[94] This disillusionment made many gravitate towards the newly formed Likud, including young voters aged 25–39 but particularly the Sephardi community, whose sense of injustice over decades of discrimination at the hands of the Ashkenazi Labour elite reached a tipping point. With many Sephardim still on the lower rungs of the socio-economic and educational ladder, they considered Labour responsible for their inability to advance in Israeli society, a feeling exacerbated by wider issues like corruption, labour unrest, inflation, and housing shortages. A survey by the Israeli Institute of Applied Research showed that in September 1973, 62 per cent of Sephardim supported Labour, a figure which fell to 43 per cent by December 1973, and was clearly reflected in gains made by the Likud in the 1973 elections.[95]

This ideological shift from left to right was consolidated over the next four years, leading to a ground-breaking Likud victory in the 1977 elections. In his analysis of this shift, Akzin notes that in addition to the aforementioned issues, "squabbles within the Labour Party (after Golda Meir's resignation) and the indifferent public image of the new prime minister, Yitzhak Rabin, created the impression of a cabinet and a ruling party rent by serious disagreements and incapable of dealing effectively with the problems of the day."[96] Moreover, when a number of high-profile corruption scandals came to light, the Labour Party was popularly perceived to have been "sucked into a vortex of corruption which permeated its entire structure."[97]

While Shapiro and Mendilow certainly acknowledge the importance of long-term issues like the Sephardi shift, they also emphasise the broader systemic change in Israeli politics of the previous decades, in which party clustering brought about the demise of a dominant party system. Menachem Begin's coalition building and the eventual creation of the Likud in 1973 was thus crucial, as a credible alternative to Labour rule was required in order to translate this dissent into a power shift.[98] Though Begin certainly benefited from his fair share of fortunate timing, his religiosity, populism, and patriotism appealed to the Sephardim and other religious segments of society, embodied in his uncompromising stand on the retention of Judea and Samaria.[99]

Although an unlikely candidate to relinquish territory, even Begin came to accept that peace with Egypt was preferable to continued Israeli control of the Sinai. In a paradoxical way, the war brought peace between Egypt and Israel. On both sides, the attitudes which informed the immobilism of the pre-war diplomacy and which prevented any settlement were altered and opened the door for negotiations. When one considers the similarity between the disengagement agreement of 1974 and the proposed interim agreement of 1971, the transformative significance of the war becomes quite clear. While one can argue that what was offered to the Egyptians in 1978 could have been offered earlier, this neglects to take into account the mental barriers that existed and the significant effects of the war.[100]

Moreover, it omits the crucial role of the US. One of the most significant legacies of the war was the strengthening of the Israeli relationship with the US, which significantly influenced Israeli policy. Although Israel was not comfortable being a piece in the wider game of Cold War politics, they were nonetheless grateful to the Americans for their support, which played an important role in the course of the war and its end. The heightened American role in the region and their political commitment to changing the status quo was clear to see as Kissinger and then President Carter continued to mediate. This role as Israel's strongest ally in the international community remains highly significant to this day.

The overarching lesson of the October War, however, that territory does not equate to security, and that in fact security can sometimes only exist by giving up territory, has not been fully absorbed. Following the conclusion of the October War, there was a monumental rise in defence spending. In 1976, nearly half the country's GNP went towards defence, and still constituted 30% by the time of the Camp David Accords of 1978.[101] Although this figure has since fallen, Israeli defence spending continues to be one of the highest in the world, at least in part due to the traumatic memory of the October War. However, the threat of another large-scale conventional war along those lines has become negligible, and questions must be asked whether maintaining old conventional forces is the most effective way of dealing with the threats that Israel currently faces.[102] Furthermore, is the military the key to solving the underlying problem which gives rise to those threats?

Ultimately, Eban was correct in his assertion that the post-1967 borders were a guarantee of future wars. The continued Israeli occupation of the West Bank and the Golan Heights constitutes a significant stumbling block to Israel's ability to exist peacefully in the region and be accepted by its neighbours. As long as it continues, Uri Avnery's prophecy is likely to remain valid, and although the blood shed is predominantly not Israeli, this is nonetheless a tragedy for the Jewish state. The fundamental question of Zionist objectives which was asked following the Six Day War has yet to be resolved, and though it remains a highly divisive issue, it must be actively addressed. One can only hope that war will not once again be a prerequisite for future peace in the region.

4

THE OCTOBER WAR
AND EGYPT'S MULTIPLE CROSSINGS

Yoram Meital

The October War was a momentous event in the modern history of Egypt. The crossing of the Suez Canal was used as a metaphor for the awakening of Egyptian society from the gloom that swept it after the crushing defeat in the Six Day War, and for the ability of the Egyptians to achieve successful "crossing" in other fields as well. Following its defeat in the June 1967 war, Egypt lost Sinai; its armed forces were in total disarray; the Egyptian economy was dealt a mortal blow by the loss of transit fees through the Suez Canal, the loss of the Sinai oil fields as well as the near total cessation of tourism. Investments also declined steeply, while defence expenditures increased sharply. Moreover, a sense of insecurity spread throughout the population, and a crisis of legitimacy was discernible in certain quarters of the public who began to doubt the leadership's ability to extricate the country from the crisis. The war had turned into a crisis of Gamal 'Abd al-Nasser's personal, charismatic leadership and of that of his associates, and had called into question the regime's symbols as well as its legitimacy.

When Anwar al-Sadat replaced Nasser (October 1970), a gradual change in Egypt's overall strategic policy emerged. The new president had to deal with numerous problems. Internally, social and economic distress signals were apparent; depression was exacerbated by the defeat in the 1967 war with Israel and by challenges to Sadat's decisions from various sectors. Externally, Egypt's political manoeuvrability was restricted because of its unstable relations with many Arab states and with the superpowers (including the severing of its relations with the United States). In the struggle against Israel, the status quo of "neither peace nor war" had continued since the ceasefire that ended the War of Attrition (August 1970). Egypt's decision-makers recognised that dealing with the problematic internal situation would entail adopting an overall economic and political policy that would differ from the one identified with the Nasserite regime. In efforts to break the harmful status quo, Sadat tended to go to the greatest possible length with regard to both political and military action. He took pains to affirm his personal interest in promoting peace, and already on February 1971 the president stated: "We want peace, and I have already said several times that I am ready to go to the end of the world to prevent a single soldier of ours from being wounded."[1] The failure of the "year of decision" led to utter deadlock in the political process. From the autumn of 1972 till the summer of 1973 two new lines of development emerged which came to have an impact on Egypt's policy: in foreign affairs, the process of global détente became more marked; while at home, pressures to overturn the status quo by some method or other mounted steadily.

Cairo recognised that a political solution to the conflict with Israel could only be attained through the US; and that effective US aid in reaching it could only be gained by curtailing relations with the Soviet Union. However, the lack of political progress caused Egypt to revert to planning for war; and warlike operations in turn required large-scale Soviet military aid. On 6 July 1972, Sadat convened a meeting of the Armed Forces Supreme Council to review the current capabilities of the Egyptian army. The meeting pointed to two old dilemmas still determining Cairo's choice: the lack of an offensive option likely to lead to the desired results; and, in consequence, the need to define a limited operation which could be quickly turned to political advantage. The head of military intelligence, Ahmad Isma'il, told the meeting that Israel's "superiority, especially in the air, was such that Egypt's armed forces were in no position to mount a successful assault."[2] Sadat's subsequent summing up is crucial for an understanding of his concept of the expected battle.

He said: "We must distinguish between politicians and soldiers. You as soldiers must concentrate your efforts on preparing the troops for the coming battle. I realize, and General Sadiq agrees with me, that we must not go into battle unless we have the capacity to deter Israel from attacking our interior. The problem which confronts us is what to do if we are obliged, politically, to go to war before we have that deterrent?"[3]

Two days later a decisive meeting was held between the Egyptian president and the Soviet ambassador. Sadat protested against delays in the delivery of promised weapon systems, and added that, just as he would not receive a diktat from the US, neither would he accept one from the Soviet Union. At that point the president asked his national security adviser, Hafez Isma'il, to tell the ambassador there and then that he was ending cooperation with the Soviet Union as of the date of the conversation, and that the employment of Soviet advisers would be discontinued at the end of two weeks. As a result more than 15,000 advisers returned to the Soviet Union. This dramatic message led to a severe crisis developing in Soviet–Egyptian relations.

Two main reasons seem to have led to the dismissal. One was the US–Soviet summit of May 1972 and its outcome; the other was the fundamental distrust and irritation which had developed on the part of Sadat towards the Kremlin leadership. Sadat assumed that the expulsion would be welcomed by Washington and cause it to respond by a commensurate gesture towards Cairo. And indeed, we learn from American sources that during the rest of 1972 there were frequent US–Egyptian exchanges, some public, some covert, for the mutual clarification of positions.[4] The ensuing contacts convinced Sadat that the US was clinging to its former positions, namely that, on the one hand, the US considered itself able to contribute to a constructive discussion between the sides; but that, on the other hand, the US (1972 being an election year) was not in a position to pressure Israel to change its attitudes. Such a change could only result from contacts between the parties themselves. A deadlock being thus in the offing, Sadat endeavoured to mend, at least to some degree, his relations with the Soviet Union. Following an exchange of messages with Moscow (through the good offices of Syria), Prime Minister 'Aziz Sidqi left for Moscow on 22 October 1972. Simultaneously, Cairo informed the Soviet military attaché that it was unilaterally prolonging the agreement on port services for the Soviet navy for another five years. These were the first indications of the Soviet-Egyptian rift being repaired. They were also signals meant for the US, telling Washington not to think of the present difficulties between Cairo and Moscow as a permanent break likely to benefit the US alone.

During the summer of 1972, Sadat came to the conclusion that, as a matter of principle, the status quo needed to be broken by a military operation. It was now incumbent upon him to decide on its precise scope and its timing. The decision raised further major questions, such as the number of fronts on which the operation should, or could, be conducted: its intended duration: the type of weapons needed and their availability. The latter consideration led to the question of whether Egypt ought to go to war with the arms it then possessed. On 24 October 1972, Sadat convened the Armed Forces Supreme Council. The concept he put forward at the meeting was made clear by his reply to a question from the quartermaster-general, who wanted to know whether the object of the planned operation was "the liberation of the occupied territories or is it merely a resumption of military activities so as to give you a better chance of a political solution?" Sadat told him that the object was "breaking the ceasefire." Several senior participants at the meeting opposed Sadat's belief that an immediate operation would only lead to a new defeat. But the majority argued that at the current time the army was not ready for war. Sadat found that some of the senior officers did not have a clear understanding of his authority as president and ultimate decision-maker, and of their own responsibility for implementing precisely the policy he was laying down. Angrily, he told the Deputy War Minister, Hasan 'Abd al-Qadir: "You don't have to tell me what to do and what not to-do...Keep to your limits. You are a soldier, not a politician."[5] Following the meeting, Sadat dismissed the war minister, his deputy, and the commander of the navy. However, the importance of the meeting lay in Sadat's making it clear that he intended to launch a war with the means then at the army's disposal. While military preparations were thus going forward, contacts with the US continued in 1973. A most important conduit was that between Hafez Isma'il and Henry Kissinger. On 24 and 25 February 1973, Isma'il and Kissinger held three secret meetings. The Egyptian side, though appreciative of the importance of the contacts in themselves, felt that they had failed to bring a settlement nearer, since they had given no indication of a significant change in US positions. Sadat summed up his impressions as follows: it was impossible for the United States to make a move if Egypt itself didn't take military action to break the deadlock.[6]

THE OCTOBER WAR AND EGYPT'S MULTIPLE CROSSINGS

Two fronts war

Once Egypt had decided that war was the only way to overturn the status quo, it was incumbent on its decision-makers to decide on operational objectives commensurate with the means at their disposal and with the given domestic, regional and global constraints. Sadat assumed that Syria held the key to their improvement: if Damascus could be convinced of the justice and correctness of the Egyptian position and be rallied to Cairo's side, then a war on two fronts would become possible. If this came to pass, Arab solidarity would be restored; and even though other Arab states might not join in the war, they would at least assist the Syrian-Egyptian war effort. In operative terms, the first move for Egyptian-Syrian wartime coordination was the trip to Damascus by Egyptian War Minister Ahmad Isma'il in mid-February 1973. He presented to President Hafez Al-Asad a plan for the simultaneous launching of a joint attack against Israel by the two states. Egypt proposed three possible dates for the attack: May, August or September-October. A biographer of Asad's career wrote that the Syrian president agreed on the spot. "The only reservation he expressed was regarding the date, May 1973. Asad argued that he would need several more months to have his army ready."[7] The following month, Isma'il completed the Egyptian war plan, and large arms delivery contracts were signed with the Soviet Union.

A long series of coordination moves ensued, both within Egypt and between Cairo and Damascus. During March and April 1973, Sadat gave the war plan firmer shape, both with regard to the military objectives and to its role as part of the political effort, merging the two aspects into a single strategy. The war was to begin with a surprise attack on both the Egyptian and the Syrian fronts, meant to reach limited objectives in the field, but to be sufficient to shatter the Israeli security doctrine. The Suez Canal was to be crossed at several points and bridgeheads were to be established on its eastern bank. The Bar-Lev Line was to be overpowered and the new Egyptian line be held according to instructions from the political leadership. The longer the Egyptian forces succeeded in holding a strip of land east of the canal, the greater the chance for intervention on the part of the great powers, as well as by the Arab states. The overall international, as well as regional, situation would thus undergo a radical transformation. Under the new circumstances, steps leading to a political solution could be set into motion on much more favourable terms than had been possible before. Moreover, the success of the initial attack would mark the rehabilitation of the army and the restoration of its prestige and its morale.

The decisive deliberations on launching the war took place at cabinet level on 5 April 1973. The majority of the participants spoke for war. Sadat reviewed the international situation and stated that, even though the US had the strength to solve the Middle East problem, it lacked the will to do so and endeavoured instead to impose its views on the Arabs. He added that the battle would extend to Arab fronts other than Egypt's, and that the post-war political contacts would reflect the achievements of the fighting. Following Sadat's words, War Minister Isma'il reported on his recent trip to Arab capitals; his impressions were that the Arab states "are not enthusiastic about joining a war, being apprehensive that what had happened in 1967 would happen again." Neither had he discerned a desire on their part to assist the war effort financially or in other ways.[8]

At this stage it also became clear that Damascus's concept of the coming war was totally different from Cairo's. Egyptian leaders were able to gauge President Asad's views during the latter's visit on 23 and 24 April. The decisive talks were held at the presidential rest home at Burj al-'Arab, west of Alexandria. Asad declared himself ready to take part in a joint military move, provided its aims were defined as follows: for Egypt, crossing the canal and occupying western Sinai up to, and including, the Giddi and Mitla passes and Sharm al-Shaykh; for Syria, the occupation of the Golan Heights. Sadat was convinced that only a war on two fronts could deal Israel a real blow and lead to the intervention of the powers. He therefore ordered two plans to be prepared. One would eventually be given to the Egyptian army command for execution; the other, envisaging an operation on a larger scale calculated to satisfy Syrian demands, would be submitted to the Syrians who were to think of it as the real operational plan. The first stipulated crossing the canal and holding a narrow strip on its eastern bank; the second envisaged an Egyptian advance as far as the Sinai passes. When the war minister instructed Chief of Staff Sa'ad al-Din al-Shazly to draw up the broader plan, the latter tried to dissuade the minister by pointing to the army's inability to carry it out. He demanded to know why the previous plan was being changed; the war minister told him that "it was a political instruction…If the Syrians realized that our plan was limited to the capturing of a line less than ten miles east of the Canal, they would not go to war alongside us." Shazly went on to say that eventually a compromise was reached: he would add a second phase to the "real" plan which would cover the advance to the passes. Its details, the war minister told him, "would serve to satisfy the Syrians. But he promised that [the second phase] would never be implemented except under the most favorable conditions." On a more personal note, Shazly added that he was "sickened by the duplicity. But I was bound to obey and to keep the secret. Even in this memoir, I have been reluctant to divulge it…The truth was that neither I nor any of my subordinates dreamed the second phase would be carried out."[9]

On 22 August 1973, the top echelons of the two armies opened six days of staff talks in Alexandria, held under conditions of stringent secrecy. These meetings reached agreement on all questions except for two, which were left for the two presidents to decide. These were: the date the battle was to be launched, and the precise hour for it to start. The joint command recommended two alternatives: between 7 and 11 September, or between 5 and 10 October. The final date, 6 October, was only set at a secret meeting of the two presidents on 12 September; it was the hour, rather than the day, which remained undecided until 3 October (when it was set for 2:05-p.m.). Another important step for the inter-Arab preparation of the war was Sadat's visit to Saudi Arabia, also in August. King Faisal was at first hesitant about the two countries going to war, but when Sadat detailed his war plans, he let himself be persuaded. He did, however, make one suggestion: the war must last long enough to build up a united Arab front. Sadat agreed and said that he had nothing to ask of Saudi Arabia except that it should work for the creation of just such a united Arab front. Sadat also visited Kuwait and Qatar. It is still unclear how much Sadat and these oil-rich states leaders agreed to use the oil embargo as part of the Arabs' war plan.

A significant meeting on the war and its objectives took place only a week before the start of the battle, on 30 September, when the National Security Council was convened at Sadat's private residence in Giza. Obviously, it was not meant to decide whether the country should go to war or not: by the time it met, the senior officers had already been advised of the date of D-Day. The war minister's remarks concisely summed up Cairo's concept. Even at that late date, however, Sadat did not inform the participants that the date for launching the war had already been set for a week later. On 3 October, Sadat gave the Soviet ambassador a hint of the imminent outbreak of war. As a result, the families of the remaining Soviet staff in Egypt were ordered home.

The Egyptian concept of the conduct of the coming war and of objectives is set out with great clarity in two documents Sadat gave the war minister, on 1 and 5 October, The earlier document stated that the strategic objective was "to challenge the Israeli Security Theory by carrying out a military action according to the capabilities of the armed forces aimed at inflicting the heaviest losses on the enemy and convincing him that continued occupation of our land exacts a price that is too high for him to pay." Consequently the Israeli security theory, based on psychological, political and military intimidation, would be seen as no longer capable of protecting it. Challenging the Israeli security theory would in the short term make it possible to reach "an honorable solution for the Middle East crisis." In the long term, it might lead to a "basic change" in Israel's thinking, morale and "aggressive tendencies." The second directive was somewhat more specific, instructing the army to attain three aims:

A) To end the present military deadlock by breaking the ceasefire as from October 6, 1973; B) To inflict the greatest possible losses on the enemy, in personnel, arms and equipment; C) To work for the liberation of the occupied land in successive stages in accordance with the growth and development of the potentialities and capabilities of Armed Forces.[10]

War zone

Egypt's actual military and political wartime moves from 6 to 16 October show that Sadat himself and the forces under his command clung with great accuracy to the aims he had laid down. The surprise offensive was launched in the early afternoon of 6 October. By 8 October, the Egyptian army had reached most of the tactical aims of the first stage: the achievement of surprise, the crossing of the Suez Canal, the establishment of several bridges over it, and the transfer across them of infantry and armoured forces with their equipment. The fighting qualities and discipline of the Egyptian army were considerably higher than at any time in the past; so were the technological level of their arms and their ability to use them. Israel for its part had for long become prey to erroneous military and political thinking, supported by the public mood of large segments of the population. Its concept was that it was capable of foiling every Arab attempt to go to war against it. More than that: that no Arab state was considering going to war. These convictions caused the Israeli government to ignore clear intelligence warnings until almost the last moment.[11]

The initial Egyptian assault was carried out by five divisions who established three bridgeheads and, exploiting the advantage of surprise, conquered most fortified posts along the Bar-Lev Line during the first few days of fighting. The surprise factor was not only the result of the Israeli intelligence failure, but also of the use of unexpected, novel strategy. This enabled the Egyptians to bring across the canal much larger bodies of troops than had been anticipated and, once they had rapidly crossed over, to conduct their operations by means of tactics unforeseen in Israel. The Egyptian army was able to stand up to the Israeli armour by sophisticated use of infantry equipped with anti-tank weapons and trained in the rapid preparation of defensive positions in the open, sandy ground of Sinai. This was often done at night (a period of full moonlight having been chosen to open the war). Consequently, initial Israeli losses of armour were heavy. Moreover, the Egyptian troops east of the canal were protected from air attacks by a dense deployment of ground-to-air missiles on its western bank. Their range virtually neutralised the Israeli air force in the zone of the initial fighting. The Israeli armour and the Bar-Lev strong points, by contrast, were thereby deprived of effective air cover.

All the while, other aspects of the combined military–political approach were not neglected. On 7 October, Sadat decided to use the direct channel to the US established by Hafez Isma'il and to transmit to Washington a message saying that Egypt's "basic objective remains as always, the achievement of peace in the Middle East and not to achieve partial settlements." Cairo, he continued, "does not intend to deepen the engagements or widen the confrontation." Therefore, the Egyptian position was as follows: "Israel has to withdraw from all occupied territories." If it did so, Egypt was ready to participate in a peace conference at the UN, under appropriate auspices. Egypt "agree to the freedom of navigation in the Straits of Tiran", and, except as a guarantee, "an international presence for a limited period." Kissinger replied the following day, saying that the US position was "to bring about a cease-fire without at the same time taking a position which might produce a confrontation with the Egyptian side." Kissinger added a few general points, apparently from a desire to keep the channel open. Isma'il answered the questions on 9 October. His reply indicated that Egypt was trying to establish a linkage between the call for a ceasefire and the US commitment to obtain an Israeli withdrawal to the pre-1967 lines. He repeated the demand for a complete Israeli withdrawal, went on to say that subsequently a peace conference could convene for the purpose of "final peace agreement (*ittifaq salam niha'i*)", and added that Egypt would agree to an international presence at Sharm al-Shaykh for a limited period, and to supervision of shipping through the Tiran Straits. On 10 October, Isma'il sent Kissinger another message reflecting Cairo's stand at that time (a stand marginally more flexible than three days earlier). He stated that Egypt would agree to a ceasefire and total Israeli withdrawal according to a fixed timetable and under UN supervision. The completion of the Israeli withdrawal would coincide with the termination of belligerence by Egypt. The Gaza Strip would be placed under UN control, pending the grant of self-determination. Following the end of belligerence, a peace conference would convene under UN supervision and with the participation of all sides, including the great powers and the Palestinians, in order to search for ways to ensure sovereignty, security and freedom of navigation.[12]

In this early stage of the war, Sadat's consideration in rejecting the ceasefire appeals was to demonstrate his resolve to create a new situation. The change in the circumstances, he felt, should be incisive enough not to be perceived as merely temporary, but rather to compel the sides to adopt completely new attitudes. He also wished to exploit to the full the advantage he had gained over Israel by the success of the first surprise moves in the field. On 10 October, the Soviet ambassador transmitted a request from Moscow for a ceasefire, arguing that an immediate ceasefire would both maintain Egypt's political advantage and enable it to continue coordinating developments on the Syrian and the Egyptian front. The Soviets reiterated their request late at night on the 12 October. At the same time, Britain made a similar appeal. Sadat rejected that appeal, too.

Sadat's political decisions must also be seen against the background of events at the front. The initial success might have made it possible for Egypt to move deeper into Sinai, towards the Giddi and Mitla passes or even towards the international boundary with Israel. These possibilities were discussed at high command meetings on 8, 9 and 10 October, but eventually the meetings followed Sadat's lead and decided not to move forward. His main ally in declining a further advance was War Minister Isma'il. Sadat argued that the army should not deviate from the original plan of seizing a strip of only 10 kilometres, and should also take into account the possibility of a quick recovery of the Israeli forces from the initial shock, and of US support for them. Moreover, an advance would diminish the effectiveness of the present air protection for the Egyptian troops. During the first week of the fighting, the Syrians began to understand the nature of Cairo's war aims and to grasp that its intention was to remain close to the canal. Therefore, as the Israeli military pressure on the Syrian front grew in intensity, Syrian demands for Egypt to keep to its original commitment (as Syria understood it) and to remain faithful to the concept of a genuine two-front war became ever more urgent. The Egyptian army, Damascus clamoured, must resume the offensive and move deeper into Sinai. Both sides understood that a serious threat to the depth of Sinai would bring marked relief to the Syrian front. When the scope of the Israeli counter-attack on the Golan Heights (11–13 October) became clear, the Egyptian army tried, on 14 October, to push forward again. The attempt turned into a costly failure and ended in retreat. After the event, Egyptian senior officers blamed Sadat for the failure, arguing that he had held back the army when an advance was still possible (on 10 October) but had, under pressure from Damascus, pushed it into an offensive when it was too late.[13]

In the meantime, the issue of superpower support for the warring sides had also come to the fore. The Soviet Union started a massive air lift to both Syria and Egypt, beginning on 10 October. This, and the heavy losses in the battlefields, led Israel to appeal to the US to accelerate deliveries of urgently needed munitions, as well as to grant it emergency economic assistance. On 14 October, the US responded positively. Its principal motive was to prevent a situation in which an ally of the Soviet Union, equipped with Soviet weapons, might defeat a US ally equipped with US weapons. At the same time, the US wished to signal to the Arab states, first and foremost to Egypt, that they would not be able to decide the fate of the Arab–Israeli conflict by the use of force.

The turning point in the course of the war came on 16 October and was marked by two events: the Israeli breakthrough to the western bank of the Suez Canal near Deversoir (not far from the town of Ismaïlia), and Sadat's statement the same day. The breakthrough created a dilemma with severe implications, both militarily and politically. Egypt's troop strength on the western bank of the canal was not sufficient to over-power the Israeli units which had crossed over near Deversoir. (Already, on 19 October, they numbered three divisions, including armour.) To do so would have required a massive re-deployment of Egypt's general reserve from the area of Cairo and perhaps also the transfer of troops from Sinai back to the western bank. Chief of Staff Shazly recom-mended doing so. As against this, there was the consideration that the basic military and political strategy of the war had been to secure, at any price, a strip of land—east of the canal. To maintain the advantage already gained necessitated the continued deployment in Sinai of all the troops already there. Sadat, as well as some senior officers, therefore held that the original strategic objectives must be maintained despite the breakthrough. Even though it might be good tactics to bring some units back to the western bank, it would, in their opinion, be bad strategy. The internal debate ended with the acceptance of Sadat's point of view and with the decision not to pull back troops from Sinai to the vicinity of Deversoir. Also on 16 October, Sadat made a speech in the People's Council addressing himself directly to the president of the US. He put forward an Egyptian proposal, of which the following was the pivotal passage: "We are prepared to accept a cease-fire on condition that the Israeli forces withdraw forthwith from all the occupied territories to the pre-June 5 1967 lines, under international supervision…We are ready, once the withdrawal from all these territories has been carried out, to attend an international peace conference at the UN…We are willing, at this hour,…to start clearing the Suez Canal to open it to international navigation…Throughout all this we are not prepared to accept ambigu-ous promises or flexible expressions."[14]

After the Deversoir breakthrough, the oil-exporting Arab states began making determined use of the oil weapon. Led by Saudi Arabia and Kuwait, they cut down oil exports to the West as a means of exerting pressure on the US, the industrial Western countries and Japan. They proclaimed that the embargo would continue until it produced the fol-lowing results: a halt to US aid to Israel; consolidation of the ceasefire; and Israel's consent to implement Resolution 242. Following a series of appeals by the powers for an immediate ceasefire, the Security Council eventually adopted Resolution 338, on 22 October. Its terms stipulated a ceasefire in the positions being held by the sides at the time; an immediate start to the implementation of Resolution 242; and the opening of negotiations, under appropriate auspices, "aimed at establishing a just and durable peace in the Middle East." Cairo accepted the resolution the day it was passed.

As soon as Resolution 338 was passed, Sadat was in frequent communication with President Richard Nixon. He asked for the president's help in getting the Israelis to allow medical and food supplies through to the nearly entrapped Third Army Corps. He requested that a US military attaché from Tel Aviv proceed to the front lines to verify Israel's observance of the ceasefire. This is corroborated by Hafez Isma'il, who himself dealt with transmitting the Egyptian messages to Washington. On 23, 24 and 25 October, he passed on a note from Sadat to Nixon demanding US action for the immediate application of the ceasefire by Israel. If this was not done, Sadat declared, Cairo would in future regard all US promises to Egypt with a great deal of scepticism. Nixon's and Kissinger's replays emphasised that the US informed Israel that "any further offensive operation would lead to a severe deterioration of relations between the Israeli and the U.S. Government."[15]

When it became clear that fighting was going on despite the ceasefire resolution, the Soviet Union placed an airborne division stationed in Eastern Europe on high alert. In a note to Nixon dated 24 October, Brezhnev threatened military intervention. The US reacted by placing its own forces on alert. It also informed Brezhnev that "sending Soviet troops to the Middle East would be considered a violation of article II of the agreement on the prevention of nuclear war of June 22, 1973."[16] At the same time, Nixon informed Sadat that the US would impose the observation of the ceasefire on Israel. Yet for a moment it looked as if one or the other of the powers might lose control and that a global conflagration—might ensue. The following day, 25 October, the Security Council passed a renewed, more stringent cease-fire call (Resolution 340) and fighting ceased there and then. On 27 October, Kissinger informed Cairo that Israel was ready to enter direct negotiations on arrangements to implement the ceasefire, and that Egypt was at liberty to choose the time and place for doing so. Sadat responded positively and appointed General 'Abd Al-Ghani Al-Jamasi to represent Egypt at the talks.

When the ceasefire took hold, Egypt was in possession of two bridge-heads east of the Suez Canal, totalling about 1,000 square kilometres, but the more southerly one was cut off from the rest of the Egyptian forces. It was held by the Third Army, whose approximately 20,000 men no longer had any supply lines open, either to the other force in Sinai or to the western bank of the canal. Israel for its part held some 1,600 square kilometres west of the canal. Israel had lost 2,691, the Arab armies nearly 18,000 dead; 305 Israeli and 8,370 Arab soldiers had become prisoners of war. The total number of wounded was estimated at several tens of thousands.

The multiple crossings

In Egypt's hegemonic narrative, the crossing (al-'ubur) of the Suez Canal by the victorious Egyptian forces was linked to the great energies latent in Egyptian society that would enable it to make a "crossing" over into new "territory" in other fields as well, first and foremost in the economy. These concepts were fully articulated in a novel overarching policy entitled "the Opening" (al-infitah), which spoke explicitly of taking advantage of the wartime momentum in order to deal with Egypt's domestic challenges. On the economic front, steps were taken to introduce a market economy, expand the activity of the private sector, lure foreign investments, and decrease the dominance of the public sector. Yet another major aim was the restoration of national self-confidence, and the strengthening of the regime's legitimacy in the eyes of the public.

In terms of Egypt's foreign policy, the relationship with the US was crucial for achieving the aims of the "Opening" policy. The rapprochement with Washington was part and parcel of an overall re-orientation of the country's global policies, which resulted from a broad reassessment of national priorities. The need to deal with conflict with Israel, as well as the economic and monetary challenges facing Egypt, were the factors underlying the turn towards the US. Sadat argued that in the prevailing global, regional and domestic circumstances, Israel's positions could not be changed by force of arms alone; even less was it feasible to seek a radical solution such as the elimination of Israel. Quick and realistically attainable results could only be the outcome of a more reasonable policy towards the US and other Western countries. Such a policy was capable of producing pressure on Israel, at least up to a point. In view of Israel's dependence on the US, Cairo averred that Washington could be made to bring pressure to bear on Jerusalem, provided the Arabs knew how to present their case to the US administration and public opinion. Sadat had no illusion that Washington was on the point of foregoing its traditional support of Israel, and was quite aware that American military and economic assistance to Israel continued to be on the increase. If Egypt's aim was a political settlement, Cairo had first of all to reach an understanding with Washington.

The American administration quickly saw the golden opportunity to advance its own interests through turning Egypt into a close ally. Following the 1973 War, both Cairo and Washington revised their attitudes towards each other. Washington abandoned the policy of upholding the status quo in favour of the creation of a US-launched diplomatic momentum; moreover, the US administration attributed increasing importance to Egypt's positions in the regional system. The change stemmed both from US considerations and from a certain increase in Cairo's influence in Washington after the war. The revised US policy had two principal aims: to ensure the flow of oil to the West; and to weaken the Soviet hold in the Middle East. Egypt's pivotal role in this strategy found expression in bilateral steps. First, on 28 February 1974, diplomatic relations (severed during the 1967 war) were restored. In April, Nixon asked the US Senate to grant Egypt $250 million in economic aid, stressing that the funds "would be used for the tasks which come with peace: clearing the Suez Canal, repairing the damage in adjacent areas, and restoring Egyptian trade."[17] The Senate agreed to make the grant.

Controversies at home and abroad

Cairo's claim that the October War had opened the road towards a peace settlement with Israel encountered a great deal of criticism from various Arab quarters, as well as in Egypt itself. On the Arab scene, Egypt's principal critics were Syria, Iraq, Libya and the PLO. They demanded that Egypt should be isolated, and its policies shunned, on the Arab scene. Within Egypt most of the criticism was directed towards the settlements with Israel, the increasingly close relationship with the United States, the adoption of the "Opening" policy and the limitations imposed by the government in the political domain. The political steps taken by Sadat were portrayed as a real blow to political and national interests (both Egyptian and Arab), and his economic decisions were described as a deathblow to the lower classes. Sadat's critics argued that his decisions mirrored inability to transform the victories on the battlefield into better political advantages. As Mohammad Hassanein Heikal, an intimate friend and adviser to Nasser and an influential contemporary writer on Middle East issues, argued:

In the October War politics defeated and betrayed arms, just as in 1967 arms defeated and betrayed politics. I believe that the mistake President Sadat made in the October War, notwithstanding its cause, was his inability to distinguish between the battle and the war. The battle has to do with the exchange of fire between tanks, cannons, missiles and air fighters, while the war is a completely different matter. The war is a struggle of wills that exploits everything, including the battlefield outcomes, in order to gain political advantages …I regretfully acknowledge that in the history of modern wars I cannot recall any similar case such as the October War where the outcome was so different from the beginning and its progress so contradicted its ending.[18]

Al-Shazly, the Egyptian chief of staff during the October War who was released from the army on Sadat's orders in December 1973, also questioned the achievements attributed to Sadat in the official narrative of the war. He claimed that Sadat appropriated the war's achievements to advance political goals detrimental to Egyptian national interests in particular and Arab ones in general. As Al-Shazly argued, "The heroic details of the crossing [of the Suez Canal] were ignored in a chorus of sycophancy proclaiming all was the leadership of one man."[19] In a book entitled *Autumn of Fury* (1983), Heikal suggested that Sadat's image in the West as "the Hero of War and Peace" derived from ignorance of his failure to adapt his political, economic and social policies to Egypt. Refuting Sadat's image as a visionary leader who was ahead of his time, he argued that the October War had indeed been a rare opportunity to achieve much of significance for Egypt, but Sadat "threw it all away."[20] According to Heikal, Sadat's declaration that the 1973 October War was the last between Israel and the Arabs had tied Egypt's hands and allowed Israel to exercise force against the Arabs. Thus, the entire Arab world had paid the price for the separate peace between Egypt and Israel.[21] Similarly, Ahmad Baha al-Din, another renowned publicist, also criticised that declaration as having imbued the Egyptian public with false hopes of an imminent era of peace, promising that resources formerly dedicated to war would now be used for domestic development.[22] According to Hasan Nafi', a political scientist in the University of Cairo, Sadat's political errors had annulled Egypt's achievements in the October War. The simplistic equation that Sadat and his supporters had wished to make between peace and ensuing economic achievements and prosperity had been intended to "market" the peace with Israel to the public as a therapeutic means of bringing solace to Egypt's ills.[23] Nafi', like Heikal, attributed Sadat's political failures to his personality and simplistic way of thinking. In this context, he argued that Sadat's famous claim that his visit to Jerusalem (November 1977) was intended to break down the "psychological barrier" between Israel and the Arabs had served to market the delusion that a large part of the Arab–Israeli conflict originated from fear and suspicion between the two peoples. However, this claim had failed to convince most Egyptians, and the opposition parties on both the right and the left, as well as independent speakers, had harshly criticised Sadat's political path. Consequently, the gap between Sadat's vision of a peace policy leading to economic prosperity and the stand held by most of the Egyptian public and its leaders, had gradually increased.[24]

For most Egyptians, however, *the October War* or *the Ramadan War* (the two common names for the 1973 war in Egypt) was an unquestioned victory. Following the surprise offensive of 6 October, the Egyptian army had achieved most of its tactical aims: the crossing of the Suez Canal, and the massive crossing of infantry and armoured forces with their equipment into the Sinai peninsula. The initial attack's success marked the rehabilitation of the army and the restoration of its prestige, dignity and morale. Egypt's major achievement was that it had broken the status quo against the efforts of Israel and the superpowers to perpetuate it. The war had given proof, many Egyptians pointed out, of the hollowness of Israel's concept viewing the post-1967 lines as "secure boundaries." The defeat of the Israeli security doctrine was the measure of Egypt's victory. For others, Cairo's major achievement was that it had succeeded in breaking the status quo against the desire of the superpowers who had wanted to perpetuate it.

Naguib Mahfouz had this to say on the matter:

Did we win the battle or were we defeated?…Let us ask ourselves what criterion to apply to the question of victory or defeat?…I say that the objective laid down for it is the criterion for any war…; the aim, not the land or the casualties or even the [course of the] fighting…There is then no doubt that the outcome is a victory for the Arab armies. It is certainly not a defeat, even if it is not the final victory which will only be attained by another, crushing victory, or else by just and honorable peace.[25]

Even writers formerly as sceptical as Tawfiq al-Hakim now sounded a different note. On the third day of the war, he wrote: "When we crossed into Sinai, we "crossed" the defeat [of 1967). Whatever the outcome of the fighting, the important thing is that we have cleansed ourselves. That is the meaning of the slogan: "Egypt always remains Egypt." The world thought [Egypt] had sunk into torpor; but its spirit had not become inert. If it dozed for a while, it woke up quickly, roared, and stood on its feet."[26]

If measured in terms of the targets they had set themselves, then both Egypt and Israel had indeed cause to claim significant achievements, if not complete victory. Egypt's objective had been to overturn the status quo and to accelerate political efforts, and Cairo had indeed succeeded in doing both. Israel for its part regarded the war primarily as a military challenge and its chief aim was to foil the Egyptian military threat; it, too, therefore attained its most important war aim, even though it was eventually not strong enough to eliminate the Third Army's bridgehead in Sinai, opposite Suez city. Another aspect of the war was the time factor. In the short term, what counted was the Egyptian–Syrian threat to Israel's security, and in this regard it must indeed be said that the Arab offensive called into question the Israeli concept of security and the reliability of its intelligence services; this remains true, even though Israel eventually gained tactical military superiority. It ended the war holding Syrian territories beyond the 1967 ceasefire line in the Golan Heights (halting only some 40 km from Damascus), as well as large Egyptian areas west of the Suez Canal, coming within 100 km of Cairo. In purely military terms, these were the marks of victory. But if we look at the outcome from the perspective of a longer time span, and under the aspect of its broad political and strategic results, we find that Egypt, aiming specifically at long-term targets, made undeniably important strategic gains. Egypt's strategic aims had been to break the status quo; to cause the US to substantially change its policy towards the Arab–Israeli conflict; and to create circumstances in which a political solution would now become feasible that was more advantageous to Egypt than would have been possible before the war. Following the war it became clear that it was the change in US policy which turned out to be Cairo's most desired achievement. However, the strategic relations with the US, the peace treaty with Israel, and the Opening policy have all been highly controversial in Egypt since the October 1973 War.

5

SYRIA AND THE OCTOBER WAR

THE MISSED OPPORTUNITY

Eyal Zisser

The offensive the Arabs launched on 6 October 1973 gave them one moment of joy and hope, but after only a few days this was replaced by worry and frustration. Thus, the hope of victory turned to a fear of defeat, which did indeed materialize, not because of the losses the Arabs suffered on the battle-field, but because of the collapse of the alliance between Egypt and Syria. This gave Israel self-assurance and confidence, and increased its aggressiveness toward the Arabs, and especially toward Syria, Lebanon, and Palestine.

> 'Abd al-Halim Khaddam (Syrian Vice President), *My Memories*,
> *al-Safir* (Beirut), 17 February 2003)

Introduction

The tremors that seized the Arab world with the outbreak of the "Arab Spring" at the beginning of 2011 heralded the end of a lengthy era in the history of the region. This era was characterised by, or perhaps stood in the shadow of, strong and stable authoritarian regimes that ruled high-handedly for generations. Of these regimes, the Egypt regime signed a peace agreement with Israel in 1979 that it has been careful to adhere to over the years. The Syrian regime, on the other hand, has refrained from reaching a peace agreement with its southern neighbour. At the same time, however, it has been careful to maintain absolute quiet along their shared border. The upheavals in the region that started at the beginning of 2011 signify that it has entered into a new era, which is presently marked by a lack of stability and great uncertainty, not only in the domestic affairs of the Arab states, but also in their foreign relations, both on the regional and the Arab-Israel arenas.

It is clear that the upheavals in the region brought about by the "Arab Spring" called into question many of the basic assumptions of the last several decades in regard to the Middle East in general, and especially in regard to Israel-Arab relations. It goes without saying that the present turmoil makes it possible to reconsider from new perspectives a number of events that over the years have been perceived as being of crucial importance in the history of the region. One of these is, of course, the October 1973 War. This war, which is the most recent all-out conventional war between Israel and the Arab states, was a major factor influencing Arab-Israel relations in the decades following it and right up until the 2011 "Arab Spring."

The October 1973 War has particular importance in relations between Israel and Syria, but also for the Syrian state itself. The war began on 6 October. For Syria, the importance of that date does not lie just in the fact that it was the birthday of the founder of the modern Syria, Hafez al-Asad (born in Qardaha on 6 October 1930). Its importance stems primarily from the implications of the war on shaping Israeli-Syrian relations for the last four decades. These years have been characterised by complete quiet along the Golan Heights front, while at the same time, in the Lebanese arena, both sides have been very active, finding that country a convenient venue for exchanging blows indirectly via Lebanese agents. But there is another point that must be emphasised: the October War has weighed heavily on how the Syrian state has shaped its image domestically and on how Syria's rulers, both Hafez al-Asad and his son Bashar, have made their choices—or avoided making choices—regarding the course the state should follow since then and right up to the present time.

Syrians view the October War (the October War of Liberation, *Harb Tishrin al-Tahririyya*) as a significant and important landmark in the history of modern Syria. For here, for the first time, the Syrians took their fate into their own hands, instead of leaving it to others, as in the past. The Syrian army was revealed as a worthy adversary to the Israeli army. It even scored significant, if only limited and temporary, achievements at the start of the fighting, which were adequate to remove the stain of defeat that had adhered to it since the Six Day War. It is no wonder then that 6 October, the day the war broke out, was declared a national holiday celebrating the miraculous achievements of Syria led by Hafez al-Asad during and after the war. In spite of all this, one will generally find it difficult to find evidence—whether from the time of Hafez al-Asad or even from the time of his son Bashar—that a holiday atmosphere reigned in Syria and among its citizens on the special date. And certainly there is no comparison between the way the outbreak of the war was marked in Syria and the way it was marked in Egypt, Syria's sister Arab state, and the senior, even if problematic, partner in this war.

The melancholy with which the Syrians greet the anniversary of the outbreak of the October War is not necessarily connected to the heavy price the Syrians paid in the war, around 6,000 dead, nor to the severe material damage of almost $3.5 billion done to the country.[1] The melancholy lies in the realisation that this war achieved nothing for Syria, neither a settlement of the Arab–Israel conflict nor, of course, the return of the Golan Heights to Damascus.

Indeed, at the end of the day, Syria, in complete contrast to Egypt, failed in its efforts to sustain the military successes it achieved at the start of the war and even worse, it was unable to translate those successes after the war into political achievements (that is, the return of the Golan Heights). No less important is the fact that the October War was not used as a springboard for radical social, political and economic change at home, or in foreign policy, such as the great changes Anwar Sadat brought about in Egypt. As a result, over the years Syria has remained fixed in the same place it found itself at the end of the war. It is no wonder, then, that the feeling aroused in Syria by the remembrance of the war is, in particular, the sense of a missed opportunity.

This impression is particularly noticeable in the description of the war and the events that unfolded in its aftermath found in Patrick Seale's biography of Hafez al-Asad, *Asad: The Struggle for the Middle East*. Seale is considered to be the Westerner closest to Asad, and it was the Syrian president himself who gave Seale the task of writing his biography. Indeed, Seale, based on statements by Asad, does not hide the feeling that this war gained nothing for Syria. In his book he sums up Asad's comments with these words: "Although Asad did not know it, his enterprise with Sadat was flawed from the start, because behind the impressive façade of cooperation there was no unity of mind, and on this hidden reed the Arabs' great hopes were to founder.[2]

The road to war—Syria between 1967 and 1973

The rise of Hafez al-Asad to power in Syria in November 1970 was a turning point in the history of the state. Asad succeeded in establishing a strong central authority that achieved stability such as Syria had never known since becoming independent in April 1946. Backed by this stability, Asad was able to turn Syria into an influential regional actor and promote Syrian political interests—vis-à-vis its Arab neighbours, Turkey, the Palestinian arena, and even vis-à-vis Israel.[3]

There is no doubt that along with establishing his regime at home and giving it a firm foundation, Hafez al-Asad also viewed the Arab–Israeli conflict as a central concern on both his personal agenda and the agenda of the state he headed. This centrality was, of course, a direct consequence of the Six Day War. This war was fixed in the Syrian collective memory as a national trauma because of the humiliating defeat suffered by the Syrian army, which led to the loss of the Golan Heights, sovereign Syrian territory.[4]

Thus, the main conclusion that Hafez al-Asad drew from the Six Day War was the need to strengthen Syria's military power. But he also wanted to establish a unified Arab front that would enable the Arabs to compete with Israel on the battlefield. This was an early adumbration of the "strategic parity" concept Asad adopted in the 1980s. Indeed, building Syria's military power and, along with this, establishing and strengthening cooperation among the Arab states, especially Egypt, were the first goals Asad set for himself.

Syria's military build-up In the six years following the Six Day War, and especially following Asad's coming to power in 1970, up to the October War, Syria's military strength almost doubled. On the eve of the war the Syrian army counted 170,000 soldiers, compared to 70,000 soldiers at the outbreak of the Six Day War. The Syrian army had also been supplied with advanced Soviet equipment and had greatly improved its ability in the spheres of artillery, armour and air defence.[5]

Strengthening Cooperation between Syria and Egypt From the time of Hafez al-Asad's accession to power, and especially during the years 1972–3, cooperation with Egypt increased. It should be noted that the relationship between Egypt and Syria was always characterised by tension, suspicion, and even mistrust. These negative features can be traced back to a series of episodes from the far past that cast a dark shadow, including the episode of the United Arab Republic (UAR, the unification of Egypt and Syria established in February 1958, from which Syria resigned with great fanfare in September 1961), but a much more serious influence was Syria's conduct on the eve of and during the Six Day War.[6]

The rise to power of Anwar Sadat in Egypt and Hafez al-Asad in Syria at the end of 1970 opened a new page in relations between the two states. These two leaders were determined to ignore the residue of the past in order to advance the policies they considered most appropriate for their respective countries. It seems that during 1971 Asad and Sadat reached an understanding about going to war against Israel together. This understanding was consistent with Sadat's strategic thinking, as well as Asad's, that only a military campaign could jolt the region out of the status quo into which it had fallen and generate a political process that would return to the Arabs—in the present context, to Egypt and Syria in particular—the lands they had lost in the Six Day War. Still, it is a fact that it took the two states over two years to translate this understanding into action.[7] The Syrians, of course, take pains to represent Asad as the initiator of the path to war, and to claim that he might have acted even without the aid of Egypt if Sadat had not agreed to be an ally in this campaign. This was because of Asad's determination to avenge the humiliation of the defeat suffered by Syria in the Six Day War, as well as his commitment to return the Golan Heights to Syrian control. In his memoirs 'Abd al-Halim Khaddam testifies, for example, that just a week after Asad's rise to power the new president initiated a meeting with Sadat, during which he raised the idea of going to war jointly. However, Sadat, according to Khaddam, was involved in advancing an interim arrangement with Israel based on an Israeli withdrawal from the banks of the Suez Canal. Thus, Asad was forced to wait until Sadat gave up the hopes he had pinned on this process and returned to the war option. Later, according to Khaddam, Syria had to wait until the breach between Egypt and the Soviet Union—caused by Sadat's impulsive expulsion of Soviet advisers from Egypt—was mended.[8]

Despite these claims, it seems that Sadat was really the driving force behind the move to go to war. This assumption is based on the behaviour of the leaders during the following years. Sadat acted vigorously, with initiative and daring. In contrast, Asad's behaviour over the years was characterised by caution, anxiety and often inaction and passivity in the face of events. Sadat states in his memoirs that he and Asad came to a concrete decision to go to war—as opposed to the agreement in principle reached previously about the necessity of a military campaign against Israel—during their April 1973 meeting in Burj al 'Arab, near Alexandria. Sadat testifies that at this meeting "I told Assad that I had decided to go to war this year, and I asked his opinion about this, and he answered me that we would go together and that he meant it."[9] It should be noted that even before this meeting, in February 1973, Egyptian Minister of War Ahmad Isma'il 'Ali had visited Damascus and revealed to Asad, for the first time apparently, Egypt's concrete intention to go to war at the end of the year. According to Egyptian sources, the Syrians wanted to delay the war for a few months and not begin it in the autumn of 1973. This was because they wanted to procure arms that would allow them to confront the Israeli air force. Indeed, only after Syria obtained such arms from the Soviets was it possible to advance the war plan.[10]

From 21 to 23 August 1973, the high military command of Egypt and Syria met at the headquarters of the Egyptian navy in Ra's al-Tin for final discussions before going to war. Syrian Chief of Staff Yusuf Shakkur and Egyptian Chief of Staff Sa'ad al-Din al-Shazly signed a document containing the agreements that the two sides had reached. At this point Syrian Minister of Defence Mustafa Talas, accompanied by the commander of the Egyptian Air Force, Husni Mubarak, flew to Syria to report to Presidents Asad and Sadat, who were meeting in Bludan, west of Damascus, on the agreements that had been reached. It was evidently at this meeting that the two presidents made the final decision about when the war would begin—October 1973. According to Egyptian sources, the Syrians requested that the opening of hostilities be delayed for 48 hours, for the purpose of making final logistical arrangements, in particular in order to empty the fuel reservoirs near Damascus. However, the Egyptians succeeded in convincing them to start the attack at the agreed-upon time.[11]

It turns out, incidentally, that the Egyptians suspected the Syrians of not intending to go to war at all, just as had happened in 1967, when the Syrians hesitated in joining the battle. On the eve of the October War, Muhammad Basyuni, who later served as Egyptian ambassador to Israel, was serving as Egyptian military attaché in Damascus. He testified that he was the official in charge of coordinating the collaboration between the two Arab countries. He reported that on the eve of the war he was summoned to Cairo and brought before a battery of high-ranking Egyptian officers who wanted an answer to one question only—would Syria go to war alongside Egypt at the moment of truth.[12] It seems, therefore, that the Egyptians questioned Syria's willingness to go to war alongside them. The Syrians, for their part, naturally try to claim that the Egyptians were the ones who were problematic allies. Their proof for this is their assertion that the Soviets, when informed by Asad about the agreement to go to war that Egypt and Syria had reached, asked Asad over and over again if he was convinced that the Egyptians would fight alongside him.[13]

The war's aims

According to Asad's biographer, Patrick Seale, the objective of the war, as Asad envisioned it, was "the return to the Arabs of the territories Israel captured in 1967".[14] The Syrians planned the war as one operational move, whose final aim was to reach the Jordan River. It is possible that the Syrians intended to cross this line. Alternatively, they may have only intended to seize the slopes running down from the Golan Heights to the river and from this position to defend the territorial advances they had made. Syrian Minister of Defence Mustafa Talas indicates in his memoirs, *The Story of My Life* (*Mir'at Hayati*), that, according to the plan of attack prepared in Damascus, the Syrian army was supposed to establish a bridgehead west of the Jordan River in order to prevent Israel from staging a counter-attack that would expel the Syrian forces from the territories they had taken on the Golan Heights.[15]

As noted above, the Syrians did not coordinate their operational and tactical plans with the Egyptians, and, as a matter of fact, the partners never held any detailed and penetrating consultations. Consequently, there was never any real discussion about the final goals of the war or what might happen after the hostilities. Seale states in his biography of Asad, based upon what Asad told him, that it was agreed that each state would be free to plan the campaign on its front as it saw fit. At the same

73

time, according to Seale, an understanding was reached between the Syrian and Egyptian leaders that: "The goal was the retrieval of territory which Israel occupied in 1967. Each country was free to plan its offensive on its own front, but it was agreed that Syria's aim was the recovery of the Golan while the Egyptian objective was to reach the Sinai passes in the first stage before regrouping for the reconquest of the whole peninsula. This was what Sadat and I decided and it was on this principle that we went to war"[16]

This is the source of the manifest Syrian claim that Egypt misled Syria and enticed it into undertaking an all-out attack that exposed the Syrian army to the Israel Defence Forces (IDF). Syria's assumption was that Egypt would launch an all-encompassing operation at the same time as Syria, which would reduce the danger confronting Syria. What actually happened, however, was in complete contradiction to what, according to the Syrians, had been agreed upon. The Egyptians launched only a limited operation that focused on the eastern banks of the Suez Canal, and when Israel perceived this—Seale hints that the Syrians believe that the Egyptians even gave Israel signs that this was their plan—Israel was able to concentrate its forces against the Syrians and deliver a decisive blow.[17]

The Syrian claim is backed, at least partially, by the testimony of some of Sadat's aides who later became his rivals, for example, former Egyptian Chief of Staff Sa'ad al-Din al-Shazly. At one time Egypt had embraced the concept of a "comprehensive war," but abandoned it as the war approached. However, on the eve of Asad's April 1973 visit to Egypt, according to Shazly, he was instructed by Sadat to revive the old concept and present it as if it were now Egypt's plan. When the Syrian delegation headed by Hafez al-Asad arrived in Cairo, Operation Plan "Granite 2" was presented to it. According to this plan, the Egyptian army would advance to the Giddi and Mitla passes, then, depending on how the battles developed, even deploy to liberate all of Sinai. The goal of this whole presentation was, as noted above, to convince the Syrians to participate in the war. As is well-known, the Egyptian military leadership had come to the conclusion that it was doubtful whether the Egyptian army was strong enough to advance beyond the passes. This being so, the most Egypt hoped for was to activate a political process that would lead to the return of Sinai. Accordingly, the Egyptian leadership decided to adopt a different operational plan, called "High minarets," according to which the Egyptian army would take control of just a few kilometres, perhaps only ten, beyond the canal.[18]

The October War—the Syrian front

On 6 October 1973, at 14:00 hours, the armies of Egypt and Syria opened coordinated attacks along both the Golan Heights and the Suez Canal fronts. At the beginning of the war the Syrian army scored impressive victories, limited and temporary as they were. These included breaking through the Israeli defensive line along the Golan front, gaining control of significant portions of the Golan Heights to within a few kilometres of the Jordan River passages, and the capture of the Mount Hermon (Jabal al-Shaykh) outpost. In addition, and perhaps even most importantly, during the first days of the war the Syrian air defences on the Golan front were able to block Israeli air force attacks and inflict heavy losses. The Syrian assault was carried out along three parallel divisional attack axes based upon the three first echelon Mechanized Divisions, 5, 7 and 9. These were followed by Armour Division 1 as the second echelon. Armour Division 3 was left as a reserve near Damascus, to defend the regime from any potential domestic threat. At the same time as the attack of the mechanised divisions, the Syrians landed commando forces that captured Israel's Mount Hermon outpost. They also planned to land commando forces with the aim of capturing the passages over the Jordan River and the routes ascending to the Golan Heights. However, this plan was not executed at the beginning of the war, and during the subsequent fighting all such attempts were thwarted by the Israeli forces.[19]

The outbreak of the war, which caught the Israeli forces (two Israeli tank brigades, numbers seven and 188 with a total of 178 tanks) by surprise, was marked by dramatic successes on the part of the Syrian forces, which had around 600 tanks in the first echelons of the attack. On 6 and 7 October 1973, Syrian Divisions 5 and 9 succeeded in breaking through Israeli lines and advancing deep into the Golan Heights. Division 9, under the command of Hasan Turkmani, reached the Khushniyya and were in arm's each of Gesher Hapakak (Bustan al-Khuri bridge) and Arlik bridge (al-Hasil bridge) on the Jordan River, while Division 5, under the command of Ali 'Aslan, did even better, with its advance units managing to reach a line from which they were able to overlook the routes ascending from the Jordan River to the Golan in the area of Ma'aleh Gamla and al-'Al. The Syrians poured the second-echelon troops of Division 1 into the areas where breakthroughs had been achieved. In contrast to all this, Division 7's attempt, under the command of 'Umar Abrash, to break through in Emek HaBakha (the Valley of Tears) opposite Mas'ada, and the efforts made to move Division 9 to the aid of Division 7, failed. Division 7 was pounded and in fact annihilated during the battles.[20]

The Syrians failed to take advantage of their successes during the first and second days of the war and did not overrun the Jordan River, something they were perhaps capable of doing at that stage of the fighting. The fact that the Syrian forces came to a halt just a few kilometres before the capture of the passages over the Jordan River, and perhaps even before they had established a bridgehead on the western side of the river, later evoked a scholarly debate. The question was asked, what prompted the Syrian forces to halt and refrain from overrunning the western slopes of the Golan Heights leading down to the Jordan River? There are those who claim that the Syrian forces came to a standstill on account of the bitter defensive battles the retreating IDF forces were fighting against them. Others maintain that this halt came about because the Syrian General Staff found it difficult to deviate from the plans made before the war. It was thus unable to take advantage of the stunning successes the Syrian forces achieved during the first stage of the war, successes that far exceeded the Syrians' expectations and initial planning. Some maintain that the halt came about because the Syrians suspected a possible Israeli ambush, otherwise, how could one explain the great ease with which the Israeli defensive lines were breached? Finally, there are even those who explained the Syrians' premature standstill by claiming that they were afraid Israel would use the nuclear weapons in its possession if the Syrians crossed the 1967 lines—which presumably constituted red lines for Israel—and thereby threatened the very existence of the state of Israel.[21]

After two days of difficult fighting, during which the IDF relied upon its regular army units deployed on the Golan Heights, the Israeli reserve forces began to arrive. These troops enabled the IDF to block the Syrian assault, and later, on 8 and 9 October 1973, even to return the situation to what it had been before the Syrian attack. The Syrians were pushed out of the areas they had overrun in the southern Golan Heights, and the conditions that had prevailed previously were reestablished. On the basis of its successes, the IDF was able to prepare itself for a counter-attack aimed at taking the war into Syrian territory and even at creating a ground threat to Damascus. The attack was undertaken even though it was clear to the Israeli planners from the start that not enough forces were being allocated for this mission. And indeed, the Israeli move did not fully succeed, because of fierce Syrian resistance and also because of the arrival of Iraqi expeditionary forces. Immediately upon their arrival these troops were sent to the front to fight the Israelis. Despite this resistance, the IDF still managed to breach the Syrians' first line of defence on the Golan Heights and to come within 40 km of Damascus. In a move meant to apply pressure on the Syrian leadership, IDF artillery shelled the suburbs of Damascus.[22]

Thus, after three weeks of fighting, Israel was able to take back the territories the Syrians had captured on the Golan Heights, including the Mount Hermon outpost, and even to move over into territory on the Syrian side of the Golan, with the aim of using it as a bridgehead towards Damascus. At the 40 km line, the Syrians finally succeeded in halting the Israeli effort at a breakthrough towards Damascus. Deadlock ensued and, since both sides were quite exhausted, the fighting on the Golan Heights came to an end.

The false alliance between Egypt and Syria

The disagreement between Egypt and Syria over the degree of their commitment to each other arose once again while the war was still in progress. The Syrians quickly claimed that Egypt had started conducting negotiations with Israel, via the Americans, from the very first day of the war, and had finally concocted a ceasefire behind the back of Damascus, about which it avoided informing the Syrians. This, the latter claimed, was how Egypt started the process that ended in the signing of a peace agreement with Israel in March 1979, all of this behind the back of Damascus, and to a great extent at Damascus' expense.

As a matter of fact, on 16 October 1973, two days after Egypt's failed offensive in Sinai of 14 October, President Sadat turned to President Nixon during a speech in the National Assembly and called upon him to intervene and bring the war to an end and settle the Arab–Israeli conflict. Seale states that this came as an unpleasant surprise to Asad. What really surprised Asad was Sadat's willingness to stop the fighting subject to the good will of the United States and his willingness to make himself dependent on the good will of that country.

Asad was informed by Sadat about his readiness to accept a ceasefire with Israel in a cable he sent him on 19 October 1973, in which he wrote: "We have fought Israel to the fifteenth day. In the first four days Israel was alone... but during the last ten days I have, on the Egyptian front, been fighting the United States as well, through the arms it is sending. To put it bluntly, I cannot fight the United States or accept the responsibility before history or the destruction of our armed forces for a second time... my heart bleeds to tell you this..."

To this Asad immediately answered: "I received your message yesterday with deep emotion. I beg you to look again at the military situation on the northern front and on both sides of the canal. We see no cause for pessimism. We can continue the struggle against the enemy forces, whether they have crossed the canal or are still fighting east of the canal. I am convinced that by continuing and intensifying the battle, it will be possible to ensure the destruction of those enemy units that have crossed the canal..."[23]

However, this exchange of letters was not enough to stop the Egyptians, and especially not the Americans. Thus, as early as 20 October 1973, US Secretary of State Henry Kissinger went to Moscow for talks with the Soviets, during which a ceasefire agreement that was supposed to take effect on 22 October 1973 was formulated. As it turned out, Israel continued fighting for several more days.

Sadat explained to Asad that his readiness to accept the ceasefire resulted from the fact that it was an agreement reached between the two superpowers and therefore he could not ignore it. Asad complained that no one had informed him about this agreement. Sadat replied that he had assumed the superpowers would be the ones to inform the Syrians. Asad replied that he had gone to war in order to fight alongside Sadat. He also asked why Sadat was ready to accept the ceasefire, to which Sadat replied that he hoped to get his territory back. Asad, according to Seale, didn't believe this and answered, "I haven't seen any sign of this."[24]

When Asad learned, not from his Egyptian ally, but from Henry Kissinger, about the way Sadat was conducting himself vis-à-vis the American secretary of state, he hastened to cable Sadat: "I would have preferred to have seen the proposals outlined by you to the People's Assembly before these were made public... it gives me no pleasure to write these words, but I wish to hide none of my thoughts and opinions from you since we are engaged together in a battle of life and death."[25]

The Egyptian version of the story stands opposed to the Syrian version. According to the Egyptians, it was the Syrians who proved to be the problematic partner. At the end of the first day of battle, according to the Egyptians, the Syrians were already looking for a ceasefire. Egypt's successes were still limited and just beginning. The Syrians, meanwhile, had succeeded much beyond their expectations, having breached the Israeli defensive lines and in effect overrun the entire Golan Heights. And just at this point, say the Egyptians, the Soviet ambassador in Cairo, Vladimir Vinogradov, presented himself to Sadat and notified him that the Syrians had already asked the Soviet Union, via the Soviet ambassador in Damascus, to work for a ceasefire. All they wanted was to be allowed to keep the territory they now held on the Golan Heights. And this was done, the Egyptians complained, without any consideration whatsoever for the situation on the Egyptian front. Sadat, of course, quickly rejected this request and contacted Asad directly to find out the meaning of the Soviet move. Asad denied turning to the Soviets with such a request. However, the Soviet ambassador in Cairo approached Sadat a second time with the issue of the Syrian request, which led the Egyptian president to believe that the Syrian denial was false.[26]

The Syrians explained that the incident was the result of a misunderstanding by the Soviets. According to the Syrians, they and the Egyptians had agreed that Asad would be responsible for informing the Soviets about the Arabs' intention to go to war, because of the poor relations between Cairo and Moscow. In his message to the Soviets Asad added the following, which allegedly had also been agreed upon earlier with the Egyptians: if the two states achieved their territorial aims on the battlefield, they asked the Soviet Union to intervene at that point and work to impose a ceasefire agreement via the United Nations Security Council. This agreement should enable Syria and Egypt to preserve their achievements and lay the foundations for the return of their lands. It is possible, claimed the Syrians, that this message created the confusion or misunderstanding on the part of the Soviets that led to their attempt to achieve a ceasefire. Syrian analyses of the war also do not rule out the possibility that the Soviets decided to act on their own initiative on behalf of their clients as soon as they got news of the Syrians' achievements on the first day of battle. An examination of Sadat's memoirs shows that he did not accept these explanations and conjectures, and believed that the Syrians did indeed ask the Soviets to act on Syria's behalf without any consideration of Egypt's interests.[27]

The war of missed opportunity

Israel and Egypt acted rather quickly and signed a ceasefire agreement on 12 November 1973, and a disengagement of forces agreement on 18 January 1974. Egypt also participated in the Geneva Peace Conference that convened on 21 December 1973. On the Syrian front, however, the war formally ended only on 31 May 1974. With the war's end, Egypt set out on a new path, at home and abroad, and the term "*'ubur*" (which initially signified "crossing the Suez Canal") became a key term signifying the introduction of wide-ranging changes in the country. These included a new political, social and economic openness and major changes in the country's international orientation, namely, the abandonment of the Soviet Union, drawing close to the United States, and, finally, even achieving a peace agreement with Israel.[28]

In contrast to Egypt, Syria failed to use the war as a springboard for change and the advancement of Syrian political interests—the return of the Golan Heights, in particular. The disengagement of forces agreement signed in May 1974 did not lead to the opening of a political process, and, of course, the Golan Heights remained in Israel's hands. All Syria got in the framework of the May 1974 agreement was the city of Quneitra, which was turned into a memorial and pilgrimage site in an effort to perpetuate the memory of Israel's "crimes." Asad also failed to take advantage of the war to institute radical economic and social reforms. Instead, he allowed Syria to remain in a state of stagnation for many more years. Moreover, Syria emerged from the war convinced that it had fallen victim to an act of betrayal by its ally, whom it viewed as its senior, Egypt. The Syrians believe that Egypt worked hand-in-hand with the US, and, in practice, even with Israel, behind the back of Damascus, and thus brought about the Arab defeat in the war.[29]

There is no surprise, therefore, that a Syrian official version of the story of the October War is hardly to be found. Apart from Hafez al-Asad's own testimony, which appeared in Patrick Seale's *Asad's Syria*, all other Syrian political leaders or military commanders refrained from giving their own version of what had really happened on the Syrian side of the hill in October 1973 (Khaddam is an exception), partly due to the fact that the same leaders and commanders, including Hafez al-Asad himself, continued to rule Syria for another three decades and probably found the question of Syrian conduct during the war too embarrassing and clearly too controversial.

Why did Hafez al-Asad refrain from using the war to put Syria on a different path? It is possible, of course, to place the blame for Syria's stagnation on Anwar Sadat, or on Henry Kissinger, or even on Israel, but the question still remains, what was Asad's part and, even more so, his responsibility as Syria's leader, in the failure to exploit the 1973 war? There are many answers to this question. Some focus on Asad's limitations as a politician and statesman, limitations rooted in his personality, his world view, and the style of his political conduct. Others focus on the domestic situation in Syria during those years.

The later 1970s were difficult years for the Ba'ath regime in Damascus. Domestically it found itself facing an Islamic rebellion (1976–82) that at its peak became a real threat to the regime's existence. In Lebanon, starting in June 1976, Syria got bogged down in the treacherous swamp produced by the civil war in that country. Then, in March 1979, Israel and Egypt signed their peace agreement, thus removing Egypt from the forefront of the struggle with Israel. As early as the mid-1970s Asad had started working to establish an eastern front with Lebanon and Jordan against Israel. Following the Egypt–Israel peace treaty, Asad started working to establish an Arab rejectionist front based on the Damascus–Baghdad axis. However, Asad's efforts bore no fruit. Syria's relations with Jordan and the Palestine Liberation Organisation (PLO) became embroiled in crisis, and the Syrian regime also found itself in a life and death struggle with Saddam Hussein's Ba'ath regime in Iraq. The Iran–Iraq war that broke out in September 1980 also weakened Syria, since it removed the strategic depth that Iraq could have provided in case of a confrontation with Israel. That war also harmed Syria's relations with the Gulf States, which did not hide their anger at Damascus for its support of Iran in the conflict with Iraq.[30]

Another related question that deserves to be treated in a separate study, is the question of Israeli–Syrian relations after the October 1973 War. Indeed, Asad did signal at the time that he might be ready to consider a peace treaty with Israel, for example, in the well-known interview he gave to *Newsweek* magazine in 1975, where he spoke about his desire for peace. But Damascus also sent out other signals at the time. In any case, it was obvious that Asad needed someone from the outside to help him clear the path to peace. But Israel, Egypt and especially the US, were all focused at the time on the Israeli–Egyptian front, where the chances for progress appeared much more promising. Furthermore, Sadat was more amenable to American advances than Asad. Still, even though both Egypt and Israel were obviously ready for a peace treaty, it is a fact that several more years had to pass after the war before such an agreement could be concluded.[31]

How is the war to be remembered?

From the Syrian point of view, their disagreements with the Egyptians were among the war's most outstanding features. The disagreements grew greater and greater until they became an unbridgeable chasm following Sadat's visit to Jerusalem in November 1977. For the Egyptians this constituted a kind of closure to the events stemming from 1967, but for the Syrians, Sadat's visit became just another element in their sinking into a narrative of abandonment and Egyptian treachery.

In sum, the Syrian narrative regarding the October War is a story of daring, courage and military victories having far-reaching strategic ramifications, but at the same time it is the story of a missed opportunity, mainly because of Egypt's treachery. From this angle, the October War narrative became another stratum in the general narrative of Syria's history that has been held since practically the state's beginnings, which views Syria as a small state, standing alone, surrounded by enemies, and often betrayed.

That this is the case is indicated more than anything else by the report on the war prepared by former Syrian vice-president 'Abd al-Halim Khaddam. In this report one also finds a kind of justification of why Syria's leaders did not foresee that Egypt would betray Syria, and why, in spite of their misgivings, they gave Egypt their agreement to go to war together.

"There is no doubt that Syria confronted a difficult and complex dilemma, but it did not allow doubts to govern it, and it acted in accord with the understandings that were reached with Egypt. This was done despite the suspicion that Egypt's president would take part in the war, but place the historic responsibility for its results on Syria. In any case, the severe injury caused to the Arab nation as a whole during and after the war, was caused without any connection to any decision that Syria might have taken.[32]

6

US FOREIGN POLICY AND THE
KISSINGER STRATAGEM

Asaf Siniver

More than any other foreign policy crisis which confronted the Nixon administration, the October War brought to the fore the indisputable position of Henry Kissinger as the embodiment of American foreign policy. A series of domestic crises which coincided with the onset of the war on 6 October 1973 not only signalled the beginning of the president's downfall, but also catapulted Kissinger, his national security adviser and recently-appointed secretary of state to a position of unparalleled power in projecting American interests abroad.

On 10 October Vice President Spiro Agnew resigned from office following charges of tax evasion and bribery. Two days later the US Court of Appeals ordered Nixon to release a series of White House tapes to Archibald Cox, the Watergate special prosecutor. On 20 October the "Saturday Night Massacre" took place, with the resignations of Attorney General Elliot Richardson and his deputy William Ruckelshaus, and Nixon's firing of Cox over the court's order to hand in the tapes. The inevitable consequences of the coinciding major foreign policy crisis with the domestic turmoil were not lost on Nixon. By his own admission he was eager to "relieve the domestic crisis in order to reduce the temptation the Soviets would feel to take advantage of our internal turmoil by exploiting the international crisis in the Middle East."[1] Nixon's chief of staff, Alexander Haig, maintained during the war that he knew "of no knowledgeable person who does not believe that one of the important reasons the Kremlin put the crisis in motion was its calculation that the president of the United States was so distracted and disabled by his domestic problems that he would be unable to react with adequate force and dispatch..."[2] Indeed, from the first moments of the war Kissinger was evidently concerned whether the president would be able to follow the flow of events and keep control of the situation, and whether he was mentally stable to make critical decisions on the spot. Kissinger waited two and half hours on the morning of 6 October before he alerted the president to the outbreak of war in the Middle East. He informed Alexander Haig, who stayed with Nixon in Key Biscayne, Florida, that "I want you to know... that we are on top of it here", and to ensure that Nixon would not be seen to be out of the loop, he urged Haig to tell the media "that the President was kept informed from 6 a.m. on... I think our domestic situation has invited this war."[3]

The Nixon administration's policy towards the Arab–Israeli conflict between the Jordanian crisis of September 1970 and the outbreak of the October War three years later has been widely described as complacent.[4] The civil war in Jordan ended with the defeat of the Palestinian guerrillas and the Syrian forces, and the strengthening of the pro-Western regime of King Hussein, who received the tacit support of the US and Israel during the three-week crisis. A few weeks later President Gamal Abdel Nasser of Egypt passed away and was succeeded by his unassuming deputy, Anwar Sadat. This turn of events in effect transformed Washington's policy from one of even-handedness during the first year of the administration, to a policy explicitly dedicated to the containment of Soviet influence and Arab aggression in the region by ensuring Israel's qualitative military superiority vis-à-vis the "radical" regimes of Egypt, Syria and Iraq. The inevitable result of this policy was a sense of complacency in Jerusalem and Washington towards the prospect of a diplomatic breakthrough. Moreover, the American reluctance to apply pressure on Golda Meir's government to move away from diplomatic intransigence proved decisive in convincing President Sadat that the only way to bring Israel and the United States to the negotiation table was by going to war with Israel and forcing the Nixon administration to take part in the post-war negotiations.

US FOREIGN POLICY AND THE KISSINGER STRATAGEM

Henry Kissinger was the undisputed architect of US Middle East policy in the period leading up to the war, during the war, and in the post-war negotiations which took place from November 1973 to early 1975. As the president's national security adviser Kissinger controlled and managed the flow of information and advice from the defence and foreign policy bureaucracies to the White House; his appointment as secretary of state in September 1973, in place of the docile William Rogers, had formally cemented his position as the president's top foreign policy adviser. By that point in the life of Nixon's second term in office, Kissinger was already heralded as the mastermind of America's most dramatic diplomatic success, including the opening to China, the détente with the Soviet Union, and the negotiations with the North Vietnamese to bring an end to the bloody war in Vietnam—the latter effort winning Kissinger the 1973 Nobel Peace Prize. Kissinger's ascendancy to fame and power proved a major source of consternation for Nixon, who believed that Kissinger's reputation was being built at his expense. During the early years of the administration Nixon tried to contain Kissinger's apparent appetite for power with the help of his two trusted gatekeepers, Chief of Staff Bob Haldeman and adviser for Domestic Affairs John Ehrlichman. In September 1970 Ehrlichman informed Kissinger that he was not allowed to give any more televised briefs to the press on policy issues, and Nixon himself mused whether "Henry needed psychiatric care."[5] By October 1973, however, both Haldeman and Ehrlichman were forced to resign following the revelations of the Watergate scandal, and were later convicted of perjury, conspiracy and obstruction of justice. Nixon became more embattled and less attentive, and ultimately lost his grip of the foreign policy machinery, leaving Kissinger's authority unchallenged.

The Kissinger stratagem during the October War rested on four principles: to ensure Israel's continued superiority in the balance of Middle East military power; to prevent the Soviets from gaining ground in the region; to dismantle the threat of an Arab oil embargo; and most importantly, to make the United States the principal actor in the post-war diplomacy. The effects of this stratagem are demonstrated by four events before, during and after the October war: the pre-war diplomacy of stalemate; the airlift to Israel during the second week of the war; Kissinger's trip to Moscow on 20 October; and the infamous "nuclear alert" towards the end of the war.

THE OCTOBER 1973 WAR

Pre-war stalemate diplomacy

During 1971–2, as secret negotiations were underway with the Soviets, Chinese and the North Vietnamese, the Nixon administration was understandably cautious about opening another diplomatic front in the Middle East, and was reluctant to pressurise Israel to respond in kind to President Sadat's overtures to break the no-peace-no-war stalemate. Washington was also suspicions of Sadat and had little confidence in his ability to lead Egypt. When Sadat entered office in late 1970, Under Secretary of State Eliot Richardson estimated that he would not remain in power for more than four to six months, while Kissinger saw him as little more than an "interim figure".[6] As a result this pre-war period has consequently been described in the literature as one of "missed opportunities."[7] In an address to the Egyptian National Assembly in February 1971 Sadat signalled his willingness to reopen the Suez Canal and resume negotiations with Israel based on UN Resolution 242 in exchange for an Israeli withdrawal from the Sinai peninsula. The Israeli government rejected Sadat's proposal and the Americans were sceptical of Sadat's intentions. In May 1972 Sadat learned that at a Moscow summit Nixon and Brezhnev had agreed on the need for a "military relaxation" in the Middle East, which in effect meant the slowing of supply of Soviet arms to Egypt. Two months later Sadat expelled more than 10,000 Soviet personnel from Egypt, and returned to Moscow military equipment. He told the Kremlin that the expulsion was an inevitable consequence of the growing interference in Egypt's domestic affairs, and the slow pace of Soviet military assistance.[8]

The Soviet exodus from Egypt was received in Washington with some satisfaction, but with an even greater sense of suspicion. With the presidential elections due in four months, it was obvious that a Middle East initiative would damage Nixon's chances of re-election given the slim chances of success. Kissinger assured Sadat that after the elections the White House would launch a new peace initiative, though he still had little faith in the Egyptian president. According to William Quandt, who worked under Kissinger at the NSC, "Kissinger wasn't interested. He had a very contemptuous attitude towards Sadat; he thought 'why would he kick the Russians out for nothing? If he was smart he would have come to me first'; he thought Sadat was weak and wanted to keep the pressure on."[9]

Following Nixon's landslide re-election in November 1972, Kissinger opened a back channel to Cairo, through Hafez Isma'il, Sadat's national security adviser. However, by mid-1973 Sadat had already made a decision to go to war, while Kissinger was busy nailing down the final details of a ceasefire in Vietnam. Kissinger later conceded that when he met Isma'il for the last time, in May 1973, the Middle East "was heading toward war. We did not know it. But he did."[10] The Kissinger-Isma'il talks were doomed to fail in any case, given that the general elections in Israel were due to take place in October 1973, and, as noted above, US domestic developments soon took precedence over foreign policy, meaning that neither Prime Minister Meir nor President Nixon were receptive to negotiations. Sadat made no secret of his frustration with Washington's refusal to put pressure on Israel and enter a constructive dialogue, as he explained in an interview to *Newsweek* in April 1973:

My main difficulty with the US… has been to get the Administration to take a position in the conflict and put it on paper. Everyone has fallen asleep over the Mideast crisis. But they will soon wake up to the fact that Americans have left us no way out… Everything in this country is now being mobilized in earnest for the resumption of the battle—which is now inevitable.[11]

The airlift

Despite the growing reports in the months preceding the war about the mobilisation of Egyptian troops along the western bank of the Suez Canal, both Israelis and Americans seemed confident that the Arabs were not foolish enough to start another war. In May 1973 the NSC submitted to Kissinger a report about Egyptian moves which could be interpreted as "a pattern of action that could be preparation for hostilities against Israel." These actions included the mobilisation of surface-to-air SA-6 missiles, bombers and jet fighters. Nevertheless, the report concluded that "whatever the Egyptian and Arab leaders intend at this stage, the pattern of their actions thus far does not provide the Arabs with a rational basis for an attack at an early date".[12] Kissinger too did not expect Sadat to go to war, asserting to Israeli Foreign Minister Abba Eban that the Egyptian leader "shows no capacity for thinking moves ahead".[13] The Americans were captivated by Israel's *Conceptzia*—the intelligence Concept which estimated, even as late as two days before the war,—that there was a "low probability" of war, and it would remain so until the Arabs improved their airpower capabilities and acquired more effective ground-to-air missiles, which, according to "the Concept", would not happen before 1975.[14] Even only hours before the joint Egyptian–Syrian attack on Israel, American intelligence refused to question the Israeli paradigm, as William Quandt reported to Brent Scowcroft, Kissinger's deputy in the NSC: the intelligence services "have continued to downplay the likelihood of an Arab attack on Israel and still have no signs that such action is imminent. They appear to favor the alternative explanation of a crisis in Arab–Soviet relations."[15]

The war presented Washington with a dilemma. While it was important to prevent an Israeli defeat on the battlefield, it was crucial that Israel did not win too decisively, as another Arab defeat could prompt Soviet intervention. Moreover, the risk of an Arab oil embargo became a real possibility. As intelligence significantly lagged behind events during the first hours of the war, there was some uncertainty as to the identity of the aggressor. The Washington Special Actions Group (WSAG), the administration's interdepartmental crisis management group, struggled to match the reports of a coordinated Egyptian–Syrian offensive on two separate fronts with the intelligence estimates that the Arabs were not prepared to go to war at this point in time. CIA Director William Colby, Defense Secretary James Schlesinger and Chairman of the Joint Chiefs of Staff (JCS) Admiral Thomas Moorer argued that Israel initiated the hostilities. Roy Atherton from the State Department argued that it was inconceivable that Israel would start a war on Yom Kippur, the holiest and most solemn day in the Jewish calendar. Kissinger was convinced that the war was a result of Arab aggression, and told the Soviet ambassador Dobrynin that the Egyptian claims to the contrary were "baloney". His first orders to the WSAG were to make plans for the advancement of the Sixth Fleet to the eastern Mediterranean, and to prepare for the evacuation of American embassies in the region.[16]

Despite the Israeli losses on the battlefield in the first days of the fighting, Washington was still confident that the war would end with another Arab defeat, and so Kissinger preferred not to pressure Israel to accept a cease-fire in place. In the first days of the fighting the loss ratio on the southern front was nine Israeli tanks to a single Egyptian tank; and in the north by 9 October more than 120 Israeli tanks were destroyed, leaving only fifty tanks to defend the entire Golan Heights. In the first two days of the fighting alone 724 Israeli soldiers were killed—more than during the entire Six Day War.[17] On Tuesday 9 October, Kissinger explained to the Israeli ambassador in Washington, Simcha Dinitz: "Our strategy was to give you until Wednesday evening, by which time I thought the whole Egyptian army would be wrecked.'"During the meeting Dinitz asked for planes, tanks and "general information" about the movement of Iraqi forces towards Syria.[18] At the end of the day Kissinger met Dinitz again to report that Nixon had approved the entire list of "consumables" Israel had asked for, including ordnance and electronic equipment (except for laser bombs). Nixon also promised to replace all the tanks and planes Israel had lost.[19] This decision in effect signalled Washington's realisation that the war was far from over and that there was no diplomatic solution in sight.

The Soviets had made a decision to resupply the Arabs in the first days of the war, and the first planes took off for Egypt and Syria on 8 October. From that point a massive airlift and sealift took place almost on a daily basis. Furthermore, various Arab countries also supported Egypt and Syria's war effort.[20] At the same time in Washington, despite the promise to replace Israeli losses in planes and tanks, Kissinger decided to hold back on a full military commitment to Israel on a similar scale to the Soviet operation. It was not until the second week of the war, on 14 October, that constant supplies on a massive scale began to reach Israel. One reason for the delay was the administration's desire to keep its options open at the end of the war. Assessing the situation on 9 October, William Quandt wrote to Kissinger that, "if we act too early or too visibly on this key issue, we will insure attacks on US citizens and an oil embargo in key Arab states". At the same time, Quandt recognised that should the US fail to respond positively to a genuine Israeli request for arms, the US would not enjoy sufficient leverage over Israel at the end of the war.[21] Accordingly in his meetings with Ambassador Dinitz, Kissinger preferred to explain the reason for the delay as "bureaucratic difficulties". Specifically, he blamed Defense Secretary James Schlesinger and the Pentagon for acting slowly: "That's a bigger problem now than we thought. I must tell you, don't go running around Defense. Scowcroft will handle it."[22] He assured Dinitz that he was "a true friend of Israel" and that he had taken the matter to the president, who had agreed "in principle" to replace any losses in arms.[23] He even advised Dinitz to urge the Israeli government to go on the offensive "as quickly and as strongly as possible" before a ceasefire would take place.[24]

Remarkably, Dinitz did not question Kissinger's assertion that his hands were tied by the bureaucracy. As arguably the most powerful man in Washington at the time, it is unlikely that Kissinger was constrained by Defense Secretary Schlesinger, who at the time had been in office for only three months.[25] According to Quandt, it was in fact Kissinger who ordered Schlesinger not to resupply Israel:

> I remember Kissinger saying to Schlesinger in one of the meetings, "You are going to have to bear the responsibility for whatever delay there is because I have to deal with the Israelis on the diplomatic front. Nixon and I cannot be viewed as the problem; right now is not the time"… It wasn't Schlesinger, he was doing what he was told: "get ready to do it but don't do it!", and so he had to take the fall.[26]

Moreover, Schlesinger himself insisted that there was "simply no half way house" and that the US would have to use its own military aircraft to resupply Israel, rather than use commercial airlines which would attract less attention, as Kissinger preferred. His view was supported by Admiral Moorer who believed that a Military Aircraft Command (MAC) would be more efficient and easier to control than commercial charters.[27] On 13 October Haig warned Kissinger that Schlesinger was "ready to move MAC aircraft in there immediately. I think that would be foolish." Kissinger replied, "That would be a disaster, Al. How can he fuck everything up for a week… I think it's stupid."[28]

On 13 October a desperate Dinitz warned Kissinger: "If a massive American airlift to Israel does not start immediately, then I'll know that the United States is reneging on its promises and its policy, and we will have to draw very serious conclusions from all this."[29] This explicit threat to seek support for Israel in Congress achieved the desired result, as the embattled Nixon did not wish to add a foreign policy scandal to his domestic travails. For the first time since the outbreak of the war, the president became personally involve in managing it, and ordered Kissinger to push ahead with the airlift to Israel: "Goddamn it, use every one we have. Tell them [the Pentagon] to send everything that can fly."[30] Nixon's personal intervention brought an end to Kissinger's manipulation of the bureaucracy, the Israelis and the president himself, to whom he claimed that the Pentagon was responsible for delaying the transfer of arms. Within hours Kissinger convened the WSAG in the morning of 14 October to "settle the technicalities of the airlift once and for all".[31] By the end of the day—the first day of the airlift—Israel had received 148 tons of supplies. By the end of the fighting on 25 October the US had delivered nearly 12,880 tons of supplies to Israel, along with forty F-4 Phantom Jets, thirty-six A-4 Skyhawks and twelve C-130 transport planes. By contrast, by this date the Soviets had delivered to the Arabs 11,174 tons of supplies, even though the Soviet airlift had begun on 10 October.[32] As expected, the airlift had an immediate impact on the fighting, and by 16 October the Israelis had completed a successful counter-offensive in the Sinai and crossed the Suez Canal—a feat they failed to achieve even during the Six Day War. As Kissinger observed, the atmosphere in Washington was now more "relaxed"—so much so that he took the WSAG members to the Oval Office for a pep talk with the president. Nixon thanked the group for the hard work, and explained that his decision on the airlift was not made out of love for Israel, but was in fact a leverage tool for the post-war negotiations: "In order to have the influence we need to bring Israel to a settlement, we have to have their confidence. That is why this airlift… We can't get so much to them that they will be arrogant, but we can't be in the position where Israel puts pressure on Congress for us to do more." Despite the looming oil crisis, the mood at the meeting remained positive. Kissinger declared that "this has been the best-run crisis since you have been in the White House", and Deputy Secretary of Defense William Clements applauded Nixon: "your military services have just reacted in an out-standing fashion, Mr President".[33]

Kissinger's ploy ultimately proved successful: the Arabs had made considerable gains on the battlefield during the first week of the war, whilst the Israelis were grateful that he came to their rescue with the airlift. As far as Foreign Minister Eban was concerned, "Our heroes were Nixon and Kissinger. Our enemies were the Pentagon and Schlesinger."[34] Dinitz also believed that Kissinger was infallible. He "surrendered completely to Kissinger's solicitations and personal charm. He was flattered that the powerful, brilliant Kissinger called him frequently, consulted him… Without desiring it, without even being conscious of it, Dinitz turned into Kissinger's man… ultimately he believed that Kissinger was pure; that the wolves were in the Pentagon."[35]

The Moscow agreement

Following the airlift and the change of fortunes in favour of Israel on the battlefield, there was some concern in Washington that the "smell of victory will not make Israel welcome a ceasefire".[36] The Soviets, however, were even more worried about the developments on the battlefield, and on 19 October Brezhnev asked Nixon to send Kissinger to Moscow to negotiate an immediate ceasefire, as the situation in the Middle East was harmful to détente. En route to Moscow, Kissinger learned that Nixon had communicated to Brezhnev that he would come to Moscow with the president's "full authority… the commitments that he may make in the course of your discussions have my complete support".[37] Kissinger feared that his new privileged position at the negotiation table would severely limit his manoeuvrability in the negotiations: "I was horrified. The letter meant that I would be deprived of any capacity to stall…[it] made it impossible for me from Moscow to refer any tentative agreement to the President for his approval—if only to buy time to consult Israel… History will not record that I resisted many grants of authority. This one I resisted bitterly".[38]

By 21 October Egypt's Third Army was nearly encircled by the Israelis and Sadat desperately pleaded with Moscow to agree to a ceasefire in place. When Kissinger and Brezhnev met for the third and last time, over breakfast on 22 October, it did not take them long to work out a joint text, which was later passed in the United Nations as Security Council Resolution 338. The resolution called for a ceasefire in-place within twelve hours, and the implementation of Security Council Resolution 242.[39]

Kissinger's diplomatic success in Moscow was not appreciated at his next stop, Tel Aviv. Prime Minister Meir was "absolutely mad with Kissinger" for dictating an agreement on which she was not consulted.[40] Peter Rodman from Kissinger's NSC staff recalled that "Israel felt [it] had been shafted [in Moscow] by the United States".[41] Kissinger wisely decided to begin his meeting with Meir by reassuring the prime minister and her countrymen. Rather than forcing Israel to abide by the Moscow understanding, he explained his grand strategy for the post-war negotiations. There were no "side understandings" on the implementation of Resolution 242 as it was referred to in Resolution 338. He had Brezhnev's "word of honour" that he would "use his maximum influence" with the Arabs to release Israeli prisoners of war within seventy-two hours. He had given "direct orders" that the airlift to Israel would continue. He even promised Meir that he would publicly ask the International Committee of the Red Cross to bring to Israel 4,000 Jews from Damascus.[42]

But Kissinger's most important reassurance to Meir concerned the implementation of the ceasefire. First he confided that with regard to the exact meaning of the phrase "standstill ceasefire" as it appeared in Resolution 338, he had not "thought it through yet". He then explicitly suggested that Israel would not be recriminated if it failed to observe the ceasefire immediately: "You won't get violent protests from Washington if something happens during the night, while I'm flying. Nothing can happen in Washington until noon tomorrow." Meir replied, "If they don't stop, we won't", and Kissinger then responded, most tellingly, "even if they do…"[43]

Remarkably, Kissinger did not stop there. After successfully negotiating an agreement in Moscow which subsequently materialised into a binding Security Council resolution, he now actively advocated that the Israelis disregard it and finish the job along the Suez Canal so as to reach the negotiation table from the strongest possible position. When Israeli generals joined the meeting and confirmed that they would need two or three days to destroy the Egyptian forces on the east bank of the Suez Canal, Kissinger replied, "Two or three days? That's all? Well, in Vietnam the ceasefire didn't go into effect at the exact time that was agreed on."[44] After deliberately delaying the supply of much-needed arms to Israel during the first week of the war, Kissinger was now willingly turning a blind eye to a hypothetical Israeli violation of the ceasefire.

The Israeli generals in the room did not ask Kissinger for clarification. Whether implicitly or explicitly, they received a green light from the US secretary of state to advance their offensive on the southern front. When Kissinger arrived in Washington on the morning of 23 October, he learned that the ceasefire had collapsed, three hours after it went into effect. The result was the complete encirclement of the 25,000-strong Egyptian Third Army on the eastern bank of the Suez Canal, the cutting of the Egyptian supply routes, and the opening of the road to Cairo to Israeli forces.[45] The Soviets had no doubt about the chain of events which had led to this result, and expressed outrage, pointing the blame at Kissinger. According to Dobrynin, the Israeli offensive "was a premeditated violation of the agreement from the start", whereas Brezhnev was even less subtle: "Here, in Moscow, Kissinger behaved in a cunning way. He vowed fidelity to the policy of détente, and then while in Tel-Aviv he made a deal with Golda."[46] According to Quandt, Kissinger's gambit was essential to bring the Israelis and the Arabs to the negotiating table at a position which would be most propitious to American interests: "The stakes were no longer to defeat the aggressors… this is a crisis and [Kissinger's] goal was to ensure that this ends in a way that opens the door to an American-led diplomacy. He doesn't want the Russians to be in it, and obviously Israel cannot be defeated. But Sadat should not be defeated either, because if you humiliate the Arabs it would never work."[47]

The "nuclear" alert

The final component in Kissinger's stratagem during the war was his decision to place American armed forces on the highest state of alert since the 1962 Cuban missile crisis, a decision he took while the president was in bed. As the fighting continued along the Suez Canal following the violation of the ceasefire, the Egyptian Third Army was on the verge of annihilation. On 24 October a desperate Sadat pleaded for the superpowers to send a joint task force to the region to enforce the ceasefire.[48] Brezhnev responded by urging Nixon to accept a Soviet proposal to "urgently dispatch to Egypt Soviet and American military contingents, to insure the implementation" of the decision of the Security Council. Nixon and Kissinger promptly rejected the proposal, which they viewed as a dangerous precedent of Soviet presence in the region, and an obstacle to American post-war grand diplomacy.[49]

Nixon and Kissinger were particularly alarmed by what they read to be a Soviet ultimatum. Brezhnev's message read: "I will say it straight that if you find it impossible to act jointly with us in this matter, we should be faced with the necessity urgently to consider the question of taking appropriate steps unilaterally."[50] The president interpreted the message as "perhaps the most serious threat to US–Soviet relations since the Cuban missile crisis eleven years before".[51] The Kremlin, however, had no intention of sending troops to the region, as the Soviet diplomat Victor Israelyan Kremlin recalled: "Nobody liked or supported the idea. 'We have already made a principle decision not to be involved in the Middle East war, and there are no reasons to change our decision', noted Brezhnev. Thus any military involvement unilateral or together with the United States, was ruled out."[52]

Whilst the Soviets hoped that the threat of unilateral intervention would propel Washington to act jointly on the matter and influence Israel to stop the fighting, Brezhnev's message had the opposite effect on Washington. Kissinger convened a meeting of the NSC/WSAG at which it was decided to place American forces around the world on increased alert—all this while Nixon was in bed, at the height of the crisis. Kissinger's response to Brezhnev's message had been described as "illogical", "incredible", and "an alarmist interpretation that represented a worst-case interpretation of the facts".[53] Other accounts, however, defend Kissinger's actions given the high stakes and uncertainty in which he found himself. According to Chief of Naval Operations Admiral Elmo Zumwalt, "The Soviets presented us with what certainly looked like an ultimatum, and it would have been negligent indeed in such a situation not to assume a posture of readiness"; whereas William Bundy described Kissinger's calculations during this episode as "spelled out and balanced, more frankly and carefully than at any other critical point in his active career".[54]

Before convening the crucial meeting just before midnight on 24 October, Kissinger said to Alexander Haig, "You cannot be sure how much of this is due to our domestic crisis... I don't think they would have taken on a functioning president... Don't forget that is what the Soviets are playing on. They find a cripple facing impeachment and why shouldn't they go in there."[55] Although a crisis was clearly looming, Kissinger did not believe it necessitated Nixon's presence at the meeting, as he told Haig: "I don't think we should bother the president." Haig cautioned: "He has to be part of everything you are doing', but when Kissinger asked, "Should I get him up?", Haig replied curtly, "No."[56] There are multiple sources suggesting that the president was intoxicated during this episode and was in no condition to chair this crucial meeting. According to Raymond Garthoff, "Nixon had been drinking heavily and was not in condition to participate in the meeting. I had been told this independently by two members attending the WSAG/NSC meeting... and who say they were told by Kissinger at the meeting."[57] According to Quandt, Nixon was so unstable that Defense Secretary Schlesinger ordered the military to ignore any presidential orders which might come during that night:

Schlesinger, I've been told, in that meeting, said "we have to make sure that no unauthorised communications come from the White House to the Joint Chiefs of Staff, so I am going to tell the Chairman of the JCS not to carry out any orders except from me, including no calls from the President." They didn't think Nixon was in any shape to function, so Schlesinger told the Chairman of the JCS, "if the President calls you, don't do what he says." I don't think it's constitutional, but I think that's indicative of how worried they were that psychologically and perhaps physically Nixon wasn't functioning that well.[58]

These accounts of the night are supported by evidence of Nixon's condition throughout the crisis. For example, on 11 October Kissinger ordered his deputy at the NSC, Brent Scowcroft, not to transfer a call to the president from British Prime Minister Edward Heath: "Can we tell them no? When I talked to the president he was loaded"—even though this was at only 8 o'clock in the evening.[59]

The meeting lasted for more than three hours, until 2 o'clock in the morning of 25 October. The group included Secretaries Kissinger and Schlesinger, Admiral Moorer, DCI Colby, Assistant Secretary of State Sisco, Scowcroft, Haig and Commander Jonathan Howe from the NSC.[60] It was firstly agreed to send a reply to Moscow that would be "conciliatory in tone but strong in substance".[61] To achieve the latter, the group unanimously agreed to increase the readiness of American forces worldwide to a level which would be noticed in Moscow. Descending from DefCon (Defense Condition)1, which means maximum readiness for war, to DefCon 5, American forces are normally placed on DefCon 4 or 5. Just before midnight Admiral Moorer ordered all military commands to move to DefCon 3, which implied the highest stage of readiness during peacetime. The Strategic Air Command, normally at DefCon 3, was moved to DefCon 2 (attack is imminent). In addition the 82nd Airborne Division in Germany was alerted for possible movement; the carrier *Franklin Delano Roosevelt* was ordered to move from the coast of Italy to join the *Independence* in the eastern Mediterranean, while the carrier *John F. Kennedy* and its escorts were ordered to move from the Atlantic Ocean towards the region.[62] These military measures had a clear political aim, and their principal advantage was their high visibility. They were accompanied by a strong message to Brezhnev, in Nixon's name, in the early hours of the morning of 25 October. It rejected the Soviet proposal and warned that a unilateral action by Moscow "would produce incalculable consequences which would be in the interest of neither of our countries and which would end all we have striven so hard to achieve".[63] The more conciliatory approach was directed at Sadat. The group drafted another message in Nixon's name, urging the Egyptian leader to "consider the consequences for your country if the two great nuclear countries were thus to confront each other on your soil".[64]

Within hours Sadat replied that he accepted the American position. Kissinger and Haig then went to brief Nixon on the previous night's events, and the president approved of the measures taken during the night. By noon, however, they were no longer necessary, as the UN Security Council passed Resolution 340 which called for an immediate ceasefire, a return to the 22 October lines and the implementation of Resolution 338. The following day, 26 October, the DefCon order was rescinded, after Kissinger had reassured Ambassador Dobrynin that the order was not a "hostile act" on behalf of the US, and—much like his management of the crisis throughout—explained that it had been "mostly determined by 'domestic considerations'".[65]

The Kissinger stratagem during the October War was unique even in comparison to the traditional accounts of Kissinger as a grand strategist, a manipulative and power-hungry individual. In the absence of a functioning and engaged president, Kissinger often made important decisions without prior consultation with Nixon, or with a presidential *carte blanche* to make decisions on his behalf. Kissinger's unique position as the secretary of state and national security adviser put him in a most opportune position to control the bureaucracy while he still enjoyed the confidence of his interlocutors abroad. Whereas criticism of Kissinger's conduct during the war is not without merit, it is impossible to dispute the fact that the legacy of Kissinger's management of the war served well to enhance American interests in the Middle East in the long run. Washington gained the trust of Egypt whilst its support for Israel continued; the Soviets lost ground and were pushed to the sidelines of Middle East diplomacy; the Arab oil embargo, which was announced during the last week of the war, had lost momentum as Kissinger's shuttle diplomacy was bearing fruit. Undoubtedly the most important legacy of this episode was the United States becoming the principal mediator of Arab–Israeli peace. Kissinger's success in negotiating three interim agreements between Israel and Egypt (January 1974 and May 1975) and Israel and Syria (May 1974) paved the way to the Egyptian–Israeli peace treaty of 1979, and ultimately created an environment in which the US is the ubiquitous partner in Arab–Israeli negotiations. However, the degree to which it can maintain the position of an honest broker in the conflict remains questionable, especially against the background of the succession of failed diplomatic efforts since the early 1990s. It may ultimately necessitate a re-examination of one of the most enduring axioms of Arab–Israeli diplomacy over the past four decades—that American involvement is both necessary and desirable to achieve success.

7

THE SOVIET UNION AND THE OCTOBER WAR

Galia Golan

Introduction

Soviet foreign policy was guided by a number of sometimes conflicting interests, be they of a political, economic, strategic military, ideological or else domestic nature. It is not always easy, even with archival sources, to determine just which interest dominated each foreign policy decision, particularly since the results of many decisions failed to reflect (or achieve) the presumably chosen objectives. At the time of the 1973 War, the leaders in Moscow were juggling all of these interests as they sought to preserve a regional presence while, at the same time, pursuing a global détente. The Soviet policy of détente, which was generated primarily by economic necessity, did not rule out competition with the West. Indeed, it was intended ultimately to strengthen the Soviet Union in this competition, militarily as well as economically, but détente did require cooperation, especially with the US, and a far-less tense, non-polarised international environment. Thus a major issue was how to achieve and maintain global cooperation and relaxation while at the same time maintaining a competitive position, primarily military but also political in the Middle East. An additional complicating interest was the now occasionally violent Sino–Soviet dispute, which, on the one hand, was a contributing factor in favour of the policy of détente for the Soviets (a need for quiet and security in Europe while moving forces to the east; in time, also dampening the emerging US–Chinese rapprochement); but which on the other hand placed Moscow on the defensive regarding its commitments to Third World countries and revolutionary parties. To this mix one must add that for each side of the conflicting interests there were advocates within the Soviet establishment, including even within the military, pressing for or against détente.[1]

It is my contention that détente far outweighed the regional interest in this period—before, during and immediately after the 1973 War, and was intended by Moscow to apply also to the Middle East. In extending détente to this region, the idea was to transform but not eliminate Soviet positions there, whether because the Arab–Israeli conflict had become too volatile or because Soviet continued presence was too precarious, particularly after the death of Nasser (and Syria's continued refusal of a friendship treaty). The way to achieve this transformation was to work jointly with the US for a settlement of the conflict, but a settlement that would include superpower guarantees that would allow for some kind of continued presence. At the very least, activity towards a settlement might, on the one hand, prevent a war and, on the other hand, ward off an Arab (specifically Egyptian) turn to the Americans (out of despair that Moscow would ever be able to get the Arabs their territories back for them). At the same time, the divisive nature of the issue for Soviet–American relations—possibly a threat to détente—might be reduced if not entirely eliminated. As we shall see, the wish to prevent the Arab–Israeli dispute from becoming a source of even political, much less military, confrontation between the superpowers was evident in Soviet–US communications during the war itself.

The Soviets' effort to juggle their global interests with their regional interests ultimately led to their loss of both or, more accurately, a division of détente for the Soviets that later destroyed détente altogether. Despite efforts during the war by both superpowers to preserve détente, the regional competition led—unintentionally—to their confrontation at the end of the war, and this in turn would greatly handicap détente in the broader international arena, in part by strengthening opponents to the policy in both countries. Subsequent progress in the global arena (for example, the 1975 European Security Conference) was accompanied by stiff competition in the Middle East, with the Soviets almost begging for the extension of détente to the region so as to be included in—rather than totally excluded from—the emerging agreements between Israel and Egypt. At the same time, however, Moscow's own division of détente, namely its aggressive moves elsewhere in the Third World, finally led to the collapse of détente. One may suggest that it was not Soviet wartime behaviour (the attempted juggling) that led to Moscow's exclusion from post-war dealings in the region, inasmuch as both Kissinger and Sadat were set on side-lining the Soviets. Nonetheless, Soviet efforts before and during the war suggested a belief that détente could be maintained at both the regional and global levels.

Pre-war period

The Soviet interest in détente with the US was apparent from the earliest days of the Nixon administration as the two began to deal with trade, especially Most Favoured Nation status (MFN) and credits, disarmament, Strategic Arms Limitation Talks (SALT), the Non-Proliferation Treaty (NPT), a nuclear test ban treaty, Germany, Berlin, the European security conference, Vietnam, Cambodia, Laos, and other issues along with the Middle East. Priorities were obviously not the same for both superpowers, and Kissinger's insistence on linkage tended to serve his more specific interest in avoiding significant progress on the Arab–Israeli issue out of the conviction that eventually, once the Arabs saw that their reliance on the Soviets was not succeeding in getting them back their territories, they would turn to the US. None of the available information provides answers to the questions as to whether or not Moscow was aware of Kissinger's tactics regarding the Middle East, or even when the Soviets began to believe that a settlement of some kind was needed in the Middle East lest, on the one hand, they be dragged into another war there; or, on the other hand, their investment (military bases) in Egypt be lost.

But the US, specifically Kissinger, was not interested in a Soviet–US deal and for the most part avoided lengthy discussion of the Middle East even at the summit in May 1972. And thus the summit produced the laconic reference to maintain "military relaxation" in the Middle East, a formula for the status quo that infuriated Sadat. For the Egyptian leader this was the final blow in what had been more than a year of frustrating Egyptian requests and Soviet promises for the arms necessary for war.

Sadat had clearly understood that the Soviets' global interests, specifically détente, were more important than Egypt's interests. The result was Sadat's July 1972 demand for the withdrawal of the Soviet troops stationed in Egypt.

The fact that Brezhnev had actually proposed withdrawing his troops as part of an eventual agreement suggests that the Soviets may already have decided that their need to have such a force in Egypt did not outweigh the problems and risks involved (of involvement in a war, for example), particularly if Sadat were determined to have them go.[2] At the time of the expulsion, the Soviets had actually improved their capabilities with regard to protecting and servicing their fleet in the Mediterranean (and countering NATO there), possibly rendering the Egyptian bases less critical for them. Moreover, aside from alternatives in Syria, the Soviets were shifting much of their military (and economic) attention further south and east, to the Horn of Africa, Persian Gulf, and Indian Ocean areas. Whether welcomed or not, Sadat's order left the Soviets with few options (they certainly were not going to try to stay by force in a non-Marxist country far from Soviet borders). The option they chose was one of anger, pulling out not only the military contingents but also almost all of the advisers, trainers and equipment, including SAMs and SA3s, along with the Soviet ambassador. The freeze they initiated in relations (and arms deliveries) may have been designed, or believed, to demonstrate to Sadat that the Egyptian military was dependent upon the Soviet Union. In any case, mediation efforts by Syrian President Hafez al-Asad produced only a minor thaw in the autumn of 1972, with the Soviets returning a few hundred advisers and some SAMs.

The freeze continued actually until early 1973. Having chosen (in January) alternative dates for a limited war across the Suez Canal,[3] in February Sadat sent first his national security adviser, Hafez Isma'il, and then his war minister, Ahmed Isma'il, to Moscow to patch up relations and seek renewal of arms deliveries. The Soviets did comply, resuming arms deliveries and returning still more advisers. However, despite what appears to have been assistance (for example, transporting Moroccan troops to Syria in April 1973), they (a) did not provide all of Sadat's requests (for example advanced MIG-23s, while Scuds came only in September 1973; and (b) continued to try to dissuade Sadat (and also Asad) from going to war. This was more than amply documented by

Sadat in interviews and comments both before and after the war.[4] The US also acknowledged this in high-level bilateral talks before the war. Most importantly, Brezhnev repeatedly communicated his concerns to Nixon regarding what he called the "explosive" situation, almost pleading with the US to agree at least to principles for an agreement that could be conveyed to the Arabs in order to deter them from going to war—with all that such a development would mean, negatively, for détente.[5] Soviet efforts to restrain both Egypt and Syria were so serious that a decided deterioration occurred in relations with both countries during the summer and autumn, prior to the October attack.[6] When the Soviet ambassador in Cairo was informed by Sadat on 3 October that war was imminent, Moscow began an airlift of its civilian personnel out of the country—an act which Ahmed Isma'il later accused the Soviets of having conducted openly and intentionally in order to ruin the element of surprise and thereby, possibly, necessitate cancellation of the attack.[7]

The 1973 War

While Soviet global policy, namely détente, was moving relatively smoothly, ups and downs on various disarmament and trade issues notwithstanding, Soviet relations with both Egypt and Syria were experiencing difficulties when the war that Moscow had hoped to avoid erupted on 6 October 1973. Moscow's priority objective was most likely to limit polarisation and damage to détente as much as possible and, of course, prevent a direct Soviet–US military confrontation; but the Soviets would also have to be careful to preserve—even improve, if possible—their relationship with the Arabs. Such objectives would presumably be best served by an early end to hostilities, particularly since Soviet estimates (like those of the US) were that Israel would be quickly victorious. The correspondence between Moscow and Washington indicates that neither was actually interested in turning to the UN Security Council for a ceasefire in the first two days of the war, conceivably because each was waiting to see how the first days' battles would turn out, and they hoped to be able to avoid a confrontation between them at the UN.[8] However, the Soviets did try to prevail upon Sadat to agree to a ceasefire even on the first day of the battle, and virtually every day thereafter, for Moscow was convinced that, early gains notwithstanding, the

Arabs would face defeat (and call for Soviet assistance). In Moscow there were reportedly even some within the military who expressed satisfaction over this—to prove to Sadat that he could not in fact do without the Soviets militarily.[9]

The Soviets' first official statement on the war came only on the evening of 7 October, after they had received Sadat's negative response to a Soviet bid for a ceasefire (conveyed by Soviet ambassador Vinogradov when he was finally able to meet with Sadat, six hours after the beginning of the war), and we know from various sources, including Sadat and Vinogradov, that this pressure on Sadat continued on 7, 8 and 10 October and again at dawn on 13 October.[10] From the first day, according to Sadat, the Soviets told him the Syrians had already agreed to a cease-fire. The 13 October ceasefire bid was actually a Soviet–American initiative, to be proposed both to Sadat and in the UNSC by the British.[11] Sadat's angry response was that this was just one more attempt in which the Soviets were lying to him about ostensible Syrian agreement. There is little information on Soviet–Syrian contacts at this time, but there were claims later that there had in fact been a discussion between the Soviet ambassador to Damascus, Nuritdin Mukhidinov and Asad about the Soviets' call for a ceasefire after the first 48 hours of the war.[12]

Initially, the Soviets and Americans had agreed not to propose a ceasefire resolution at the UN so as to avoid divisive polemics that might hurt détente. But the Soviets were also reluctant to annoy the Egyptians further by proposing a ceasefire without Sadat's agreement (especially with the embarrassing likelihood of a Chinese veto). Brezhnev had told Nixon on 10 October that Moscow was ready for a ceasefire, but if the US tabled a resolution, the Soviets would have to abstain since the Arabs had not agreed. Abstaining rather than vetoing would be a détente-motivated gesture (as Brezhnev pointed out)[13] that would have cost the Soviets with their Arab friends, had Washington proceeded. The Soviets intensified their efforts with Sadat, dispatching Kosygin to Cairo suddenly on 16 October. The reason for the urgency was, apparently, the failed Egyptian attempt to break out of its positions on the eastern side of the Suez Canal on 14 October, and the successful Israeli counterattack. Yet Sadat kept Kosygin waiting in the embassy several times, finally meeting him on 18 October, at which time Sadat must have been aware of the fact that Israeli forces had successfully broadened their 16 October bridgehead on the western side of the canal.[14] Nonetheless,

Sadat was still unwilling to agree to a cease-fire, and Kosygin left Cairo empty-handed. Sadat's agreement came only the next day, but, significantly, even without this the Soviets had already asked Kissinger to come to Moscow to work out an immediate ceasefire.[15] Relatively quickly the Soviets abandoned their demand for Israeli withdrawal to the 4 June 1967 lines,[16] and a joint cease-fire resolution was worked out, to go into effect from early evening on 22 October. Syrian President Asad claimed that he had not been consulted (later denied by Moscow), and he was in fact angry since he had been planning a counter-attack with Iraqi and Jordanian contingents.[17]

The fate of this ceasefire will be discussed below, but first an apparent contradiction must be examined. On 8 October Brezhnev sent messages to Arab leaders reportedly urging them to come to the aid of their Arab brothers. Together with a Soviet re-supply effort to Egypt and Syria that began on 10 October, this would appear to have been an effort to prolong the war, rather than end it quickly. Brezhnev claimed to Nixon that he was merely seeking the opinion of Arab leaders on the matter of a ceasefire, but in fact Brezhnev was answering a query from Algerian President Boumedienne about what the Soviets planned to do to assist Egypt and Syria. Thus the 8 October messages actually spoke more of the need for "Arab solidarity," adding that the Algerian leaders "understood" the "complexity" of the situation (implying that it was up to the Arabs, not the Soviets, to provide assistance). Indeed later Moscow said that "the Arab countries should be worrying about solidarity with Egypt and Syria rather than lecturing the Russians on how to help them."[18] Yet, the resupply effort did begin on 10 October, and it did both puzzle and displease the Americans.

Sadat claimed later that only medical and other non-weapon supplies were sent (until 15 October), and that Moscow actually demanded hard currency payments.[19] He also said that the Soviets had sent only equipment previously ordered and spares from nearby stocks. Indeed, during a 14–15 October visit to Moscow, Boumedienne provided hard currency, as did Abu Dhabi, and the Soviet airlift to Egypt actually doubled the number of aircraft beginning 15 October. The increased deliveries might, however, have been connected with the beginning of the US airlift to Israel at the same time.[20]

In any case, the fact that at the same time as the resupply effort was taking place the Soviets nonetheless continued—even stepped up—their efforts to persuade Sadat to agree to a ceasefire suggests that, rather than trying to prolong the war, Moscow was trying to shore up the Arabs so as to prevent a defeat, before a ceasefire could be achieved. Even the more hawkish Grechko argued that aid would help until a ceasefire was achieved (although the decision was that aid should not exceed existing contracts). Moreover, the aid—even if disparaged by Sadat—was also a way of demonstrating Soviet loyalty, and value to the Arabs, particularly in view of the pre-war problems. What is more, the Soviets were increasingly alarmed as the expected Israeli victory began to materialise with the 14 October counter-attack and then the crossing of the canal during the night of 15–16 October. Their concern was reflected not only by Kosygin's sudden visit to Cairo and augmentation of the airlift, but also by the dispatch of additional Soviet ships into the Mediterranean. But, as the Americans were to point out, the Soviets did "everything to stay out" of the conflict, including initially shifting their ships westward (while the Americans moved theirs eastward, with both [augmented] fleets assuming holding positions next to each other off the island of Crete).[21] Admiral Bagley (commander of US naval forces in Europe) commented after the war that the Soviet naval posture had been "restrained and considerate," and, like the Americans, ready to pre-empt if necessary.[22]

Actually, as they were shoring up the Arabs—for political as well as military reasons—the Soviets were concerned about the negative repercussions in Washington. A Brezhnev message to Nixon on 17 October (the same day that four more Soviet amphibious marine ships entered the Mediterranean), noted the anti-détente sentiment in Washington, presumably in response to US press claims that the Soviets had violated détente by not warning Washington of impending war. Brezhnev elaborated on his pre-war warnings. But he also spoke of what he called "hysteria," that is, hawkish views in Washington that sought to exploit the different loyalties of the two superpowers to produce polarisation in the Soviet–American cease-fire efforts and cause irreparable damage to détente. For evidence, he referred directly to a comment Nixon had made a few days earlier (in a 15 October speech) in connection with the Middle East crisis, recalling the US landing of the marines in Lebanon in 1958. There is no other sign that Brezhnev believed this to be a veiled threat of American action, but he did apparently perceive it as a strengthening of anti-détente voices in the US and therefore a reason to emphasise the cooperation achieved so far and the need to protect détente.

THE SOVIET UNION AND THE OCTOBER WAR

The concern over anti-détente forces in Washington suggests another explanation of the apparently contradictory ceasefire/assistance dualism. As in the pre-war period, this may have been the result of differences of opinion within the Soviet leadership, linked to pro-and anti-détente positions (the latter believing that détente would weaken the Soviets, militarily, politically or ideologically). There may have been differences over risk-taking or classic hawk/dove approaches, and there were those who did not believe that non-Marxist Third World leaders (like Sadat) should be trusted (or aided). There were in fact signs of differences of opinion regarding the meaning of the war with regard to détente. In speeches on the very same day, 8 October, Grechko characterised the war as a sign of the continued aggressiveness of imperialism, while Brezhnev, at another venue, praised what he termed the relaxation of world tensions and the trend towards détente. Granted that Grechko was addressing a military event and Brezhnev the visiting Japanese premier, but similar differences could be found in additional pronouncements during the war and in the reporting of the military paper *Krasnaya zvezda* as distinct from *Pravda*—in fact, *Pravda* failed to carry some of Grechko's anti-détente speeches.[23] There were differences of opinion in the Politburo discussions of 15 October that led to Kosygin's departure for Cairo on 16 October. According to Soviet diplomat Viktor Israelyan, who was present on behalf of the Foreign Ministry, the pro-détentists (Brezhnev, Kosygin, Gromyko) proposed a high-level emissary to convey a strong message on the need for an immediate ceasefire. Grechko favoured, rather, a prolongation of the war in the form of a war of attrition, while KGB head Andropov and President Podgorny were more concerned that pressure on Sadat would harm Soviet relations with the Arab world. (Primakov has written about earlier differences with Podgorny, who seemed to have more confidence in Sadat as an ally than most other Soviet officials.)[24] In the end Kosygin was chosen to go, with instructions from Brezhnev to be careful with Sadat so as not to harm relations with the Arabs, but also to be firm about the imminent danger of defeat (and remind Sadat of the Soviet warnings that a war would have grave consequences).[25]

While the Soviets, and Washington, saw their joint ceasefire resolution as an achievement of détente, as well as a sign that they had weathered the war without damaging détente, this was not the way others viewed it. For the Soviets, a problem was not just Asad's dissatisfaction but also accusations by the Chinese, the PLO, Iraq, Libya, Kuwait and Algeria that Moscow had "colluded" with the US in the interests of détente.[26] Thus, when the ceasefire broke down, with Israel continuing its conquest of the west bank of the canal, ultimately also surrounding the 20,000-strong Egyptian Third Army trapped on the eastern side of the canal, Moscow was on the defensive politically. Moreover, Brezhnev was now faced with the very dilemma he had hoped to avoid throughout the war (and before), as Sadat pleaded for intervention to enforce the ceasefire and save the Third Army.

Sadat called for joint Soviet–US intervention, which at first both Moscow and Washington believed could be accommodated instead by UN observers in the area. Brezhnev's concern was expressed in his using the hotline to the White House twice on 23 October, calling on the United States, as "co-guarantor" with the Soviet Union, to restrain the Israelis; but the tone was still one of cooperation invoking preservation of détente. During that day Sadat contacted both the Soviets and the US (the latter by a back channel) with the request to intervene, even with military forces. At this point the discussions between the US and Moscow were over wording of a new ceasefire resolution, with no sign of tension between the two countries (as clearly indicated by Kissinger's briefing to his State Department staff late afternoon on 23 October).

The next morning (late afternoon Moscow time), 24 October, Brezhnev sent another message to Nixon again expressing concern over continued Israeli advances even after the new cease-fire and beseeching the US to control Israel. As the day progressed, however, Sadat informed both the Soviets and the US that he planned to ask the UNSC to dispatch a Soviet–American force to implement the ceasefire. Washington informed Sadat of its opposition to this, while, in the meantime Brezhnev sent still another message urging Washington to control Israel, commenting that he was certain the US could do this. Subsequently, Dobynin informed Kissinger that the Soviets would support Sadat's request in the UN. This message was followed a few hours later by still another message from Brezhnev, but this time of a more threatening nature.

…Let us together, the Soviet Union and the United States, urgently dispatch to Egypt Soviet and American military contingents, with their mission the implementation of the decision of the Security Council of October 22 and 23 concerning the cessation of fire and of all military activities and also the understanding with you on the guarantee of the implementation of the decisions of the Security Council.

It is necessary to adhere without delay. I will say it straight that if you find it impossible to act jointly with us in this matter, we should be faced with the necessity urgently to consider the question of taking appropriate steps unilaterally. We cannot allow arbitrariness on the part of Israel.

We have an understanding with you which we value highly—that is to act jointly. Let us implement this understanding on a concrete case in this complex situation. It will be a good example of our agreed actions in the interest of peace. We have no doubt that all those who are in favor of détente, of peace, of good relations between the Soviet Union and the United States will only welcome such joint action of ours. I will appreciate an immediate and clear reply from you. (US translation)[27]

It was this message that led to the crisis and US alert declared at 3 a.m. US time. The alert decision was intended to convey to Moscow that the Americans would not tolerate the introduction of Soviet troops into the region, whatever form this might take. The Americans spelled this out in their response to Brezhnev's letter, without mentioning the alert. The signs that had concerned Washington were: Soviet airborne divisions on alert (three since 12 October at least, others since the beginning of the war); a halt in the Soviet airlift—possibly freeing planes to transport the airborne divisions; the spotting of eight transport planes on their way to the region.[28] However, in a post-war press conference, Secretary of Defense Schlesinger said that the airborne divisions were not the cause of the US alert.[29] Indeed, it would have taken the Soviets several days to place such a force in battle, hardly in time to stop the Israelis or save the Third Army. It was thought, according to Schlesinger, that at most the Soviets might have intended to place a limited, symbolic but politically significant force around Cairo.

The question here, however, is not why the Americans did what they did, but, rather, what did the Soviets actually intend to do? The frequent communications from Brezhnev to Washington on 23 and early 24 October, themselves a response to Sadat's near panic, were a sign of Moscow's increasing concern over the failure of a cease-fire for which it was in part responsible (and being criticised). The tone was still that of a partner, rather than an adversary, but a growing frustration was clearly apparent over what the Soviets may genuinely have believed to be American hesitation, rather than inability, to control the Israelis. The Soviets were now faced with the dilemma they had sought to avoid: how to maintain their credibility with the Arab world without intervening militarily to save the Egyptians, but also without destroying the relationship with Washington. During the night of 22–3 October and then again during the day of 23 October, the Politburo debated its options. The correspondence with Washington was the outcome of these meetings, along with a warning to the Israelis "of gravest consequences" should they fail to "stop their aggression". In the first discussions, a suggestion by Grechko to send a joint Soviet–US force to enforce the ceasefire was not, according to Israelyan, tabled.[30] The critical discussions came on 24 October, in response to further entreaties by Sadat. It was decided initially to send a group of seventy military observers (including twenty interpreters) to Egypt (the US had told Moscow it was sending military observers from the embassy in Tel Aviv). Grechko reportedly again urged "a demonstration of our military force in Egypt and Syria," supported by Podgorny but strongly opposed by Kosygin and Gromyko.[31] Kosygin reportedly repeated an earlier proposal to send a joint Soviet–American group of several hundred observers. Some accounts of the meeting claim that this was a serious proposal, but Israelyan reports that most participants in the discussion considered it unrealistic, since the US would never agree to a joint force. Chief of Staff Kulikov reportedly commented that by the time a joint force or even a unilateral Soviet force reached the area and achieved battle readiness, Cairo would have fallen and the war would be over. In any case, he reportedly opposed any force going there until Egyptian and Israeli troops were separated.[32] Nonetheless, as we have seen, the proposal of a joint force was included in the letter to Nixon, probably for propaganda purposes, so that the Americans could be blamed, rather than the Soviets, for the rejection of Sadat's plea. There was reportedly a discussion of a unilateral Soviet action, but Brezhnev favoured a cautious approach, and the idea of sending troops was not supported. Nor was there any decision to threaten the sending of Soviet troops. According to several accounts, two things were decided. One was to order air force manoeuvres in the Caucasus.[33] This could have been a measure simply to make a threat to use force more credible, but one military source has claimed that orders were given to prepare contingency plans for the "optimal use of airborne troops," and another, civilian, source said that contingency plans were drawn up for the dispatch of two or three divisions to save the Third Army. Other Soviet sources denied this emphatically, and Gromyko said much later (in 1989) that the only troops considered would have been to form a cordon around Cairo.[34]

The other decision adopted was to continue to press the Americans, by means of a stronger letter than previously. Reportedly, the letter prepared by Gromyko was purposely vague and conditional ("…faced with the necessity urgently to consider…"), using the words "contingents" rather than "troops."[35] As Gromyko said in 1989, "some of my colleagues might have said that [the letter] was only a form of political pressure." More importantly, the letter drafted by Gromyko did not contain the threatening "I will say it straight…" sentence. This was added at some point by "someone" (according to Primakov and Dobynin) or by Brezhnev himself (Israelyan).[36] Lest this sound like excessive "Kremlinology," I suggest it is of great importance, since it is this sentence that alarmed Kissinger, leading to the DefCon 3 alert and ultimately strengthening the voices of the anti-détentists in Washington.

Inasmuch as the Politburo members apparently believed the letter to Washington was to have been relatively cautious, it is understandable that they were surprised by the American reaction that came in the form of a high-level alert. In a meeting on 25 October to consider their response, Brezhnev was said to have been not only surprised but also indignant over the US alert, while anti-détentists characterised it as unprovoked Western aggressiveness. Grechko, reportedly, again suggested sending Soviet forces to the region, but this idea was soundly rejected by Kosygin and Gromyko on the grounds that it would lead to American intervention and escalation. Grechko then suggested mobilising 50,000 to 70,000 troops, but this and similar ideas were abandoned in favour of a purely political response. Brezhnev finally decided simply to ignore the American alert and thereby avoid confrontation. Since no decision had in fact been taken earlier to engage militarily, there was no point in getting into a dispute with Washington now. Instead, Brezhnev sent a message that, in accord with the Americans' suggestions earlier in the day, the Soviets would send seventy observers (and the US as well) and agree to a UN non-permanent Security Council members' peace-keeping force. By the end of the day the ceasefire was holding, and water and plasma had been allowed into the Third Army—both possibly because of Kissinger's discussions with Israel about Soviet threats to intervene. By midnight the US DefCon 3 was removed.

Brezhnev was able the following day to open the World Peace Congress (which he had postponed by one day) with a tribute to détente. But in fact détente had been badly damaged by the war, and particularly by the threatening letter. The letter—meant to help the relationship with the Arabs, strengthened anti-détentists in the US (even Kissinger had momentary doubts when he read it)[37] while the US response (the alert) strengthened anti-détentists in the Kremlin. Also, the Soviet effort to maintain its relationship with the Arabs, namely the resupply effort, created problems for cooperation with the US (that is, the appearance of seeking to prolong the war), while the simultaneous cooperation with the US for a ceasefire (primarily but not only the pressure on Sadat) prompted Arab resentment and even accusations of Soviet–American collusion in the interests of détente. On the whole, the Soviets' attempt to juggle their basically contradictory interests failed, though my conclusion is that (a) they gave priority to détente throughout the war; (b) they believed that their aid to the Arabs, including the letter, would not stretch détente beyond its limits (that is, they underestimated the possible US response or interpretations); and (c) they misunderstood the fragility of their position in the Middle East. Thus, it may be that the Soviets miscalculated both Sadat's intentions—to shift to the US—and also the Americans' interest (or lack of interest) in continuing détente cooperation in the Middle East. In other words, it is possible that no matter what the Soviets did during the war vis-à-vis the Arabs or the United States, the former (specifically Sadat) was determined to be rid of Moscow; and the latter (specifically Kissinger) was also determined to exclude the Soviets from subsequent dealings in the Middle East.

Post-war decline and legacy

In the long term, the Soviet Union's position in the Middle East declined significantly after the war, as did Soviet–US cooperation in the region and, in time, even détente at the global level. None of these developments was a foregone conclusion from the Soviets' point of view, nor were they all necessarily or totally attributable to the war, given the long-standing inclinations of both Sadat and Kissinger. Yet the superpowers' policies during the war did play a role, at the very least as contributing factors, to the deterioration of the Soviet position in the region and, ultimately, the demise of détente, despite subsequent efforts by Moscow at damage-control.

Almost immediately after the war, Moscow began to sense a change in the American attitude, remarking specifically on what it correctly perceived as an American attempt to exclude the Soviets from post-war deliberations and to encourage an Arab break with Moscow. This was generally treated in a low key (if at all) by Soviet pronouncements, as Brezhnev and the supporters of détente strove to ignore publicly (and defend privately) any US actions that might be viewed as contrary to détente, notably the crisis of 24–5 October, and later Kissinger's solo achievements of Arab–Israeli disengagement agreements. For example, Kissinger's shuttles back and forth to Damascus to achieve Israeli–Syrian troop disengagement were virtually ignored by the Soviet media, while Soviet visits to Syria were credited for the agreement eventually reached.[38] In conversations and correspondence with Washington, however, Moscow's growing concern—and anger—was explicit. This took the form not only of demands for inclusion in the disengagement talks, but also the demand to be co-guarantors with the US of any Arab–Israeli settlement reached. Indeed Gromyko insisted to Kissinger (during a February 1974 visit to Washington) that such a role had already been agreed upon and was meant to be taken literally. To this end, the Soviets repeated what they insisted was their genuine interest in seeing resolution of the Arab–Israeli conflict (pointing, among other things, to the more favourable position they had taken vis-à-vis Israel at the post-war Geneva conference).[39] Their interest in resolution of the conflict stemmed primarily from concern over the risks that the ongoing and basically uncontrollable conflict could and did cause to Soviet–US relations. The issue between Moscow and the US, however, was not Soviet sincerity regarding a settlement of the conflict, but, rather, Kissinger's intention of ejecting the Soviets from the region altogether.

Thus, the Soviets found themselves in a contradiction somewhat similar to but more difficult than the one they had experienced before the war: how to maintain their presence in the region as the champions of the Arabs while seeking cooperation with the US. They sought to prove to the Arabs that Moscow was needed, arguing that only the Soviet Union could press the US to pressure Israel, and only the Soviet Union supported all the Arab interests (a comprehensive settlement) while the US would only provide partial satisfaction. At the same time, they had to demonstrate to the US (and possibly Israel) the need to include Moscow. The Soviets did this by moderating certain of its positions (namely, Gromyko's speech at the Geneva conference), but also by claiming to control the military option via its influence in the Arab world. It is doubtful that Sadat could have been persuaded in any case, but the Soviets' loss of credibility in the eyes of all the Arab states during the war greatly crippled Moscow's efforts. Not only did Sadat pursue his original intention of gradually shifting to the US and ending the treaty and relationship with Moscow, but Syria, for example, angry over the quality and types of arms it had received and over what it claimed had been the precipitous Soviet agreement to a ceasefire[40] opened interest sections with the US in 1974 (following a visit to Damascus by Nixon), and sought to diversify its arms suppliers. Even the PLO agreed to secret talks with the US.

Neither Syria nor the PLO, however, abandoned the Soviets. In fact, the Soviets were able to strengthen their relations with each, providing both of them with greater assistance as a counter-balance to the loss of Egypt. One might argue that in this sense Moscow's position in the region was not hurt. In fact, however, not only Moscow's credibility but also its influence—always tenuous at best—was reduced. Syria continued to refuse to sign a Friendship Treaty (until 1981) and blatantly rejected Moscow's opposition to its policy in Lebanon;[41] the PLO continued to maintain its independence (from Communist parties as well as Moscow), refusing (until 1988) to accept UNSC resolution 242 or other Soviet-supported positions on a resolution of the conflict. More importantly, the Soviets were not only unable to find a way into Middle East deliberations, they were also unable to impede Washington's successes, most notably the 1975 Interim Agreement and later the Egyptian-Israeli peace agreement. This loss—to the gain of the US—of the most important country in the region limited (though it did not eliminate) Moscow's strategic position in the region. This may not have been critical for the Soviets inasmuch as they were becoming less dependent strategically and even less interested in the eastern Mediterranean, as their strategic and economic interests moved south-southeastward to the Persian Gulf, Horn of Africa, Indian Ocean area.[42] But it did seriously hurt the Soviets' political position, as Washington proved that it could "deliver" where Moscow had failed, that is, in getting Israel out of Arab territory. The continued importance of this was reflected in Moscow's near constant demand to the US that détente be extended to the Middle East, meaning that the Soviets be included in the Middle East deliberations. When that proved a hopeless cause, with Kissinger's achievement of the 1975 Egyptian-Israeli interim agreement, Moscow adopted a more blatant adversarial role towards the US in the region.

If the Soviets finally despaired of an application of détente to the Middle East, they did not give up on détente at the global level.[43] All the Soviet-US détente-related negotiations (on trade, arms, and so forth) continued after the 1973 War, prompted as they were by American as well as Soviet interests. Indeed, global détente even appeared to reach remarkable success with the convening of the 1975 Helsinki Conference on European Security—an achievement long-sought by Moscow and one of the main objectives of Brezhnev's détente policy. Yet, détente was far from secure, due, in some part, to the 1973 War.

Opponents to détente in both Moscow and Washington had been strengthened by the war. In Washington this facilitated the passage of the Jackson–Vanik and Stevenson amendments limiting Soviet–US trade (mainly US credits), constituting a serious blow to Moscow. Even after this victory for the American opponents of détente, domestic pressure continued on the White House regarding SALT and other negotiations. This was aided by Moscow, however, for there too anti-détentists had been equally reinforced by events of the war (especially the alert). Brezhnev was hard put to deny that his pursuit of détente during the war had worked to the disadvantage of the Soviet position in the region. (His opponents might have pointed out that it had already worked against Moscow even earlier, having precipitated Sadat's expulsion of the Soviets troops in 1972.) Possibly in response to such criticism at home (and from Third World leaders), the Soviets appeared to adopt more hard-line policies in the Third World, for example, Angola, Ethiopia and later Yemen. Successful assaults on détente in Washington[44] fuelled similar assaults in Moscow, and vice versa. Ultimately it was just this type of hard-line policies—culminating in the Soviet invasion of Afghanistan—that destroyed détente. It may be argued that by the time of that event, détente had been significantly crippled (namely, the problems over SALT II), and, moreover, many of the mutual hardening of positions might have occurred even without the blows to détente occasioned by the 1973 War. Nevertheless, the strengthening of the opponents of détente in both countries in connection with and as a result of the war contributed to the gradual demise of détente. In this sense, the war may have constituted a turning point not only for the Soviet role in the Middle East, but also, more importantly for Moscow, a turning point for their relationship with the United States and global détente.

It is difficult to speak of a legacy of this experience for the Soviets inasmuch as an entirely new concept of rule—and foreign policy—was introduced by Gorbachev beginning a few years after the collapse of détente. Believing that international relations should be based on a balance of interests, he put an end to the adversarial relationship and competition with the West and advocated the removal of outside powers from regional or local conflicts, such as the Arab-Israeli conflict. These, he claimed, should be resolved by a balance of interests between the protagonists themselves. It might be argued that the experience of the October War contributed to Gorbachev's understanding that détente, that is cooperation with the West, could not be conducted side by side with competition for influence in various areas of the world. There is no specific reference by Gorbachev to such a conclusion related specifically to the Middle East, but it did underlay Gorbachev's "New Thinking" in foreign policy and his attitude to the Arab-Israeli conflict and other conflicts.

8

JORDAN'S WAR THAT NEVER WAS

Assaf David

Three recently published books have added valuable information and analysis to the somewhat scanty literature on Jordan's symbolic role in the 1973 War. Using secondary sources and personal interviews, Curtis Ryan described the domestic, economic and foreign policy considerations that were behind Jordan's policy choices before and during the war. Avi Shlaim and Nigel Ashton, in their biographies of King Hussein, drew on direct access to the king and declassified British and American documents to provide considerable information on Jordan's actions during the war.[1]

The aim of this chapter is twofold: first, to present a critical synthesis of the various perspectives on Jordan's role in the 1973 War; second, to provide additional insight into Jordan's foreign policy in the months preceding the war and into its military considerations and actions during the war. This information is based mostly on recently declassified documents published in a special volume of the Foreign Relations of the United States dedicated to the 1973 war.[2] So far, the FRUS documents on Jordan have not been explored by scholars, apart from a "tentative first stab" at them.[3]

THE OCTOBER 1973 WAR

Approaching the storm

With its small military severely beaten in the 1967 war, and its institutions and civil society seriously damaged and divided following the 1970–1 civil war, Jordan could ill afford the adventure of a new war in 1973. Also, since Jordan enjoyed the backing of the United States and Israel in its confrontation with the PLO, it was hardly considered by Egypt, Syria and Saudi Arabia as a natural partner for a new Arab military campaign against Israel. Moreover, Jordan's decision-makers feared that if the course of the war turned against the country, Egypt and Syria would leave the kingdom's territory to the mercy of Israel.[4]

Considerations of political economy also limited Jordan's policy choices. With the exception of Saudi Arabia, the rich Gulf monarchies had terminated their financial aid to Jordan following the civil war, and by 1973 the state budget was suffering from a chronic deficit. Britain and the United States, on the other hand, increased their level of aid to the kingdom to such an extent that the Americans felt that Jordan was becoming addicted to excessive public expenses and generous foreign aid.[5] As a result, Jordan found its security and foreign policy decisions severely restricted by its Western benefactors.

In terms of foreign policy, Jordan could not have been further from Egypt and Syria in the wake of the 1973 War. While Sadat refused any interim agreement with Israel in the Sinai, and secretly opted to launch a surprise attack on Israel along with Syria, Hussein embarked on a diplomatic offensive. In March 1972, he proposed the establishment of the United Arab Kingdom, a Jordanian-Palestinian federation on both banks of the River Jordan. Widely interpreted as a scheme to deprive the Palestinians of real statehood, the plan was condemned by the PLO and other Arab states.[6] Israel, too, showed no enthusiasm for the plan. However, the plan did trigger the resumption of the secret dialogue between Israel and Jordan, and over the course of 1972 top officials from both sides met three times to discuss the nature of a possible settlement between them. Israel proposed the Allon Plan, a "security blueprint for the restoration of a truncated West Bank to the kingdom",[7] which the king was unable to accept. Therefore, the two sides agreed to disagree on the issue of peace and moved on to discuss other issues, widening the scope of their dialogue to include security, civic and even environmental problems.[8]

Aware of Hussein's secret dialogue with the Israeli leadership, Sadat was hostile to, and even contemptuous of, the king.[9] The president of Egypt was also aware of Jordan's firm position against the resumption of hostilities against Israel, though he appeared to understand Jordan's standpoint and even urged it not to "become involved in Egypt's war of attrition," lest Israel invade the East Bank and destroy the Jordanian army.[10] Hussein had hoped to gauge the support of Egypt and Syria for an American-led peace plan, but the Americans doubted his chances of success.[11] In fact, the State Department, reassured of Jordan's moderation, favoured concentrating first on the Egyptian-Israeli track and postponing the Jordanian-Israeli track till later, a position they shared with the king himself.[12] As Kissinger elegantly put it to the king, "the trouble with you Jordanians is that you are so reasonable!"[13]

Hussein's meetings with the Israeli leadership in May and August 1973 focused on the general situation in the Middle East, as well as on economic and business cooperation, leading the Americans to conclude that he had decided on "a long-term strategy of tacit collaboration with Israel while he strengthens his own country."[14] Moreover, Hussein assured Prime Minister Meir that Jordan would not "in any way" alter its policy concerning the resumption of hostilities or Fedayeen activity.[15] He even requested Israeli intelligence on Syrian and Egyptian military movements, indicating that Jordan "has plans for pre-emptive strikes in the event of threatening troop movements."[16] Pleased with the tightening bond, Israel assisted Jordan's efforts to secure more American aid, and even promised to arrange economic aid for Jordan through third parties.[17]

The summer of 1973: clouds of war

Throughout 1973, the king constantly warned the United States and Israel of an imminent war. In February, he informed Ambassador Brown that "Sadat has begun recently to think of war as a serious alternative."[18] Three months later he warned that "a major international military fiasco in the area is inevitable," providing Israel with details on Arab forces headed for Egypt and Syria, as well as on the Syrian military build-up, battle orders and secret military plans.[19] Unfortunately, the Israelis believed that the king tended "to exaggerate, to be alarmist."[20] In June, the king told Kissinger that "the situation grows steadily worse and that the eruption on a military basis appears to be most imminent."[21] A month later, he made similar comments to the British prime minister, Edward Heath, and forwarded yet another warning to Israel.[22]

Sadat, Asad and Hussein met in Cairo in mid-September to discuss their future plans. Brown reported that Hussein had come out the "winner" at the summit: Jordanian–Egyptian relations were normalised, and the relations with Syria were to follow suit. The three leaders agreed that no unified command would be established, neither Egyptian nor Syrian troops would be stationed in Jordan, and there would be no deal between Jordan and the Fedayeen.[23] The Americans observed that the aim of Jordan's "new foreign policy" was to ease internal pressures and enhance the king's standing in the Arab and Palestinian sphere. A first step was an amnesty for all political prisoners and prominent Fedayeen leaders.[24] Prime Minister Rifa'i claimed that war was discussed in the summit only in general terms and "as a possible option [...] after proper preparation," adding that Jordan was supposed to "play a purely defensive role" and deter any potential Israeli attack.[25] The official Jordanian position holds that the king was excluded from the actual war plans.[26]

Hussein's meeting with Meir and top Israeli officials in Tel Aviv on 25 September, during which he allegedly warned the Israelis of an imminent Egyptian–Syrian attack, remains the subject of much controversy among historians. The known facts are that Fathi Abu Taleb, director of military intelligence of the Jordanian army (and later chief of staff), accompanied the king and met separately with Israeli intelligence officers, including the head of the Mossad. Hussein disclosed to the Israelis detailed information from a "very, very sensitive source in Syria"[27] on pre-jump positions of all military units in Syria, adding, in response to Meir's question, that it was unlikely that Syria would start anything without Egypt. The latter point is sharply disputed, since Israeli sources insist that the king did report a Syrian–Egyptian coordination.[28] Hussein's mysterious source was Abboud Salem, an Iraqi pilot who defected to Jordan in the early 1960s and became a Jordanian intelligence officer. Salem, who served as the commander of the Jordanian air force from 1973 to 1976, was related through his wife to a Syrian division commander, whom he had recruited as an agent long before the war.[29]

The fact that Israel did not heed the king's vague warning leads his biographers to argue that he had not told the Israelis anything they did not already know. Shlaim also echoes the king's assertion that he could not possibly have divulged the plan of attack to the Israelis, since he knew nothing about it and had himself been caught "completely off guard" when the war broke out.[30] Shlaim and Ashton,[31] who enjoyed direct access to the king and to his personal letters, seem to have gone out of their way to exonerate Hussein regarding his meeting with Meir. The same is true of Jack O'Connell, the former CIA chief officer in Amman, who insists in his newly published autobiography that Hussein's meeting with Meir was essentially a "fishing expedition" which "picked up nothing about a planned attack by Egypt and Syria".[32] Ashton even suggests that Hussein's goal was "most certainly not to able them [the Israelis] better to prepare for war and preserve the status quo," concluding that "in view of what he [Hussein] knew about Syrian plans what is more remarkable is how little, not how much, he told the Israelis".[33]

However, Gai Gavra, whose research paper on the Hussein–Meir meeting was a basic source for Shlaim's analysis, concluded that Hussein did effectively warn Israel of an imminent attack. This was also the impression of the head of the Jordan branch in the Israeli military intelligence, who watched the meeting secretly through CCTV. Years later, Hussein and a Jordanian prime minister (possibly Rifa'i) even told Israeli officials that had the king been summoned to testify in front of the Agranat Commission, he would have turned its conclusions upside down.[34]

In the days following the meeting in Tel Aviv, the king continued to be extremely worried and anxious about the "strange activity" in the Syrian army.[35] However, Jordan only received official, albeit vague, notification of the upcoming attack on 3 October, when General Nofal of the Egyptian army visited Amman and conveyed to the chief of staff of the Jordanian army, Zeid Bin Shaker, "a veiled warning of portentous events to come," in the words of Ali el-Edroos, the semi-official historian of the Jordanian army. However, el-Edroos insists that "the scope, scale and ferocity of the Syro–Egyptian strategic offensive" took Jordan completely by surprise.[36] Abu Daoud, the military commander of Fatah who had been imprisoned in Jordan since 1972, provides a different account. According to him, the king came to visit him in jail on 18 September, and told him: "I return from Cairo and the brothers might go to war, which I honestly do not approve of. If Sadat loses Cairo he could retreat to Aswan, and if Asad loses Damascus he could retreat to Aleppo. But if I lose Amman, where can I go to? The desert?" Declaring that he would not participate in the war, the king released Abu Daoud from jail along with 2,500 other Fedayeen, seeking to empty Jordan's prison cells of Palestinian combatants before war broke out.[37] However, Abu Daoud's account has yet to be corroborated by other sources.

Avoiding entrapment

As Ryan convincingly argues, Jordan's limited involvement in the war was "designed to avoid entrapment into a more direct war with Israel, while also skirting charges within the Arab camp and Jordanian society that the regime had abandoned its Arab neighbours".[38] As Sami Khazendar pointed out, "Hussein had learned and realised from the 1967 war that political gains could be achieved by symbolic military participation and by making the army technically alert, without paying the military cost of a weakened army and state".[39] The king had promised the Americans and the Israelis in advance that "in a condition of war, Jordan will maintain strict control and non-involvement by Jordanian troops unless Jordanian territory is violated."[40] His stance was affected not just by the foreign policy and political economy considerations discussed above, but also by subjective military reasons.

The Jordanian army had suffered severe losses in personnel and equipment in the 1967 war, and until 1969 its borders were "virtually defenseless".[41] Moreover, it was punished by the United States for entering the war, and it was only at the end of 1968 that the Americans began to re-equip the Jordanian army, mostly for fear of losing Jordan to the Soviets. Jordanian–American relations and full military cooperation were fully restored only after September 1970.[42] By 1973, Jordan was busy securing a large package of American military equipment,[43] rendering the kingdom more militarily dependent on the United States than at any other time in the past; with no effective aerial defence system, it could not even contemplate joining a war.[44] Jordan reminded Sadat of this fact when he pressed them to intervene in the war.[45]

During 1973, the king reassured the Americans that he needed to improve his army's firepower and mobility—not against Israel, but "in order to meet the ever present Syrian and Iraqi threats to our territory", particularly in the event that Jordan entered into "some negotiations or form of settlement with the Israelis."[46] The United States, for its part, had been effectively dissuading the king from any thoughts he might have had in mind on leading his army to war, putting it under Arab command or allowing the Fedayeen back into the kingdom.[47]

Hussein was clearly aware of these three restrictions, as he reiterated to the Americans that he would follow them and even refused Saudi subsidies in return for letting the Fedayeen back in Jordan.[48] Pressures from the Gulf to hand over the command of the Jordanian army to Egypt mounted as the war drew near,[49] but the king was keen on avoiding what he and other Arab leaders considered "a piece of jackassery by Sadat and Asad," in the words of the director of the CIA, "which doesn't necessarily have to involve all good Arabs."[50]

The existing literature on the war devotes little attention to the civilian and military officials involved in Jordan's decision-making processes. Prime Minister Rifa'i and Amer Khammash, the former chief of staff and the powerful minister of the Royal Court during the war, were the king's main envoys to Egypt and Syria at the time. Both strongly objected to Jordan's participation in another war with Israel. Khammash, a highly respected professional officer who had led a revolution in the Jordanian army's strategic planning and organisational processes since 1962, became Hussein's closest military adviser. The king's uncle, al-Sharif Nasser Bin Jamil, and Field Marshal Habes al-Majali, both of whom also served as chiefs of staff during the 1960s, seem to have excelled more in politics than in military affairs, and their power waned gradually following the civil war.[51] In 1973, Majali occupied the essentially symbolic position of commander in chief of the army, while the real commander of the armed forces was the chief of staff, Zeid Bin Shaker.

Little is known about the standpoint of Bin Shaker and other top military officers on whether to join the 1973 War, and at least some of them feared that opening a third front with Israel might cost Jordan the East Bank.[52] However, Shlaim argues that Mreiwed Tall, the king's private secretary, together with "a number of army commanders," believed that Jordan should fight.[53] Nahed Hattar, a famous Transjordanian intellectual and a close friend of Tall, insists that the king "rejected pressures from the Jordanian army's command" to open a third front with Israel.[54] On the other hand, Khammash's objection to entering the war is well documented, and he even reminded Sadat and Asad of their armies' mediocre performance in the past.[55] The fact that the king used the services of Khammash to communicate with Sadat and Asad on military affairs before and during the war, although Khammash was no longer a military official at the time, is the best testimony to the king's thoughts and calculations in the summer of 1973.

"Not to engage heavily in battle"

During the first four days of the war Hussein was, in Ashton's words, "little more than a concerned spectator," given the initial success of the Egyptian–Syrian attack.[56] However, the American ambassador to Tel Aviv, Kenneth Keating, observed that "pressures are obviously mounting in Jordan to join the battle." Warning that Israel might try to "outflank Syrian forces by going through Lebanon or Jordan," Keating suggested to "talk to both Israelis and Jordanians soon" in order to prevent a clash between them.[57] Hussein had already rejected a "semi-hysterical" request from King Faisal of Saudi Arabia to allow the movement of Saudi forces to the Syrian front, explaining that his troops were needed in Jordan. However, the king told Brown that this was the sort of pressure he was increasingly subject to from "virtually every Arab state,"[58] begging, along with Rifa'i, for a prompt call for a ceasefire at the Security Council "even if it was not adhered to completely."[59]

By the evening of 8 October, the pressure was taking its toll on the king. Citing Hussein's self-admitted "incoherent" mood, Brown argued that the psychological atmosphere at the Jordanian army's war room "must be taken into account." Hussein was afraid that Israel would try to reach Damascus, warning that this could "drag Jordan in willy-nilly." He also demanded that Israel stop its constant over-flying of Jordan, since "his pilots feel increasingly humiliated." Brown asked the king to resist emotional calls to enter the war, reminding him the Jordan might lose "its people, its armed forces, and its future development plans." Hussein argued, in response, that without an immediate ceasefire followed by meaningful efforts at reaching a settlement for the Middle East, "the Arabs will sit back for a short while, convince themselves that they could have won the war with a slightly greater effort, and then re-launch it. Who would be running what country then," the king concluded, "I cannot guess."[60]

The next morning the Soviet chargé met the king and told him that they believed that "all Arab states should enter the battle now." Hussein replied that Jordan was acting in accordance with its own national interests,[61] but the Americans worried that his resolution would waiver.

Kissinger sent him a personal message, commending him for his stead-fastness and assuring him of imminent and meaningful peace efforts.[62] Meanwhile, Israeli military officials delivered a "well-rehearsed tirade" stating that if Hussein entered the war, "Israel would dedicate the IDF to the task of completely destroying Jordan, its air force, army and infra-structure."[63] Brown mentioned the threat to the king who "took it seri-ously".[64] However, Hussein was under growing pressure to send transporters that would carry Iraqi tanks to Syria. Although he felt that Jordan still had "sufficient sound military arguments" to maintain self-control, he wondered how long he could go on.[65] Gradually, the Ameri-cans realised that "Jordan seems to be drawing closer to possible involvement in the fighting."[66]

The next day the king lamented that "no matter how the war goes he will be the goat and probably the pariah of the Arab world," requesting American military and financial assistance in the event that the Arab states cut him off. Brown warned the king that "the Israeli generals are in a bitter, nasty mood," adding that they will look at him "as a Mus-solini who stabbed them in the back and the retribution will be unbear-able." Crown Prince Hassan, who together with al-Sharif Nasser strongly opposed any Jordanian involvement in the war,[67] concurred that "Jordan could not even dare contemplate military action against the West Bank." However, Brown noted that the king "was getting in deeper and deeper."[68]

Brown's assessment was correct, but Hussein solved his dilemma by choosing a much more convenient military alternative: dispatching an armoured brigade to the southern Golan. The king thought that this was "the least he could do under the circumstances," but he still hoped that Israel would not attack Jordan in reprisal.[69] Therefore, the Jordanians tried to identify a safe route that would allow their units to proceed and retreat without having to engage Israeli forces.[70] Prince Hassan even suggested that the king inform the Israelis of the deployment, provide them with exact coordinates, and assure them that "Jordan had no inten-tion of having the Jordanian unit come into contact with Israeli forces."[71]

Meanwhile, Israeli officials continued to send ominous messages. They threatened to "crush Jordan if Hussein was foolish enough to inter-vene in the war," to which Rifa'i replied mockingly that "he had heard the same warnings given to Egypt and Syria in the past," but "Israel did not seem able to carry out those threats as rapidly as people supposed."[72]

The Americans reminded Israel that they had a shared interest "not only in Hussein's non-intervention in the war but also in his survival,"[73] but were indeed concerned that Hussein's move would give a casus belli to Israel. The king promised to put the 40th Armoured Brigade on alert for the time being, amused by the fact that it was the same brigade that had withstood the brunt of the Syrian attack in 1970.[74] In the worst-case scenario, he planned to offer the brigade to take over duties east of the Golan and on the Jordanian border in order to free Syrian units for combat. Emphasising that he was just "trying to cover himself with the Arabs if the situation deteriorates rapidly," Hussein told Brown that he had sent the Iraqis the tank transporters they had asked for "after Syrians had said they would do no good."[75]

Late on 10 October, the king received an urgent call from Sadat asking him to intervene militarily and stating that "the fate of the Arab world depended on his decision."[76] Kissinger attempted to delay the king's decision for at least 36–48 hours,[77] but Hussein received another plea from the Syrians for immediate dispatch of a full armoured division, to which he reacted by sending liaison officers to Syria in an attempt to buy time. Under constant Saudi pressure to take action, the Jordanians warned the Americans that the existence of the Hashemite regime might be at stake.[78]

On the afternoon of 11 October, the decision was made. The king informed Brown that "before Syrian war ends, Jordan has to be in." Hussein admitted that he could delay matters for 36 hours unless there was an imminent possible collapse of Syria, hoping that "the Secretary could work miracles."[79] In fact, the king preferred sending the brigade to Syria to accepting Sadat's alternative offer to let the Fedayeen back into Jordan and attack Israel from there.[80] The king politely asked the British ambassador to find out "before it was too late" whether the Israelis considered his "gesture" to Syria a casus belli. He and the crown prince reiterated to the British[81] and the Americans that the survival of the Hashemite regime depended on the move, though the king tried to further rationalise his decision by stressing that the presence of Western-oriented Jordan and Saudi forces in the battle area "will prevent complete radicalisation of Arab world in direction of Soviets."[82] The next day, Hussein authorised a night travel of the Saudi forces through Jordan to Syria.[83]

The Jordanians notified the Syrians and Sadat that they could not afford to send a division, offering to send a brigade to be stationed on the left flank of the Golan. As planned, Jordan chose safe routes of access and supply that would keep its forces out of direct contact with Israeli forces.[84] Seeking to reassure the Israelis, Hussein sent a detailed letter to Prime Minister Meir, explaining his reasons for moving the brigade to the north and asking Israel "to refrain from attacking this unit if at all possible." The king emphasised that he had sent "a relatively small force" to an area adjacent to Jordan's frontiers with Syria, promising that "this would not affect the outcome of the fighting there, and would give Jordan the political cover it needed for remaining outside of the present conflict." Most importantly, it would keep Jordan and Israel away from going to "senseless war" against each other.[85]

Recognising that Hussein had made up his mind, the Americans and the British consulted each other on how to convince the Israelis to show restraint.[86] British Prime Minister Edward Heath argued that Hussein's move "is the best arrangement really. Let him appear to be doing something when he really isn't".[87] Explaining to the Israeli ambassador to Washington, Simcha Dinitz, that the Jordanians "did not care what the Israelis did," Kissinger still requested that Israel not attack the Jordanian brigade, since it would not fight but "just stand there".[88] Tel Aviv's answer was negative, though Dinitz admitted that this did not mean that Israel would attack Jordan, but simply that its advice to the kingdom was "not to move the unit".[89] Kissinger could then reassure President Nixon that Israel was "not looking for an excuse to attack Jordan."[90] In his memoirs, he noted that "only in the Middle East it is conceivable that a belligerent would ask an adversary's approval for engaging in an act of war against it".[91]

Back in Amman, the Jordanian leadership showed great disappointment at the United States' failure to advance a ceasefire that would spare the 40th Brigade the actual fighting. The king became very emotional, stressing that he could not "see himself creating another country and another army out of the rubble." He told Brown that he was "leaving for the front with the 40th Brigade," stressing that he was "neither mad nor sick but he would rather die with his soldiers than live in a dishonoured, ruined country under the thumb of the Soviets."[92] After calming down, Hussein notified both Kissinger and Meir that the 40th Brigade had arrived at the Jordanian–Syrian border on the morning of 13 October, and that "its moves from then on are to be slow and deliberate."[93]

That same day, Israel assured Hussein, through the Americans, that if he did not move his forces into Syria, Israel would take no military action against Jordan."[94] Israel also asked the king, through the British, to give it "the best assurances possible that you will not open fire." The king could not be reached, as he had left the war room to head to the front, along with Bin Shaker, the moment he heard that Idi Amin was on his way to Amman.[95] Prince Hassan was afraid that some of the forces had already entered into Syria, but the British ambassador, whom the Americans considered the main mediator between Israel and Jordan, sent the Israelis the exact location of the 40th Brigade. Notably, while Hassan wanted to avoid bloodshed "but have Jordanian presence on the front now that king has so decided," Rifa'i privately admitted to Brown that "what is required is that there be Jordanian martyrs."[96]

By 15 October, the king could no longer stand Asad's pressing demand that the 40th Brigade withdraw or engage in fight. He called Meir, using a direct line installed by an ex-CIA officer after the civil war,[97] and informed her that "Israel should consider the Jordanian expeditionary force of the 40th Armoured Brigade as hostile as of yesterday morning." Hussein made it clear that the brigade would inevitably be involved in action, noting that the "many contradictory orders" the force had been given made it impossible to predict where it will be at any given moment.[98] Apparently, this was a response to an earlier Israeli suggestion to provide the Jordanian brigade with the precise coordinates which it should not cross if it wanted to avoid fighting the Israeli forces.[99] Dinitz thought that, under the circumstances, "the least harm would be done" if no additional force was sent to the front and "the existing Jordanian force there would receive instructions not to engage heavily in battle."[100] Prince Hassan and al-Sharif Nasser both concurred that "it would be madness for Jordan to commit more troops to Syria."[101]

After three days of relative silence on the diplomatic channels between the United States and Jordan, and following the successful crossing of the Suez Canal by Israeli forces, Kissinger sent a long, encouraging letter to the king. He expressed his and the president's admiration for Hussein's statesmanship, implying that "history will confirm a crucial role in any fair settlement to Jordan's prudence and restraint in these difficult times." Kissinger promised the king in no uncertain terms that Jordan's interests would be fully protected in the future fundamental settlement of the conflict.[102] The king greatly appreciated the message, but was increasingly worried by the Israeli advances in the Sinai and the Golan, since he believed that this would generate great pressures on him to open a Jordanian–Israeli front, "which he knew would be suicide."[103]

In the battlefield, Jordan received another reminder of the disarray its forces had suffered under the Egyptian command in 1967. At the outset, the Syrians could not give the 40th Brigade precise plans for deployment, and the brigade commander was instructed by his Jordanian superiors to maintain the cohesion of his unit and not take direct orders from the Syrians.[104] The Israelis, for their part, had information that the 40th Brigade would work with the Iraqi forces and in fact become part of their movement in the area.[105] Khaled Hajhouj al-Majali, the brigade's commander, admitted later that they were initially placed under the command of an Iraqi armoured division, and that only on 17 October were they placed under the command of a Syrian infantry division.[106]

After three days of battle, the king's "annoyance at the Arab disorganisation" and chaos had grown. The Saudis got lost in the desert and the Jordanians had to send camels to find them, and the CIA reported that "the Iraqi and Syrians started shooting at each other and the Jordanians were chewed up by the Israelis."[107] The Israelis heard "rumours" that many Jordanian tanks were hit by the Iraqis,[108] and Majali lamented the fact that they were "indiscriminately shelled, bombed and rocketed by Israelis and Arabs alike".[109] Kissinger, however, pointed out that for Hussein "the more chaos there is, the better his alibi."[110] By the evening of 18 October, the 40th Brigade had returned to defensive positions, where it remained until the end of the war.[111]

In fact, the king's situation was not as convenient as the Americans predicted: as he saw it, the moment he subordinated his troops to Arab command he lost a great deal of control over their fate. Thus, when Kissinger cheerfully updated him, on 21 October, on the agreement he had reached with the Soviets on the text for a Security Council Resolution on a ceasefire,[112] the king replied that though he shared Kissinger's hopes for a joint resolution, he had already sent a tactical command of the 99th Brigade to Syria. Its aim was to establish a "phantom division," enabling Jordan to assert that it had sent major forces to Syria before the ceasefire.[113]

As the cease-fire came into effect, Hussein faced a serious dilemma regarding the Syrian and Iraqi refusal to accept the agreement. He was also concerned about the continued deployment of Iraqi troops into Syria, but felt that he could not withdraw his troops from Syria at that time, nor remove them from Syrian command.[114] The king informed Brown that he could not accept the American request to announce a complete ceasefire, adding that Jordan could accept this on its own territory, but "so far as its forces in Syria are concerned they are under Syrian command." Brown attempted at length to persuade the king that he was allowing his policy to be determined by Syria, which had not accepted Resolution 242 in the first place. "It would be ironic and non-understandable in history for Jordan to enter Syria with its forces in order to thwart Iraqis and then have its policy on Middle East peace determined by those Iraqis," the ambassador claimed.[115]

Brown also warned the king that Jordan's participation in the planned Syrian–Iraqi–Jordanian attack at dawn, a few hours after cease-fire, "could be disaster for us all." Anxious and uncertain of the king's decision, he noted that Hussein and Prince Hassan "feel like pawns in an immensely large chess game where no one has told them what the rules are." As Brown left the room, he had only one request from the king: "For God's sake, do not let your army get into a fruitless attack tomorrow morning and have the wrath of the world descend on you."[116] The State Department suggested in response that the king at least "pass his assurances to the Israelis that his forces would adopt a strictly defensive posture if the Syrians continued to fight."[117]

Later that night, the king informed Brown that he and Sadat had not been able to reach Asad, and accordingly "plans for tomorrow's operation still underway." Hussein also declined to promise Brown that his forces would only be in defensive positions,[118] responding with "Inshallah" to Brown's request that Jordan not violate the ceasefire. After a while the king reported that he had talked to Asad and told him that "the superpowers had warned him that any action tomorrow would be in violation of the ceasefire." Asad promised to discuss this with his group, so the king was still unable to commit himself to observing the ceasefire.[119] The British embassy observed that the king was undoubtedly "reluctant to destroy his new-found standing in Syria and elsewhere by withdrawing from the battle without Asad's agreement".[120]

Helplessly, Brown requested that Kissinger send an immediate message to the king telling him that any military action by Jordanian forces would be "viewed most seriously by world community." Admitting his failure to convince Jordan's leaders not to take the wrong course "after having done well by themselves up to now," Brown revealed that "certain ones are claiming that we are talking for ourselves and not for the United States government, and that Jordan has clashed with Israel at other times during this war and has not paid for it." The ambassador concluded that a message from Kissinger "may be the only way to stop this foolishness."[121]

A few hours later, Kissinger sent Hussein a message in this spirit,[122] but the king had already informed the Americans that the Jordanian and the Iraqi forces had been instructed by the Syrians to stand down for the time being. Hussein added that if he received any further messages to the contrary, he would "stall until he heard from Kissinger."[123] Yet the story was far from over. Commenting on Kissinger's message to the king, Rifa'i argued that "Jordan would have to fight if the Syrians and Iraqis went into battle, since the Jordanians were under Syrian command." Brown reminded the prime minister that Jordan had ultimate responsibility for the actions of its forces, and that if they violated the ceasefire they would not be able to plead non-responsibility. He also stressed that the Jordanians had to make sure that their role in Syria was one of pushing Asad towards acceptance of the ceasefire "and not as bystanders."[124]

Shortly afterwards, the king expressed his deep concern to Brown over Syria's delayed acceptance of the ceasefire. He informed him that he was about to send a delegation to Syria, carrying a letter to Asad on Jordan's withdrawal from Syrian territory "unless decision forthcoming." The king believed that Baghdad, which had the "closest links with Moscow," was the real trouble-maker, urging Kissinger to ask Brezhnev to impose the ceasefire on Syria and Iraq.[125] Hussein sent another delegation to Cairo, and then a second one to Damascus.[126] The Jordanians were finally able to withdraw their forces from Syria thanks to Rifa'i's scheme to send Khammash to Asad in order to request the Jordanian troops back, allegedly because of intelligence reports that suggested that Israel was about to expand its violations of the ceasefire into the East Bank. The routes of the retreating Jordanian forces were passed again via the Americans to the Israelis.[127] The total losses of the 40th Brigade in the war were twenty-seven casualties, fifty wounded and fourteen tanks disabled beyond repair.[128]

Conclusion

Jordan's symbolic participation in the 1973 War was a joint venture between Jordan, the United States and Israel. It was determined in advance not just because of foreign policy and political economy considerations, but also because of Jordan's growing military dependency on the United States, its professional assessment of the Arab–Israeli military balance, and its tightening secret dialogue with Israel prior to the war. Above all, the Jordanian leadership was afraid of being dragged into another futile Arab–Israeli war that would cost it the East Bank. The Americans and the Israelis, for their part, made sure that Hussein understood what was at stake during the first few days of the war.

While Israel could not, for obvious reasons, welcome King Hussein's decision to dispatch a brigade to assist the Syrian forces, it ultimately accepted the move and attempted to minimise the danger of direct clashes by assuring that the brigade was idle. The Jordanians, for their part, took every step to ensure that their troops operate as slowly and distantly as possible, but at the same time recognised that in order to win the cause they would have to sacrifice a small number of martyrs. Jordan's reluctance to fully accept the ceasefire and its willingness to suffer more losses, and possibly the wrath of Israel and the United States, adds another dimension to the king's initial insistence on not repeating the 1967 debacle by putting his troops under the control of Arab command.

Are there any lessons that can be gleaned from Jordan's "war that never was"? First, in terms of historiography, King Hussein's new biographers play down his warning to Israel or dismiss it altogether, possibly because of the obvious political sensitivity. This is perhaps a living testimony to the reluctance of scholars who have been given direct access to key players to judge the latter's actions for what they were. Moreover, any new historiography is expected to shed light and dispel myths, and one wonders whether it added a professional motivation for the new interpretations of King Hussein's meeting with Golda Meir.

Second, Jordan's policy choices before and during the war are a remarkable example for the resolution of a realist Arab leader, who was prepared to do whatever in his power to save his country from total destruction. King Hussein preferred to betray the Arab cause in order to be loyal to his citizens and his country, and not just to his own rule. In other words, his decision to stay out of war was responsible and courageous rather than a show of treason and cowardice.

The FRUS documents on the 1973 war and its aftermath also expose the fascinating story of Jordanian and American gradual acceptance of the Palestinians' right for self-determination on the West Bank following the war. This aspect should form the focus for future research. Another topic that has not been sufficiently illuminated in this chapter, and which merits future research, is the Jordanian selective historiography of the war, on which there are ample primary Jordanian sources from the past decade.

9

PALESTINIAN POLITICS IN TRANSITION

THE CASE OF THE OCTOBER WAR

Philipp O. Amour

Introduction

While there is a consensus among analysts that the October War of 1973 initiated a change in the Middle East's political balance, most accept that it also had knock-on effects for the Israeli–Palestinian conflict.[1] Yet when conducting a literature review, the author noticed that academic attention is concentrated on two issues above all others: the impact of the war on the region in general, and on the two main actors of the war in particular: Egypt and Israel. Remarkably, the Palestinian role in the October War either stays untouched, or there is no in-depth analysis. This is explained by several reasons.

First, the war was not primarily a Palestinian–Israeli war, and thus the focus of literary analysis has been on the major parties in the conflict, rather than the Palestinians. References to Palestinian considerations are oblique and limited in extent. Whereas from the perspective of Palestinian studies, the 1970s was an intensive decade for historical events. Western analysts have made only limited efforts to cover those events, and there are still many gaps, for example, the effects of the October

War, the institution building process of the Palestine Liberation Organisation (PLO), or the social and cultural history of the Palestinians in exile. Related to this is the fact that the Palestine Liberation Organisation (PLO) is a resistance movement leaving few records for analysts to follow. Within the Palestinian territory, any access to research records is difficult, because of the hostile and risky environment. It is a common fact that revolutionary situations usually damage contemporary documents or make them unattainable for some time, and that they disperse the people who could serve as witnesses. These conditions make the notion of a domestic archive virtually impossible.[2] Any gathering of oral history will be time-consuming and the costs will be high.

As I have shown elsewhere, there is a correlation between the presence and availability of historical records, on the one hand, and our understanding of the unfolding situation on the other hand.[3] For example, during the Lebanese civil war (1975 and beyond) or the clashes between Palestinians in the refugee camps during the 1980s, it was not easy for Western academics to follow intra-Palestinian politics, so for this reason the impact of the October War on the Palestinians has rarely been the subject of Western publications. Whereas it has been a common subject for domestic publications, written by local researchers, academics and politicians; the war and its consequences initiated many debates among Palestinian intellectuals and politicians that are easily available through published books or journal articles. For instance, Nazeih Abud Nidal's books present some of the most important critiques of PLO developments and the historical figures of Fatah, as does Habash's book on the problems facing the Palestinian revolution. Naji Aloush ably covers the doctrinal clashes between the Palestinian factions. All of these books are positive examples of publications that can help in our attempt to understand the impact of the October War, especially on recent and current Palestinian politics.

Some of these works focus on the disputes and negotiations that took place in relation to policy-building and leadership of the PLO leadership pre- and post-war. Others review the advances and setbacks of the transition period in Palestinian policy. However, in these local publications one often notices a lack of any deeply critical view or objective distance to the topic. Sometimes there is heated sentiment running through the polemic. The writers tend to be leftist critics of the political changes to come. But despite the lack of self-reflective perspective and depth of social analysis, most of the publications are of value due to the first-hand witness they deliver.

The best contemporary journals from this time (in Beirut) are the prestigious *Shuun Filastiniya* (Palestine Affairs) that was run by the Palestine Research Center, and the *Journal of Palestine Studies*. Both institutions held workshops and published related articles that are indispensable for the analysis of contemporary affairs. However, readers are advised to bear in mind how polarised the political and intellectual climate in Beirut was in the 1970s: writers belonged to particular factions, as will be elaborated below. Despite these considerations, such local publications are of great value in helping our attempt to understand and analyse the recent history of the Palestinians and how it influences the present situation.

This difference between the angles of local and Western literature illustrates the importance of fieldwork and empirical research, language skills, and the availability of domestic archives in order to make the analytical literature truly comprehensive and to be able to come to accurate conclusions.[4] Thus, this chapter reveals new findings and creates points of synthesis with the standard literature, by exposing materials from previously unused archives and local sources.[5] We hope the historiography will evolve further in order to supplement some of the overlooked or neglected chapters of Middle Eastern history.

This chapter will examine developments in the politics of the Palestine Liberation Organisation (PLO) in the context of the October War of 1973 and beyond. It will explore how the Palestinians are attempting to restore and rebuild their homeland from two different points in time: both before and after the turn of the decade (1970). This evaluation will help explain how Palestinian leadership and the prevalent factions transformed themselves over time, and how the legacies of this transformation reflect on previous and current Palestinian national identity.

The thesis of the chapter is that the Nakba (the National Tragedy of 1948) was the prime cause of the policy the Palestinians chose up to the end of the 1960s. Two main principles were formed in the course of the military resistance against the Zionist movement: a military approach as the means of restoring Palestine; and cultural reinforcement as a means of activating society and preparing it for the future Palestinian state. However, the conditions of Palestinians in exile around 1970, and the political awareness of the Fatah leadership, resulted in the emergence of a third principle: political settlement with Israel.

As far as this third principle is concerned, the changes in the balance of regional politics after the October War, in conjunction with the will of the superpowers during détente to foster peace in the region, resulted in the third approach developing more quickly and becoming a core element of Palestinian state-building policy after 1974. In historical retrospect, it can be seen that this transitional period managed to paralyse the PLO and fragment the party landscape; it resulted in a war of principles between the national institutions of the Palestinians.

Palestinian political thought before the October War (1948–70)

The Palestinian National Tragedy—the so-called Nakba—characterised a significant shift in national history, due to the erosion in politics and culture. In retrospect, it marked the start of modern politics and cultural and social advancement for Palestinians. From that point, a widely educated generation of Palestinians with comparatively new qualities and potential seized the initiative and took on the leadership. In contrast to pre-Nakba, the new Palestinian National Movement (PNM) is more consistent and is led by educated, determined figures, with the support of the intelligentsia (for example, Edward Said, Ibrahim Abou Loughood, Hisham Shurabi).

This younger and more cultured generation made the point (according to the Nakba literature)[6] that the social and political decline that had been responsible for the loss of the homeland had to be reversed by efforts to modernise Palestinian society and strengthen its political and military capabilities. They demanded fresh cultural and socio-economic development, and a political distancing from the older generation and from Arab countries. This younger generation believed that building a Palestinian state was part of a more elaborate programme, encompassing socio-cultural, military and diplomatic elements.[7] As a result, two main principles came to dominate the political approach of the Palestinians until the end of the 1960s.

The first was a rational/institutional principle. It was developed by the younger generation who completed their education at the time of the National Tragedy; they gained their social standing by gradually filling the gap left by the political leadership who went into exile. Almost immediately after the Nakba, education was seen to be of immense value to young Palestinians, for the role it played in the regeneration of the people and their awareness of national identity. They recognised the role of education in creating the basis for a future Palestinian state, a basis that could help them rebuild Palestinian society from exile, and eventually initiate the restoration of Palestine. This belief manifested itself in the establishment through the 1950s-60s of various social institutions, like kindergartens, schools, health centres and even sewing salons.[8] The culmination of this drive was the establishment and institutionalisation of the PLO,[9] which then led to the systematisation of socio-cultural changes and economic processes resulting in changes in the related fields.[10]

The founders of the PLO and the members of its first executive were rooted in this rational/institutional culture, which may come as a surprise for orthodox historians.[11] But actually it was a perfectly logical outcome: these people were doctors, lawyers and academics, so they aimed to improve the areas of diplomacy, research and social development above all. The earliest institutions and unions to be established are evidence of the intentions, policies and politics of this group of professionals: their first achievements were the national fund and diplomatic missions to Lebanon and China; then the National Research Centre (1965) and the General Union of Palestinian Woman (1965) and of Students (1966).[12] During the 1950s these pioneers believed that the Palestinians could not rise to the financial, political or military capability to confront or compete with Israel.[13]

The second principle we shall examine is the historical/military principle that set as its target the complete restoration of the historic Palestine of Mandate or even Ottoman times. The followers of this principle argued for armed liberation, and thus Palestine should dedicate itself to military success. Although this strand of political belief became evident soon after the National Tragedy, it came to play a more active role in Palestinian politics after the emergence of the PNM. This ideology of military resistance was interwoven with the Fatah ideology of "Palestinism".

The Fatah party was strong-willed and chose to take another path of national identification. Their choice of political ideology for Palestinism was national independence from the Arab countries and national self-activism. This initial spark of Palestinism was fanned by the defeat of Arab troops in the Six Day War of 1967, and the alleged victory of the Fatah by Karma over Israeli troops. For many Arabs, the PNM, and post-1968 the PLO, represented a revolutionary beacon, from which revolutionary changes might spread to the rest of the Arab world. Indeed, the PNM did prove itself a secure haven for many suppressed and exiled Arabs.[14] The military characteristic established itself as a strong part of Palestinian identity, and hence was perceived as the best approach for restoring the homeland and maintaining freedom of movement for Palestinians and Arab revolutionaries across borders. However, the first, more intellectual strand of belief nevertheless recognised that military capabilities were useful for the protection of diplomatic and socio-cultural institutions from outside risks.

Both these political strands were united in their efforts to create a Palestinian nation state in the territory of historic Palestine, and both agreed that this state should be modern in all aspects. Both believed in the capability of the Palestinians to build a better future, through the combination of armed resistance and building social institutions; this could be the formula to boost people's morale and bring the Palestinians to independence.[15] The PLO leadership in Beirut apportioned its income between these national projects, deciding between institution-building and military self-sufficiency, from its exile in Lebanon.

The war of attrition in Jordan in 1969–70 marked a shift in how the mainstream leadership of the PLO (and the Fatah leadership) perceived the Palestinian–Israeli conflict. The leadership became aware again of the challenges it had to face, both in opposing the policy of Arab regimes against the PLO, and within the plurality of Palestinian political thought.[16] Furthermore, Fatah's members were aware of the fact that the military actions against Israel were effectively no more than small-scale military incursions that would hardly lead to the restoration of historic Palestine. From today's perspective, we can see that a political settlement with Israel—after leaving Jordan—might have been a better policy for the consolidation and institutionalisation of the PLO.

Factors relating to realism, pragmatism and frustration about the Arab alliances gave rise to a third stream of political opportunism: the realist/pragmatic strand of thought. Significant members of Fatah, among others Yasser Arafat and Abu Iyad, joined this faction. They were already holding secret discussions with others about this strategy, which was aimed at political settlement as the means to build a Palestinian state, prior to the October War.[17] However, the Fatah leadership could not state their opinion publicly because the political climate in the Arab states was against a treaty. More importantly, the majority of Fatah was against such reconciliation and not yet ready to adopt this policy; they did not want to offer any further reasons for splitting and weakening the Palestinians so shortly after the expulsion from Jordan.[18]

Instead, Arafat and Abu Iyad encouraged others to articulate this option and thus stimulate debate through a third party.[19] They also spoke to the international media, as for instance Abu Iyad did with *Le Monde* in 1972. He proposed "a negotiated settlement with Israel based on a two-state solution, one in which a Palestinian state would live alongside and in harmony with its powerful Israeli neighbour".[20]

The October War gave this more ideological strand a definite boost. All parties in the conflict (PLO and Israel) saw themselves confronted with this new situation of having to react to regional and international pressure and eventually adjust their own ideology. For the Palestinian decision-makers a new situation was emerging, and they had to examine the new regional configurations and consider how to transform their own standpoints.[21]

The standard literature of the period hardly explains the background to the transition of the political beliefs of the Palestinians, and it usually refers only to 1974, when the situation became clearer.

Palestinian politics in transition: the case of the October War

During and after the October War, the issue of Palestinian national self-interest began to be mentioned in debates about the possible out-comes of the war, the direction of peacemaking, and its potential effect on the Palestinians. These debates evoked many interpretative points of view, which created obvious difficulties in dealing with the post-war era. The war reinforced Palestinian views of nationalism, while leading others to perceive that the situation had changed from before. In retrospect, we can see the adjustment in perception by the Palestinian leadership towards fulfilling national aspirations for Palestine, and this change led, in my opinion, to the integration of the PLO into the regional and, to some extent, the international system.[22]

All three ideological strands acknowledged the advancement of Arab capabilities in strategic warfare, and were aware of the impact on local balance of power. But their positions on how Palestinians should react to this new situation differed.

The historical/military strand believed that military resistance was now confirmed as a viable strategy by the outcome of the war. They saw this new situation as an opportunity for Arabs and Palestinians to enhance their military efficiency, their weaponry, their tactical and strategic capabilities, so that they could launch future wars.[23] They saw the alleged siege as evidence of being on the right path ever since Karamah, and that changing the nature of the national approach was not justified at this point. Thus, the historical/military faction opposed a peaceful political settlement of the Palestinian problem, as many felt this would result in a reduction in the natural rights of the Palestinians and would require compromises in future negotiations. However, they failed to consider the potential of the Camp David Accords in their calculations and the consequent neutralisation of Egypt, which suggested they would not be able to liberate Palestine using their more officious approach.

The newly emerged moderate camp was at the opposite of the ideological spectrum and believed that the Arabs' demonstration of their capabilities in the war suggested both strengths and weaknesses. They considered the alleged siege as exaggerated and doubted that the Arabs would be able to support their expectations in the near future. The Fatah mainstream leadership and the PLO leadership believed that changes in the political situation in the Middle East required a re-examination of Palestinian principles and the favoured approach towards building a Palestinian state. In their eyes, diplomacy was the better path for the Palestinian cause, as it would open channels of communication with the Western superpowers; whereas missing this opportunity would provide an excuse for regional and international exclusion, and would sustain the stereotypes of Palestinian isolation.

The key Fatah figures were keen on Israeli politics and believed that the Israeli strategic circles and ruling élites intended to rescind from the PLO and were opposing a Palestinian (mini) state.[24] Nevertheless, they believed that missing the opportunity to make post-war changes would damage the PLO politically and lead to stereotypes about Palestinians continuing to be upheld: the aversion to political settlement.

While the realist/pragmatic strand was aware of the importance of Western support for their cause and was trying to persuade Western key powers that the Palestinians were a trustworthy partner for peace,[25] the historic/military strand was more susceptible to pressure from the superpowers to make peace. The first faction was thus more interested in following new political opportunities through adapting the Palestinian approach to the new political situation, while the second faction chose isolationism—hoping for the support of the Soviet Union.[26]

The rational/institutional strand was split: the left wing was on the side of the military faction, while the right wing inclined towards the moderate camp. However, the centre followers of this strand believed that the process of socio-cultural advancement should take priority and should not be compromised by political diversions. These differences in interpretation, expectation and ideology over the wartime and post-war periods illustrate the clashes within the Palestinian political and intellectual landscape from the 1970s up until the present time.

The impact on Palestinian politics and the para-state-building process

The post-war era brought both serious problems and potential benefits to the Palestinians. The following sections will summarise the main points.[27]

The psychological siege and Palestinism

The war redefined the balance of power in the Middle East. Up until 1973 Israel had won every war against Arab troops, so in the perception of both the Arab public and the West, Israel's army was invincible. The October War showed that despite the military superiority of Israel, the Arabs could still match up in a competitive situation. For the Arabs it became clear that they could improve their position and they were capable of making advances in military and strategic affairs. Thus Arab self-confidence increased and many felt that Arab dignity had been restored. This narrative is still evident amongst the Arab public: for instance, the theme was part of a TV series called *Naji Atallah's Squad* [on MBC] during Ramadan in 2012.

This "moral siege" had a positive effect on Palestinism, as both the Palestinians and Arabs could confirm again (after Karamah) that they were able to win a war and the psychological battle against Israel. For all Palestinian political factions, the outcome of the October War resulted in a confirmation of Palestinism as the correct approach to follow, to lead to the establishment of the Palestinian state. Furthermore, the October War illustrated the importance of mechanics and the need for science and strategy throughout society. Since Karamah, Palestinism has been an integral part of the national discourse, and this was confirmed again after the October War. But this should not detract from the differences between the camps: the extremist camp was seduced by Arab capabilities and romanticised the "invincibility of revolutions", while the moderate camp still had their doubts.

This belief gave the PLO leadership another reason to support institutional developments and socio-cultural projects in Lebanon and elsewhere, while in exile. Even in the first few years after the flight to Lebanon, the PLO succeeded in becoming the representative authority for all regional and international organisations dealing with Palestinian affairs in exile. This shows how successful the building of a "para-state" was in creating an image of respectability for the PLO. Along with the diplomatic initiatives of the PLO, this smoothed the way for the official acknowledgment that came in 1974.

Transition of the national approach and international recognition

After the start of the October War, international protagonists intervened in order to resolve it, to put an end to the Arab–Israeli conflict, and at its core the "Palestinian problem". In the wake of these initiatives the Palestinian parties created a novel political programme that remained part of Palestinian politics throughout the following decades—the so-called ten points programme.

The ten points programme was a way of uniting the intentions and expectations of all political factions. It enabled both main strands to remain loyal to their beliefs and principles, while being flexible enough to consider other political ideas and the expectations of the regional and world powers. The programme was meant to satisfy the historical points of view by reassuring the hard-liners that they could still attain the restoration of Palestine by means of military liberation; while the moderate stream pursued their new track, of political settlement. The programme should allow soft-liners the possibility of establishing a Palestinian state on the parts of Palestine that Israel had left or had taken; while leaving the possibility of restoring historic Palestine using military resistance. The programme was ratified by the 12th Palestinian National Council in Cairo in July 1974, and was mainly supported by the right wing of Fatah and the Democratic Front for the Liberation of Palestine (DFLP).

The realist/pragmatic stream was able to achieve this due to the charisma of historical figures, their key positions in the PLO, domination over economic resources and, last but not least, their leadership style.

This more balanced approach was a fundamental departure from the mainstream view that military resistance was the only way to liberate historic Palestine. This political transition for the PLO became the foundation for further diplomatic successes. Arab solidarity increased after the war in 1973 and supported the acknowledgment of the PLO.

In October 1974 the Arab League assured the PLO that it was the sole legitimate representative of the Palestinian people, and affirmed the right of the Palestinian people to self-determination and their right to return to their homeland. In accordance with the ten points programme, the Arab League also guaranteed the right of Palestinians to establish an independent national authority over each part of Palestine under the direction of the PLO. This recognition went beyond the local arena. In November 1974 the United Nations General Assembly issued Resolution 3236 in which it affirmed the inalienable rights of the Palestinian people, including the right of self-determination and the right to national independence and sovereignty. Then with Resolution 3237 the UN gave the PLO observer status and full membership in all sub-organisations of the UN.

With local and international recognition of the PLO, the Palestinian national aspirations gained strength. The PLO succeeded in articulating Palestinian rights as a people and as a nation, with this public acknowledgment of the rights of the Palestinians to their own state. Additionally, Palestinians celebrated a diplomatic triumph against Jordan and Israel for the first time. Jordan itself had no alternative but to accept the decision of the Arab League regarding the new position and role of the PLO in regard to Palestine and the Palestinians. The Arab and Islamic solidarity caused an intolerable climate for the Jordanian government, inhibiting any acts of sabotage against related efforts of the PLO.[28] The PLO also succeeded in putting Israel increasingly under pressure through its own diplomatic initiatives and its accepted place in the UN. These gains would have been hardly imaginable without the shake-up in regional politics after the October War. Publicly, Israel became known for denying Palestinians the right to their own state and for refusing to negotiate with the PLO.

However this shift in international perception came at a high price. Their opponents took the opportunity to sow doubt about the quality and legitimacy of the Palestinian leadership and the PLO. This doubt persists amongst some observers until the present.

Splintering of the political landscape

The acceptance of the ten points programme through the National Council did not entirely dissipate tensions between the different factions. Opposition emerged (for example, from the PFLP, the PFLP-General leadership, the Arab liberation front) against the new national policy. These groups froze their memberships and activities in the PLO committees and, in the same year, established a so-called "denial front", which was intended to unify the followers of the historical/military principle under one umbrella. Their goal was to work against what they viewed as a compromise programme and to restore what was, from their perspective, the natural right of the Palestinians. Some radical factions even tried to subvert the transition process through sabotage and assassination, which undoubtedly damaged the image of the Palestinians. The denial front received financial support from Libya, Iraq and Syria.[29] Although they returned in 1979 and participated in the 14th PNC, an inevitable crisis within the political landscape has loomed ever since.

However, the influence of the denial front is considerable and deserves more attention than is usually given it by the standard literature. The front denunciated the position and historical role of the Fatah leadership and questioned the legitimacy of the PLO on its current trajectory. The front also attracted members from the left wing of Fatah, and gave them a platform to organise themselves and to establish contacts with the regimes in Libya, Iraq and Syria.

So the majority of the left wing of Fatah refused the new political programme. Individuals like Naji Aloush or Munir Shafiq were influential because they were theorists and writers, which is what attracted many members of Fatah, like the student movement.[30] The historical/military faction believed that the new orientation and the inclinations of Fatah and the PLO were straying from the national and historical path.

The political mainstream, as represented by individuals like Yasser Arafat and Ubu Iyad, had to look out for the rebellious attitudes of some of these members and military leaders. The steady rise of Fatah did not come without a hefty price, which came about in 1983. The result was a remarkable split from the mother party, and an attempt to take over Fatah in Lebanon with the help of Syria.[31] The problems of the PLO got even worse when it was caught up in the vortex of the Lebanese civil war (1975), putting further pressure on the Palestinian leadership. While the mainstream leadership of the PLO had tried not to involve itself in the Lebanese civil war,[32] the denial front was determined to step in on the side of the Lebanese national movement against the kata'b bloc. This attitude put the PLO leadership in a tight spot, and pushed it to enter alliances with the Lebanese movements against kata'b and its allies.[33] There are two explanations behind this move. First of all, the mainstream did not want to repeat the mistakes it had made in Jordan, where it failed to have a unified policy against impending threats; and, secondly, it wanted to ally itself with indigenous partners.

The pressure on the PLO also increased after the peace negotiations between Egypt and Israel, as the role of Egypt in the Arab–Israeli conflict was redefined. For Palestinians of all political convictions it was clear that they should not lose the Lebanon as a "last bastion" for potential military engagement with Israel. As we shall see in the next section, the dissent among the Palestinians during the 1970s also influenced the socio-cultural process.

Stagnation of the institution-building process

After their removal from Jordan, the Fatah mainstream began to consolidate itself in Lebanon and to install the PLO as a para-state organisation for all Palestinians. It was arguably successful in accomplishing a high level of institutional development and achieving a good basis of legitimation. The prevailing political consensus towards the basic issues in the years 1970–3 had a positive impact on the development of the Palestinian quasi-state, causing intensified and more widespread socio-cultural, economic and political processes among Palestinians.

The issue of maintaining control over the national institutions became relevant after the breakout of what I call the conceptual war in the context of the ten points programme post-1974. A conceptual dispute broke out, and old tensions such as Arabism versus Palestinism were revived. The institutions were divided into positions for and against the transitional programme as well. Despite the adoption of the ten points programme by the PNC, the majority of the Palestinian left wing and the Pan-Arabists opposed it vehemently because they either considered it an abandonment of Palestinians' natural rights, or they viewed the political alliances as not yet ready for a settlement with Israel. Their opposition, however, did not remain as purely individual; it also became incorporated within the national institutions they worked in or were responsible for. They dominated most institutions related to research, journalism, and even the national, social, welfare and education systems. As a result, the members of such institutions started writing theoretical and polarising articles and books, delivering arguments in opposition to the pragmatists.[34]

Given the charisma of these figures (for example, Naji Aloush or Munir Shafiq) and their powers of mobilisation, there was a risk that the domination by the mainstream leadership would diminish and that they would lose this conceptual war. The historical Fatah leadership had reasons for concern, as some of the PLO institutions applied censorship against articles advocating the Two-state solution or attacked such books in their publications.[35] The historical leadership thought that the "intellectual opposition" was misusing its role in the national institutions by not supporting the directives of the client, the Palestinian National Council, which had already adopted the ten points programme.

As the conceptual war intensified, the PLO leadership tried to co-opt the opposition by all possible means, putting pressure on them to express their loyalty to the national programme.[36] In the wake of the verbal and financial pressure against the National Research Center and the think tank, both directors (Anis Sayigh[37] and Nabil Sha'th)[38] resigned from their jobs. From then on, the PLO mainstream tried to force the nomination of candidates (for example, to the General Union of Palestinian Authors) through complicated manoeuvring, or to hire people for the national institutions who were loyal to its political programme. Apart from getting rid of directors who were not loyal, the PLO leadership was successful in convincing many employees, whether field workers, researchers or authors, to avoid any collision with the executive leadership and to focus primarily on their tasks.

However, the containment and takeover of oppositional institutions put the credibility of the PLO as a bipartisan organisation into question. The rift between ideological factions was widening and the political disputes, together with the Lebanese civil war, led to the stagnation of socio-cultural, politica, and economic processes in exile.[39]

Epilogue: The legacies of the October War

After the withdrawal of the PLO from Lebanon to Tunis (a non-front state to Israel), the pro-military faction was in sharp decline, while the pro-negotiation faction went from strength to strength. The PLO mainstream then focused on nation and institution-building in the occupied Palestinian territories and tried to open negotiating channels with the USA and Israel from Tunis. Thus, it was not surprising that the PLO leadership was able to support the first Intifada and take control over its acclaimed local leadership straightaway.

The historical opposition faction, on the other hand, rallied round the military liberation wing that surfaced during the 1980s and 90s, reviving that former policy position, and while it rejected military entanglements in the Palestinian (and Arab) hemisphere, it welcomed financial and other support from the Ba'ath regime in Syria (for example, the PFLP or DFLP and later Hamas) and from the Qaddafi and Hussein regimes (for example, Fatih al-Intifada lead by Abu Musa). The Ba'ath regime tried to acquire a dominant position in the Palestinian hemisphere by supporting the splits within Fatah, and offered military help to the disputes against the mother party. But this process scarcely jeopardised the internal order of the movement.

The principle of military resistance does not owe its survival solely to ideological or moralistic reasons. For hundreds of thousands of Palestinians in exile it is their reason for existence. It has enabled those in refugee camps and along the front line with Israel to defend themselves against Israel's acts of war, and against domestic upheavals like the civil war in Jordan and in Lebanon. For many, abandoning this principle would threaten their very existence: the idea of military resistance guarantees the right to return for millions of Palestinians.

The start of the Intifada in 1987 has changed the nature of Palestinian politics from exile-centred to domestic. The Intifada of stones and its local leadership were more oriented towards peaceful resistance and thus closer to the moderate camp than the extremist one. Yet the establishment of Hamas in the Palestinian territories in 1988 gave weight to the historical/military approach. Making use of the new situation after the start of the Intifada, the PLO proclaimed a Palestinian state on the basis of UNO Resolution 181 and then recognised UN Resolution 242 in 1988. While the ten points programme of 1974 showed flexibility on the issue of territorial compromise and methods of restoration, there was a shift in national policy with the proclamation of 1988, as Israel and the Two-state solution were expressly mentioned. These developments and the end of the Cold War forced both conflict parties to the negotiating table. After much bargaining and brainstorming in Madrid and Oslo, the Oslo Accords were signed, and have been determining the relationship between Israel and the PLO ever since.

The Oslo Accords not only enabled the Palestinians to establish a governmental body in the Palestinian territories, but also to hold elections, and to set up the governmental and juridical basis for a Palestinian state. The pragmatist stream felt that their positions were confirmed, and they thus felt that the Oslo Accords recognised the rights of the Palestinians accurately and would enable the creation of a Palestinian state by the end of the interim period. From today's perspective, it can be said that, since the return of the PLO leadership into Palestinian territories in 1993, nation and state building (after the political settlement with Israel) became the ultimate approach for creating the Palestinian state, whereas the PLO leadership previously in exile used a multiple of fault lines of militant resistance and peaceful diplomacy. With this in mind, the success or failure of the Accords were and are connected to the historical legacy, credibility and historical consciousness of all the ideological streams described.

The opposition (including Hamas) rejected the Oslo agreements for many reasons. They perceived the agreements to be curtailing the rights of Palestinians in an unconditional concession to Israel, while in their opinion not respecting even their most basic aspirations. This rejection of the Oslo Accords also had a significant implication on Palestinian politics; this opposition rejected any political cooperation with the PNC and reaffirmed its right to continue national resistance against the Israeli occupation. According to this orientation, radical rejectionist groups partook in a string of violent actions and suicide bombings during the interim period in Israel that endangered the peace process. In reaction to this, the Palestinian security services of the established PNA had to crack down on other Palestinians to stop them from conducting "resistance/radical actions" against Israel. Historically this marked a dawn in Palestinian politics, hence national disputes were used to set upon personal encounters or ideological conflicts (for example, DFLP and PFLP or Fatih intra conflicts), but not upon "resistance" against Israel.

After the end of the interim period and the Oslo Accords failing to result in the creation of a Palestinian state, the central opposition felt confirmed, and former figures like Yasser Arafat lost their reputation. Radical forces gained strength due to the increase of Israeli restrictions on settlement and the confiscation of Palestinian land, which caused a new Intifada to break out. It was radical and militaristic, deriving from the historical/military strand of ideology. Although they were not able to restore historic Palestine, they considered the retreat of the Israeli army from the Gaza strip in 2005 as an achievement for which their military inspiration was responsible. As for political advances for the opposition, Hamas and other parties took part in and won the parliamentary elections in 2006.

The national government that emerged represented a unity of both streams and—for the first time in the Palestinian territories—gave the Palestinians a chance to merge and unify both poles, or at least bring them closer together. However, this opportunity was missed, due above all to international pressure and imposed financial sanctions. Israel and other international powers did not recognise a government that included Hamas, and they made their political and financial support dependent upon Hamas recognising the existence of Israel. Hamas refused, and the international powers and Israel failed to acknowledge that Hamas could be, in my view, on a transitional path similar to Fatah's. To push the argument further, it could be said that Hamas is now where Fatah was around 1973. International politics did not consider this and asked Hamas for an immediate recognition of Israel, disregarding the need for Hamas to prepare the majority of their members for it, as Fatah did in the context of the ten points programme. In my opinion, there is little reason to believe that Hamas would deviate from this pattern.

After the economic and political sanctions imposed on the Palestinian government by the international community, and the Egyptian regime initiating a siege on the banks of Gaza, the situation between Hamas and Fatah escalated, resulting in the *coup d'état* by Hamas against the PNA in 2007. So now there are de facto two Palestinian autonomies, both acclaiming their legitimacy. The soft-liners have their own national autonomy on the West Bank and feel that their ideology has been confirmed. For them, Israel and the opposition are responsible for the failure of the Oslo Accords. Then there is a second Palestinian national autonomy on the Gaza strip, run by the hard-liners. Similar to the soft-liners, they too feel that their ideology of military resistance has been confirmed, as they were able to resist the Israeli attack in 2008. This situation has effectively produced a stalemate between the two streams, at least from the perspectives of the different parties, and future studies should examine this, taking into consideration the implications of the Arab Spring. Along this and from current perspectives I believe that both blocs seem to be lacking a viable strategy to achieve the national aspiration of self-determination.

Depending on how the Arab Spring develops and what adjustments the Middle East will experience, this stalemate situation could change. The extent and level to which a change could occur is dependent on the weaknesses and strengths of evolving democracies in the region, and also the Iran bloc. The democracies in the region would rather support the moderate camp and foster a balanced negotiation with Israel. But it is possible that the new governments could back up Hamas and help it to implement its ideologies, maybe not as Fatah but towards a Palestinian consensus. However, such scenarios are unlikely in the short or mid term, as such developments are bound to be a long process.

10

FARAWAY CAUSES, IMMEDIATE EFFECTS

THE WAR AND EUROPEAN CONSEQUENCES

Rory Miller

In the immediate wake of the Arab invasion of Israel on 6 October 1973 some member states of the European Economic Community (hereafter, EEC or Community) called for "immediate consultations" to be held.[1] However, no special meeting was convened to deal with the outbreak of war. Instead, the matter was addressed in the course of the pre-scheduled Political Cooperation (EPC) meeting of 11–12 October.[2]

The only official Community statement on the matter had no more substance. It restated support for UN Security Council Resolution 242 of November 1967. This clarified little, given the differing interpretations of that resolution among EEC member states. Even the previously outspoken French decided on a "wait and see" policy, which prompted a letter from Colonel Muammar Qaddafi of Libya condemning France's "reserved attitude".[3]

As the conflict progressed, it became apparent that no European country was willing to follow the US precedent and provide any practical support to the Jewish state. Nor did any Community member agree to allow the US air convoy sent to resupply Israel during the war to use its airspace or territory for landing or refuelling.

155

Despite this cautious approach the 1973 War would subsequently pose the most serious challenge to the EEC's existence since the French vetoed British entry into the organisation a decade earlier. This was especially true in relation to four interconnected issues:—the evolving European attempt to consolidate political and economic cooperation among member states; Europe's policy towards the Israeli–Palestinian conflict; the Euro–American strategic relationship; and Euro-Arab relations.

Crisis politics

Following a meeting on 17 October 1973, Kuwait, Saudi Arabia, Iraq, Abu Dhabi, Qatar, Libya and Algeria (Arab members of the oil-producing cartel, the Organisation of Petroleum Exporting Countries, or OPEC) announced that they would cut back oil production by 5 per cent every month until Israel withdrew from occupied Arab territories and restored Palestinian rights.[4] Kuwait and Saudi Arabia went further and threatened an immediate reduction of 10 per cent.

Two days later, all seven Arab states declared that they were in the course of drawing up a list of their "friends" and "enemies" in Europe. Oil exports to the "friendly" nations of France, Spain and the United Kingdom would remain at September 1973 levels. All other European countries would face a 5 per cent monthly cut in deliveries until Israel agreed to Arab demands. All European countries, that is, except Portugal and the Netherlands who, along with the US, faced an immediate and total Arab oil embargo—Portugal for providing the US with permission to re-equip Israel from the Azores, and the Netherlands for its status as the most pro-Israeli nation in Europe.

This "selective embargo",[5] as French Foreign Minister Michel Jobert termed it, directly challenged the Community's attempt to consolidate cooperation in the foreign policy sphere that had been gradually evolving since the late 1960s. Member state governments refused Dutch requests for help in meeting its oil shortage. British Foreign Secretary Alec Douglas-Home justified his government's refusal to supply Holland from its reserves on the grounds that it would only have drawn the rest of Europe onto the Arab boycott list.[6] The French government fully subscribed to this view. During a visit to London in November 1973, President Georges Pompidou told Prime Minister Edward Heath that standing by those allies who were singled out by the Arab oil producers "was more likely to result in [us] being attacked by the Arabs and treated by them in the same way".[7]

Abandoning the Dutch was not enough to guarantee the favour of the oil suppliers. On 6 November 1973, the Community went further. It issued a declaration on the Arab–Israeli conflict, which it described as its "first contribution" to the "search for a comprehensive solution".[8] This statement called for both sides to return to their 22 October 1973 positions and for negotiations along the lines of UN Security Council Resolutions 242 and 338.[9]

The November declaration expressed support for the right of each state to live in peace within secure and recognised borders, and an implicit acceptance of Israel's right to exist. However, this was linked to a much more explicit statement that there would only be a just and lasting peace if the "legitimate rights of the Palestinians" were taken into account. It also stressed the need for Israel to "end territorial occupation" of land gained in 1967.[10]

In the immediate wake of the publication of the November 1973 declaration Foreign Office officials argued that the British position "had not moved a centimetre". The European statement, they argued, was simply a reiteration of British support for UN Security Council Resolution 242.[11] In truth, it was anything but the standard inoffensive and bland joint communiqué traditionally issued at the end of EEC get-togethers. Rather, it was the first time since 1967 that the Community collectively placed the Palestinian issue at the centre of the political debate.

Most importantly, and directly challenging British official claims at the time, was the fact that by stating "the need for Israel to end the territorial occupation which it has maintained since the conflict of 1967", the November declaration was lining up the newly enlarged Community behind the French position since 1967: that UN Security Council Resolution 242 could only be interpreted as a withdrawal from all the territories occupied by Israel in the June war.

This would have major repercussions for future British involvement in the politics of the Palestine question. In mid-1975, for example, the French government found it "difficult to understand" the British reluctance to support any European guarantee of a peace that called for a full Israeli withdrawal to June 1967 borders on the grounds that the Heath government, in endorsing the November 1973 declaration, had accepted the French reading of Resolution 242.[12]

The same was true for West Germany. In the summer of 1971 Foreign Minister Walter Scheel was adamant that in regard to UN Security Council Resolution 242, there were "differences between the French and West German positions … the attitude of Bonn supports the interpretation given by Washington and London".[13] But in endorsing the November declaration, Germany was now "walking a tightrope"[14] between its commitment to Israel and its obligations to its EEC partners. Even the Dutch government, despite subsequent denials to the contrary by Foreign Minister van der Stoel, appeared to accept the French position on Resolution 242 by supporting the November statement.[15]

Just weeks into his new job as US secretary of state, Henry Kissinger took a dim view of the Community's November declaration, which he had only heard about while on a visit to Cairo. Israel reacted even more negatively. Foreign Minister Abba Eban urged the Community to "reconsider the content and spirit of their declaration", adding that the EEC's new-found interest in Palestinian rights had more to do with "oil for Europe … than peace for the Middle East".[16]

Douglas-Home rejected such accusations as "nonsense"[17] but Eban had a point. Subsequently, Heath would have no reservations in acknowledging the link, at least in his mind, between the 6 November 1973 Middle East declaration and the oil crisis, noting that "in recognition … we were treated, along with France, as a 'friendly' nation".[18]

On 1 November, just five days before the EEC declaration, Libya, which along with Saudi Arabia provided two-thirds of West Germany's oil needs, threatened Bonn with a total boycott if it failed to show what it termed "positive neutrality".[19] While just two days before the November declaration, eight of the ten OAPEC member states met in Kuwait to discuss tightening the oil embargo.

Given this, even *Le Monde*, which was generally supportive of the European approach throughout the crisis, published an article criticising the declaration as a "revelation" of the political impotency of Europe[20]— a view provided credibility by the fact that public Arab threats regarding possible future reductions of up to 25 per cent in oil supplies to Europe ceased immediately following the publication of the 6 November declaration.

At their summit meeting in Algiers in late November 1973, the Arab heads of state characterised the EEC's declaration as "significant".[21] Secret clauses excluded from the original Algiers Declaration, but published subsequently in the Arabic press, called for the "Arab nation" to build on what President Anwar Sadat of Egypt termed "signs of understanding" in Europe in order to "develop the political stance".[22]

The Algiers meeting was important for other reasons also. It agreed to set up PLO information offices in Community capitals under the auspices of the Arab League. Also, by designating the PLO as the "only legitimate representative of the Palestinian people", a resolution officially confirmed by the Arab summit in Rabat in October 1974, this gathering of Arab leaders placed the Palestinian question and the role of the PLO at the top of the Arab agenda. This would have a significant impact on both Euro–Arab and Euro–American relations over subsequent years.

Prior to the 1973 War, the Arab governments had been frustrated over what they saw as their inability to gain political influence in Europe. Following a visit to Europe in late 1972, Egypt's recently appointed foreign minister, Muhammad Hassan al-Zayyat, acknowledged that the continent-wide Arab effort to improve diplomatic ties with Europe had failed in the face of counter-efforts by pro-Israel forces inside the Community.[23]

Events of late 1973 altered forever the relationship between the oil-exporting Arab nations and the industrial West. Senior Arab officials suddenly found that they had unfettered access to Europe's most senior policy-makers. On 5 November 1973, al-Zayyat met with Pompidou and Jobert in Paris. This was followed by a tour of European capitals by Saudi oil minister Ahmed Zaki Yamani and Dr Beleid Abdul Sallam, the Algerian minister of industry and energy. In these meetings European leaders pleaded for the Arab world to refrain from jeopardising European unity.[24] In turn, the two Arab representatives pressured their hosts to take a firmer stand against Washington's policy in the Middle East in order to protect Europe's oil and other strategic interests in the future.

Transatlantic tensions

Such demands did not fall on deaf ears. One major consequence of the oil crisis was that it highlighted the very different realities that Europe and the US faced *vis-à-vis* the Middle East. The first and most immediately apparent difference related to dependence on Arab oil. Pompidou told Kissinger at the height of the crisis: "you only rely on the Arabs for about a tenth of your consumption. We are entirely dependent upon them."[25] The French president was actually overestimating US reliance at this time. In 1973, the US imported just 4 per cent of its oil from the Arab world, whereas Britain imported 30 per cent, West Germany 38 per cent, France 53 per cent and Italy 60 per cent of their oil from the same suppliers.

The Arabs had originally planned to use the embargo to punish the US. But the focus of the boycott quickly switched to Europe when it became apparent that it was far more vulnerable than the US, because it relied far more on oil imports and used a higher proportion of imported oil for essential consumer and industrial needs.[26]

The Arab hope was that if Europe began to feel the impact of an oil shortage, it would pressure the US into rethinking its policies towards the Middle East. Or if that did not work, then the aim was to isolate the US and place it in an untenable position among the Western states.

This strategy benefited from the fact that even prior to the 1973 conflict it was already widely accepted inside the Community that the US was largely indifferent to the damage its Middle East policies were doing to European interests. In May 1973, for example, a diverse group of parliamentarians, academics, churchmen and writers from across Europe published an open letter to President Richard Nixon claiming that Europe, not to mention the US, had "suffered because of the subordination of American policy in the Middle East to Israeli interests".[27]

Once the crisis got underway, this argument gained increased currency. Tensions were compounded by the wave of statements emanating from administration officials, congressmen, Middle East experts and newspaper columnists charging Europe with having disgracefully capitulated to oil blackmail and having "hurried to subscribe to political formulations demanded by the Arabs",[28] as one prominent US academic put it at the time.

Transatlantic differences had other deeper, more profound roots. By 1973 the Nixon administration had shifted its foreign policy priorities away from South East Asia and towards a diplomatic initiative in the Middle East. America's disentanglement from the Vietnam quagmire raised concerns in Europe over the impact it would have on EC-led efforts to develop a common foreign policy independent of Washington on a wide-range of issues, not least the Middle East.

Many now agreed with Jobert that the US "did not have the slightest desire to bring to life a super-national Europe like the USA"[29] and that

Kissinger was taking "evident pleasure"[30] in using events in the Middle East to re-assert US dominance over Europe in the region.

This major deterioration in US-European relations was all the more notable and noticeable because it occurred at a time when Downing Street was home to the most Eurocentric and least pro-American British prime minister since World War II. The war certainly provided Heath with an opportunity to consolidate his pro-European credentials and to underpin his government's efforts to promote a united EC policy on the Middle East.

In late September 1973 Pompidou had proposed the convening of a Community summit to lay the basis for European political cooperation and to demonstrate Europe's "capacity to help in settling the world's problems".[31] In late November, Pompidou and Heath endorsed such a meeting in response to the Middle East crisis.[32]

The upshot was that the EEC heads of government and state gathered in the Danish capital of Copenhagen in mid-December 1973. This meeting discussed all aspects of the Middle East crisis, not simply the oil issue, and was attended by four Arab foreign ministers who had been deputised by the recent Algiers summit to represent the Arab position on both oil and the Arab–Israeli conflict.

On one level the Copenhagen summit was a failure. France and Britain vetoed the calls from the Dutch, Danes and West Germans for joint Community action on oil; a meeting of EEC foreign ministers three days later was no more productive. The summit did, however, provide the opportunity for European leaders to agree to "meet more frequently", to "speak with one voice in important world affairs" and to "decide on the means by which a common position should be worked out quickly in times of crisis".[33] Copenhagen also saw discussions on the convening of a joint Euro–Arab conference, possibly at summit level, something that the Arab representatives attending the meeting in the Danish capital had pushed for repeatedly.

The Community's Middle East declaration of early November and its December meeting at Copenhagen may well have been a consequence of the panic over oil that had plunged Europe into a recession. It may have shown the world the extent of Europe's dependence on the oil sheikdoms of the Gulf. But it also brought home a greater truth. The Community had no hope of increasing its international influence without increasing cooperation in the foreign policy sphere. Developing a new, extensive, relationship with the Arab world would be an important component of this.

Arab policy-makers and diplomats, as well as their supporters in Europe, saw all this as providing a tremendous opportunity for increased cooperation between Europe and the Arab world. In January 1974, voices emanating from near King Faisal of Saudi Arabia were hopeful that after the turmoil of the recent past mutual ties would now rapidly improve.[34] But almost immediately European plans and Arab hopes faced a major setback when the Nixon administration announced that it was convening a conference in Washington for all the major oil-consuming countries.

There was scepticism across the Community over whether the US goal of an agreement between those nations reliant on Arab oil was achievable in this period of instability in the international system. Nevertheless, it was difficult to reject the American invitation, given the fact that Europe's overriding economic and political priority was stable energy supplies at affordable prices.

Adamant that the best way forward was direct negotiations between Europe and the oil-producing countries free of US involvement, France challenged the support for the Washington meeting in London and Bonn. In response, West German Chancellor Willy Brandt warned Pompidou that cooperation on energy must be the immediate priority because "if the Community cannot agree on this, it is nothing".[35]

A difficult dialogue

Paris was extremely relieved when the Washington talks failed to reach a conclusive agreement. This allowed France to fill the vacuum by insisting that the Community now convene a mechanism, named the Euro–Arab Dialogue (EAD), that would allow Europe to deal directly with the Arab world.

The short-term objective of this new framework was "stable oil supplies at fair prices".[36] In March 1974, within weeks of the Community adopting the French call for the establishment of the EAD, the Arab oil-producing states meeting in Vienna agreed (against the wishes of Libya and Syria) to ease their oil restrictions on Italy and West Germany, who were added to the list of "friendly" nations. The embargo against the Netherlands remained in place, as did the special limitations on exports to Denmark. By this time the continuing oil restrictions had no real impact even on the Dutch or Danes. The Community, which in April 1974 had failed to agree on a French proposal for future discussions between oil consumers and producers, could take little credit for this. Rather, it was due to the fact that by now the oil available on international markets exceeded demand to the extent that European ports were finding it hard to accommodate all arriving oil tankers.

It was only in September 1974, almost one full year after the beginning of the crisis, that the EEC concluded its first substantive agreement to work towards a joint energy policy. But even this plan was a long way from the French goal of seeking a dialogue and concertation with the producer countries. It was limited to reducing petroleum dependence from a projected 60 per cent to 40 per cent of total consumption and only gained grudging acceptance because of the desperate need to address the rising cost of oil.[37] The European Parliament for one was not impressed. In early 1975 it issued a resolution expressing its "dismay" that the "governments of certain member states appear to have lost the will to achieve a common energy policy, thus weakening considerably their own advocation of European Union".[38]

The immediate preoccupation with oil notwithstanding, the overriding objective of Community policy-makers was that the EAD framework would lead the Arabs to have a "kindlier view" of Europe, or at least "make the Arabs think twice, if not three times, before taking discriminatory action against us".[39]

It was hoped that this could be achieved by using the EAD to build up Euro–Arab economic and cultural ties. As a French memorandum put it, "economic cooperation will be the principle theme [of the EAD]".[40] Thus, the official objectives of the framework excluded politics and focused solely on developing economic, technical and cultural cooperation with the Arab world, especially in the areas of agriculture, rural development, industrialisation, trade, basic infrastructure, finance, science and technology.[41]

During the summer of 1974, the EAD began to take shape. In June the Community delivered an aide-memoire to all Arab states that framed the EAD in terms of the request by Arab representatives at Copenhagen for a new relationship. In September, EEC foreign ministers attending the annual UN General Assembly meeting in New York hosted a lunch for their Arab counterparts. By November 1974, the permanent EAD working groups and the EAD General Commission were in place.

Altogether, twenty-one Arab states took part in the EAD under the auspices of the Arab League. In mid-1975, nineteen Arab countries presented the EEC with a "shopping list" of what they wanted to gain from economic cooperation under the new framework.[42] The Arab League followed this up with a request for the signing of a comprehensive trade convention between the Community and the Arab world under the auspices of the EAD.[43]

But, as EEC diplomats acknowledged, the overriding reality was that the Arab world was sharply divided between a minority who "wish to discuss the practical business of cooperation" and a majority "who wish to make political points".[44] Those who adopted the latter approach argued that while Europe had little influence over Israel compared to the US and could in no way match the Soviets in regard to economic and military aid to the Arab nations, it still had a key role to play in the politics of the Arab–Israeli conflict. In particular, there was hope that via the EAD a united Community led by Britain and France could be convinced to exert significant influence on future US policy in the Middle East. As the Baghdad paper *Al Thawra* put it in May 1975, one Arab objective of the EAD was to make the EEC states "use pressure on the USA to stop helping the Zionist entity".[45]

Following a meeting with Arab League Secretary-General Mahmoud Riad in Cairo in late 1974, French Foreign Minister Jean Sauvagnargues reported back to a meeting of EEC foreign ministers that the Arabs "could not make a distinction between the political problem and the economic issues".[46] The most serious political obstacle to the success of the EAD was the Arab demand that the Palestine Liberation Organisation (PLO) play a central role in the nascent framework. In 1971–2, the PLO opened offices in London, Paris, Rome and Geneva as part of its attempt to promote its image as the diplomatic representative of the Palestinian people, as well as a revolutionary guerrilla organisation struggling for the liberation of its homeland. The PLO benefited from the Community's wide-ranging statement on Palestinian rights in its November 1973 declaration and from the decision of the Arab summit in Algiers in the same month to declare the PLO the "only legitimate representative of the Palestinian people". As an editorial in *Le Monde* noted, this decision meant that for the first time PLO leader Yasser Arafat had been "accorded equal status with the heads of [Arab] states".[47]

In November 1974, the same month that the EAD General Commission was established, the Arab leaders at their summit in Rabat, Morocco, endorsed the PLO as the "sole legitimate representative of the Palestinian people" and authorised it to set up an "independent national authority" on any liberated Palestinian territory.[48] In the words of a *London Times* editorial, this decision of the Arab states to line up "behind the flag of the militant Palestinian guerrilla movement"[49] fundamentally influenced the situation in the Middle East by establishing the PLO as a "leading formal actor" in the region.[50] The Rabat decision also gave a boost to the Arab League's insistence that the "Palestinians must have the right to attend any meeting in the framework of the Dialogue…[there can be]… no retreat by the Arab states on the Palestine issue".[51]

The PLO Factor

It was quickly dawning on the Community that, in the words of one of its own diplomats, PLO participation was the "only political issue on which they [the Arabs] are interested in discussing".[52] While France and a number of other EEC member states (notably Ireland and Italy) were sympathetic to including the PLO in the process, the British, Dutch, Danes and West Germans were far less flexible and were "not prepared to make political concessions to the Arabs in this context".[53] This resulted in the indefinite postponement of the first plenary meeting of the EAD's General Commission, originally scheduled to take place at ambassadorial level on 26 November 1974.

One key reason for the divide in the Community over the role of the PLO in the EAD was the post-war success of Washington's highly ambitious and ultimately successful attempt to cement its position as the predominant external party in the Middle East through peacemaking. In these terms, by July 1974, the same month that a high-level Arab delegation travelled to Paris to discuss the EAD, the US was increasingly concerned that the nascent dialogue could pose a real danger to, or at the very least complicate, American efforts to broker an Egyptian–Israeli settlement.

In a January 1975 discussion on the EAD with British Foreign Secretary James Callaghan, Kissinger "accepted, with regret" that the dialogue would take place. But he was also adamant that Europe would be dragged down a "slippery slope" and he doubted whether the Community could prevent the Arabs from turning the EAD into a "political forum".[54] In a meeting with Chancellor Schmidt and Foreign Minister Hans-Dietrich Genscher of West Germany the following month, Kissinger addressed the matter of the EAD in the context of the "European obsession" with the PLO and reiterated the administration's distaste over both.[55]

The Community's sensitivity to Washington's "immense and slightly hysterical interest"[56] in the EAD put it in a very difficult position. Torn between internal divisions over the legitimacy of the PLO, the maximalist demands of the Arab states and the minimalist expectations of the US, during late 1974 and 1975 the Community struggled to find an acceptable solution to the problem of the role of the PLO in the EAD.

This was only resolved in early 1975, when the French suggested the convening of study groups consisting of experts chosen by the EEC and the Arab League who were not official representatives of governments, as this would allow for the inclusion of Palestinians in the Arab delegation.[57] Community ministers endorsed this proposal for the creation of "non-governmental expert groups"[58] on condition that it was made "quite clear" to the Arabs that the EEC "would not regard the presence at the meeting…of PLO experts as implying European recognition of the PLO's claims".[59]

Once in place, the "Dublin Formula", as this compromise agreement was known, allowed for the convening of the first EAD plenary session in Cairo in June 1975. During this meeting, members of the PLO's finance department, the Palestine National Fund, participated as part of the Arab delegation. To blur the affiliations of those attending yet further, all delegates were identified, if at all, by function rather than nationality.

At the conclusion of the Cairo meeting, both sides described the EAD as the "product of a joint political will that emerged at the highest level".[60] This became the catchphrase of subsequent EAD meetings in Rome in July and Abu Dhabi in November 1975.[61] But from its first meeting the EAD found itself a hostage to relentless attempts to force the normalisation of relations between the Community and the PLO onto the agenda.

The polite deceptions of Euro–Arab diplomacy could only go so far. By the time of the Tunis EAD meeting in February 1977, Ismael Khelil, the Tunisian delegate, was warning the Community that there could be no progress towards greater economic cooperation between Europe and the Arabs if there was no progress on political questions.[62] The final communiqué of the October 1977 meeting in Brussels underlined this impasse. For the first time the Arab delegation insisted on explicitly using the EAD to call on the Community to endorse the principle of Palestinian statehood.

Even if they had been in favour of such a move, Community officials had very little authority to expand on the foreign policy positions of member state governments that had been agreed at the Council of Ministers, the forum for heads of member state governments which met three times a year. Despite calling for the strengthening of EEC institutions and arguing that a collective approach was key, national governments had little appetite for ceding power to European institutions in matters of foreign policy.

Despite Arab frustrations over the failure to gain explicit EEC endorsement of the PLO and a Palestinian state through the EAD mechanism, the framework did have its benefits. It provided the Arabs with the prestige of having a special relationship with Europe, which was denied to Israel: while the strategy of placing the PLO at the heart of official meetings between Community and Arab representatives meant that the Palestine issue was always at the top of the Euro–Arab agenda. The EAD also provided PLO officials with numerous opportunities to attend inter-parliamentary meetings and unofficial Euro–Arab conferences alongside senior Arab officials and, more importantly, current and former senior European figures attending these events in a personal capacity.

Alternatives to Camp David

On 29–30 June 1977, the Community published its London communiqué on the Palestine issue. The longest section in this statement addressed the "legitimate right of the Palestinian people to give effective expression to its national identity". But there was also an implicit reference to the PLO when it demanded that the "representatives of the parties to the conflict including the Palestinian people must participate in the negotiations in an appropriate manner".[63] One year later, in June 1978, the Community issued a statement on the Middle East which called for representatives of the Palestinians to participate in negotiations and for Israel to grant "effective expression" to Palestinian national identity and to "recognise the legitimate rights of the Palestinian people" in the context of an overall settlement of the conflict.[64]

The following September, the Community welcomed the unprecedented 12 days of substantive peace discussions at Camp David between US President Jimmy Carter, Israeli Prime Minister Menachem Begin and Egyptian President Anwar Sadat as "a further major step towards… settlement", and offered "strong support" for the process.[65]

However, there was serious concern inside Europe that by this time the Camp David discussions primarily focused on achieving full Israeli withdrawal from the Sinai in return for Egyptian recognition of Israel and a normalisation of bilateral relations. Israeli Prime Minister Menachem Begin had no interest in linking self-determination or even autonomy in the West Bank and Gaza with a bilateral agreement with Egypt. Neither, in the final account, had Sadat. Despite his consistent attempts to promote the Palestinian position, his priority was regaining territory rather than immersing himself in "West Bank haggling".[66] Ultimately Sadat was even willing to forgo a date for the beginning of Palestinian autonomy in the occupied territories in order to secure the return of his prized Sinai.[67]

On 26 March, 1979, Carter hosted Begin and Sadat on the north lawn of the White House to mark the signing of the Egyptian–Israeli peace treaty. Celebration of this defining moment in the history of the modern Middle East was tempered by one overriding reality. As the *Financial Times* noted, this treaty offered "peace without agreement" precisely because the concept of Palestinian autonomy as set out was not defined or integrated into a comprehensive framework.[68]

There was little that the Carter administration could do about it except play up the success of the bilateral agreement and lobby allies for support. European ambassadors in Washington were briefed on the agreement and were requested to ask their governments to refrain from sabotaging the treaty.[69] Some were more obliging than others.

France made no secret of its distaste for what Foreign Minister Jean François-Poncet dismissed as "the bilateral peace treaty".[70] The communiqué issued by the French Council of Ministers on 29 March noted that the peace deal did not address a number of key issues concerning a comprehensive peace.[71] The Élysée Palace told Washington that while it would continue to provide bilateral technical aid to Egypt, it would not do so through the Camp David framework. The West German govern-ment was less openly hostile to the agreement, but Chancellor Schmidt was unwilling to give explicit backing to Camp David or to provide financial support to Egypt under the framework unless it was part of an international aid effort, so as to avoid being seen as pro-Camp David by Arab opponents of the treaty.[72]

From the day the Camp David agreement was signed, Europe's cor-ridors of power were rife with predictions of its imminent collapse. But fearful of the US reaction, neither the Commission nor any member state government was willing to break explicitly with it. The Commu-nity's unenviable position of having to navigate a course that took US interests into account was made worse by the fear of alienating Arab opponents of the Israeli–Egyptian peace, which perhaps explains why no Community statement ever called on the Arab world to accept Camp David.

Concerns over ongoing European dependence on Arab oil aside, the EEC's reluctance to embrace Camp David also came at a time of unprec-edented public sympathy for the Palestinian cause in Europe. This was also reflected at a political level and, in September 1979, the Community called, for the first time, for "representatives" of the Palestinians to "play a full part in the negotiations of a comprehensive settlement".[73]

The Camp David process had significantly undermined the EAD framework. No Egyptian representatives attended the fourth EAD General Committee in Damascus in early December 1978. Worse, on 31 March 1979, nineteen Arab League members (including a Palestin-ian delegation) ejected Egypt from the League for signing a separate peace with Israel. This put an end to French efforts during its 1979 Community presidency to boost the EAD by offering to convene a meeting of the framework at ministerial level, something that the Arabs had been lobbying for since late 1974 and France itself had been "push-ing" since 1975.[74]

On top of this, after expelling Egypt, the Arab League transferred its headquarters from Cairo to Tunis. This forced the Community to ignore requests from both the rump Cairo office and the new Tunis office for EAD documentation, lest it be seen to be taking sides. In April 1979, the new Tunis headquarters informed the Community that EAD meet-ings at all levels would be suspended until the Arab League reorganised itself fully in the wake of Camp David.[75]

By the end of 1979 the EAD had ceased to function without having officially been disbanded. Talks in February 1980 on reviving it came to naught in the face of Arab demands that the Community now address politics as a priority and use the EAD to speak out against Camp David in more explicit terms.[76] A further meeting under the framework in Rome in early March 1980 made no more progress and led one Arab delegate to denounce the EAD as "nothing but a hoax" that was now "at a complete standstill".[77]

Bet in Venice

Convinced that Camp David was "dead as a doornail"[78] and spurred on by a desire to rescue the EAD, by the spring of 1980 the Community was increasingly willing to challenge the bilateral Egyptian–Israeli peace. At a meeting in Luxemburg on 28 April 1980, the European Council issued a statement: "Conscious that Europe may in due course have a role to play", it had "instructed the foreign ministers to submit a report on this problem on the occasion of its next session at Venice". By the first week of May 1980 it was an open secret that the Community was preparing to make a major statement on the Middle East in order to keep "momentum" in the peace process following the inevitable collapse of Camp David.[79]

In April 1980 Khaled al Hassan, the head of a PLO delegation visiting Strasbourg, outlined the role that he wanted the EEC to play once Camp David had officially collapsed. Europe, he explained, should refer the issue back to the UN Security Council, which would then vote to force Israel to make a complete withdrawal from all occupied territories. This in turn would be followed by the birth of a Palestinian state.[80]

Speaking in a television interview at the end of May, President Carter was clear: "We are asking the European allies not to get involved in the negotiations for the time being … my predication is that without very much delay we will be back at the negotiating table, making progress."[81] He also warned that, if necessary, he would not hesitate to veto any draft resolution submitted by the EEC to the UN Security Council in order "to prevent this Camp David process being destroyed or subverted".[82] In early June, Carter again threatened to veto any European attempt to push through a Security Council draft resolution on Palestinian self-determination.

Carter's multiple threats to veto any draft resolution on Palestinian self-determination were enough to deter the EEC from opting for the UN route.[83] However, the Community was still in favour of setting out a major new policy declaration on the Palestine issue at its June summit in Venice. The long-anticipated Venice Declaration was published on 13 June 1980. As André Fontaine, editor-in-chief of *Le Monde*, noted, "most of the Nine had already said more or less the same thing, but each in its own way, and in less solemn circumstances".[84]

Though acknowledging Israel's right to exist it contained outspoken criticism of Israeli "territorial occupation" since 1967 and condemned settlements built outside pre-1967 borders as illegal under international law. In a reference to the political claims of the Palestinians it rejected the traditional view that the Palestinian problem was "simply one of refugees" and it called for the Palestinians people to be allowed to "exercise fully its right to self-determination". Most controversially, it also called for the PLO to be "associated with" future negotiations.[85] This broke new ground in so much as it was the first Community statement on the Middle East conflict to include explicit support for Palestinian "self-determination".

But it also played safe by calling for PLO association rather than participation in future peace negotiations. In these terms the Venice Declaration failed to provide a real alternative to Camp David because it refused to give formal recognition to the PLO or to express explicit support for the establishment of a Palestinian state. This left the Community with no more influence over the PLO after the document had been published than before. At the same time, the position adopted by the Community in Venice contributed to a significant worsening in Euro–Israeli relations. As an Israeli foreign ministry report written in the wake of Venice summed up, "the political principles of the European Community are destructive and unacceptable and stand no chance of being considered viable by Israel".[86]

Nevertheless, from the European perspective the Venice Declaration was the most significant consequence of the 1973 War. As one Arab commentator explained, it had succeeded "in keeping the Arab world from total alienation from the West".[87] For British Foreign Secretary Lord Carrington, a moving force behind the declaration, it was an acknowledgement that "the PLO enjoys considerable Palestinian support [and] …cannot be left out of account"; and as such it attempted to place a "proper appreciation of the Palestinian aspect".[88] It was also, as Carrington later explained, a response to the "political vacuum" in the Middle East when the Camp David process was "in the doldrums",[89] and the US was "having a sabbatical and moderate Arabs, in particular, needed to see that somebody, somewhere, was alive to the problem and wanted to help".[90] President Giscard d'Estaing of France echoed Carrington's sentiments and described the Venice Declaration as "a major contribution" to "the emergence, or rather re-emergence, of a European presence, acting in its own way and for its own ends".[91]

As a new decade dawned, the Venice Declaration served notice to the international community of Europe's intent since the 1973 War to develop a distinctive voice as an external player in the Arab–Israeli conflict in order to consolidate internal political cooperation, improve relations with the Arab world, and challenge the US for influence across the Middle East.

Israel's speedy military victory over the Arabs in 1967 redrew the map of the Middle East and provided Europe with the hope that it could now take advantage of the new regional dynamics to transform its economic power into political influence on the ground. The 1973 War put paid to this hope. Since then, and to the deep frustration of successive generations of European policymakers, engagement in Arab-Israeli conflict in general, and the Israel-Palestine conflict in particular, has shone an all too-bright light on the limits of European political and diplomat power in its "near abroad". In fact, nowhere has the gap between European rhetoric and action been more obvious than in its involvement in this festering conflict since 1973.

Moreover, forty years on it is now possible to see clearly that the 1973 war, and its intended and unintended consequences, has had a huge influence on Europe's internal development as a political force on the world stage, as well as on its engagement with the US in the Middle East. The 1973 War illuminated the inherent, perhaps even structural, weaknesses of Europe as a global political actor. Now, as then, Europe also continues to play a deeply unsatisfying supporting role to the US in a political process that continues to falter in its efforts to facilitate peace between Israel and its Arab neighbours.

11

OIL AND THE OCTOBER WAR

David S. Painter

The 1973–4 oil crisis altered the balance of power in the world economy and threatened to upset the overall balance of power. In response to US support for Israel during the October 1973 Arab–Israeli War, the Organisation of Arab Oil Exporting Countries (OAPEC) imposed an embargo on oil shipments to the United States and the Netherlands and cut back production, reducing the amount of oil available for export.[1] Although serious oil shortages did not occur, oil prices quadrupled, harming economies around the world. The differential impact of the crisis on the United States and the Soviet Union affected the course of the Cold War.

The crisis

On 6 October 1973, Egyptian and Syrian forces launched simultaneous attacks on Israeli forces occupying the Sinai and the Golan Heights. The attacks caught the Israelis by surprise, and in the initial fighting Egyptian troops broke through Israeli lines and established positions on the east bank of the Suez Canal, and Syrian forces recaptured much of the Golan Heights.

The Palestine Liberation Organisation, radical nationalists in the Kuwait national assembly, and the Iraqi Ba'ath party immediately called for Arab oil producers to wield the oil weapon against Israel and its supporters, and oil workers in Kuwait threatened to stop production completely unless shipments to the United States were cut by at least 50 per cent. Iraq nationalised the share of Exxon and Mobil in the Basrah Petroleum Company (BPC) in retaliation for US support of Israel, and Algeria declared an embargo on oil exports to the United States. Both actions were largely symbolic. The Iraqis had nationalised the main foreign oil company in Iraq in 1972, and they offered compensation and allowed Exxon and Mobil continued access to oil from the BPC. Algeria sent very little oil to the United States so its action also had little impact. In addition, the Saudi government directed the US-owned Arabian American Oil Company (ARAMCO) to supply crude oil and products to Egypt and Iraq to aid the war effort. Fearing retaliation if it refused, ARAMCO complied with the request.[2]

Despite the war, representatives from the oil companies and the Persian Gulf producers met as scheduled in Vienna on 8 October to discuss revisions to the 1971 Tehran price agreement. The Gulf States wanted adjustments in the price of oil to compensate them for inflation and to restore the 80/20 profit-sharing ratio that had prevailed at the time of the Tehran agreement. They rejected the companies' offer of a 15 per cent increase in price, a revised inflation-adjustment rate, and a small premium for low-sulphur crude; and demanded a 100 per cent increase, an improved inflation-adjustment formula, and a mechanism for keeping the posted (tax reference) price 40 per cent above the market price as it had at the time of the Tehran agreement. With the two sides so far apart, the company representatives left Vienna on 9 October to consult with their home governments. The representatives of the Gulf States left Vienna for an emergency meeting of the Organisation of Arab Petroleum Exporting Countries (OAPEC) in Kuwait.[3]

Founded in 1968 by Saudi Arabia, Kuwait and Libya as a means to separate oil from politics, OAPEC's purpose changed after the overthrow of the Libyan monarchy in September 1969 and its replacement by a radical regime. In 1970, Algeria, Bahrain, Qatar, Abu Dhabi and Dubai joined OAPEC, followed by Iraq, Egypt and Syria in 1972, giving the majority to states that favoured the use of oil as a political weapon.[4]

Reports from Saudi Arabia indicated that King Faisal was thinking about cutting back oil production in order to force the United States to pressure Israel to withdraw from the territories it had occupied in 1967. Faisal had been under pressure from Arab radicals for years to use the kingdom's vast oil resources as a weapon on behalf of the Arab cause. During 1973, the Saudis repeatedly warned that they could be forced to take action unless the United States put pressure on Israel to withdraw from the Arab lands occupied in 1967 and recognised the rights of the Palestinian people. In August 1973, Faisal met with Egyptian President Anwar Sadat and promised to use the "oil weapon" in the event of a war with Israel.[5]

The Central Intelligence Agency (CIA) warned that if Israel began to win major victories and the United States actively aided Israel by resupplying it, US oil interests in the Arab world would be in jeopardy. Moreover, if the Saudis and the other major Arab oil producers cut production to pressure the United States and its allies to change policy, it would have a serious impact on Western Europe and Japan, and to a lesser extent the United States. The heads of Exxon, Mobil, Texaco, and SOCAL also warned that US military aid to Israel would harm US oil companies and undermine the US position in the Middle East.[6]

The United States began a full-scale airlift of military supplies to Israel on 14 October in response to Soviet resupply of Egypt and Syria and urgent Israeli requests. Aware that this action would cause problems with the Saudis, US Secretary of State Henry A. Kissinger wrote to King Faisal that the United States "had no alternative" but to begin an airlift of supplies to Israel following the "massive" Soviet airlift of arms to the Arabs. Kissinger asked Faisal to understand that the airlift was not intended to be anti-Arab, and pledged that the United States would stop its airlift as soon as the Soviets stopped theirs. The Saudis rejected Kissinger's explanation and warned that continued US support of Israel would result in economic sanctions in the form of production cuts.[7]

Kissinger, however, refused to believe that the Saudis would take action against the United States, a view seemingly supported by CIA Director William Colby, who told the Washington Special Action Group (WSAG) on 16 October that King Faisal was just blowing off steam and his anger at the United States would be temporary. At the meeting, the WSAG decided to increase the US airlift to Israel until the rate of delivery was 25 per cent ahead of Soviet deliveries to the Arabs. By the end of the fighting on 25 October, the United States had delivered around 12,880 tons of supplies to Israel, as compared to Soviet deliveries to the Arab states of 11,174 tons.[8]

On 16 October, with the tide of battle turning against his forces, Egyptian President Anwar Sadat called for an immediate ban on Arab oil exports to the United States. In addition, the Saudis informed European countries that they were planning to reduce the quantity of oil that they would make available for export. They realised that this would hurt European nations more than the United States, but they expected the Europeans to bring pressure on the United States to adopt a more even-handed approach to the Arab–Israeli dispute. At the same time but independently of the war, the Gulf exporting countries unilaterally raised the posted price of oil from $3.01 a barrel to $5.11 a barrel, a 70 per cent increase.[9]

At the OAPEC oil ministers meeting in Kuwait on 17 October, Iraq called for nationalisation of all US oil companies in Arab countries, withdrawal of funds from US banks, and a total embargo of oil shipments to the United States. Syria and Libya also supported nationalising US companies in the Arab world. Reluctant to cut their ties with ARAMCO and the United States, the Saudis, supported by the Egyptians, opposed the Iraqi proposals and convinced the conference to adopt a proposal that called for each Arab state to cut its oil production by at least 5 per cent from September levels, warning that "the same percentage will be applied in each month compared with the previous one, until the Israeli withdrawal is completed from the whole Arab territories occupied in June 1967 and the legal rights of the Palestinian people restored." To ensure that this action would not harm states that assisted the Arab cause, the conferees promised to provide friendly states with the same amount of oil that they had been receiving.[10]

Saudi Arabia, Kuwait, Qatar, and Algeria reduced their production by 10 per cent, and Libya and Bahrain cut production by 5 per cent. Iraq, whose representatives had walked out of the conference when their proposals were rejected, refused to cut production, arguing that the production cutbacks would harm friendly as well as hostile countries. Iraqi production had long lagged behind other Middle East producers, especially after Iraq's nationalisation of over 95 per cent of the Iraq Petroleum Company's concession in December 1961. Moreover, Iraq did not have large foreign exchange reserves that would allow it to cut back production.[11]

The conference also adopted a secret resolution calling for "most severe cuts" on supplies to the United States, but left each member free to decide on its own whether and when it would embargo exports to the United States. Abu Dhabi declared an embargo on exports to the United States on 18 October, followed by Libya and Qatar on 19 October. Libya also raised the posted price for its oil to $8.925 per barrel. Discounting warnings from the Saudis that further aid to Israel would result in an embargo, President Nixon on 19 October requested from Congress $2.2 billion in grant military assistance for Israel. The next day Saudi Arabia declared a total embargo of oil shipments to the United States and warned that it would continue as long as Israel occupied Arab territory outside its 1967 borders. On 21 October, the Saudi extended the embargo against the United States to include all indirect shipments and deliveries to refineries supplying US military forces in Bahrain, Italy, and Greece. Within a few days, the remaining Arab producers, including Iraq, declared embargoes against the United States. OAPEC extended its embargo to the Netherlands on 23 October in retaliation for Dutch support for Israel. Iraq also nationalised Shell's share in the Basrah Petroleum Company (Shell was 60 per cent Dutch owned).[12]

The Saudis exercised strict control of the destination of their exports. They required tanker captains carrying Saudi oil to sign affidavits stating their destination and to confirm delivery upon their arrival in order to prevent mid-ocean diversions. Arab diplomats also monitored public records of oil imports by country of origin. Saudi oil minister Sheikh Ahmad Zaki Yamani made it clear to ARAMCO officials that the company had to follow the Saudi government's orders on enforcing the embargo and production cutbacks. Noncompliance would result in nationalisation. Company officials complied, arguing that cooperation would maintain the flow of Arab oil to non-embargoed nations.[13]

By the end of October the cutbacks and embargoes were firmly in place, creating three classes of countries: embargoed countries received no Arab oil; "friendly countries," defined as countries that aided the Arab cause, would receive 100 per cent of their September level of imports; and "neutral countries," would get what remained after the embargoes, cutbacks and the needs of friendly states had been met. Yamani summarised Arab oil policy as follows: "If you are hostile to us you get no oil. If you are neutral you get oil but not as much as before. If you are friendly you get the same as before."[14]

The net impact on crude production was almost 20 per cent, because Saudi Arabia and Kuwait calculated their cutbacks after reducing their production by the amount going to the United States and the Netherlands. At its meeting in Kuwait on 4 November, OAPEC increased the cutback level to 25 per cent, 20 per cent plus the promised 5 per cent monthly increase for November. The ministers decided, however, to include the volume of embargoed oil in the 25 per cent, thus reducing the actual impact of the increase.[15]

Sharing the pain

Unlike the supply disruptions in 1956 and 1967, the 1973 disruption occurred at a time when there was little spare productive capacity outside the Middle East. Proven oil reserves in the continental United States peaked at 39.9 billion barrels in 1968, and US oil production peaked in 1970 at 11.3 million barrels per day (bpd).[16] Alaskan oil would not be available until the mid-1970s, and North Sea oil was also not yet available. Venezuelan reserves declined during the 1960s as the oil companies shifted the focus of their operations to the Middle East, and Venezuelan production began a gradual decline in 1970. In contrast, oil reserves in the Middle East (including North Africa) increased from 126.2 billion barrels in 1955 to 433.7 billion barrels in 1972, around two-thirds of the world total. Middle East (including North African) production reached almost 24.7 million bpd in 1973, around 42.2 per cent of world oil production of 58.5 million bpd and over half of non-Communist world production. The major Arab oil producing countries accounted for almost one-third of world oil production in 1973, with production of over 18.7 million bpd.[17]

As a result of these changes, Middle East oil had come to play a crucial role in the world energy situation. In Western Europe and Japan oil had replaced coal as the chief source of energy, and by 1973 accounted for 58.5 per cent of total energy consumption in Western Europe and 75.1 per cent in Japan. Around 70 per cent of Western European and 40–45 per cent of Japanese oil imports came from Arab producers; thus Arab oil accounted for over 40 per cent of total Western European energy consumption and over one-third of total Japanese energy consumption. Arab oil constituted a much smaller share of US oil imports and energy consumption, but the high absolute level of US oil consumption and the key role of oil in transportation made even this small amount significant in the face of supply difficulties. After the United

States ended its Mandatory Oil Import Program in April 1973, the import share of US oil consumption rose to 36.3 per cent for 1973, with about 25 per cent coming from Arab producers, including products refined in the Caribbean and Europe (1.6 million bpd out of 6.6 million bpd). Oil supplied around 45 per cent of US energy consumption, with Arab oil accounting for around 5 per cent of total US energy consumption.[18]

Thus while the embargo targeted the United States and the Netherlands, Western Europe and Japan would be the hardest hit by the cutbacks in production. In addition, the embargo on the Netherlands magnified the impact of the cutbacks because Rotterdam played a strategic role in the European oil system. Around 80 per cent of the crude oil imported by the Netherlands, some two million bpd, was re-exported to other European countries as refined products. Although OAPEC sought to mitigate this situation by promising other countries supplies to compensate for the loss of oil going through the Netherlands, logistical and other problems made it difficult to replace oil from there. As a result, the embargo against the Netherlands also disrupted supplies to Belgium, Luxembourg, and West Germany.[19] If the cutbacks continued and were increased, there was little that Western European countries could do to avoid oil shortages in the short run.[20]

As a result of these actions, Arab oil production in November 1973 was around 5 million bpd less than in September. Other countries, including non-Arab OPEC members increased their production slightly, so the net decline was around 4.4 million bpd. Due to the differences in shipping times—it took tankers around a month to travel from the Persian Gulf to Western European and the United States and three weeks to reach Japan—countries like West Germany, which imported large amounts of oil from Libya, were affected earlier than countries whose imports came from the Persian Gulf.[21]

In 1956–57 and 1967, governments in the consuming countries had taken the lead in allocating oil supplies to deal with the disruptions. This worked largely because there was ample spare productive capacity outside the Middle East. In addition, in the earlier instances overall Arab production remained steady or declined only slightly. Therefore it was possible, if complicated, to rearrange supply routes to make sure countries got the oil they needed. The problem in 1973 was that there was almost no spare productive capacity outside the Middle East, and Arab producers cut back production at a time when oil consumption was increasing at a high rate. Therefore any allocation scheme would have to focus on sharing less oil.

The British and French, along with most members of the European Economic Community (EEC), opposed government oil-sharing plans because they feared that government action would lead the Arab states to extend the embargo to them as well as to the Netherlands, thus reducing the total amount of oil available to Europe.[22] In addition, the Europeans and the Japanese argued that any allocation scheme should be based on the percentage of total energy supply each country lost as a result of the embargo and cutbacks. Under such a scenario, the United States would have to reduce its imports even further to help its allies make up for their losses. The United States argued that an allocation scheme should be based on the volume of lost imports. Under such a scenario, more oil would be diverted to the United States due to the embargo against it.[23] Given the political obstacles to either scheme, the United States and the other consuming countries let the oil companies handle the allocation process.

The companies decided to "spread the pain" by allocating existing supplies as equitably as possible among importing countries. The oil companies feared that failure to redistribute supplies equitably could provoke consuming country governments to take measures that would curtail their operational freedom and profits. On the other had, they feared that if they violated the embargo they would suffer nationalisation or less favourable participation agreements. In these circumstances, the companies essentially decided that they would try to comply with the letter of Arab directives while meeting the requirements of the embargoed nations by spreading the reduction in supply due to the embargoes and the production cutbacks throughout the world and not targeting specific nations.[24]

On 6 November, the European Economic Community (EEC) issued a statement calling for Israeli withdrawal from the occupied territories in accordance with UNSC 242 and recognition of the legitimate rights of the Palestinian people. Two weeks later, OAPEC announced that in appreciation of EEC support for a settlement based on UNSC 242, the planned cutback in production for Europe in December would not take place. After the Japanese government issued a similar statement on 22 November, the Arab states announced that Japan would also be exempt from the December cutbacks. A week later, the Arab states added South Africa, Rhodesia, and Portugal to the embargo list.[25] Although the OAPEC decision to cancel the production cutbacks for December mitigated the European and Japanese supply situations to an extent, Western governments remained concerned about what would happen if the cutbacks resumed and/or increased.[26]

The US response

The United States wanted to break the Arab oil boycott, but had little success convincing the Saudis to end the embargo. King Faisal remained angry at the United States for supporting Israel and determined to maintain the embargo until Israel withdrew from the occupied territories, allowed the return of the Palestinians to their homes, and gave up its claim to sole sovereignty over Jerusalem. Faisal also insisted that any settlement would have to have the support of Kuwait as well as Egypt and Syria.[27]

The crisis gave added urgency to efforts to change US energy policies to make the nation less dependent on imported oil. On 7 November, President Nixon delivered a nationwide address urging energy conservation and proposing "Project Independence." Invoking "the sprit of Apollo" and the "determination of the Manhattan Project," Nixon set the goal of the United States developing by the end of the decade "the potential to meet our own energy needs without depending on any foreign energy source." In the short run, Nixon called for greater use of coal, conservation of oil, relaxation of environmental regulations, more funding for oil exploration and development, and increased production from US naval oil reserves. Nixon also asked Congress to approve long-pending legislation that would authorise construction of the Alaskan pipeline, promote the use of natural gas, and relax standards for mining coal. On 16 November, Congress passed the Trans-Alaska Pipeline Authorization Act with newly sworn-in Vice President Gerald Ford casting the tie-breaking vote in the Senate. Congress also extended mandatory allocation authority to all fuels. Present Nixon signed both measures into law in late November.[28]

It would take a long time for most of these measures to have an impact. Meanwhile, there were discussions within the US government over the possibility of using force to end the embargo. Secretary of

Defense James Schlesinger discussed use of military force to secure Middle East oil during bilateral meetings with members of the NATO Nuclear Planning Group in early November, emphasising that the United States would not let itself "be driven to the wall" and would not tolerate "blackmail." On 15 November, Schlesinger told the British ambassador to the United States, Lord Cromer, that "overt acquiescence in Arab bullying" by the Europeans had strengthened the Arab position, adding that British actions would cause the first Lord Cromer, nineteenth century British statesman Evelyn Baring, to roll over in his grave. Lord Cromer replied that they were no longer living in the nineteenth century, "when gunboats were in fashionable use." Clearly upset about being "pushed around," Schlesinger argued that Arabs would use similar tactics in the future since they were getting away with it, and that "it was no longer obvious to him" that the United States should not use force.[29]

Kissinger publicly aired the possibility of US use of force at a 21 November press conference, stating: "if pressures continue unreasonably and indefinitely, then the United States will have to consider what countermeasures it may have to take. We would do this with enormous reluctance, and we are still hopeful that matters will not reach this point." In his memoirs, Kissinger wrote, "These were not empty threats. I ordered a number of studies from the key departments on countermeasures against Arab members of OPEC if the embargo continued. By the end of the month, several contingency studies had been completed."[30] The Saudis complained about Kissinger's remarks, and Yamani warned that if the United States tried to use force to counter Arab oil policy, the Saudis would destroy their oil facilities, thus denying the West access to its oil for many years.[31]

Schlesinger, who had raised the possibility of occupying Saudi Arabia as early as 10 October, later told interviewers that he had been prepared to invade Abu Dhabi, because its location made it a good spot from which to project power into the rest of the region. Schlesinger apparently planned to make use of already scheduled military exercises in the Persian Gulf as a cover for intervention.[32]

Evidence on this matter is scarce, and somewhat contradictory. At times, Kissinger seemed sympathetic, though at other times he seemed opposed to the idea. In a staff meeting on 26 October, for example, Kissinger stated: "I know what would have happened in the nineteenth century. But we can't do that. The idea that a Bedouin kingdom could hold up Western Europe and the United States would have been absolutely inconceivable. They would have landed, they would have divided up the oil fields, and they would have solved the problem."[33] After White House Chief of Staff Alexander Haig told Kissinger on 27 October that Schlesinger had mentioned "putting troops in crucial states to get oil." Kissinger responded that Schlesinger was "insane," and added, "I do not think we can survive with these fellows in there at Defense— they are crazy." At a meeting on 3 November, Kissinger brought up the topic of seizing oil fields himself, though possibly only to please Schlesinger who was present.[34]

The British government took Schlesinger's statements seriously and commissioned a study on the possibility of the United States using force against Arab oil producers. The British study concluded that if the United States intervened before exhausting all possibilities of a peaceful settlement, the consequences for European interests would be "disastrous," especially if the intervention curtailed rather than expanded access to oil. While Schlesinger apparently thought that seizing Abu Dhabi would intimidate the other producers, the British believed that the only way intervention would succeed would be to seize all the fields, with the Saudi fields being the most important. This would be a huge task that would take some time, increasing the likelihood of major damage to the oil fields.[35]

Although Kissinger and Schlesinger continued to mention using force in private meetings, the United States did not take military action, in part because analyses indicated that US military action would probably result in destruction of the oil facilities the United States was trying to control. Moreover, as the British analysis made clear, most European countries would oppose the use of force except as the last resort. The ongoing talks between Egypt and Israel also lessened tensions and raised hope that drastic actions could be avoided.[36]

What impact, if any, these threats of military action had on the Saudis is difficult to evaluate in the absence of Saudi sources. The Saudis decided to allow ARAMCO to deliver oil to US military forces in the Pacific and the Mediterranean as long as they did so discreetly. Fiercely anti-Communist, King Faisal was especially determined that US forces in South East Asia continued to receive the oil they needed. ARAMCO was able to do this without drawing any attention, though the deliveries were interrupted briefly in late December after the head of ARAMCO let the secret slip to lower level Saudi officials and word got back to Yamani. The Saudis agreed to overlook the indiscretion and quickly resumed deliveries.[37]

The Saudis also decided to accept a US guarantee of Israeli withdrawal from Arab lands rather than completion of withdrawal before they would end the embargo and production cuts. Reflecting the Saudi position, OAPEC issued a statement on 9 December that linked the ending of the embargo against the United States and the production cutbacks to US guarantee that Israel would withdraw from the occupied territories, including Jerusalem, according to a negotiated timetable. Saudi Arabia also announced that it would postpone its scheduled 5 per cent December cutback. After the meeting, Yamani explained that production increases could begin as soon as Israel accepted the principle of withdrawal from all Arab lands and the United States guaranteed Israeli compliance.[38]

To put further pressure on the Arab states, Kissinger urged the main oil consuming nations to coordinate their policies in a speech in London on 12 December. Kissinger called for the creation of an international Energy Action Group (EAG) composed of producers and consumers to explore ways to ways to increase production and use energy more carefully. Concerned that such an organisation would antagonise the producers and that the US policies were the source of the problems, the Europeans were reluctant to agree to the US plan. In addition, the Europeans correctly suspected that Kissinger wanted to use the oil crisis as a means of re-asserting US leadership of the Western alliance.[39]

Higher prices and continued embargo

The Persian Gulf members of OPEC met in Tehran in late December to discuss the price of oil. Iran had received over $17 a barrel for oil it offered on the spot market earlier in the month, and the shah argued that oil prices should be set at the value of alternative sources of energy. On this basis Iran proposed a price of $11.65 a barrel for Arabian light crude, which was now designated as the "marker" crude, the base from which to calculate differential prices for other crudes. This would yield a government share of $7.00 a barrel. Iraq and Algeria, which sent a delegation to the meeting although it was not a Gulf country, wanted a government share of at least $10 a barrel, which would result in a posted price of $14 a barrel. OPEC's Economic Commission argued for a government take of $14 a barrel, which implied a posted price of around $23 a barrel. The Saudis argued that the high prices cited by the Iranians and others were not true market prices but rather represented the unique conditions created by the embargo and production cuts. Higher prices, they warned, could ruin the economies of the oil importing countries, leading to a reduction of their demand for oil, which would damage the oil exporting countries. Saudi Arabia suggested a government share of $5 a barrel, which meant a posted price of around $8 a barrel. In the end, however, the Saudis went along with the Iranian price as a compromise between the higher and lower proposals. Due to the way the oil companies' taxes were calculated, the companies' margins on total sales, and hence their revenues, increased automatically as prices rose.[40]

According to Kissinger, the price increase was "one of the pivotal events in the history of this century." The CIA had already estimated that the oil price increase announced on 16 October would raise the US and Japanese oil import bills by about $3 billion a year each and Western Europe's bill by $8 billion. The new price would double these amounts for the developed countries and have a sharply negative impact on oil-importing developing countries. The shah's role in pushing for higher prices put the United States on the spot. Iran did not participate in the embargo or production cutbacks, and increased Iranian production played an important role in mitigating their impact. In addition, the United States looked to Iran to take over Britain's role of guardian of Western interests in the Persian Gulf. These factors made it difficult for the United States to oppose the shah openly. Although Kissinger later tried to minimise the shah's role in the price increases, he sent a messages to the shah in the president's name on 29 December that argued that the price increases would have a "catastrophic" impact on the world economy and strongly urged that the increases be reconsidered. The shah, however, believed the new prices were justified, and refused to consider lowering them.[41]

In an OAPEC meeting a few days later, the Arab states announced that they were reducing their production cutbacks from 25 per cent to 15 per cent effective from 1 January 1974, and were cancelling the 5 per cent cutback scheduled for January 1974, thus making more oil available on world markets. They also granted a few "friendly" countries, including the United Kingdom, which was experiencing a nationwide coal strike, preferences to allow them more than their September 1973 import level, creating a fourth category of countries: most favoured countries that received their current demands rather than just their September 1973 level. Britain, France and Third World countries that had broken relations with Israel were in the new category. The embargo against the United States, the Netherlands and the others would, however, continue.[42]

President Nixon wrote to President Sadat on 28 December that unless the embargo against the United States was lifted at once, the United States would find it difficult to continue to support the peace process. Nixon sent a similar letter to King Faisal the same day.[43] On 2 January, Kissinger publicly called for an end to the embargo in a press conference, noting that the United States was not considering countermeasures "at this moment." Five days later, Schlesinger publicly warned that reprisals against the oil producers were possible. In a press conference on 10 January, Kissinger let Schlesinger's threat stand by remarking that the secretary of defense was speaking about contingencies that might arise, noting that the point where the United States might take action had not yet been reached. In response, Yamani and the Kuwaiti minister of foreign affairs warned that their countries would destroy their oil installations in the event of US military intervention.[44]

Concerned that the Europeans and Japan were weakening the consumers' position by seeking bilateral deals with the Middle East, President Nixon on 9 January 1974 invited the major industrial nations to participate in an energy conference to be held in Washington. The public US position was that the conference of consumers was not aimed at OPEC, and Nixon proposed that all OPEC members should meet with the consumer nations ninety days after the consumer conference. The clear purpose of the conference, however, was to develop a consumer group to improve the bargaining position of the consumer nations, as Kissinger bluntly admitted at a staff meeting at the end of January. As noted earlier, Kissinger also hoped to use the oil crisis as a means of reasserting US leadership of the Western alliance.[45]

The main consuming countries met in Washington from 11 to 13 February. Most European nations, including the United Kingdom, desired a more independent role for Europe, but also were reluctant to follow the French in openly opposing US policies. Unable to promote alliance cohesion by providing oil to its allies, the United States resorted to threats and warnings to try to gain cooperation. In his toast at the beginning of the conference, Nixon suggested that failure of Europe and Japan to follow US leadership on energy matters encouraged isolationism in the United States and those who called for the United States to withdraw its troops from Europe. Kissinger warned that failure to solve the energy problem cooperatively "would threaten the world with a vicious cycle of competition, autarky, rivalry, and depression such as led to the collapse of world order in the 1930s." The conference approved the creation of an energy coordination group, which resulted in the creation of the International Energy Agency in November 1974.[46]

Although Nixon announced in his state of the union address at the end of January that the embargo was about to end, the Saudis insisted that the embargo would not end until a disengagement agreement had been reached on the Syrian front as well. At a press conference on 6 March, Nixon warned that if the embargo against the United States was not lifted at the OAPEC meeting scheduled to begin in Tripoli on 13 March, the US diplomatic effort would be undermined. Privately, however, the United States moved to strengthen its military and economic ties with Saudi Arabia. In addition to military training and technical assistance, the United States recommitted itself to protecting the Saudi regime against its internal as well as its external enemies. Although the agreements were not signed until June, Nixon and Kissinger saw them as a way to influence Saudi oil policies. The Tripoli meeting agreed to ease restrictions, and the Arab states agreed to end the embargo on 18 March. The same day the Saudis announced that they would immediately increase oil production by 1 million barrels a day. Syria and Israel signed a ceasefire agreement on 31 May.[47]

Assessing the impact

Although the effects of the embargo and production cutbacks were barely noticeable by the time they ended, initially they sharply reduced the amount of oil available in international markets. Arab oil production in November 1973 was around 5 million bpd less than in September, but after November, Arab production rose gradually until the end of the embargo in March 1974 because after November the Arab states decided not to implement the 5 per cent cuts each month as originally threatened. Also, as noted earlier, Iraq refused to participate in the production cutbacks, and between September and December, Iraqi production increased 7 per cent. Non-Arab oil production expanded modestly through January 1973 and then remained constant. As a result, world crude oil production increased after November 1973 though it remained below September levels.[48]

Crude oil production, September 1973 through March 1974
(In millions of barrels per day)

	9/73	10/73	11/73	12/73	1/74	2/74	3/74
Arab	20.8	19.8	15.8	16.1	17.6	17.9	18.5
Non-Arab	38.4	38.9	39.0	39.3	39.6	39.5	39.5
Total	59.2	58.7	54.8	55.4	57.2	57.4	58.0

Source: *FEA Report*, 7.

In addition, declining demand in the consuming countries blunted the impact of the Arab supply restrictions. The drop in oil consumption resulted from a combination of milder than usual winters in the United States and Western Europe, higher prices, conservation measures, and an impending recession. The decline in oil consumption in the major oil importing countries varied. Consumption in Japan and Canada increased between January and April 1974, compared to the same period in 1973. US consumption over the same period fell by 6.9 per cent, while consumption in the United Kingdom, France, West Germany and Italy fell by 11 per cent.[49]

Consumption in major consuming areas (in millions of tons)

	1–4/73	1–4/74	Change
United States	220.9	205.8	−6.9%
United Kingdom, France, West Germany, Italy	152.2	135.4	−11.0%
Canada	26.4	28.1	+6.5%
Japan	81.5	82.4	+1.0%
Total	481.1	450.7	−6.3%

Source: *FEA Report*, 8.

In the period, December 1973 to April 1974, the United States received 12 per cent less oil (crude and products) than in the same period in 1973. Western Europe received 13.6 per cent less oil while

Japan received 1 per cent more. Although these figures seem to indicate an apparent inequity in the allocation of restricted supplies, they do not take into account different growth rates in energy demand. Before October 1973, Japanese energy demand had been growing at an annual rate of approximately 17 per cent, compared to a 5 per cent growth rate in the United States and Western Europe. When the projected growth in demand is taken into account, the US shortfall was 17 per cent, the Western European 18.0 per cent, and the Japanese 16.0 per cent.[50]

As noted earlier, the oil companies sought to distribute the shortfall in supplies equitably. The most difficult logistical problem was how to supply the embargoed countries. The United States was importing around 2 million bpd of Arab oil when the embargo began and received almost no oil from Arab producers during the embargo. Although this represented only a small percentage of total US oil and energy consumption, in absolute terms it was a large amount of oil. To replace embargoed Arab oil, the companies increased the flow of oil from Venezuela, Iran, Nigeria and Indonesia to the United States, with the embargoed Arab oil going to markets in Europe. US imports from Venezuela increased 3.3 per cent, from Iran 41.8 per cent, from Nigeria 66.9 per cent and from Indonesia 28.8 per cent. US imports from the Caribbean, mostly transshipped Iranian oil but also some Arab oil, increased 131.4 per cent. Without these shifts, US oil imports would have declined almost 30 per cent.[51]

Although Western Europe received from 13.8 to 18 per cent less oil (depending on how the shortfall is calculated) during the period October 1973 to March 1974, the impact was minimal after November 1973. Indeed, Western Europe as a whole maintained stocks of 80 days' consumption throughout the period. The oil companies, mainly Shell and BP, rerouted non-Arab oil (mostly from Iran and Nigeria) to the Netherlands, and, in general, took care to spread the pain of the cutbacks. As a result of the sharing Britain and France did not receive the full benefit of being considered friendly countries by the Arabs. Britain received slightly more oil than the European average, but this result was due to the response of the oil companies, with OAPEC's blessing, to provide more oil to Britain during the energy emergency created by the national coal strike. Japan's needs were met by crude oil from Indonesia and Iran, though after Japan joined the ranks of friendly states some Iranian oil destined for Japan was replaced by oil from Qatar.[52]

Redistributing Arab oil required changes in tanker runs. Fortunately, the embargo occurred at a time of surplus capacity in the tanker market. Although the lack of deepwater ports in the United States made the redistribution of supplies more complicated, the development of refinery and trans-shipment facilities in the Caribbean helped mitigate this problem. There were also technical constraints on redistributing oil supplies. Refineries were set up for specific crude oils, and processing crude oil with different sulphur content and/or different gravity could cause serious damage to refineries as well as reduce their efficiency and profitability. This limited ability of the oil companies to change crude inputs. Pipelines were also designed for certain types of oil, thus adding to the complexity of redistributing oil supplies.[53]

The disruptions that occurred were largely due to the difficulty and expense of rerouting so much oil and to government policies. Most governments were wary of drawing down reserves, since they did not know how long the crisis would last. Governments also tried to protect their economies by securing favoured treatment from the oil companies or by imposing restrictions on the trans-shipment of supplies. Despite having national oil companies, Britain and France fared little better than countries that were forced to rely entirely on the international oil companies, although BP, at the request of the British government, discreetly redirected some shipments to Britain. In the United States, efforts to cope with reduced supplies were complicated by price controls on oil (originally imposed in August 1971), and by regulations that sought to protect independent oil refineries and to achieve a geographically even sharing of the shortfall.[54]

It is difficult to assess the political impact of the embargo and production cutbacks. While use of the oil weapon helped focus attention on the problems of Israeli occupation and the plight of the Palestinians, the Arabs gained little politically in the long run, in part because Kissinger was not interested in solving these problems.[55] In addition, while serious oil shortages did not occur, the embargo and production cutbacks caused disruptions and contributed to the sharp increase in the price of oil, which further undermined sympathy for the Arab position in Western public opinion.

Higher oil prices intensified the economic problems faced by the United States and the other Western industrial countries in the 1970s, especially inflation, which was now accompanied by stagnation and increased unemployment. The cost of importing larger amounts of more expensive oil also had a significant impact on economic growth and the balance of payments of the United States and other importing countries.[56] The economic effects of the oil crisis contributed to the collapse of Keynesianism and a new era of conservative political hegemony and to increasing inequality in most countries.[57]

Although the oil producers' success in increasing their revenues encouraged Third World demands for a new international economic order, the long-term impact undercut the position of most developing countries.[58] Non-oil-producing developing countries were hit especially hard as they had to pay higher prices for oil at the same time as demand for their exports dropped, due to the impact of high oil prices on the economies of their key customers. The United States opposed efforts to set up compensatory funding arrangements through the International Monetary Fund, managing to keep such funding at a very low level. As a result, petrodollars were recycled through the private banking systems. The banks, flush with petrodollars from the oil-exporting countries, were eager to lend and offered low interest rates, and many countries borrowed more than they could afford, a move that contributed to the Third World debt crisis of the 1980s when interest rates rose sharply in late 1979.[59]

The sharp rise in oil prices resulted in greatly increased revenues for the major oil-producing countries. OPEC members' revenues jumped from $13.7 billion in 1972 to $22.6 billion in 1973 to $87 billion in 1974, and reached $122.5 in 1977. Increased revenues allowed the major oil-producing countries to take over ownership, and thus full control, over their oil resources. In almost every case, the producing countries already owned their oil reserves. What the oil companies possessed were concessions that allowed them to control the production and distribution of the oil. In the late 1960s, the major producing nations declared their intention to participate in the ownership and control of their respective oil industries, calling for a gradual and compensated takeover of the oil facilities in their countries. The oil crises, by providing the producing countries with extra revenues and the confidence to assert their prerogatives, led to a massive buy-out of the major producing firms and the establishment of national oil companies in the producing countries. In 1970, national oil companies owned less than 10 per cent of their oil industries; by 1979, the figure was almost 70 per cent.

Full ownership of all aspects of their oil industries gave producing countries greater control over such factors as the pace of development of their reserves, the rate of production, and the destination of their exports.[60]

The increase in Iranian oil revenues, from $2.4 billion in 1972 to $17.8 billion in 1974 and $21.2 billion in 1977, spurred extravagant military spending, inflation, massive rural–urban migration, and increases in already sharp inequalities in wealth and income. The weapons systems bought by the shah also brought thousands of Western technicians and military advisers into Iran, inflaming conservative fears of corrosive Western influence and swelling the ranks of the shah's opponents. A decline in real oil prices in 1978 and decreases in government spending caused economic problems and sparked the outbreak of widespread demonstrations against the shah. By the time the US government realised what was happening, it was too late to save the shah, who fled Iran in January 1979.[61] The turmoil surrounding the Iranian Revolution disrupted oil supplies and markets, and led to a further doubling of oil prices.

The oil crisis also influenced the course of the Cold War. Conservative critics of détente erroneously viewed the October War as an attempt by the Soviets to expand their influence. Coinciding with the US withdrawal from Vietnam, the Watergate crisis, a wave of revolutions in the Third World, the Soviet Union's achievement of nuclear parity with the United States, and the decline of US manufacturing as a result of increased competition from Western Europe and Japan, the oil crisis reinforced perceptions of a weakened United States. In addition, US popular culture tended to equate the private automobile and personal mobility with individual freedom, so high oil prices seemed to strike at the American way of life.[62]

In contrast, the Soviet Union benefited from higher oil prices. As new fields in western Siberia entered production, the Soviet Union overtook the United States as the world's leading oil producer in 1974. Although most Soviet oil exports went to Eastern Europe, Cuba and Vietnam, hard currency earnings from oil exports to Western Europe and Japan rose sharply and by 1976 were responsible for half of the Soviet Union's hard currency earnings. The windfall from higher prices allowed the Soviets to import large amounts of Western grain and machinery. On the other hand, the cost of developing Siberian oil, including the necessary transportation infrastructure, drained scarce capital from other sectors of the economy. Oil earnings also tended to mask the Soviet Union's increasingly severe economic problems, and by giving the illusion of continued viability to a system that was already in serious trouble reduced incentives for undertaking sorely needed structural reforms. The revenue gains from oil earnings may also have helped finance increased Soviet involvement in the Third World in the 1970s, actions that proved costly not only in terms of resources but also in their negative impact on détente.[63]

Finally, the sharp increases in oil prices in the 1970s set in motion a series of developments that over time lessened the influence of Middle East oil in the world oil economy. Higher prices led to more efficient use of oil, a slowing in the growth of oil consumption, and the replacement of oil with other energy sources, especially coal and nuclear power, in electricity generation. Higher prices also spurred development of oil fields outside the Middle East, and the collapse of the Soviet Union led to increased production and exports from the Caspian and increased exports from Russia. The result was a decline in the Middle East share of world oil production.

Middle East Share of World Oil Production (Percentage)

1973	1975	1980	1985	1990	1995	2000	2005	2010
42.2	40.2	35.6	23.8	32.4	35.1	36.5	36.6	35.7

Source: *BP Statistical Review of World Energy, 2012.*

In addition the United States set up a Strategic Petroleum Reserves to guard against future shortages. In 1980, President Jimmy Carter announced that the United States would use military force if necessary to defend access to Persian Gulf oil, and three years later the United States established a new military command dedicated to this mission. Although these developments reduced the likelihood of a reoccurrence of the oil crises of the 1970s, the Middle East still contained a large portion of world oil reserves and productive capacity and still played a vital role in the world oil economy. Maintaining access to Persian Gulf oil was a key objective of the U.S. response to the Iraqi conquest of Kuwait in August 1990, and concerns about oil were a factor in the US decision to invade Iraq in March 2003.[64]

12

ASHRAF MARWAN AND ISRAEL'S
INTELLIGENCE FAILURE

Ahron Bregman

Dr Ashraf Marwan, President Gamal Abdel Nasser's son-in-law and later President Anwar Sadat's close adviser was recruited by Mossad, the Israeli Intelligence Agency, in 1970, and went on to provide his Israeli handlers with startling information on Egypt's preparations for war. Within Israel's intelligence community he was regarded as "a miraculous source". But a growing school of thought maintains that Marwan was a double agent, planted by Egyptian intelligence to feed Israel false information—the jewel in their crown and crucial to Egypt's plan of deception in the lead-up to the October 1973 War. This article analyses the role Marwan played in the years leading up to the war, assesses his contribution to Israel's intelligence failure before the war, and argues that whether Marwan was loyal to Israel, or an agent planted by Egypt, the result was the same: namely that Israel fell into the trap of raising his status to such an extent that he became a "super-source", blinding Israel to those other intelligence sources that could have saved her from being caught by surprise on 6 October 1973.

A personal note

In a chapter on the October War in *Israel's Wars*, published in 2000, I hinted at the identity of a senior Egyptian who was, as I put it, "the right-hand man" of Egypt's President Anwar Sadat, but who was also a Mossad agent.[1] I contended that this person, whose name was still top secret, was actually a double agent who was serving Egypt at a time when Israel considered him a super-spy on her behalf, and that he successfully misled Israel's intelligence services in the run-up to the 1973 War. In a *History of Israel*, published two years later, I again referred to this mysterious spy by saying, this time, that he was "a very close family member of Egypt's President Nasser" and that in Israel he was dubbed "The-Son-in Law".[2]

On 2 December 2002, the Egyptian newspaper *Swat al Umma* asked Nasser's son-in-law, Dr Ashraf Marwan, to answer whether he was the person at the heart of my story. Marwan's reply that it was all "a silly detective story" upset me a great deal and I responded by giving a counter-interview to the Egyptian newspaper *Al Ahram al Arabi* where I confirmed that the "Son-in-Law" in my book is indeed Ashraf Marwan, the son-in-law of President Nasser. Noting Marwan's dismissive remark regarding my claims as being "a silly detective story", I said that "I have to defend my good name as a historian and I cannot accept this". I added that "Ashraf Marwan was a model spy. He was a very professional spy. He succeeded in tricking Israel. He is the person who more than anyone else should be credited with Egypt's success in deceiving Israel before the October 1973 war."[3] The interview was published in Egypt on 21 December 2002 under the heading, "Ashraf Marwan a perfect spy and national hero", and with that the identity of the most important spy who ever worked for Mossad and perhaps in the Middle East was revealed.

Soon after this public spat someone phoned me at home identifying himself as "the man you've written about"; the person on the line was Ashraf Marwan. We had a polite but brief conversation at the end of which Marwan added: "I want to say three more things to you: One, I'm not challenging you [regarding your double-agent claim]. Two, you have your enemies and I have mine—don't listen to my enemies. Three, we should meet up when I'm better ... but don't listen to my enemies".[4] This was the beginning of a five-year relationship, which included one face-to-face meeting on 23 October 2003 at the Intercontinental Hotel on Park Lane in London and scores of telephone conversations, some of which I noted down for the record.[5]

On 26 June 2007, Marwan telephoned me three times within an hour and a half, and each time he phoned he left me a voice message; this was very unusual as in the five years I had known him he had never left me an answer machine message.[6] Later in the afternoon we had quite a long telephone conversation and arranged to meet up the next day near King's College London, where I teach; Marwan said he would phone my office to confirm exactly where and when we would meet.[7] But the next day he failed to make contact and later, after I had given up waiting for him and returned home, I learned that around the time we were due to meet Marwan had fallen to his death from the balcony of his London home in Mayfair.

A police investigation ensued, during the course of which I was interviewed three times by Scotland Yard detectives, keen to know more about my relationship with Marwan, the meeting that never was, and the manuscript of his memoirs on which he had been working and that mysteriously disappeared on the day he died (I had been helping him put them together). After a three-year investigation, the police handed over their findings to a judge whose task it was to determine what had happened to Marwan on that fateful day. At the request of the Marwan family I was summoned to give evidence: to testify about our planned meeting and about the manuscript of his memoirs. But at the end of three days of deliberations the judge failed to determine whether Marwan killed himself or was murdered; whether he jumped or was pushed.

In hindsight, to unmask Marwan as a spy was a colossal error of judgement on my part, but the positive outcome of what came to be known as the "Marwan Affair" is that it opened up the gates to a huge amount of new writing about the October War and the crucial, though not yet fully explained, role Marwan played in it.

Marwan and his work with Mossad

Ashraf Marwan was born in Egypt on 2 February 1944 into a middle-class family. He studied chemistry, served in the Egyptian army, and in 1966 married President Nasser's third daughter, Mona. In 1968, Marwan started to work in the Presidential Information Bureau, where he served under the information secretary, Sami Sharaf. The bureau's main task was to gather intelligence on political, military, social and other matters and give it directly to the president. Towards the end of 1968, the Marwans moved to London where Ashraf embarked on his Master's degree, and during this time he also carried out special diplomatic missions for his father-in-law, the president; he was a charming but also a very decisive and daring young man.

In July 1970, while in London, Marwan contacted the Israeli embassy asking to talk to a security person; twice his request was rebuffed as the Israeli representative failed to recognise him. But Marwan tried again, left his name and, in December, when the matter was reported to Shmuel Goren, head of the Mossad centre in Europe, he at once identified that the caller was President Nasser's son-in-law and a meeting was arranged.

Marwan offered to spy for the Israelis, and the impression they received was that money was an important motive in offering his services.[8] In Tel Aviv, the director of Mossad, Zvi Zamir, and his head of the Humint (human intelligence) department, Rehavia Vardi, decided to take a risk and recruit Marwan in spite of him being a "walk-in"—a person who volunteers to work for an espionage agency rather than being recruited on the agency's initiative after much hard work. Walk-ins are notorious for being potential double agents and the Israelis were aware that this could be an Egyptian plot to deceive them.[9] But Zamir and his team believed that Marwan was probably not a double agent: first, because it is difficult to handle double agents for a long period of time and only very professional intelligence agencies can do so; the Israelis thought that the Mahabharat, the Egyptian intelligence agency, was not sophisticated enough to carry out such a task successfully. Second, from an Egyptian point of view, using the president's son-in-law as a spy carried with it too many risks; he could be killed or taken prisoner by the Israelis. Third, already in his first meeting with the Israelis Marwan had provided them with such extraordinary information that the Israelis thought he was just too good to be given to them voluntarily by Egyptian intelligence—even as a way to try and plant a spy among their ranks.[10] Yet, to reassure themselves that Marwan was reliable, the Israelis tasked him with bringing key documents that would prove his bona fides; indeed, the papers—and oral explanations—Marwan subsequently provided, which included, among others, protocols of talks between President Nasser and Soviet leaders during Nasser's secret visit to Moscow in early 1970, impressed the Israelis a great deal; when Marwan's information was checked against data obtained from other intelligence sources it proved to be reliable.[11] Still careful not to fall into an Egyptian trap, the Israelis set up two committees, one of Mossad members, the other of joint Mossad and Military Intelligence members, to keep an eye on the contact with Marwan.

In subsequent weeks and months the connection between Marwan and Mossad was institutionalised: he received a code name, "The Angel", after the popular British TV series "The Saint", which in Israel was translated as "The Angel", starring Roger Moore as Simon Templar. Also, a case officer was appointed; his name was Dubi Asherov, but Marwan only knew him as "Alex": he would serve as Marwan's handler throughout his career with Mossad. Israel's Military Intelligence was also involved in handling Marwan; an officer, expert on Egyptian affairs, Lt. Col. Meir, would often join meetings with Marwan to ask specific questions. Mossad director Zamir would meet Marwan too, in part in order to impress on him the importance Israel put on his services and also to reassure himself that Marwan was reliable.

Under Nasser's successor, Anwar Sadat, Marwan was promoted to replace Sami Sharaf as the head of the Information Bureau, a promotion, of course, which also benefited Mossad, as the new post would give Marwan even better access to Egypt's top secrets. Indeed, in August 1971 Marwan handed over to his case officer Asherov, the Egyptian war plan, an extraordinary document detailing how in a future war Egyptian forces would cross the Suez Canal over five bridges. Marwan also provided the Israelis with a detailed document on the commands, formations and units of the Egyptian army, as well as the weapons used by the various units.

Marwan and the birth of "the Concept"

On the basis of Marwan's extraordinary information the Israelis soon recast their entire pre-October War strategy—to be known as "the Concept".

At its heart was the thinking that Egypt would not wage war against Israel without first acquiring from the Soviets certain "deterring" weaponry, namely fighter bombers with a capacity sufficient to drop large bombs on Israeli cities and Scud missiles to deter the Israeli air force from attacking Egyptian centres of population, lest Egypt retaliates in kind.[12]

199

Indeed, in November 1971 Israel's Military Intelligence, basing its assessment on Marwan's documents, observed that "the absence of certain weaponry to attack deep in Israel ... is one of the strongest restraints ... Holding back the Egyptian regime from authorising an immediate resumption of war against Israel ..."[13] Additionally, according to "the Concept", Egypt would not launch war against Israel on her own without direct Syrian participation, as success in war against Israel required an attack on her from two directions to force her to split her forces.

Adhering to "the Concept" meant that, practically speaking, all Israel had to do was monitor Egyptian airfields and other entries into the country for evidence that the above weapons had arrived in Egypt, for if the Egyptians were to acquire such weapons, and if the Sinai were still in Israeli hands, then after a period of training and assimilation, Egypt would be ready for a military attack on Israel and would most likely strike. But until such time, Israel felt that she was safe from attack.

That this strategy (which later came under intense criticism) was not a mere theory invented by the Israelis themselves, but that it came entirely from their best spy, Marwan, we also know from Moshe Dayan, Israel's legendry defence minister on the eve of the 1973 War, who said in a later interview:

The "Concept" was not the invention of a mad-genius in Israel's military intelligence, nor of the head of Military Intelligence, nor of the Defence Minister, but it emerged from very critical information which we thought was the best one could have acquired ... this information which became the foundation of the "Concept" was checked in every possible way and was found out to be authentic and accurate. I can say in full confidence that any intelligence agency in the world, and any defense minister or chief of staff who would have got this information and would have known how it was obtained [a reference to Marwan—AB] would have come to the same conclusions.[14]

"The Concept" which formed the essence of the Israeli strategic thinking before the October War is a prime example of just how dominant Marwan and his information had become in Israel's decision-making process in the years before the October War.

Marwan's warnings of war

Within a very short period of time after his recruitment, the Israelis started regarding Marwan not just as a provider of critical information but also as a "warning agent" who would raise the alarm should an attack on Israel become imminent. Indeed, in subsequent years Marwan would provide Mossad with warnings of imminent attacks, and because the Israelis held him in such high esteem they took his notices very seriously and often acted upon them even when they had other contradictory information.

In November 1972, Marwan reported to his Israeli handlers that President Sadat had decided to launch a war against Israel and that it would happen "before the end of the year".[15] This warning caused a huge stir in Israel, where the military increased its state of alert; but no war broke out. Then in April 1973, Marwan warned again that war was imminent—and he even provided his Mossad case officer Asherov with a specific date, 19 May; the arrival in Egypt on 7 April of a squadron of sixteen Hunters and sixteen Mirage warplanes served to strengthen the view in Israel that Egypt would indeed strike. In response to Marwan's warning—and against the advice of Military Intelligence—the Israelis, on 19 April, embarked on a massive mobilisation of their reserve forces, speeded up military purchases and crystallised preparations for war. But the Egyptian attack did not materialise and on 12 August the forces were dispersed. This futile mobilisation cost Israel a fortune, some $45 million, and irritated many, in particular the minister of finance. But these two false warnings of war that never actually materialised did not in any way damage Marwan's status in Israel, where he continued to be held as a most reliable super-spy.

But there were also, as we now know from information that has been released over the years, at least two critical events in Egypt of which Marwan must have been aware but which he failed to report to the Israelis, or when he did there was something unusual about his reports. The first took place on 23 August 1973 in Alexandria, where a joint Syrian–Egyptian armed forces supreme council took—indeed, for the first time—a firm decision to embark on war against Israel and put a date on it. The second event took place on 28 August 1973, when Marwan was the only Egyptian official sitting in a secret meeting between President Sadat and King Faisal of Saudi Arabia, where—following the aforementioned Alexandria meeting—Sadat notified the Saudi king that Egypt would launch war against Israel, "soon, very soon..." Strangely, in his report Marwan said that Sadat had decided to postpone the war.[16]

On 4 October 1973, Marwan contacted his case officer Asherov from Paris, where he was on a visit with an Egyptian delegation, to report that he wanted to discuss "lots of chemicals", which was an agreed code word for a warning on war, and added that he would like to meet in person "the general", which was a reference to General Zamir, director of Mossad, on the following day.[17] Zamir hurried to London, landing there on 5 October, and met Marwan for more than an hour, receiving a specific warning from him that Egypt and Syria would strike on Yom Kippur, 6 October.[18] Marwan's warning reached Israel at 2.45 in the morning of 6th October and triggered Israeli preparations for war which, as it was understood from Marwan's report, would start at sunset.[19]

The trap of the master spy

> "I'm not a superman"
> Marwan to Bregman, 6 October 2006 [20]

Ever since the 1973 War there has been a heated debate in Israel between two opposing schools of thought: those who maintain that Marwan was a double agent and the linchpin of a shrewd Arab deception that for years leading up to the war fooled the Israelis into believing war was unlikely; and those, notably the director of Mossad in 1973 and one of Marwan's handlers, Zamir, who insisted that Marwan was a valued agent and "Israel's best source ever".[21]

A double agent?

Of course there was always the fact that Marwan was a "walk-in": an agent who offered his services to Mossad unprompted, rather than being selected and recruited by them. This is one reason to suspect that he might have been a Trojan horse, planted by Egyptian intelligence. Mossad agents who followed Marwan's movements in London before and after meeting his handlers testified that they were astonished by his self-confidence: he would arrive at meetings, some of which took place close to the Egyptian embassy, driving an Egyptian diplomatic car, and walk straight into the meetings with the Israelis without so much as glancing over his shoulder. This can be seen as recklessness—and indeed there was such a streak in Marwan's character—or else perhaps as confidence that he was safe meeting the Israelis, in the knowledge that he was really there on Egypt's behalf.

After the October War Israel's Military Intelligence was blamed for failing to see that war was in the offing; amidst this fallout they embarked on an attempt to establish whether Marwan was a double agent, as some of them had suspected all along. Their investigation was "inconclusive", which—putting it differently—showed that they were at least unable to rule out the possibility that indeed Marwan has fooled them.[22]

And there are other indications to show that Marwan might have been a double agent, working primarily for the Egyptians. As shown, he provided Israel with the data which would become the foundation of "the Concept", the view in Israel before the October War that obtaining certain weapons—Scuds and long range bombers—was an absolute precondition for Egypt to go to war against Israel. However, when President Sadat realised that the Soviets would not provide him with the required weapons and decided, in principle, to embark on a limited war against Israel without the Scuds and bombers, Marwan, who must have known about the change in policy, failed to notify the Israelis. He thus left them clinging to a strategy ("the Concept") which was no longer valid and which led them to neglect any contradictory information showing that war was on their doorstep, and so directly endanger their own security.[23] So much so that, even when war was on their doorstep— less than two weeks before it broke out—on 24 September 1973, director of Military Intelligence General Zeira still observed that acquiring bombers to strike deep into Israel continued to be, from the Egyptian point of view, "a precondition to go to war and this precondition is unlikely to be realised before 1975".[24]

A further indication to strengthen the view that Marwan was misleading Israel is that twice before the war, in the autumn of 1972 and spring of 1973, he warned them that Egypt would embark on war, but in both cases war failed to materialise. Both warnings led to major preparations and mobilisation of forces in Israel, and the maintenance of a high state of alert before the units were eventually dispersed. Those who suspect that Marwan was fooling Israel maintain that Marwan provided these warnings in order to lessen Israel's apprehension of war by increasing the effect of the "cry-wolf syndrome"; and also to enable the Egyptians to monitor how Israel would react in such emergency situations so they could recast their own military plans accordingly.[25] What strengthens this point of view even more is that, as described above, the first time a firm decision to embark on war against Israel was actually taken—by the joint Syrian–Egyptian armed forces supreme council meeting in Alexandria on 23 August 1973—he failed to mention it to his handlers. The question is on what evidence was Marwan acting when he provided Israel with the November 1972 and April 1973 warnings? We now know from information released in Egypt after the war that the Egyptians had no intention of going to war during these months; for instance, in his memoirs President Sadat writes that he had no intention of starting a war in the spring of 1973, "but as part of my strategic deception plan I launched a mass media campaign then and took various civil defence measures which led the Israelis to believe that war was imminent".[26] General Gamasy, the Egyptian director of operations, also said, referring to the spring 1973 activities in Egypt that led to the Israeli mobilisation, that the actions were "something we did … to deceive Israeli intelligence".[27] And General Fuad Awidi of the Egyptian army intelligence service said in an interview: "The exercises and mobilisations in [the spring of] 1973 were part of our deception plan."[28] Given these testimonies, it seems plausible that Marwan's false warnings that fooled the Israelis twice were part of that Egyptian deception plan; and this would explain why, when on 28 August Sadat sat down with the Saudi king and told him that war against Israel would happen "soon, very soon", Marwan—who had been in the room with Sadat and the king—reported to the Israelis that Egypt had delayed plans for war. Why else, if not to deceive them?[29] Director of Military Intelligence Zeira, a prominent member of the school of thought that believes that Marwan was a double agent, writes in his memoirs that the fact that Marwan concealed crucial information by failing to report, for instance, on the 23 August Alexandria meeting, while at the same time sending soothing signals to the Israelis that war was delayed, indicates that Marwan was indeed "the jewel in the crown of the Egyptian deception plan."[30]

Finally, the warnings which Marwan did provide the Israelis on the eve of war, just 40 hours before it started in fact, increases the suspicion that he was misleading them. Surely, he must have known further in advance than 40 hours, and must equally have known that such a short notice period could not possibly provide the Israeli military with sufficient time to prepare fully for war and reach the fronts in time to rebuff the Arab attack. The Egyptian General Gamasy writes in his memoirs that in the Egyptian General Staff it was agreed that should Israel find out about the plans to attack her 48 hours or less before it started, then

Egypt would proceed with the attack anyway, because the Israelis could not possibly manage to bring enough reserves to the front.[31] So why did it take Marwan so long before issuing the critical warning? And why did he fail to provide a full and specific warning of war on the very day he contacted his case officer Asherov on 4 October? He said to the Israeli that he wanted to talk about "lots of chemicals", which was a code word to warn of a general, non-specific, danger of war; in his arsenal Marwan had much more specific code words which he could have used, thus leaving the Israelis more time to mobilise. Instead, he summoned the director of Mossad to come to London on the next day to whisper in his ear the specific warning of war. But that meant that this final specific warning was issued just before the outbreak of war, much too short a warning for the Israelis.[32]

And even when providing this late warning to Zamir, it seems that Marwan was misleading him again, for his warning was that war would start at "sunset" whereas in reality it opened at 2 in the afternoon. The Israelis, wanting to act on this information but also wary of revealing that they had advance knowledge of the attack, had planned to move their tanks into front-line positions at 4 p.m. But by that time on 6 October it was too late, as their positions were already overrun by the invading enemy.

A genuine spy?

Most of those who worked with Marwan in the past and some academics too, notably the leading Israeli authority on this war, Professor Uri Bar-Joseph of Haifa University who had access to authentic documents related to this period, insist that Marwan was a reliable and trustworthy agent, fully committed to Israel. He did not, they claim, intentionally cultivate "the Concept" about Egypt's preconditions for war, namely that she would only attack after obtaining Scuds and bombers which could enable her to reach Israeli population centres. Furthermore, they claim, in November 1972, when Marwan first warned the Israelis that Sadat had decided to wage war, it must have become clear to the Israelis by implication—even if Marwan did not spell it out exactly—that this precondition had been dropped.

That Marwan provided two false warnings—in 1972 and in April 1973—in order to foster a "cry-wolf syndrome" is also rejected by those believing he was a genuine spy, as Israel, they claim, also received these warnings from a number of other sources.[33] Israel, it is worth noting here, had another top spy in Egypt—an army general with superb access to all military information—and he too, most probably, provided critical information. And anyway, they go on to claim, the warning Marwan gave to Israel in 1972 reflected Sadat's genuine wish to go to war against Israel; it is known from memoirs of Egyptian military commanders that on 24 October 1972 he called them to his residence in Giza where he insisted that Egypt would have to go to war with existing weapons without waiting any longer. In the end, and for various reasons, he delayed the war. Similarly, in April 1973, Marwan's warning reflected Sadat's decision to embark on war in mid-May, a decision he was forced to postpone only because Syria, a vital ally in such an endeavour, was not ready for war.[34] Furthermore, say those who believe that Marwan was a genuine spy for Israel, to deliver intentionally two false war warnings makes no sense, since in addition to eroding Israel's war awareness, it could also erode Marwan's own credibility.

As for the warning which was given to the director of Mossad on 5 October just 40 hours before the war, claim those who believe that Marwan was not fooling his handlers, he would not have provided it at all if he was really working for Egypt; for although, as said, Egyptian war planners estimated that the Israelis needed more than 40 hours to deploy fully for war, even short notice, like that Marwan provided, was better than nothing at all. Uri Bar-Joseph, maintains that Marwan's 5 October warning was "the most important piece of intelligence which the state of Israel ever received."[35]

And then the H Hour: while Marwan said that war would start "at sunset", in reality it started at 2 in the afternoon and the question is whether, as the double agent school of thought maintains, Marwan misled Israel on purpose. However, those who believe Marwan insist that he could not have known about the change in the H hour, as the original time to start the war was indeed at sunset, but this was later changed in a secret meeting between Syria's President Hafez al-Asad and Egypt's war minister Ahmed Isma'il three days before the beginning of the war, and by that time Marwan was already in Europe and thus could not have known about the change.[36] It is interesting to note that Marwan himself, in a meeting with me, dismissed the entire thing out of hand as irrelevant; "a few hours", he said, "why does it matter at all?"[37]

What is more, claim those who believe Marwan to be a genuine spy for Israel, in their meeting in London, Marwan gave director of Mossad, Zamir, an updated Egyptian war plan—a plan that had been kept secret even from those in Egypt who knew about the coming war. This plan could have given the Israelis a major advantage when the fighting started; a spy working for the Egyptians would surely never have provided such an aid.

* * *

It seems that we will never know for sure whether Ashraf Marwan was committed more to Egypt than to Mossad or vice versa, not least because the two schools of thought have a strong case and both lack enough information—as is often the case with intelligence matters—to refute altogether the other side's point of view. And it might be, as Rafi Eitan, a former Israeli intelligence officer, claims, that even Marwan himself was not so sure whether he was working for the Israelis or the Egyptians. I believe, having known Marwan reasonably well from the day I unmasked him in December 2002 to the day he died on 27 June 2007, as I have put it elsewhere, that, "Ashraf Marwan worked for both Israel and Egypt ... he did so, in my opinion, not entirely for money, nor because of ideology ... but simply because he was intrigued by the espionage game. Having said that, when the moment of truth came to decide between Israel and Egypt, he obviously opted for the latter, because at the end of the day, he was an Egyptian and it was there his loyalty lay ..."[38]

Shlomo Gazit, who succeeded Director of Military Intelligence Eli Zeira following the latter's dismissal in the wake of the war debacle, makes the point in a recent article that, whether Marwan was a double agent, or a genuine spy committed to Israel is beside the point.[39] For Gazit, the main Israeli fault was that they elevated Marwan's position to such a high status that his views and information overshadowed whatever else was said or obtained from other intelligence sources. What strengthened Marwan's position even further, according to Gazit, was the decision of the then director of Mossad Zamir to take a step that runs against the fundamental principles of intelligence and disseminate the original reports obtained from Marwan to a group of top decision-makers in Israel: Prime Minister Golda Meir, her defence minister

Dayan, the IDF chief of staff and some others. In normal circumstances information gathered by Mossad would go first to Military Intelligence and they would produce reports based on the raw material which would then be submitted to the decision makers. Zamir, however, felt that providing Marwan's raw material to the Israeli leadership, without touching it at all, could help them to understand better how the Egyptian mind ticks. This, in hindsight, was a risky practice as it greatly increased dependency on Marwan's colourful reports, which included oral comments on the atmosphere and the moods of Sadat and others in various meetings, and inevitably weakened other estimations, notably the typically dull reports provided by Military Intelligence.

In the three weeks before the outbreak of the October War an incredible amount of information was accumulated in Israel, clearly showing that both Egypt and Syria were preparing to launch war. In normal circumstances such enemy troop movements along its borders would have led Israel to mobilise her reserves fully and move the entire nation into a higher state of alert. But nothing of the sort was done as all eyes were fixed on what the super-spy—Ashraf Marwan, would say.

If Marwan was planted by the Egyptians to fool the Israelis, then he did his job extremely well—and the Israeli failure can perhaps be understood, as it is no mean feat to catch a good double agent. On the other hand, if Marwan was not planted by Egyptian intelligence services and if he was a reliable and loyal spy to Israel, as many maintain, then Israel fell into a trap of her own making by turning him into such a powerful influence on their decision-making process at the expense of other important sources that could have prevented the catastrophe of October 1973.

The conclusion—unlike much of Marwan's life and intentions—is clear, and not linked at all to the unresolved question whether Marwan was a double agent or not: no intelligence agency or government should rely so heavily on one single source. While it is always good to have such important sources as Marwan, it is a mistake to turn them into "super-sources", because every source can in the end disappoint. As Marwan once told me, "I'm not a superman."

13

EVOLVING A DIPLOMATIC LEGACY
FROM THE WAR

THE US, EGYPTIAN, AND ISRAELI TRIANGLE

*Kenneth W. Stein**

Introduction

In advance of the 2012 congressional elections, a New Mexico senatorial candidate recently asked, "What is the most striking difference between Middle Eastern Arab political systems and ours in the United States?" The response was: "In the US, there is institutional leadership; in the Middle East, leaders are institutions themselves." For more than a thou-

---

* The interviews listed here, unless specifically noted as undertaken by another author, were carried out by me during a twelve-year research period that produced *Heroic Diplomacy: Sadat, Kissinger, Carter, Begin and the Quest for Arab–Israeli Peace* (Routledge, 1999). The Hebrew version of the book, *Medinuit Amitza* [Courageous Policy] (Tel Aviv: Ministry of Defense Publishing House), appeared in 2003. The findings from the interviews were systematically reinforced by data secured from the Freedom of Information Act, use of presidential archives, and published memoirs. The interviews conducted for *Heroic Diplomacy* have been digitised and will be made available for public use beginning in 2015.

sand years, dynastic, tribal and autocratic regimes have dominated Arab politics, bureaucracies, militaries and governments. They have existed at the local, national and regional levels." There are many examples: the Meccans, Umayyads, Buwayids, Abbasids, Fatamids, Almoravids, Osmanis, Saudis, Rashidis, Hashemites, Sabahs, Tikritis, etc. In the last century, how different would Palestinian Arab politics have been if the Mufti of Jerusalem, Hajj Amin-al-Husayni, and the head of the PLO, Yasir Arafat, had not dominated their community and undermined alternative political voices at virtually every turn?[1] Since the political upheaval that began across the Arab world in late 2010, the general public's vitriol and revulsion have been aimed at domineering autocrats. Since Mohammed Morsi's summer 2012 election in Egypt, rampant conjecture has revolved around his political direction and his relationships with the Egyptian military, the Muslim Brotherhood, Iran, Hamas, the Egyptian parliament and foreign powers. The cry for change across the region has called for reducing the dictatorial roles of imperious rulers, elite cronyism and corruption. So far, the change has focused on who rules, rather than by what rules of governance inhabitants might be assured their basic rights.

Anwar Sadat, the president of Egypt from 15 October 1970 to 6 October 1981, remains one example (among many) of an autocrat who controlled and manipulated an Arab political system.[2] Both Sadat's predecessor and his successor were equally proficient at domineering, one-man rule. Each was an autocrat with peculiar characteristics, but they were autocrats. So, also, were his contemporaries in Syria, Iraq, Jordan, Libya, Morocco, and all around the Arabian peninsula. After Sadat rebuked challenges to his presidential rule within a year of taking office, he asserted authoritarian control over domestic politics and foreign affairs. At one point prior to the October War, he made himself prime minister as well as president. He developed a historiography that glorified himself as Egypt's pharaoh of the moment. In Arab–Israeli negotiations, Sadat willingly became the essential catalyst. By sheer force of will, he drove the negotiation process forward. He was impatient, yet understood how to use other political actors, personal predispositions and political realities to achieve his single most important national objective: the full return of the Israeli-held Sinai peninsula, which had been lost by his predecessor, Gamal Abdel Nasser, in the June 1967 war. Restoration of Sinai was a necessary step towards regaining Egyptian national dignity, which was so mightily damaged in the June 1967 war. Nasser made the mistake of frightening Israel sufficiently to provoke a devastating pre-emptive military strike that lost Sinai in six days.[3] When he came to office, Sadat set about the task of righting Nasser's mistake. Without the loss of Sinai in 1967, there would not have been a territorial reason for Egypt to engage with Israel diplomatically. Thus, Nasser's decision to go to war, the loss of Sinai, and Sadat's drive to have it returned collectively culminated in partial Arab state acceptance of Israel. During Sadat's lifetime, Egypt signed military disengagement agreements with Israel in January 1974 and September 1975. From there until his trip to Jerusalem in November 1979, he kept the diplomatic process moving forward either openly, secretly, or along parallel tracks. In September 1978 and March 1979 he and Israeli Prime Minister Menachem Begin signed the Camp David Accords and the Egyptian–Israeli Treaty, respectively. The 1978 Camp David Accords were a "Declaration of Principles," or an outline on how to move forward in resolving the Palestinian–Israeli component of the conflict. It was another "disengagement agreement", only this time relating to Israel's potential disengagement from the West Bank and Gaza Strip. The 1991 Madrid Middle East Peace Conference could not have taken place if Egypt and Israel had not sustained their treaty relationship; in fact, no further diplomatic process would have been possible had Israel not fully withdrawn from all of Sinai and had the United States not remained centrally engaged in Arab-Israeli diplomacy. The 1993 Oslo Accords signed between Israel and the PLO and subsequent Israeli–Palestinian agreements provided additional substance, though not a conclusion, to that element of the conflict. The convocation of the 2007 Annapolis Middle East Peace Conference was predicated on direct negotiations between the parties—the formula that Egypt and Israel developed from 1973 through 1979; it was applied and reinforced by the 1994 Jordanian–Israeli Peace Treaty and American-led efforts in 2000 to restart Syrian–Israeli negotiations.

No analyst, casual observer, diplomat, historian or political scientist, friendly or otherwise, doubts the important function the United States played in unfolding and catalysing modern Arab–Israeli diplomacy. In these difficult and episodic negotiations, the US played many roles: critic, convener, drafter, engineer, friend, guarantor, hand-holder, mediator and postman. No other national bureaucracy had the number of skilled, knowledgeable and experienced diplomats to "work the issue." No other team of diplomats remained as intrepidly dedicated to pushing for elusive, seemingly impossible interim and final agreements. In the 1970s, Secretary of State Henry Kissinger and President Jimmy Carter were vitally important in dedicating the White House to moving Egyptian–Israeli diplomacy forwards. Both are appropriately given due praise for their dedication and accomplishments, though at times neither was fully aware of the complexity of inter-Arab political jealousies. At times, both inserted US national interests or their own personal biases into the diplomatic processes. Sometimes the US, as mediator, wanted an outcome or a pace that neither the Egyptians nor Israelis preferred. Immediately after the October 1973 War, both countries could have reached a military and political agreement if left to their own devices, but Kissinger—as will be shown below—intervened to stop the negotiations dead in their tracks. He wanted the military agreement to conclude in the aftermath of the December 1973 Geneva Middle East Peace Conference. He needed the agreement to come after the conference, so he could demonstrate his control over the negotiations; it was a means of showing Moscow who was in charge. Neither Sadat nor Israel's Begin particularly liked the Carter administration's preferences for a comprehensive agreement. Sadat had told the Israelis, according to Israeli Defence Minister Dayan, "that the question of the Palestinians, the West Bank, the refugees in general, and Jerusalem were less a priority than occupied Sinai."[4] Neither Egypt nor Israel wanted any procedure that slowed down the pursuit of a bilateral arrangement. Of course, Sadat gave public notice that he was always interested in a comprehensive peace, but when push came to shove in the autumn of 1978, he did not stop negotiations because either Syrian or Palestinian interests were not being fulfilled. Neither Israel nor Egypt wanted the Soviet Union to play a diplomatic role in renewed negotiations. That point was expressly stated in the secret Israeli–Egyptian talks in Morocco in September 1977.[5] Nor did either country want their national priorities ensnared by the spider-web of procedures that emerged from the Carter administration's diplomatic cooking.

The bottom line remains: without Sadat's presence, vision, courage, and chutzpah, there would not have been any Egyptian–Israeli agreement or series of agreements. Israeli leaders, though, were also central to agreements with Egypt. They saw the need to neutralise Egypt's military power because of its potential to put Israel's security in deep and regular jeopardy. Nonetheless, the Israelis were inherently hesitant; they never really trusted Sadat, thinking of him as "mercurial" and "unpredictable," qualities that colleagues and diplomats alike have said that he possessed in "adequate quantities." To be sure, Sadat did not wake up one morning and say to himself, "I want peace with Israel, and to do that I want to go to the Israeli parliament and give a speech with a photo of Theodor Herzl looking over my shoulder." He negotiated with Israel and signed agreements and a treaty with Israel because they were a means to an end. Harnessing himself to the US had several desirable outcomes: Washington could support his economy and help supply his military with equipment; US diplomatic engagement meant that Israel's most important friend was supportive of a negotiating process in which Israel's security remained paramount; and he could demonstrate to a highly sceptical Israeli public, particularly after decades of Nasser's publically stated hatred for Israel, that Israel should take a chance on withdrawal from Sinai. Sadat also wanted to move out from under the influence of Moscow. He knew that inching Egypt closer to the US would reduce Soviet influence in Egypt, a move that Washington found strategically advantageous in the midst of the Cold War. Peter Rodman, who was part of Secretary of State Henry Kissinger's diplomatic shuttle missions in the 1973–5 period, categorised Egypt's shift from Moscow to the US as "one of the great victories for the United States" in the Cold War. In his relationships with Washington, Sadat was a masterful strategist: he anointed Kissinger his "ambassador" to Israel, and, according to Zbigniew Brzezinski (Carter's national security adviser), later "played Carter like a violin."[6]

When Jordan's King Hussein wanted his own disengagement agreement with Israel in 1974, Sadat quietly told Kissinger to remain focused on a Syria–Israeli agreement; the Jordanians were livid.[7] Sadat was beyond clever. In the middle of 1974 and again in 1975, when he was being accused of selling out the Palestinians by negotiating indirectly with Israel through the United States, Sadat endorsed the PLO as the "sole legitimate representative of the Palestinian people." That, too, angered the Jordanians, who wanted to negotiate for the future of the West Bank and, of course, Arab Jerusalem. But Sadat knew what the Israeli response would be. If the PLO was the only possible diplomatic address for negotiating the future of the West Bank, then (given its then passionate hatred of the PLO) Israel would never negotiate the return of the West Bank and Jerusalem. That suited Sadat just fine. It kept the focus of Israel's diplomatic attention on Egypt, away from the frigid complexities of the Palestinian–Israeli relations. Sadat's consistent method was to defend the Palestinians publicly, but privately work to isolate them from negotiations or planned talks. Arafat did not make good on his private promise to Brzezinski and Carter, made through a secret intermediary in March 1977, to recognise the legitimacy of UN Resolution 242. That kept the PLO out of the negotiating mix until the Carter administration introduced the idea of Palestinian representation in a "unified" Arab delegation at a reconvened international peace conference. The resulting summer 1977 undertaking was aimed at bringing Arabs and Israelis together to resolve all issues at one time, a concept that many in the State Department thought to be totally unrealistic. Sadat, too, was not enamoured with the idea; while the Carter administration spun its wheels on this procedure, Sadat engaged in a series of secret talks with the Israelis directly in Morocco and indirectly through Romania. If the Carter administration was going to get lost in procedural matters, it was not going to keep Sadat from determining Israeli readiness to negotiate for Sinai's return.

Sadat's purpose was to gauge whether the Israelis were prepared for direct talks. When the Carter administration moved to bring the Soviet Union into diplomatic negotiations in October, after the Israelis and Egyptians had agreed in secret exchanges not to support reintroduced Soviet engagement, Sadat decided that direct talks with the Israelis was one of the only ways to maintain progress on Egypt's objectives and priorities. At Camp David in September 1978, he told Carter that he would represent the interests of the other Arabs; Carter and Brzezinski naively believed him. While the Israelis and Americans regularly became testy with each other about settlement building, Sadat simply did not care to let the settlements issue stand in the way of Egyptian–Israeli negotiating progress[8] and the ultimate return of Sinai. These were examples of unsuccessful Carter White House injections to direct the negotiating process and seek outcomes that reflected American priorities, rather than those of the negotiating parties.

Why did Sadat go to war?

Sadat used war as a means to break the diplomatic freeze. War was not his first option. Or, if it was, he cleverly disguised it by trying the diplomatic route while also preparing for war. Sadat knew by April 1973 that diplomacy alone would not ignite a negotiating process. By showing a public and private diplomatic side to the sceptical Israelis, he encouraged them to feel relaxed in their military planning. As early as 1971, Sadat let American diplomats and the media know that he wanted a diplomatic process to restore Egyptian sovereignty over Sinai. First he thought about only having several hundred Egyptian policemen stationed in Sinai. This he would reciprocate with an interim agreement with Israel—not a treaty, but something less formal. Sadat said he was prepared to "recognise Israel, *if* there would be full withdrawal from all the occupied territories, with the first step being withdrawal from the canal to the strategic Giddi and Mitla passes in Sinai."[9]

Independently of Sadat's overture, at about the same time in the late winter of 1971, Israeli Defence Minister Moshe Dayan approached Israeli Prime Minister Meir with the idea of unilateral but only partial Israeli military withdrawal from Sinai. Dayan believed that if Israel withdrew sufficiently from the canal area, then the Egyptians would have reason to rebuild the Suez Canal cities and open the canal (which had been closed since the June 1967 war), which would have been the best assurance of Egypt's intention not to launch another war; on the other hand, Dayan said that "Israel had to be in a position if they [the Egyptians] violate our expectations, within hours we will be there to take care of the situation."[10] Dayan floated the idea to some Israeli newspaper editors and then to the general public, but he was unable to convince Meir and she did not approve it. She said, if "we retreat an inch from the canal....[we] will in no time land at the international border."[11]

On several occasions in 1971 and 1972, Sadat told Donald Bergus, head of the American interests section situated in the Indian embassy, that he was prepared to negotiate with Israel. He said the same thing in 1973 to Michael Sterner, the head of the Egypt Desk at the State Department. In early 1973 he sent his National Security Adviser, Hafez Isma'il, to Kissinger to explain carefully in secret talks that he and Egypt were prepared to sign an agreement with Israel. Isma'il made it clear to Kissinger in unambiguous terms that Egypt thought that "the end of the state of war will come with the final withdrawal of Israel from Egyptian territory. We shall acknowledge respect for the sovereignty, political independence and territorial integrity of Israel and the right to live in peace ... with the final withdrawal."[12] Isma'il did not say that after withdrawal

Egypt would sign a treaty with Israel, but he was precise about how ending the "state of war" with Israel would be defined. He did intimate that Egypt was not willing to normalise relations with Israel, and would withhold full recognition until Egypt knew that agreements were on the way to conclusion with Syria and Jordan. Isma'il said nothing about the need for a Palestinian state. Sadat told a *Newsweek* interviewer on 23 April 1973, "The time has come for a shock. Diplomacy will continue before, during, and after the battle. All West Europeans are telling us that everybody has fallen asleep over the Middle East crisis. But they will soon wake up to the fact that America has left us no other way out. The resumption of the hostilities is the only way out. Everything is now being mobilized in concert for the resumption of the battle which is inevitable." That month he met secretly with President Asad in Egypt and told him, "Hafez, I am going to war this year. What do you think? He said: I am with you."[13] Sadat was moved to action because the US, or more precisely Kissinger, was not prepared to engage as mediator.

Why not? Was it Kissinger's unfamiliarity with the Arab world and Arab politics? Was it that his view of readiness for the US to become involved in negotiations was framed by Israel's Prime Minister Meir, who remained highly sceptical of Sadat or his motives? Was it that the CIA and State Department relied too heavily on the Israeli intelligence assessments that the Egyptians simply could not and would not go to war? Since Kissinger jumped into the negotiations with such gusto at the war's conclusion, what kept the Nixon administration from engaging in serious negotiations prior to it? In the days just before Nixon's summit meeting with Soviet President Leonid Brezhnev in June 1973, Kissinger (after his meetings with Isma'il) summed up the limited possibilities and liabilities for engaging in Egyptian–Israeli negotiations: "The most the US can foresee [is] persuading Israel to accept restoration of nominal Egyptian sovereignty in the Sinai with a transitional Israeli security presence at key positions. This might not be full sovereignty but it would establish the principle of legal sovereignty. The question now is whether Sadat can accept a step-by-step approach with assurance of persistent White House involvement. The US needs to avoid the kind of concrete detail that would limit the usefulness of our involvement before we have even begun." Since Isma'il had specifically asked for direct American engagement in negotiations and in a step-by-step manner, why did Kissinger (not yet secretary of state, but only NSC head) still recommend caution to Nixon in regard to Egyptian–Israeli negotiations? What is certain is that Sadat was ready to negotiate, ready to give the mediating mantle to the Americans to do so, and accurate about US reluctance to take the initiative.

There is consensus from a variety of authoritative sources on why Sadat went to war. However, with the exception of Hafez Isma'il and Egyptian General el-Gamasy, his military chief of staff at least from the sources used for this paper, did not know the degree of detail Isma'il had provided Kissinger in regard to how talks could be conducted, namely "step-by-step," and to Egypt's readiness to sign an agreement or agreements with Israel at the end of negotiations. "The war was a pro-American move where he deliberately started an international crisis, aimed at lighting a fire under the United States."[14] It was designed to cause Washington and Kissinger to take notice, become involved, and ultimately arrange for Israel's departure from Sinai.[15] Before the 1973 War, Sadat told Zaid Rifa'i, King Hussein's political adviser and later Jordan's prime minister, that in order to have the Soviets and Americans pay attention to the Middle East, he had to start a war *"harb taharik mish harb tahrir"*—a war for movement, not a war for liberation. "For me, I [Sadat] shall cross the canal and stop."[16] By contrast, Syria's foreign minister, Abd al-Halim Khaddam, said: "For Syria, it was a war of liberation, not a war of movement. The objectives of the war were to liberate Golan and Sinai. The Syrian forces advanced according to that plan. The Egyptian forces, however, just passed the canal and stopped."[17] According to Nabil al-Arabi, Sadat entered the war "not to attain military objectives, but to influence the political process."[18] As per a later assessment by American diplomat Joseph Sisco and his deputy, Roy Atherton, Sadat went to war because he could not get negotiations started otherwise. Said Sisco: "The decision to go to war was precisely to get what he wanted, namely, a negotiation" started.[19]

Either by luck, cleverness, or a combination of both, Sadat used the war's muddled outcome to promote his own national interest: to begin to achieve the restoration of Sinai to Egyptian sovereignty. Sadat told el-Gamasy that "this was not a war for the Palestinians or for the other Arabs; it was for Egypt."[20] Sadat was not prepared to make peace with Israel; according to Usamah al-Baz, later his key foreign policy adviser: "His concept of peace with Israel was something like non-belligerency, opening the Suez Canal, and ending the Arab boycott in exchange for all of Sinai with security arrangements, providing they would be under-taken astride the international border [between Egypt and Israel]."[21] In preparing for the war, Sadat was neither naive about his own military capabilities nor unrealistic about Washington's willingness to preserve Israeli security. Sadat believed that US intervention, on Israel's side, at some point during a war was likely, to prevent either an Israeli military defeat or major loss of territory. Sadat understood quite well what his limitations were militarily, even with Syria as a full partner in the Octo-ber War. Sadat realised that through military means, the Egyptian army could not dislodge Israel from all of Sinai. His war goals were limited to piercing the Israeli Bar-Lev Line on the East Bank of the Suez Canal and perhaps, if the option presented itself, driving to the western side of the Giddi and Mitla passes, some 25–30 miles into Sinai.[22] In an interview with me, Hafez Isma'il (then Sadat's national security adviser) recounted that "Sadat wanted the heat of the battle to be a force behind the politi-cal decisions which had to be taken. He was in a hurry; he would not let things cool down."[23] Sadat was the engine and motivation for Washing-ton's reengagement in Arab-Israeli diplomacy. He unfurled a negotiating process from the war to provide for Egypt's domestic needs; and he saw the possibility of a political settlement, not exclusively for Egypt, but for Egypt first.[24]

Sadat, of course, could not choreograph the actions of all the players in the conflict once the October War began. Prior to the war, he did arrange with the Saudis to impose an oil embargo on countries that supported Israel. He could not have predicted the actions of either Mos-cow or Washington, though he hoped that when the war ended Mos-cow's role in the post-war diplomacy would be marginalised. He could not have predicted that, when his troops crossed the canal so quickly, the Israelis would successfully counter-attack and surround 15,000 Egyptian soldiers of his Third Army—leaving their fate dependent upon the goodwill of Israeli leadership, which was inspired by a powerful inclination towards outright retribution against Egypt for the surprise attack on Yom Kippur day. Ultimately, the Third Army was left in the hands of Secretary of State Kissinger, who knew that the army's survival would give Sadat additional reason to depend on US diplomacy. Sadat could not have surmised when he went to war on 6 October that the US and the USSR would find themselves on the brink of conventional mili-tary, if not nuclear, confrontation over the matter of the Third Army. He could not have predicted that his capture of Israeli prisoners of war and the absolute priority of their immediate return to Israel, as demanded by Israeli Prime Minister Meir, could allow for the survival of his Third Army. Nor could he have guessed that the UN Security Council Resolution (UNSCR) 338 would be passed, sanctioning "direct negotiations between the parties." He was not yet ready to embrace such a procedure, but UNSCR 338 established an internationally sanctioned atmosphere under which indirect Egyptian–Israel talks would take place until Sadat went to Jerusalem on 19 November 1977. He could not have predicted that the post-1973 Egyptian–Israeli military talks at Kilometer 101 would evolve so successfully that he would have to countenance their early suspension—so Kissinger would have a partial agreement that he could build on after the conclusion of the December 1973 Geneva Conference. Those military talks resulted in the detail and the maps that Kissinger used in finalising the 13 January 1974 Egyptian–Israel Disengagement Agreement. Did he surmise that, by promoting Egyptian national interests, he would be opening an angry competition with Syria? Did he realise that this competition would allow Syrian President Asad to use creeping Egyptian–US closeness to deepen Syria's ties with Moscow? When Asad turned down Kissinger's invitation to attend the December 1973 Middle East Peace Conference a week before it was to commence in Geneva, Sadat achieved one of his purposes for going to war: to keep Syria from obstructing a negotiating process that promoted Egypt's interest first.

The Kilometer 101 talks to the January 1974 Egyptian–Israeli agreement: how Sadat managed his desired outcome

On 27 October 1973, a German-born Egyptian career foreign service officer, Omar Sirry, who served as deputy chief of operations in the Egyptian Foreign Ministry, was called by Egyptian Foreign Minister Ismail Fahmy. This was three weeks after the outbreak of the October 1973 War, ten days after Israel launched a counter-attack against the Egyptian army in Sinai and eventually surrounded the 15,000-man Egyptian Third Army, and one week after American Secretary of State Henry Kissinger negotiated the contents of what came to be United Nations Security Council Resolution 338 in Moscow with Soviet Chairman Brezhnev. It was only a day after the United States and the Soviet

Union had stepped back from possible military confrontation over the intervention of Soviet troops into the canal area. Fahmy told Sirry to "get a toothbrush and pyjamas and be ready" to talk with Israelis. The primary Egyptian reason for attending such talks was to find immediate relief for the Egyptian Third Army, which was surrounded by Israeli forces. The destruction of the Third Army had the potential to destroy Sadat's presidency, not to mention jeopardising Sadat's newly expanded opening to the United States. By contrast, Israel's absolute priority was effecting a swift exchange of war prisoners and arranging the return of the remains of soldiers who had been killed during the war. Fahmy told Sirry that he had to be prepared to go to Suez. Fahmy had a large ego; he did not like playing the role of President Sadat's messenger. Moreover, he was not fully informed about Sadat's objectives, and was philosophically uncomfortable about having any discussions with the Israelis. Said Sirry: "Indicative of the psychological attitude that was prevailing at the time in Egypt, after so many years of fighting and opposing the Israelis, Fahmy found it very difficult to tell me that I was going to talk to them."[25] After a pause, Fahmy told Sirry that he was to go to military headquarters, meet General el-Gamasy, and become el-Gamasy's political adviser. Sirry attended the first meeting at Kilometer 101. He was accompanied by two or three other Egyptian foreign ministry and military officials in the approximately eighteen negotiating sessions that took place between Egyptian and Israeli representatives after the October War and lasted until the end of November 1973. Sirry said, "No one understood the political significance of what we were doing."[26]

El-Gamasy, who led the Egyptian negotiating team at the Kilometer 101 talks, was a career Egyptian military officer. He was a fierce Egyptian nationalist and professional soldier. He was motivated to restore the dignity and prowess of the Egyptian army, which was so demoralised by the Arab defeat in the June 1967 war. Moreover, for el-Gamasy and other high-ranking Egyptian officials, going to war in 1973 was a measure of personal revenge against Moshe Dayan, whom they thought was the "dark side" of Israel.[27] On the same day, Israeli General Aharon Yariv,[28] recently retired as head of Israeli Military Intelligence, was summoned by Prime Minister Golda Meir to Tel Aviv. During the October War, Yariv had not held an official military position. Meir told Yariv that he would be negotiating with an Egyptian counterpart at Kilometer 101. Yariv received his instructions from Israel Galili, a very close confidant of Meir and minister without portfolio in her cabinet. Galili made sure that Yariv did not give anything, say anything, propose anything, or affirm anything without prior approval and knowledge of the government. Galili told Yariv that Israel wanted a firm cease-fire, an exchange of prisoners of war, and a lifting of the Egyptian naval blockade of Israeli shipping at the Bab el-Mendab Straits.

The pending Egyptian-Israeli talks were unique in their countries' respective belligerent relationship: Egyptian and Israeli military officials were about to negotiate the separation of their forces without the United States or another party in a mediation role, and with the United Nations relegated to a mere gopher status. Kissinger realised that the Third Army needed to be saved; that was the most pressing political requirement. He readily consented to use US government channels to connect Egyptian and Israeli negotiators. Though Kissinger is credited with shaping that agreement, it was pre-negotiated by Sadat and Meir through their military representatives at Kilometer 101. Sadat outlined the content of the meetings, Meir refined them, and the generals at Kilometer 101 added detail to their framework—before Kissinger had the talks suspended so that he could use the parties in the Geneva Peace Conference, and eventually use the content they had already agreed upon as the basis for the January 1974 agreement.

A little after 1 a.m. on a bitter cold morning of Sunday 28 October, the initial Egyptian–Israeli negotiating session took place at a wooden table under a camouflage canopy stretched between four Israeli tanks. It was 101 kilometres from Cairo. Each general made short introductory remarks, noting that both armies had fought well and honourably and that both sides should now perform admirably in making peace. The content and tone of Yariv's comments alleviated the apprehension among the Egyptians that the Israelis would be arrogant. Sirry described Yariv as "sophisticated and calm. He did not shove anything down our throats. Had he been otherwise, the Egyptian delegation would not have accepted it."[29] El-Gamasy considered Yariv "a very fine man who knew his work very well."[30] Yariv believed el-Gamasy to be "a pedantic man, but a proud officer, Egyptian, and Arab."[31] Even as the separation of forces discussions took place, elements of the two armies remained engaged. As the talks continued that first night until approximately 4 o'clock in the morning, there were intermittent intrusions of gunfire, rockets and flares. For weeks after the commencement of the Kilometer

101 negotiations, the ceasefire agreed to on 23 October was periodically broken. El-Gamasy acknowledged that most of the violations came from the Egyptian side.[32]

Replying to Yariv, el-Gamasy refrained from answering most questions, saying a response had to await instructions from Cairo. El-Gamasy customarily reported back directly to President Sadat. El-Gamasy provided both verbal and written assessments of Israeli views on a variety of issues under negotiation, and the direction in which he thought they were heading. Likewise, Yariv repeatedly excused himself to phone his superiors in order to report information and to receive further instructions.[33] While the military men were negotiating, their civilian superiors were essentially making the decisions about the content of the talks, which obviously contained political implications, including their present and future respective relationships with Washington. After the end of the first negotiating session, Sirry and Fawzi al-Ibrashi, a legal specialist in the Egyptian foreign ministry, finished their report around 6 o'clock that morning and apparently hand-delivered it to President Sadat. Sadat informed Fahmy that he would immediately go to Washington to meet with Kissinger and told Fahmy exactly what he wanted from the trip.

In his memoirs, Fahmy claimed that he conceived the ideas that became the operational outline for the tactics and strategy of Egyptian negotiating policy. But Sirry, who took the notes in this 28 October meeting, said that Sadat provided the original detailed framework for the agreement he was seeking with the Israelis. Normally, Sadat's preference was not to focus on negotiating details, but in this case he paid unique attention to the diplomatic framework he needed to save the Third Army. Apparently, not until that meeting did Sadat have a written text of what he wanted to accomplish at the Kilometer 101 talks, afterwards, or how Kissinger would take control of the unfolding diplomacy.

The framework, which Sadat dictated and Fahmy took to Washington, included the following: "Israel would withdraw to the 22 October lines; all prisoners-of-war would be released; Israel would withdraw to a line inside Sinai east of the [strategic] passes, while Egypt's forces remained in place; UN forces would be deployed between the Egyptian and Israeli forces; after Israel started withdrawing to the disengagement line, Egypt would lift the blockade of the Straits of Bab el-Mendab; once the disengagement was completed, Egypt would start clearing the Suez Canal; within an agreed time, Israel would withdraw to the international frontier; at this point, belligerency would end."[34] Also included in the framework was an outline of steps to be taken to convene an international conference, and to restore diplomatic relations between Egypt and the United States. From the outset of Egypt's diplomatic effort, Sadat wanted all substantive issues agreed upon privately before ratification at a public conference.

By the time Kissinger met with Sadat for the first time in Cairo on 7 November 1973, Fahmy had already brought Sadat's ideas to Washington and had given them to Kissinger. Simultaneously, at the Kilometer 101 talks, Sadat had el-Gamasy tell Yariv that he would agree to separate military forces in phased periods of time, establish a UN monitored buffer zone between the opposing armies, and allow the repopulation of the cities along the Suez Canal. In their two-and-a-half-hour meeting on 7 November Kissinger persuaded a positively predisposed Sadat not to settle just for a separation of forces agreement reflective of the 22 October ceasefire lines, but for a larger disengagement agreement with considerably more significance.[35] This 7 November visit was pivotal in solidifying the concept of step-by-step diplomacy because "Sadat and Kissinger devised the "strategy of interim steps ... under the mantle of a conference to bless the interim steps."[36] For his part, Sadat did not need to be convinced of the merit of the step-by-step approach; the notion of liberating Sinai through stages or phases was inherent in the Sadat–Dayan exchange via Washington eighteen months earlier, and Hafez Isma'il suggested it to Kissinger in his secret meetings earlier in 1973. Kissinger also discussed with Sadat elements of the six-point plan which he had reviewed with Meir in Washington when she visited there on 4 November. In her delegation to Washington was Yariv himself, who had taken three days off from talks with el-Gamasy. What had transpired in the previous ten days? Sadat dictated an outline that emerged from the first Yariv–el-Gamasy meetings, Fahmy took it to Washington, Kissinger then presented the outline to Meir, who had seen it already and discussed it in full with Yariv, and then Kissinger took it back to Sadat on 7 November.

Kissinger was apparently surprised that Sadat accepted the six-point plan so quickly.[37] But why not? He and Meir, through their generals, had negotiated it. It was signed on 11 November at Kilometer 101. The six-point plan agreed on 11 November and the subsequent Yariv–el-Gamasy understandings at Kilometer 101 were not Kissinger originals;

they were hybrids parented by Sadat and Meir. The disengagement agreement drafted by Generals Yariv and el-Gamasy on 11 November 1973 contained the following general six points:[38]

1. Egypt and Israel agree to observe scrupulously the cease-fire called for by the UN Security Council.
2. Both sides agree that discussion between them will begin immediately to settle the question of the return to the 22 October positions in the framework of agreement on the disengagement and separation of forces under the auspices of the United Nations.
3. The town of Suez will receive daily supplies of food, water, and medicine. All wounded civilians in the town of Suez will be evacuated.
4. There will be no impediment to the movement of non-military supplies to the East Bank [of the Suez Canal where the Third Army was surrounded].
5. The Israeli checkpoints on the Cairo–Suez road will be replaced by UN checkpoints. At the Suez end of the road, Israeli officers can participate with the UN to supervise the non-military nature of the cargo at the bank of the canal.
6. As soon as the UN checkpoints are established on the Cairo–Suez road, there will be an exchange of all prisoners-of-war, including wounded.

In the moments after the signing ceremony was completed at Kilometer 101, and while the international media were taking pictures, the dialogue between Yariv and el-Gamasy went approximately as follows: "My dear General, what do you mean by disengagement agreement? It is listed in the six-point agreement, that phrase." El-Gamasy replied, "I said it means to place the troops away from one another." Yariv replied, "No… It is a Harvard expression and it is Kissinger who will put the explanation for it, and you and I will not be able to do anything about it until Kissinger says what he means by it."[39] El-Gamasy acknowledged the accuracy of Yariv's assessment. Both generals understood that the diplomatic negotiations involving political discussions would be ultimately transferred to Kissinger's control, but neither knew when or how that would happen. Neither general was yet prepared to deliver the negotiating prerogative to him.

After the signing ceremony, Yariv and el-Gamasy continued to negotiate the details of a disengagement agreement. Subsequent el-Gamasy–Yariv meetings took place at least every two or three days, each for several hours or more. Progressively, discussions became more and more specific. As meetings became increasingly amiable, Yariv replied with even more specifics.[40] Both generals strayed beyond the scope imposed upon them by their political superiors. Through el-Gamasy, the Egyptians suggested an Israeli withdrawal of 35 kilometres deep into Sinai, with UN observers separating the belligerent forces, and a zone for the drawn-down forces of both armies. The Egyptians worked out time schedules for a full Israeli withdrawal, accompanied by one for Suez Canal repair. They included discussion about force levels in main and thinned-out buffer zones, the number of buffer zones and their sizes, the number of UN personnel and where they would be stationed, what authority the UN would enjoy in relationship to Israeli forces, when Egyptian civilians would return to the Canal Zone, etc. El-Gamasy and Yariv went further. Considerable detail about the size of the buffer zones to be established was made public in a television interview given by Meir on 16 November and repeated by Dayan to a US Congressional delegation on 19 November. Three days later, Yariv and el-Gamasy agreed that "disengagement and separation of forces should be held for 3–6 months followed by successive Israeli withdrawals until a line agreed upon in peace negotiations is reached."[41] At the same meeting, Yariv dropped Israel's insistence that the Egyptian armies on the East Bank of the canal return to the pre-war lines. El-Gamasy and Yariv agreed that the main Israeli force should be somewhere between 35 and 45 kilometres east of the canal, disengagement and separation of forces should take place within six months with Egypt wanting the first disengagement completed by 15 January 1974, and the United Nations should man the different buffer zones to be set up between their respective armies. At their 26 November meeting, Yariv and el-Gamasy had concluded several options pertaining to the content and implementation of the disengagement agreement. There were five or six different proposals for the depth of Israeli withdrawal in Sinai. Yariv stated that Israel was ready to withdraw even beyond the strategic passes if Egypt would minimise its number of troops, tanks, and artillery on the western bank of the canal. Maps were exchanged at virtually every meeting in efforts to reach implementable compromises. After the negotiations and the details discussed at meetings between 19 and 26 November, some key disagreements remained over the number of forces each side would have in the different buffer zones, and the number, range capability, and kinds of weapons each could have in those zones.

On 28 November 1973, quite abruptly, Yariv told el-Gamasy that he could no longer discuss matters pertaining to the separation of forces.

The UN representative who sometimes witnessed the talks, General Siilasvuo, was bewildered and el-Gamasy was upset; both were perplexed. El-Gamasy asked Yariv, "Why can't you discuss the separation of forces issue? We have spoken about ten principles on which we have agreed."[42] When Yariv departed from the Kilometer 101 talks, he, too, was disappointed that he suddenly had to break off his personal and substantive contacts with el-Gamasy. On the same day, Sadat publicly claimed that he was discontinuing the military talks because the discussions were "not to his liking, led nowhere, and were characterised by Israeli schemes and intrigues."[43] Many Egyptian officials, including Foreign Minister Fahmy and General el-Gamasy, saw the sudden Israeli withdrawal from the talks as a case of Israeli duplicity—making agreements one day and suspending their implementation the next.[44] El-Gamasy had no idea that Kissinger had asked Meir to stop the negotiations. At the conclusion of the talks, Sadat's advisers, historically predisposed to antagonistic attitudes toward Israel, saw the breakdown as another indication of the lack of Israeli sincerity and trustworthiness. However, when the talks ended on 29 November, 1973, virtually all the details for a full disengagement agreement were discussed and made public.

The Kilometer 101 talks ended because Kissinger wanted them ended. In his memoirs, Kissinger noted that he was "not eager for a breakthrough at Kilometer 101 before the Geneva Conference…[it] tested our patience…We never knew exactly what was happening at Kilometer 101… If disengagement disappeared from the agenda, we would be forced into endless skirmishing over broader issues on which I knew we would not be able to deliver quickly. As I cautioned [Israeli ambassador to the US] Dinitz on 3 December suppose Yariv comes out a great hero on disengagement, what do you discuss [at Geneva]?"[45] Dinitz added that "Kissinger did not value direct discussions at [Kilometer] 101 because he believed that they would be making [political] concessions there to each other without actually eliciting the full price which he could have obtained had he been choreographing the negotiations."[46] Kissinger told Eban, "For God's sake, stop the Yariv–el-Gamasy thing—put it on the Geneva level. Otherwise, we don't have an agenda in Geneva."[47] Kissinger asked Fahmy later in Washington, "What are you doing? Why did you present this [disengagement plan] to the Israelis [at Kilometer 101]?"[48] Kissinger at one point told Meir, "You don't seem to understand that they are making mistakes [at Kilometer 101].

Let me do it."[49] According to the newly-appointed US ambassador to Egypt, Hermann Eilts, political discussions had to be avoided because they "would potentially incapacitate [Kissinger's] direct and incipient intervention;" "he [Kissinger] wanted all the reins in his own hands, and was uneasy about all this progress being made and the military working group where he wasn't present."[50] The Israelis and the United States agreed to pull out of Kilometer 101. The ceasefire remained in effect, but all of the details—withdrawal, how far, and who did what to whom—were to be the subject of the Geneva Conference. "We knew," said Nick Veliotes, the deputy chief of mission at the US embassy in Tel Aviv, that "Geneva would be window dressing for what had already been achieved in the Kilometer 101 negotiations."[51] Yariv remembered it this way: "Kissinger said, "What is he [Yariv] doing there at Kilometer 101? He is proposing disengagement. I need a disengagement agreement at Geneva." Kissinger told the whole Israeli government, "I do not want a disengagement agreement now." And [I—Yariv] got instructions to say goodbye to el-Gamasy. Kissinger pressured us."[52]

Conclusions

When the Geneva Middle East Peace Conference opened on 21 December 1973, it had been sanctioned by the United Nations. The conference served as an international umbrella for the understanding reached between Yariv and el-Gamasy on 11 November 1973, at the Egyptian–Israeli Kilometer 101 Ceasefire and Troop Disengagement Talks. The conference was a public bow towards a comprehensive solution. According to former Assistant Secretary of State Sisco,

> there was no doubt in Henry's mind, in my mind, that [the negotiations had to be] step by step; that regardless of all the noises about comprehensive solutions, we knew that the most feasible step would be in the aftermath of Geneva: the talks between Egypt and the United States. We never felt that the conference per se was going to be the locus of the real negotiations. Disengagement was also a political act which could not be really achieved at 101 with that cast of characters. And to put it more precisely, if anybody was going to achieve a disengagement agreement, it was Henry Kissinger himself and his personal role.[53]

The Geneva Middle East Peace Conference sustained and confirmed Washington's domination of Arab–Israeli negotiations. It successfully checked Soviet engagement in real negotiations; it edged them to the sidelines. It formalised a gradualist, step-by-step negotiating approach through interim phases by focusing on Egypt and Israel. It gave international sanction to previously agreed-upon Egyptian–Israeli ceasefire negotiations. In the historical context of Arab–Israeli negotiations, the Geneva Conference was an unprecedented public event, dramatically occurring at a pivotal moment and forcefully advancing pragmatic diplomacy. According to Aanisuph Hareven, who handled the public relations for the Israeli delegation to the conference, "from the moment we walked into the United Nations building, this was theater, all theater, purely theater, superbly conducted by Kissinger."[54] Although Kissinger projected a public focus aimed at a comprehensive peace, he had "absolutely no intention of tackling political issues [after the October 1973 War or at Geneva]."[55] Kissinger fulfilled his promise to "assemble a multilateral conference ... to use it as a framework for ... essentially bilateral diplomacy."[56] Hafez Isma'il noted that the "1973 Geneva Conference was a tool for a military delegation to sit and work out the details of a disengagement agreement."[57] The Geneva Middle East Peace Conference served Sadat's and Kissinger's purposes: to maintain the diplomatic initiative created by the October War necessitated the abrupt end of the Kilometer 101 talks.

In the aftermath of the 1973 War, and between January 1974 and March 1979, the negotiating process was often difficult, publicly rancorous, and relatively slow. But in comparison to the extraordinary complex series of fits and starts in Arab–Israeli negotiations that followed 1979 (with the exception of the negotiation and signing the Jordanian–Israeli treaty in October 1994), Egyptian–Israeli agreements (though difficult to achieve in their time) were relatively less complex. Those later negotiations had to deal with Jerusalem, Palestinian claims to all the land west of the Jordan River, who was to speak for the Palestinians, persistent Arab and Muslim state rejection of Israel's right to exist (let alone as a Jewish state), the future of the Golan Heights, water and strategic security issues, and the issues surrounding Israel's major population centres situated so close to avowedly hostile neighbours. Perhaps it is unfair to compare the agreements of the 1970s to the heavily burdened negotiating agenda that followed.

However, three irrefutable lessons may be learned from the diplomacy that emerged from the 1973 War: First, there had to be a motivation or several motives from both sides in the negotiations for an agreement to take place. An externally imposed agreement was not possible; national

228

self-interest was required to sustain negotiations and reach negotiated agreements. Egyptian and Israeli leaders both knew what they wanted from the respective agreements negotiated. Second, despite fits and starts in the negotiations in the 1973–79 period, leaders exercised the political will to continue negotiations until agreements were reached. Sadat on the one hand, Meir, Rabin, and Begin on the other were willing to withstand negative fall-out from friends and adversaries in order to reach agreements, however imperfect they may have been from a particular national vantage point. And third, agreements were reached because there was an enormous amount of private pre-negotiations between the parties. The 1973 Geneva conference was "pre-cooked." Prior to Sadat's historic visit to Jerusalem in November 1977, from private discussions through the Rumanians and Moroccans and, notably, without knowledge or involvement of the Americans, Sadat and Begin understood that they could reach an understanding over Sinai, even if all the devilish details had not been clarified to mutual satisfaction before his November visit. Narrowing of differences between the sides about Palestinian autonomy is what the US State Department's Roy Atherton did in nine shuttle missions between Cairo and Jerusalem from January–August 1978; the July 1978 Leeds (Egyptian, Israeli, and American) Foreign Minister's conference was consumed with detail about settlements, autonomy, the transitional period, and even Jerusalem. These pre-negotiations were essential for detailed draft agreements to be crafted before Camp David commenced in September 1978. There is no doubt that the negotiations at Camp David were difficult and tiresome, but the pre-negotiations allowed the first discussions on September 5, 1978 to address detail connected to Palestinian autonomy. The treaty negotiations that took place in 1978–1979 were equally tedious. Yet, in the larger picture, without Nasser's loss of Sinai in 1967 and without Sadat's drive to start a diplomatic process out of the October War to have it returned, US diplomats might not have been challenged to push for Egyptian-Israeli negotiations. While the October War was the spark that ignited diplomacy, without Sinai in hand from 1967 onwards, Israel would not have had anything tangible to trade for a treaty. The irony is that Nasser, the great pan-Arabist and staunchest opponent of Israel and Zionism, by his actions in May-June 1967 unleashed the consequences that led ultimately to Egyptian recognition and acceptance of Israel, by Nasser's successor in 1979.

14

CLASHING NARRATIVES OF THE OCTOBER WAR

COLLECTIVE MEMORY AND GROUP PERSPECTIVE

Claudia De Martino

The Six-Day War is internationally remembered as the war that shook up an entire region and changed the political landscape in the Middle East for decades to come. Yet only six years later, in 1973, the October War brought political life in Israel to a standstill and imposed a radical shift on Israeli society. This chapter will examine the social legacy of the war, spotting out and comparing its specific short- and long-term consequences as a major collective trauma in Israeli history, while reflecting on Israel's changing image in the international arena, in reference both to the Jewish Diaspora and the West. The October War, or Egypt's October War, greatly affected the assailing country also, and a brief analysis and comparison between Egypt and Israel will be drawn.

Scientific and area studies have extensively analysed the effects of this particular war on many different levels, ranging from psychological effects of open war and low-intensity conflicts[1] to sociological aspects such as mandatory military service.[2] The "security culture", which justifies until today the continuous increase of the defence budget and the burdens imposed on Israeli citizens,[3] has as much been a subject of the

debate as the public endorsement of the feeling of defeat and of a country "dwelling alone",[4] feelings which constituted the main basis for the
new "siege mentality and its religious messianic drifts.[5] In fact, all studies
agree on defining the October War as a catalyst momentum, which
emphasised social, economic and political trends already taking place in
Israeli society. However, they all built on a solid conception of Israel as
a cohesive nation-state, as a family knit together and a so-called "community of destiny".[6]

The assumption of the nation-state as the depositary of unitary collective memory is controversial. My analysis of this concept draws on
Maurice Halbwachs' studies on "collective memory" and two of his
presumptions in particular. Firstly, he presumes that collective memory
is not something unified but rather an assortment of different groups'
memories.[7] Thus, he proposes that there is no single historical memory
in a nation but as many variations and understandings of the same event
as groups composing it. Collective memory is always a social construct,
but no coherence is to be expected in the collective memory shared by
larger, somehow artificial and "imagined communities" such as the
nation-states.[8] Secondly, he states that collective memory is never "a
revival or a return of the past as such, but essentially a remake of the past
on the basis of the present".[9]

This chapter explores the legacy of the October War in social and
ethnic terms. The premise is that the war came as a shock to all Israelis
alike, but the lessons it entailed were different for the diverse groups
constituting Israeli society. Its pluralistic social legacies emerged only
over time, but they certainly accelerated the process of social fractioning
already in progress in the 1970s. The religious, traditional and materi-
alistic middle class, the messianic pioneering circles, the *haredi* groups
and the liberal and secular left would all emerge more radical from the
war and bitterly clash on the Oslo Agreements twenty years later. Therefore, the October War has many legacies and each group drew its own
conclusions on the grounds of the existential challenge the country had
just overcome.

The collective psychological effects of the October War in comparison
with the Six-Day War will be a point of discussion. Academic debate
revolves around the question whether it was the Six Day War or the
October War that had the greater impact on Israeli mentality.[10] In fact,
the October War might be interpreted as a conflict whose force balanced

the unexpected and untenable seizure of power and territory achieved by Israel in 1967. However, there are some peculiar features linking the psychological legacy of the October War to major trauma experiences rooted in the Diaspora rather than in Zionist history. The study refers here to the definitions of "historical" and "metastorical" memory, where the first stands for a "systematic account of events" and the second for "the overarching narrative or grand récit that gives order and (collective) meaning to the historical record".[11] It argues that the Israeli legacy of the October War was built on a "metastorical" memory of events, exalting the idea of social cohesion in the country, while failing to identify the social gaps and tensions predominant in 1971–3.

The third point of this chapter will examine the international impact of the October War on the attitudes of both Jewish Diaspora groups and the rest of the world towards Israel. Jewish communities around the world rediscovered their mutual belonging and enhanced their interdependence, whereas the Western world gradually distanced itself from Israel and became more critical. Tallying to the worst oil crisis ever felt in Western Europe, it spurred open criticism towards Israel's *chutzpah* by the Western countries most affected by the oil-wavering policy of the Arab states. It was argued that the war helped shape a new form of anti-Semitism, identifying Israel as the main source of permanent instability.[12] If the "free world" was gradually parting from Israel, it was also due to the fact that the postwar era and its sense of guilt were drawing to an end.[13]

Finally, the social legacy of the October War in Egypt will be addressed, although the unfiltered oral and written documentation of the war on the Egyptian side is not as broad by for. The 1979 Egypt–Israel peace treaty was the pivotal event marking the isolation of Egypt from the Arab world, experienced as traumatic by many Egyptians, and the decline of Nasserist pan-Arab ideology. Sadat had proclaimed the war a major victory and exploited it as an opportunity to launch his "open door" policy. Thus, the domestic fallout of the October War in Egypt could not be distinguished from the realignment of the country towards the US and the radical economic reforms that followed suit, which made the liberal bourgeoisie raise its head again.[14] In light of the revolution taking place in January 2011, and the consequent ousting of Egyptian President Mubarak, it is very likely that the legacy of the October War will be revised both historically and at the level of collective memory.

Building on Kansteiner's assumption that "memories are most contested at moments of great uncertainty, because ...during periods of crisis and instability, appeals are often made to collective memory",[15] it is likely that a new account of the October War and its aftermath will emerge, but its shape remains unpredictable at this stage.

The collective trauma of 1973 and its impact on a diverse Israeli society

The belief that the Israeli Defence Forces (IDF) were unchallengeable and that consequentially the country was always militarily mightier than its neighbours was irreversibly challenged in the October War. While the 1967 war had led to euphoric expectations of long-term political stability and military security, the 1973 War revealed the "intractable nature of the conflict"[16] to the general public.

The human loss suffered by the IDF this time could not be quickly forgotten, and a feeling of vulnerability prevailed. Israel's civil society had been directly dragged into the conflict, not only because of the high number of reservists mobilised, but also because some "2,000 soldiers and officers developed symptoms referred to by the professionals as combat reactions and required professional treatment".[17] Moreover, women had to face the challenge of supporting their families through war in the absence of their husbands, and over 1,000 children became half-orphans.[18]

The War had come unexpectedly and fiercely to Israel, a real shock for a country generally living up to military challenges. It had come in a moment of increasing social and economic prosperity, when trade and consumption were rapidly burgeoning and all strata of society were concentrated on reaping the fruits of the last war's efforts, instead of pondering new threats ahead. The light-hearted psychological atmosphere prevailing between the Six Day War and the October War had something startling: in fact, war-warning signs were looming and the country had to confront new security challenges through the occupation of Palestinian territories. Yet the great majority of the population had begun to believe the time had come for the long-awaited "normalisation" promised by Zionism. Finally, Israel would become a "nation among the nations" and the foundation of public debate would be trade and development rather than war and conflict.

The October War unsettled all positive expectations and brought the country back to an emotional state of existential threat it had believed was gone for good. The public distrust towards the establishment grew vigorously, but it took a different turn compared to pre-war protests, such as those of the Black Panthers.[19] The points of concern were no longer social or economic policies, but the core political issue: the management of national security. In fact, the economic elites represented by the Labour party had betrayed Israel in its most sacred domain of action.

Rolef states that by 1977 the Israeli public was ready for a change, but to what extent was the electoral turnover of 1977 then linked to the outcome of the war? In fact, it is impossible to deny systematically the link on the ground that the first elections held after the war (1974) had favoured again the Labor party, as even the late prime minister Rabin acknowledged that the grief and the timing of the elections had played a major role in the voters' orientation.[20]

Immediately after the war, public opinion tried to make sense of what had just happened by identifying the responsibilities of the main political actors. The Agranat Commission was set up with a fact-finding mission, which first singled out only personal military accountabilities and passed a verdict on IDF senior officers, but later caused the ousting of then Prime Minister Golda Meir and Defence Minister Moshe Dayan in 1974.[21]

The religious establishment promoted a reading of the huge toll paid by the country in human losses as a collective punishment imposed by God for the hubris gained through the previous victory.[22] In their view, the main fault of Israel as a nation was the feeling of excitement collectively experienced through conquering the historical homeland of Judea and Samaria, but ascribing the success of the undertaking to human intervention and not to God. The October War put the outstanding achievements of the Six Day War in a gloomy perspective. Both wars had revealed biblical prophecy that had yet fully to unravel: a story that saw the Israeli Jews as the main protagonist, while the Arab armies were treated as supernumeraries. God was testing Israel's will of survival and repentance as a single and cohesive social unit: the Jews.

The fact that in the immediate aftermath of the war the trauma experienced by the soldiers was not addressed, neither by the authorities nor in a public debate, and that protests had targeted only the government, left the impression that its impact had not been any different from other conflicts. Most soldiers stuck to the traditional and accepted paradigm of criticising the army only from within.[23] They adhered to the custom of self-restraint upon their return and to the perception of war as a somewhat "ordinary business". Lomsky-Feder writes that "the 1973 veterans' narratives reflect the absence of social approval to express private traumatic memory".[24]

Personal and collective trauma had first started surfacing in the public debate after the return of war prisoners to Israel. The public display of Israeli prisoners,[25] dishonoured and tortured in Egyptian and Syrian prisons, reinforced a feeling of vulnerability to the whole country.[26] If Egypt apparently abided by the Geneva Protocol, Syria withheld the definitive number and names of the prisoners for months. For the first time in years, Israeli families experienced a devastating uncertainty, desperate for information about their loved ones, while Syrian and Egyptian authorities had shown no particular interest in abiding by the international protocols of the Red Cross. Israel's interdependence on official and unofficial diplomatic ties in the international, but especially in the Arab world became painfully clear.

The military vulnerability experienced in the October War traumatised Israel's *Mizrahi* Jews, who feared being subjected once more to a hostile Arab majority they had encountered previously in the accounts of their parents in their countries of origin, such as Libya, Yemen, and Iraq. The case of Arieh Segev, a Moroccan-born immigrant who served in the war as a reservist, is exemplary.[27] He also transposed his memories in the period of the Oslo Agreements: the overall tune was less epic and triumphant than the official historiography, and sometimes bitterly critical of the government and the military. His testimony did not rewrite national history from the onset; rather it provided a window into personal accounts of war. Segev for instance wrote: "The Israeli authorities have been pretty capable of honouring those who fell for the sake of their country, but have been puzzled by those who had come back alive from their custody.[28] The *Mizrahim*, as a socially disadvantaged group within Israeli society, felt even more betrayed by the Labour government than their Ashkenazi comrades.[29] The military failure weighed heavily on all ethnic groups, but in the eyes of the *Mizrahim* it revealed the inability of the establishment to defend national interest.

In addition, Arieh Segev established a link between society's inequality and defeat in the October War. In his memoirs, he describes how during captivity in Egypt he obsessively recalled an episode of power abuse while serving in *Tsahal* (IDF): he had been wrongfully sentenced to a twenty-one day prison sentence instead of his senior officer, who should have been held accountable. He had realised that corruption and bribery were also common amongst the hailed Israel Defence Forces and this impacted on IDF's ability to cope with military threats. Hence, there was no contradiction between the feeling of relative deprivation and humiliation suffered by many *Mizrahi* soldiers, mainly foot soldiers or low-ranking officers,[30] in their daily lives and the shame experienced by the country as a whole.

Thus the October War seemed to magnify and dramatise the political and psychological results of the 1967 War, pushing right-wing groups towards a more radical stance given the political and cultural vacuum left by the collapse of the left. It is certain that statist and corporative culture was already staggering, mostly due to inner drives, and had been challenged by the same Labour economic choices of the 1960s, such as Pinhas Sapir's turn to mass industrialisation.[31] Furthermore, the creation of Rafi as an independent party in 1965, and as a splinter-group of Labour, pointed towards a disintegration of the Mapai leadership, which had ruled the country for the previous thirty years and a certain blurring between Left and Right in regard to the occupation of the West Bank and Gaza, as well as in the economic domain.

Another demographic and sociological dimension must be added here, which equally contributed to the electoral success of the Right in 1977. Bernard Avishai, a sharp political observer, pointed out that the *Herut* gradually became an attractive alternative for many second-class and *Mizrahi* Jews for a number of reasons, partly linked to the psychological and political dynamics of these groups. He wrote with contempt that "they arrived as intransigent individualists, convinced of the values of the market, family-centered, and suspicious of Labour Zionism's collectivist social theories".[32] Though the latter opinion might have been more the product of a disenfranchised elite rather than historical evidence, it is certain that those groups had been ostracised by Labour for thirty years; thus their natural bent for Herut-Gahal has to be explained by the mere fact that, as Schindler posed it, "Begin allowed them to be simply Jews and didn't want to turn them artificially in 'Israelis'".[33]

Indeed, the main factor behind Herut's victory was not that its economic platform repudiated socialist ideas and working-class solidarity, but the fact that it promoted and replaced them with Jewish nationalism, a far more comprehensive and inclusive idea of society, though limited to "the Jews". It promoted the idea of the "Jewish nation" over the "Jewish state", a state whose limits and weaknesses, as Kimmerling rightly argued, had already begun to emerge right after the traumatic event of the 1973 War.[34] Israel was no longer perceived as a "strong state". Therefore, the need to regain unity and social cohesion under another banner in order to restore the original might of the State of Israel emerged; this feeling of confidence was more easily conveyed by the Right's Manichean, aggressive and pietistic views, rather than by a dishonoured and divided Left.

Another, cultural, factor was added: the feeling of deference died away towards the Ashkenazi, Western-led, secular upper class, a class that had adored listening to classical music, furnishing simple housing units with libraries, setting combat units as an example of heroism and individual commitment. The *Ashkenazim* had aspired to egalitarianism, tough without realising it. They were the ones who had believed in Zionism as a driving force towards the solution of the "Jewish question", but the majority of Israelis after 1973 no longer shared this mindset.

The messianic turn of the right—a result of the October War?

The distrust towards the Labour party's conduct of war made its leaders even less appealing to the general public. The public seemed suddenly convinced that only "the right" might be able to carry out trustworthy negotiations with the Arab world, because it was the only one endowed with the necessary moral and political authority to gain the support of both the "First" and the "Second" Israel.[35] This perception originated in the October War and still nowadays Israelis seem to consider only right-wing parties or right-wing-led governmental coalitions able to deliver both peace and security.

According to Kellerman (1993), three stages might be identified in the Zionist movement:[36] an "ideological" one, a "state-driven" one (ingathering), and, since the Six Day War, a "territorial" phase, based on the mastery of a land deemed "sacred". This third stage might be labelled as "religious", "messianic" or "revisionist".[37]

Before the October War, movements such as *Gush Emunim* and the "Land of Israel Movement"[38] would not have found the same public endorsement as after the war. The trauma and bewilderment experienced by Israeli society gave these groups both legitimacy and popularity. The war had triggered the establishment of new social movements with the aim of sharing the economic prosperity achieved in the 1967 War, while simultaneously filling a vacuum of the "left" from a cultural and political perspective. Particularly interesting is the "Land of Israel Movement" founded in 1967, but which gained a new momentum since the creation of *Gush Emunim* in 1974. The latter not only advocated the theoretical rights of the Jews to the whole land of British Palestine according to the Bible, but it also formed a new pioneering generation eager to carry out reckless settlement activity in the West Bank and the Gaza Strip. *Gush Emunim*'s ideology derived directly from the war; it was inspired by the writings of Rabbi Yehuda Amital, who tried to address the collective grief from a religious perspective.[39] He proclaimed that the war had been a punishment by God, not because of the previous arrogance of the Jews in annexing Jerusalem and Palestinian land in 1967, but for the opposite; for their lack of zeal in "liberating" the whole land from foreign presence. The October War had offered the Jews a precious opportunity to unite around the eternal values of the Bible and has acted as a reminder for the Jews as a people not to sin again.[40] This reading turned into the banner of the modern Orthodox and the National religious Jews, yet not of the *Haredim*, who felt disconnected from the state and exercised a more pragmatic approach.[41]

For many, the fate of Israel was that of a "country dwelling alone", permanently suspicious of any display of goodwill from the international community. Thus, the creation of settlements in the West Bank and the Gaza Strip, already inaugurated by the Labour party as a security measure but limited to an area close to the former Green Line, took off at full capacity with a general and cross-party endorsement by all political factions and public opinion.[42] It was both a popular and populist move, which met full acceptance by the public. This support did not mean that many Israelis would have been eager to sacrifice themselves personally for the sake of colonisation, but rather that the public, in its majority, no longer viewed colonisation as an immoral action.

Interestingly, the defeat also caused the awareness that Israel could achieve a pragmatic understanding with its neighbours at best; an approach that was not at odds with the feeling of "dwelling alone". Plans for negotiations, if not reconciliation, were mapped out, and in 1976 the Israeli Council for Israeli–Palestinian Peace was established.[43] Reservists founded the well-known Peace Now (*Shalom Akshav*) movement a few years later in reaction to the deadlock in peace talks with the Egyptians after President Sadat's visit in Israel in 1977. The concern was genuine, originating from the same firm awareness that Israel could no longer ignore the necessity of making peace with its Arab neighbours. This was, in essence, one of the solid legacies of the October War.

Nonetheless, the growing tendency to favour the right over the left was not just a result of the war, but based on the growing popularity of achieving liberalisation in the economic sphere and limiting governmental control, both goals promoted heavily by the right. The Herut's economic platform endorsed a model of a "corporate state that would arbitrate wage demands, abolish restrictions on the use of Arab labour and encourage a fully capitalist i.e. economy"[44]. It was, in fact, freeing Israelis from the Zionist dogma of "Jewish-labour only", while the occupation of the territories was providing the occasion for exploiting business opportunities in terms of construction and housing, military careers, civil administration jobs and general public services; and making cheap manpower in the form of local Palestinians readily available. Thus, a "colonial lobby" emerged, which then strongly contributed to raising consensus for the right-wing trend in politics among the wider public. The economic crisis of the late 1970s, leading the national economy to the brink of recession,[45] added to the 1973 oil embargo launched by the Arab states, and fuelled the psychological complex of "dwelling alone" even further. This perception would reach its climax with Begin after the 1977 elections.

Regional and international ramifications: the broader legacy.

The findings of a seminar on Jewish unity and solidarity across the nations[46] held in Jerusalem in the immediate aftermath of the war proved that the bond between Israel and Diaspora Jewish communities had strengthened, declaring "the willingness of young Jews to express their Jewishness openly [...as] the surest sign that this was a fact".[47] The October War heightened a sense of interdependence among Jewish communities that was there to stay. The great sociologist Charles Liebman stressed that (since 1973) "support for Israel (among Diaspora Jews) is not support for some distant state, but a symbolic expression of Jewish identity.[48]"

In 1974, a fun-draising appeal was launched by the United Jewish Appeal and triggered a never before seen monetary support. In both

Western Europe and the US, the main reason for the increase in donations had been greater identification with Israel by the Jewish communities, achieved through educational programmes and a wide range of volunteering opportunities in Israel.

However, there are additional reasons not directly ascribable to the Jewish world. The dominant cultural climate in the West had radically changed since 1967. Then, the anti-Vietnam War demonstrations were flooding Western countries, and Jewish Diaspora communities had been highly split on the issue of war in general. In 1973, conversely, the internationalist and progressive cultural climate had experienced a setback and reactionary culture worldwide was on the rise; thus, Jews had more room for publicly displaying their solidarity campaigns to Israel. Some Diaspora Jewish intellectuals and communities, who only six years before had strongly opposed Israeli policies, radically changed their minds.[49] In 1973, Jewish–American social author Michael Harrington, for instance, showed compassion for Israel's security interest by stating "… a negotiated peace with the Arabs, involving their acceptance of Israel as a Middle Eastern state, is crucial".[50]

The Arab oil embargo was perceived as a blackmailing of Western countries. It provoked a "petrol shock" in Western Europe and triggered the first main crisis since 1929. This embargo, as well as the boycott by Gulf Arab states of European States such as Germany and the Netherlands,[51] which had openly sided with Israel, made it more difficult to criticise Arab policies in Europe. The great majority of the European states, deeply aware they could not withstand economic pressure for long, tried to reactivate contacts with Arab governments by partially meeting their political demands. The two-fold heritage of the October War, thus, produced a situation where European and US Jews were more vocal on Israel's right to self-defence; but on the other hand the ECC governments, if not their people, were more distant and careful in openly showing solidarity with Israel.[52]

Moreover, a new anti-Semitism surfaced, directly linked to both the economic crisis and the newly advocated image of Israel as an imperialist country oppressing the Palestinians. This trend was nurtured by the Christian churches, particularly the Vatican, and some leftist and Catholic groups started arguing that Arab lives counted less than Israelis' because the latter felt themselves a "superior race", thus reversing the stigma that had been imposed on Jews for centuries.[53] The new anti-

Semitism emerging in Europe was directed only towards Israel. It took the shape of anti-Zionism more than anti-Semitism, but traditional racism and criticism towards Israeli policies blended in an ambiguous way. Surely, anti-Semitism in Western Europe had been simmering under the surface all along, but the events of 1973 exposed a new wave triggered by different factors. The increasing identification between Diaspora Jews and Israel showed the great majority of Western public opinion the undisputed correlation between the Israeli state and Judaism as a religion. The October War exposed *par excellence* the ambiguity of Jewish identity: as much as the war and the menace of annihilation had reunited the "Jewish family", they had also disclosed the primordial rift between Jews and Gentiles.

The October War and its social impact on Egypt

The October 1973 War was designed by Egypt as the reversal of the 1967 Arab defeat. This had been referred to in Arabic as "al-Naksa", which literally means "the setback". Sadat replaced Nasser with the double goal of rehabilitating Egyptian credibility among the Arabs and leaving pan-Arabism as the main focus of Egyptian foreign policy behind. Precisely because he wanted to revolutionise Egyptian politics from within without compromising its grounds and hindering a civil and intra-Arab war, he considered a military victory the single means to regain both popularity and freedom of action.[54]

Egyptian military echelons were longing for revenge but did not regard the complete defeat of Israel to be necessary. J.C. Moulton, then an officer in the US air force, wrote that the Egyptians succeeded in attaining their objective in the 1973 War, as they "carefully and critically examined the reasons for the 1967 loss, while Israel failed to properly determine all the reasons for its success. Egypt then corrected its mistakes and planned accordingly. The country coordinated its efforts, its military capability and all national objectives".[55] However, this claim seems to apply only to Egypt's relations to Israel rather than towards the other Arab states. In fact, Egypt failed to understand that the 1967 debacle had not been only an Egyptian breakdown, but rather a pan-Arab one.[56] This fundamental misunderstanding on the outreach of the war's fallouts led Egypt to reduce its national duty to military action, whereas this was not enough to reverse the feeling of weakness and defeat all Arab States had experienced six years before.

CLASHING NARRATIVES OF THE OCTOBER WAR

The domestic debate in Egypt between the two wars had focused on the need to reset and reorganise the army and the intelligence from scratch, and on the necessity for the country to regain its self-esteem. Since the reorganisation of the army was carried out carefully and swiftly, Sadat considered the Egyptian forces ready to cross the canal and to storm beyond Israel's Bar-Lev Line. Yet Sadat never pondered the possibility of conquering land and territories pivotal to the Palestinian cause. Thus, the Egyptian leadership viewed the October War's political victory as a national success rather than an action aimed at fully restoring the *status quo ante* existing in the Middle East before 1967. Sadat paid his choice for a national solution, rather than an "Arab" solution, with his own life, but while the Egyptian leadership was still grateful to him some twenty years later for pushing Egypt definitively out of Israeli wars, the Egyptian masses were not.

As the "myth of defeat" took off in Israeli politics and society (Liebman 1993)[57] a parallel "myth of victory" conquered Egyptian society after the October War.[58] Many intellectuals and middle-class Egyptians hoped that great military success would be followed by a period of significant internal reforms. They believed that if Egypt settled its foreign problems and initiated an economic reform of an "open door" policy, it might have the strength to concentrate on social reforms such as tackling illiteracy, which affected 50% of the population at the time, and building affordable and decent housing for the millions of rural immigrants still living in shanty town camps around the city centre.[59]

Indeed, the October War encouraged some transformations in Egyptian society. Women had played a major role in the war effort, as they had replaced men in many industrial and agricultural tasks, and they longed for more recognition and rights in its aftermath. Yet their gains were minimal and did not live up to general expectations.[60] Thus, the years between 1973 and 1981 were characterised by a strong polarisation of Egyptian society in two blocks: those advocating major changes and those resisting them. Ordinary Egyptians yearned for the tangible benefits of peace, more so than Israelis in 1967, in terms of social policies, growing labour and market opportunities for all. When those did not materialise, they felt both disappointed and betrayed by a government that had portrayed the October War as the means for Egypt to stand on its own feet again. At the end of the day, the "victory" so self-righteously announced by Sadat had brought back only land lost in

243

1967. Even though these territories, such as the oil fields of Abu Rudeis (1975), were an important win, they were only regained through negotiations with the enemy; they did not represent the key progress Egyptians were expecting from the war.

The Egyptian left, Liberals and religious groups were particularly disappointed. They had believed in the possibility of a real multi-party system and further freedom of expression, but Sadat's "carrot and stick" approach to reforms did not tackle social issues at their roots. In January 1977 riots erupted in Cairo and spread all over the country, strongly repressed by the army. Subsequently, Sadat called for a referendum on "public and order", aiming at establishing new rules banning strikes by making them punishable by hard labour.[61] The referendum was approved by 99.6% of the voters, but the support to Sadat was being challenged by some of the Free Officers' core leaders, such as Kamal el-Din Hussein, who was expelled from the People's assembly. In the place of Nasser proxies and forerunner Free Officers, a new military elite was promoted, composed of combat officers who had led the actual fighting in the October War.

Though censorship on newspapers had been lifted in 1974 and a multi-party system reintroduced in 1976, governmental policies towards freedom of expression or criticism did not really change either, and the monthly newspaper *al-Da'wa* (Muslim Brotherhood) and the weekly *Togammu al-Ahali* (leftist parties, then NPUP or National Progressive Unionist Party) were both banned in 1978 again for having voiced negative opinions on the peace process.[62] Moreover, the leftist newspaper *al-Tali'ah* estimated that the purchasing power of 80% of the population had declined sharply since the 1973 War, which caused a major erosion of real wages, while the economic rewards from foreign investments had not yet materialised.[63]

The clash on Egyptian national interests became more evident after Sadat's visit to Jerusalem. Sadat, who in previous years had vehemently supported Islamist groups in order to curb the leftist parties' power, started persecuting the former for having rejected his pragmatic approach based on the economic added value of peace with Israel. However, the Islamist discourse on the war had differed considerably from Sadat's; in fact, they had proclaimed the "October War" to be similar to "al-Badr's", a military success ensured by God's support by the mere fact it had been launched in the holy month of Ramadan.[64] According to the Muslim Brotherhood, the war had succeeded in reconciling Egypt with

its faith and thus fell into the category of "holy war".[65] They consequently disagreed on the terms of peace with Israel and turned into a
fierce opposition, promoting the peace accords as "temporary", as they
violated the Islamic principle that "Muslims could not agree on detach-
ing part of their land by voluntary sanction".[66]

Sadat soon disbanded the *New Wafd* (the Liberal party) and the
NPUP and issued the "Law of Shame" (1980), banning publications of
"all news inflaming public opinion", according to article no. 3 of the
Peace Treaty with Israel which "continuously requires Egypt to prohibit
any activity, view, thought or opinion hostile to Israel". Later on, the
newspaper *al-Da'wa* was shut down, highlighting the irreconcilability of
Sadat's pragmatic understanding of peace and the Muslim Brotherhood's
temporary understanding of peace. In July 1981, the government
arrested 1, 536 people but could not foil the attack which, nine months
later, during the official parade celebrating the anniversary of the October War, killed the president at the hand of an army officer called Khalid
al-Islambuli.

For the Egyptian public, the peace process with Israel was the real,
provocative legacy of the October War. The dispute had been on the
character of Egyptian national interest and on its final goal; while the
leadership had bet on an "Egypt only" policy and on "normalisation"
with Israel, the great majority of public opinion, ordinary people, liberals, communists and Islamists alike, would not part from Arab solidarity
and pan-Arabism to the same extent. The peace process had further
highlighted the absence of democracy within Egypt.[67]

Twenty years after the war, many columnists, amongst them Osama
al-Ba'ez,[68] remembered the feeling of national unity gained through the
war, fought by Copts and Muslims alike, and the spirit of the October
victory as a genuine drive for change and modernisation in Egyptian
society. Few critical voices examined the setback experienced during the
peace process that followed. It was evident that the media were still
heavily influenced and censored by the military establishment back
then. Since the Day of Anger on 25 January 2011, and the following
ousting of President Mubarak, new and free media bloomed in Egypt,
claiming to represent the voices and the demands of parties and segments of society silenced for over thirty years. It is likely that free oral
accounts, memories and new area studies will significantly contribute to
shed a new light on the Egyptian legacy of the October War on its for-
tieth anniversary in 2013.

Conclusion

Israeli author Avraham Hartman commented at the end of the war: "We thought of ourselves on the eve on October as being a normal society. If you analyse the nature of the political platforms that were being drawn up by the parties before the war, you will find that the issues were housing, wages and inflation. The assumption was that our external political situation was normal and we could afford to occupy ourselves exclusively with the questions of a normal society, which takes its existence and its security for granted."[69] Thus, according to Hartman, the real legacy of the October War was a reminder to all Jewish people, but especially to the Israelis, that Zionism had not accomplished its final objectives and had not freed the Jews from their curse of being loathed among nations.

War correspondent Ze'ev Schiff outlined this view further in 1974 concluding that the "post-war trauma had returned [the Israeli society] overnight to square one, where it all started". Despite all her past victories, Israel suddenly found herself again pondering dangers and realising that defeat in local battles can endanger her existence."[70] Only former President Chaim Herzog's account seems to point in the opposite direction: "The only danger is that the Arabs will not draw the correct lessons and conclusions from the war, carried away as they are in an euphoria of victory which is imaginary".[71] However, his ostensible optimism was also riddled with critical remarks: "[The war] has reduced the deterrent capacity of our armed forces. Previously, we could expect the Arabs to think twice before allowing their fingers to curl around the trigger; but in the October War the Arabs learned that, under certain conditions, they were capable of achieving some battlefield gains".[72]

Which were those "conditions" under which Israel's enemies had been capable of achieving much more than expected and predicted? In fact, they were obvious and simple: on the one hand, Israeli society and the IDF had slumped into lack of self-control, basking in prosperity and comfort, military superiority and the presumed normalisation ensured by the Six-Day War. On the other hand, the widespread feeling of a "country dwelling alone" had isolated and deceived the government and military circles to the extent that they believed Israel could perfectly do without either diplomatic or territorial adjustments with its neighbours. A pragmatic assessment of the situation had been missing.

Since then Israel had to live up to two challenges. The first was to fight inner moral corruption, which, according to many, aspired from doing as the "Gentiles" do; the second was that it should not linger anymore in optimism, and should always be on its guard against both friends and foes alike. Consequently, security became the first and foremost national and collective ethos. Militarily speaking, in the revised IDF strategy, this fact meant opting preferably for carrying out pre-emptive strikes in the presence of threats rather than waiting for the enemy's intentions to clarify.

The October War reinforced a familiar, fearful state of mind and created a further awareness in terms of the country's future. Firstly, Israel was alone and might be permanently wiped off the map by the Arabs; secondly, since its military superiority might not be tenable, negotiations for peace agreements with the surrounding Arab states ought to be explored; thirdly, no "normalisation" was awaiting Israel by the fulfilling of the Zionist national project. These conclusions paved the way for an attitude less abiding of international law but rather nourishing and emphasising Israel's national interests grounded in her original religious and spiritual sources, including the messianic, *Haredi* and neo-colonial streams. This movement made a claim of a more democratic management of the country by supporting its populist and pioneering drifts.

In sum, the October War's legacy is different from that of the Six Day War, because the collective psychological link that it established was not with Zionist history, but rather directly with the *Shoah*. If a new *Shoah* had been aired even in the first days of high alert before June 1967, its menace had been erased by the victory. Contrary to that, the October War's outcome was going to stay and be engraved in the national memory forever as the moment of maximum danger. Even nowadays, the ceremony that marks the end of the October Day (the Day of Atonement) is celebrated in the synagogues and in private houses with mixed feelings. According to the Bible, Israelis should rejoice at the end of the fast as on every other holiday; however, the memories of the fallen soldiers and the collective fear of annihilation tend mainly to overshadow all positive sentiments. Israeli TV channels air depressing programs and memorials similar to those broadcasted on the *Yom ha-Shoah;* commemorations of fallen relatives take place on the following day throughout the country. It seems that the October Day has also been set to honour the worldly condition of Israel, as a country living in constant fear of annihilation.

Even if downplayed by secular Israelis, the October War enhanced and revealed all the contradictions of Zionism between its two fold

Jewish–national and Jewish–religious identity. Its legacy followed the same path as the *Shoah* in Israeli collective memory: rather than paving the way for a more realistic assessment of the country's spiritual and military capabilities, it stamped yet another trauma into the collective consciousness, to be remembered for generations to come. In this sense, quite ironically, it had helped place Israelis "as the victim in the center of attention, [a tendency] that blinds many Israeli Jews from seeing the "other" and how another people are occupied.[73]" This legacy is common to all groups: *Ashkenazim, Mizrahim*, Russian immigrants and Ethiopian Jews, notwithstanding the different responsibilities and roles they played in the conflict.

Hence, it may be assumed that the legacy of the October War in Israel has two layers. The first is an historical memory, particularly vivid immediately after the war, which drew on the public rage and disappointment for having been betrayed by the authorities, with the *Mizrahi* Jews doubly bitter and angry with the Labour *establishment*; the second is a collective, "metastorical" memory which took off in the longer run, conveyed and boosted by the media and education, pushing all Jewish groups to identify with a traumatised people in constant fear, a collective memory of victimhood and grief.

Drawing a rough balance after 40 years, one can argue that in Israel the historical narrative of the war has been partially eroded, whereas collective memory is permeating, and the country is still waiting to regain the same feeling of self-assurance it possessed before the October War. In Egypt, conversely, the historical legacy of the October/Ramadan War is mainly that of the peace process which followed, and in the next years it will be surely disputed by emerging social groups and hybridised by alternative memories. The Muslim Brotherhood and other competing political groups that had been silenced all those years would surely seize the opportunity to express more criticism, not only of the provisions of the treaty with Israel, but also of its fallouts on domestic politics, such as the freezing of the process of democratisation of Egyptian society that it brought with it. Thus, while in the short run Israel may still cling to its self-indulgent narrative, Egypt might use the valuable opportunity of new political developments for a public debate to commence.

15

GONE BUT NOT FORGOTTEN?

THE OCCASIONAL LESSONS OF THE OCTOBER 1973 WAR

Clive Jones

Introduction

Any attempt to draw definite conclusions, yet alone "lessons", from events almost four decades ago in the Middle East is fraught with difficulty. To start with a basic methodological issue, the idea of drawing lessons is one that would be anathema to many historians imbued with a belief that all historical events are unique occurrences conditioned by time and context, whose exact constellation is hardly ever repeated beyond setting the stage for the next unique event.[1]

Scholars of International relations are undoubtedly more open to explaining the recurrence of events—most notably the timeless propensity for war across the international system—but even here, particular viewpoints regarding the resilience of enduring conflicts, not least between Israelis and Arabs, are often subject to ideological prisms that deny agency to explanations and material that do not "fit" the dominant paradigm.

Then there is the extent to which more recent events may serve to inform or indeed distort our understanding of the impact surrounding the October 1973 War on regional relations. For example, to what extent does the current challenge to autocratic regimes across the Middle East—the so-called Arab Spring—represent an end to a regional order that emerged in the aftermath of the October War? In short, beyond the hard and bitter "real" truths of the battlefield, "lessons learned" from any conflict are almost always subjective by the very nature of their political context, and as such can often act as an unreliable guide towards understanding contemporary events.

Finally, there is the degree to which memory of the actual conflict continues to shape myths which may or may not accord with the outcome of the war itself. Nowhere is this more keenly felt than in Israel where, despite inflicting severe military reversals on Egypt and Syria, the nature of its occurrence as well as the attendant human cost to the IDF has served to obscure the advantages that Israel accrued in its aftermath. The late Charles Liebman called this a *mehdal*—an omission—a term that, while falling short of an outright disaster, summarises for many Israelis a belief that "[W]hat went wrong was more likely the result of one not having done something, an error of omission, rather than having done something wrong, an error of commission."[2] Nowhere is this more evident than in the veritable cottage industry that has arisen around explaining the outbreak of the war in terms of an intelligence failure, and the ongoing controversy attached to its very historiography.[3] The enduring (and often bitter) debates are evidence enough, surrounding the relative culpability of Agaf Mo'din (AMAN, the directorate of Military Intelligence) and the extent to which the special adviser and confidant to Egyptian President Anwar Sadat, Ashraf Marwan, was or was not a double agent who intentionally deceived his Israeli paymasters over Cairo's true intent in 1973.[4]

Given these methodological hurdles, what follows is necessarily a subjective overview of the "lessons" that can be drawn from the aftermath of the 1973 War. The focus is inevitably upon Israel, given the available secondary source literature (as well as access to primary source archives) dealing with actions and thoughts of key actors in Jerusalem. While acknowledging that this gives only a partial view, this focus is perhaps unavoidable given the relative paucity (although not total absence) of accounts from Arab historians and political scientists explaining Egyptian, Syrian and even Jordanian actions during their "Ramadan War". Equally, the oil shock and the impact of the war on

Anglo–American relations have also been the subject of much scholarly enquiry elsewhere.[5] Such health warnings aside, this chapter takes as its guide the typology of knowledge first outlined by Baruch Spinoza in the seventeenth century: factual knowledge, perceptual knowledge and intuitive knowledge.[6] Factual knowledge is taken as a given by all concerned, that is to say in this case that war broke out between Israel on the one hand and Arab states led by Syria and Egypt on the other. By contrast, perceptual knowledge—how people interpret the event and intuitive knowledge, how people should "feel" about an event—provides the prisms through which lessons of history are shaped, formed and indeed reinterpreted. It is with particular reference to the interpretive and intuitive that this concluding chapter examines in brief three discreet yet interrelated outcomes of the war from which lessons of importance, weight and longevity might be drawn. These themes are intelligence reform in Israel, the impact of the war on myth and popular perception in Israel, and thirdly, lessons regarding the role of the United States and Arab–Israeli relations themselves. Inevitably, the paper compares and contrasts the outcomes of the October War with more recent events in Israel and across the region. In so doing, it makes the argument that while lessons are there to be learned, they can also be ignored or perhaps, even worse, misappropriated.

The enduring lesson of "the Concept"

Israel's intelligence community was not the only one surprised by the Egyptian and Syrian assault on 6 October 1973. In London, the director general of Intelligence at the Ministry of Defence, Louis le Bailly, was so convinced that all was quiet on the Israeli front that two days previously he had happily sent his daughter out to work on a Kibbutz for the autumn.[7] That a senior member of British intelligence appeared equally oblivious to the impending war was cold comfort to Israeli intelligence officials, and senior military officers whose performance prior to and during the first three days of the war were subjected to the government-appointed inquiry, the Agranat Commission, designed to uncover the circumstances that led to the *mehdal*. Named after its chair, Supreme Court President Shimon Agranat, the commission focused its enquiry on two key issues: 1) intelligence and interpretation of that intelligence prior to the outbreak of war; and 2) the actual state of combat readiness and performance of the Israel Defence Forces in the first three days of the war. The report, published on 2 April 1974, was excoriating in its conclusions. It placed particular blame on the director of Military Intelligence (DMI), Major General Elie Zeira, and his deputy, Brigadier General Aryeh Shalev, for their flawed intelligence assessments, and recommended the removal of the chief of staff, Lieutenant General David Elazar, and the head of Southern Command, Major General Shmuel Gonen, on the basis that they had not made their own detailed assessments of the available intelligence and had placed too much reliance on the regular forces of the IDF to provide effective defence along the Bar-Lev Line.[8]

The individual culpability of this quartet has been the subject of much debate in recent years, as the reasons for the intelligence failure have moved beyond the immediate blame cast by the Agranat Commission. However, this has tended to obscure what for many has remained the enduring "truth" of the commission: that Israeli intelligence, notably AMAN, was beholden to a particular "Concept" that denied efficacy to an Egyptian (let alone Syrian) attack without the ability to establish air superiority over the IDF. That Egypt overcame this military asymmetry by investing heavily in surface-to-air missiles (SAMs) was a military lesson Israel certainly took to heart. Subsequent research and development in electronic counter measures to blind Syrian SAM sites during the invasion of Lebanon in June 1982 is testament to that.

Such technical lessons aside, however, the importance of the Agranat Commission was in its recommendations over the future structure and composition of Israel's intelligence community and in particular AMAN. It is here, perhaps, where the appropriation of "lessons learned" has been the most problematic and reflects both bureaucratic inertia within Israel's intelligence community as well as the continued debate over the exact nature of civil–military relations in Israel. For while the Agranat Commission recommended the reduction in the monopoly exercised by AMAN over the production of national intelligence assessments and the establishment of greater pluralism across the intelligence community, moves towards this end have at best been only partial over the past forty years.[9]

Military intelligence still dominates the assessment process and, moreover, as former DMI Ahron Zeevi Farkesh suggests, tends to be self-tasking, that is to say, the political masters look to AMAN, sitting as it does at the apex of the intelligence community and consuming by far the largest proportion of its budget, as the dominant body for the production of the annual intelligence assessment, a position it has now occupied since 1975.[10] To be fair, structural constraints centred on manpower and the cost of mobilisation have meant that the emphasis upon early warning remains central to Israel's security doctrine. Equally, however, the lack of a civilian coordinating body to task, collect, collate, analyse, interpret and disseminate information—the classic intelligence cycle—has, according to scholars such as Uri Bar-Joseph, meant that interpretation of Israel's external environment is too often viewed through a military lens that, in turn, colours political assessment.[11]

Thus, despite the establishment of a small research department in the Ministry of Foreign Affairs and a rather larger equivalent in the Mossad—both recommendations of the Agranat committee—the emphasis upon military capability and intent denied that sufficient resources were focused upon reading political "signals", which were either dismissed as of little importance or interpreted as malign. A notable example is the failure by AMAN to appreciate fully Sadat's overtures for peace even up to the point when the Egyptian president arrived in Jerusalem in November 1977 to address the Knesset, although in fairness to AMAN it had not been privy to the secret contacts between Moshe Dayan and Hassam Tohami, Egypt's deputy premier, that had taken place in September.[12]

Even so, it has been argued that the current structure of AMAN remains the antithesis of the pluralism pushed for by the Agranat Commission. Despite calls for it to be made a civilian body equivalent to Britain's GCHQ and the NSA in the United States, Signals Intelligence (SIGINT), which is reckoned to produce close to 80 per cent of all intelligence-related material, remains within the gift of AMAN in the form of Unit 8200. This gives AMAN, and in particular its research division, enormous clout in terms of producing the national intelligence estimate; but equally such assessments, it is argued, continue to privilege the martial over the political, in and of itself a form of "Conceptzia". Several examples of this exist, but the most notable perhaps is Israel's own intelligence failure with regard to its assessment of Iraqi Weapons of Mass Destruction (WMD).

Alongside officials in London and Washington, Israel was convinced that Saddam Hussein had an active WMD programme prior to the

March 2003 invasion of Iraq. Moreover, some of these Israeli assessments had been fed into the British and American intelligence cycles. The failure therefore to find anything remotely akin to an active WMD programme was the source of great consternation within the Israeli intelligence community. An enquiry under Likud MK Yuval Steinitz, chairman of the intelligence subcommittee of the Knesset Foreign Affairs and Defence Committee, was convened to investigate what was widely seen as a failure of assessment, rather than necessarily a paucity of information. At the end of March 2004, the committee issued a damning report. Its key recommendations included:

- AMAN be relieved of its dominant responsibility for the NIE, with responsibility shared for its production with the Mossad. AMAN's responsibility would be confined to purely military estimates while the Mossad would be charged with overseeing the production of po-litical–strategic intelligence.
- To remove all SIGINT from the military and in turn for 8200 and its ancillary units to become a purely civilian organisation.
- The appointment of an intelligence secretary to the incumbent Prime Minister.
- To establish a Ministerial Intelligence Committee to direct and over-see the intelligence agencies.[13]

The committee itself drew criticism from some quarters for reinforc-ing what Shlomo Brom referred to as the existing tendency "within the [Israeli] intelligence community and the government to continue to act on worst case assumptions and avoiding any risk, whatever the cost".[14] This tendency towards worst-case scenarios very much remains the leg-acy of the October War and certainly informed some of the more exco-riating comments that subsequently appeared in the mainstream Hebrew press. Thus Aluf Benn could write:

The intelligence community described in the [Steinetz] report is run by a moonlighting operation in the best Israeli organisational tradition of improvisa-tion and conservatism. Military intelligence has designated itself the national assessor without this role ever having been anchored in law and in procedures. MI and the Chief of Staff decide on the targets of the intelligence gathering and research on their own without political instruction. The consumers of intelli-gence are flooded with "an ocean of material and paperwork of doubtful value to put it mildly", with trivial analysis and ambiguous assessments of known facts, and pretentious and worthless psychological portraits of the Arab leaders and their intentions.[15]

But like the Agranat Commission report, Steinitz has done very little to reform the structure of the Israeli intelligence community and, in particular, the overwhelming monopoly exercised by AMAN over the production of the NIE. For very understandable reasons, worst-case scenarios continue to dominate the immediate horizons of many intelligence communities and indeed, given the national trauma that was the October War, its impact upon AMAN has, according to Gideon Doron, been deep and long-lasting.[16]

If a lesson has been learned, it is one shaped by perceptual and intuitive knowledge that denies risk-taking, at least in terms of making overt moves towards peace. It is perhaps also indicative of a mindset that, as Yair Evron noted, sees "Arab animosity toward Israel as a constant", only mitigated by Israel's continued military predominance and vigilance. This mindset, Evron noted, served in the past to distort a more sober appreciation on the part of Israel that the "vitality of Egyptian and Syrian interests [in 1973] involved in the liberation of the Sinai and Golan Heights, far exceeded their commitment to the Palestinian cause" or indeed, the Arab nationalist cause in general.[17] Evron concludes that had Israeli policy-makers in 1973 been more sensitive to the needs to be struck between the balance of power and the balance of political interest, then the events of October 1973 might have been avoided.

Some might argue that a similar mindset determined Israel's approach towards both the *Intifada* of 1987 and certainly the overwhelming military response to the outbreak of the *al-Aqsa intifada* in September 2000, in which the culpability of Yasser Arafat in stoking the violence was taken as a given. It became what columnist Akiva Eldar in a deliberate echo of 1973 called the dominant "conceptzia" that shaped Israel's subsequent response.[18] Of course, all states have a fixed view of their external environment and the costs and opportunities to be weighed before a particular course of action is sanctioned. The concern for many Israelis, however, is that four decades after Agranat, intelligence analysis still remains unduly influenced by military concerns and interests, unable (perhaps unwilling) to concede that military capability does not always denote political intent.

THE OCTOBER 1973 WAR

From war to peace, or calm before the storm?

Undoubtedly, the massive psychological impact of the October 1973 War was exacerbated by the perception of near total Israeli dominance of its neighbours that had prevailed across the country following the triumph of the June 1967 War. Certainly, no one in Israel believed that the frontline Arab states had been disabused of their stated desire to see the Jewish state eradicated—the infamous three "No's" of the November 1967 Khartoum conference were evidence enough of this. But as Susan Hattis Rolef notes, the period between the two wars, marked by economic growth, a total belief in the efficacy of Israeli deterrence and—aside from the growth of the PLO in Lebanon—quiescence along Israel's borders, were popularly seen as "good years".[19] This popular perception however disguised the fact that, even prior to the war, public confidence in the political elites—most notably those associated with the ruling Labour Alignment—was already in decline.

Opinion polling in September 1973 suggested that, in the national elections that were due to be held in late October, Labour was predicted to lose several seats. In the event, when the elections were held on 31 December 1973, they lost five, down from fifty-six to fifty-one with the newly merged Likud increasing their share from thirty-one to thirty-nine seats. Without doubt, the outcome of the war itself (not least the conclusions of the Agranat Commission) did help accelerate the decline of the established centre-left political elite and presaged a paradigm shift across the Israeli political landscape, helped in no small part by the growing demographic clout of Oriental Jewish Israelis and their preference for right-wing parties. While we should be mindful of caricature, ethnic affiliation certainly played a part in the elections of Israel's first Likud-led government in 1977.

This is as much about political legacy as lessons to be learned but for Charles Liebman, this produced the myth: the myth that the war was a calamity for the country, exposing at worst a sclerotic political order and a profound sense of unease over the future direction in which it was heading. For Liebman, myth "imposes meaning on events", and "functions to assist the individual or society in ordering their present experience".[20] He also argued that the myth of a near calamity avoided was in part a reflection felt across society over the false hopes placed upon Israel's presumed military superiority: in short, the outcome of the June 1967 War had set the bar far too high, even though, as Liebman notes, peace with Egypt and, with it, the fracturing of the Arab consensus surrounding Israel was the end result.

Of course, the cost paid in blood was great. With over 3,000 Israeli soldiers killed and thousands more seriously wounded, Liebman perhaps underplays the disconnect between the immediate shock of such casualty figures and the later strategic awards accrued six years later at Camp David. Even so, he went on to argue that the myth of a near calamity avoided acted as a palliative to the heady expectations that accompanied the outcome of the June 1967 War, that security was now all but guaranteed, that mass *aliyah* borne on the wave of a Zionist idealism would result in economic prosperity, and that "a new self-sufficient Israel, capable of any achievement" would result. Instead, Liebman concluded, "[I]t is the suffering which resulted from the Yom Kippur war, rather than the exultation following the victory of the Six Day War, which reminds Jews about the true nature of reality and which merges the fortunes of the State of Israel into the regnant paradigms of the nature of Jewish history".[21]

Almost Hobbesian in its construct, this appreciation of a "timeless animus" directed towards the Jewish people in general and Israel in particular remains a powerful narrative in at least framing the lessons that successive Israeli leaders have drawn from the experience of the October War. We should not, of course, fall victim to a reductionism that denies agency to choice, individual or collective, offered by particular circumstance. In the case of Israel's invasion of Lebanon in June 1982, such choice, informed almost by a Clausewitzian logic, saw the use of force employed towards achieving a grandiose yet ultimately flawed political end. Even so, while Israel has remained wary of concluding formal military alliances, events both during the war and in its aftermath demonstrated the limits of Israeli "self-sufficiency" at a strategic level. As Itamar Rabinovich noted, the war demonstrated above all else "[T]he need for American supplies, and therefore the collapse of an important element in strategic US Israeli cooperation—the belief that Israel could hold its own against any Arab coalition so long as the United States deterred the Soviet Union".[22]

But ultimately, both intelligence failure and the idea of myth have tended to obscure one key lesson amid the understandable focus on the material and emotional cost of the war: the failure of Israeli diplomacy to understand (let alone explore) that there might be a partner for peace.

On 4 February 1971, Sadat announced before the Egyptian parliament his willingness to sign a peace agreement with Israel—conditioned by the immediate declaration of a ceasefire and the withdrawal of the IDF to the Mitla and Giddi Passes in the Sinai—as well as the reopening of the Suez Canal and the restoration of diplomatic relations with Washington. The response from the late Israeli prime minister, Golda Meir, was summed up by the late Israeli diplomat Gideon Rafael, who recalled that "I had strongly urged Golda to respond. In the Knesset on 9 February, she extended a finger to him—not a hand."[23] That it took a war to transform the Israeli finger into a hand might however be a lesson that Israel has yet to learn. Nearly thirty years later, and amid the carnage of the *al-Aqsa intifada*, Israel's response—or rather lack of one—to the Arab peace initiative of April 2002 (a Saudi proposal that enjoyed the support of the Arab League and the Organisation of the Islamic Conference, calling for normalisation of relations with Jerusalem in return for an Israeli withdrawal to the 1967 lines and a negotiated solution to the Palestinian refugee problem) has again been seen by some in Israel, such as Yehezkel Dror, as an opportunity missed.[24] And here might be a lesson lost or indeed forgotten from the events of October 1973. For as Elie Podeh noted:

When it comes to peace, Israel's position today [2010] is similar to its position after the wars of 1948 and 1967. The potential for negotiations was there, but the cost was considered too high. Now, too, maintaining the status quo appears to be preferable to making changes that Israelis perceive as threatening, even if they do not pose a genuine danger. In the past [decade] Israel has faced a number of initiatives: the Arab League peace plan, Syrian offers to negotiate, Palestinian willingness to move forward and even moderate declarations from Hamas. Successive Israeli governments responded to all of them with restrained indifference.[25]

One should of course accept that Podeh's analysis is partial, perhaps even intuitive. After all, the events of summer 2006 following Israel's unilateral withdrawal from all of South Lebanon hardly suggest that territorial compromise alone can assuage the hostile intent of particular states or groups. Even so, his observation contains a kernel of truth, if not an absolute lesson; that war or regional conflict is and will remain the mother of diplomatic invention. Amid the hopes and fears surrounding the Arab uprising, this lesson alone suggests that a realist peace that predominantly seeks security from the Arab world, rather than with it, will continue to dominate Israel's strategic and diplomatic horizons in the years ahead.

Insurance without a premium? The role of the United States

For many, the diplomatic outcome of the October War will forever be associated with the realist statecraft of Dr Henry Kissinger and his dual role as both national security adviser and secretary of state under the Nixon administration. Like Israel, the United States misread and misunderstood the signals coming from Cairo between 1970 and 1973: over, firstly, a willingness to embrace diplomacy to secure the return of the Sinai; and, secondly, when such overtures appeared to fall on fallow ground, the failure to listen as the drums of war beat louder. Still Washington appeared unmoved. Often it is assumed that, distracted by events in South East Asia, White House officials did not pay sufficient attention to events in the Levant. In May 1973, the Central Intelligence Agency argued that while the current situation (Israel's continued control over the Sinai) was unbearable for Egypt, the threat of military action by Cairo was meant primarily to "entice the United States to put pressure on Israel", and indeed, even if conflict broke out, "hostilities will not include extensive land combat like 1967 or a lengthy war of attrition like that fought in 1969–1970."[26]

Even so, once hostilities had commenced, American diplomacy was both swift and sure. Kissinger viewed the conflict primarily through a Cold War lens and, as such, saw the geopolitical advantages that could accrue to Washington from now engaging with Cairo. United States actions towards the conflict have been studied in length elsewhere. Suffice it to note, for the purposes of this chapter, that its relationship with Israel during this period very much equates with a patron–client relationship if, as Michael Handel argued, this is defined as the ability to make autonomous foreign policy decisions but with one ear attuned to the wishes of the great power.[27] The reluctance to incur the displeasure of Washington, even when Golda Meir and her cabinet finally realised on the morning of 6 October that war was imminent, led Jerusalem to forego a pre-emptive attack. According to Avi Kober, "The logic behind this decision was to escape any responsibility for the outbreak of war that might prompt the United States to cut off weapons supplies or limit Israel's freedom of action on the battlefield."[28]

The reward for this restraint came two years later, amid negotiations for an interim deal between Jerusalem and Cairo over the scope and pace of troop withdrawals in the Sinai. On 1 September 1975, the United States signed a memorandum of understanding with Israel which, in its scope and obligation, is the nearest the two states have come to concluding a formal defence pact. This agreement committed the United States to be "fully responsive, on an ongoing and long-term basis, to Israel's need for military equipment and other defence requirements". At the time, this also included the supply of F16 fighter planes, Pershing ground-to-ground missiles and, in *extremis*, the supply of oil to Israel aboard American registered tankers. Moreover, Washington undertook to consult with Israel over the make-up and participants in any future peace conference; and, in addition, would use its veto in the United Nations to thwart any attempt to amend Resolutions 242 and 338.[29]

Given the magnitude of this commitment (albeit one conditioned by Cold War calculations in Washington), it is tempting to see this memorandum as marking the end of the classic patron–client relationship and perhaps, as the argument of Walt and Mearsheimer might have it, the start of the Israeli tail wagging the American dog. Perhaps. But successive administrations, both Republican and Democrat, have held to the view that a strong Israel that continues to have a clear technological and qualitative edge over its regional adversaries is far more likely to make territorial compromises in the search for Middle East peace. Equally, however, when direct American interests are at stake across the region, Israel has stayed its hand militarily. The decision by Jerusalem not to respond militarily to the Scud missile attacks on Haifa and Tel Aviv during 1990–1 can be cited as evidence, although other factors probably conditioned Jerusalem's response: any attack by the IDF risked fracturing the US–Arab alliance, thereby threatening a crisis in relations with Washington; it was doubtful that Israel would have had any more success in identifying the mobile launchers and hitting them; and finally, none of the Scuds was armed with biological or chemical weapons.[30]

But if the United States remains convinced that investment in a militarily strong Israel, following October 1973, remains a *sine qua non* for regional peace, Israel perhaps has drawn different lessons. Given the human cost of the war to the state and the belief that a defensive posture had undermined, rather than enhanced, Israel's deterrent posture, virtually all Israeli military operations since 1973 have been preventative and pre-emptive:, deterrence by denial and deterrence by punishment. Thus Operation Litani in 1978, the attack on Osirak in June 1981, the invasion of Lebanon in June 1982, the strike against the PLO headquarters in Tunis in 1985, Operation Defensive Shield in April 2002 and even the attack against the Syrian reactor in Deir ez-Zor in September 2007 have all been operations of varying risk where, irrespective of Washington's wishes or position, the demands of national security have determined Israeli military behaviour. To this extent, Israeli actions both before and after 1973 represent a continuum of David Ben Gurion's famous dictum that what matters most is not what the world says, but what the Jews do. As Meron Medzini has argued:

Since the days of the Holocaust, Israel's War of Independence, the three weeks preceding the Six Day War when Israel stood virtually alone, and the delay in activating the American airlift during the 1973 Yom Kippur war, there has been a feeling in Israel that it must look out for its own defence irrespective of what the international community says or does.[31]

But while increased reliance on the United States was never meant to restrict Israel's military room for manoeuvre, it has remained a diplomatic given that the support of Washington has been integral to those formal peace treaties and agreements Israel has reached with its Arab neighbours. The "realist" peace that was the Israeli–Egyptian treaty of 1978, and the fact that, despite being remote from the initial discussions that was the Oslo process, the agreement reached between Israel and the PLO was signed on the White House lawn, are testament to that. To this extent, the lessons taken by Arab leaders from the "Ramadan" war of 1973 were until recently obvious, if not sobering: that a correlation exists between conflict with Israel, its outcome, and the extent to which Washington has been willing to engage in peace negotiations. Indeed, the involvement of the United States was crucial—despite the initial steps taken by Sadat—in brokering peace between Cairo and Jerusalem in 1978. Again, without the American-sponsored "Madrid Conference" at the end of the 1990–1 Gulf War, it is unlikely that the Oslo process would have come about.[32]

The issue today, however, is the extent to which the key diplomatic lesson of the October War—the centrality of Washington to any peace process—is a lesson of diminishing utility to the curriculum of statecraft across the wider Middle East. Sapped by the cost—human, financial and material—of its own Middle East wars, the United States is widely seen as a superpower in decline, its uni-polar moment gone as it now faces up to the global economic challenge presented by Brazil, Russia, India and China. To be sure, none can match the ability of the United States to project raw military power but, as the events of the Arab Spring have shown, Washington exercised very little real influence over the course of events that led to the ousting of President Mubarak of Egypt, much to the chagrin of both Israel and Saudi Arabia.[33]

Perhaps now any lessons to be derived from the October 1973 War lie at the crossroads of relevance. If peace can only be the result of absolute engagement by the United States among the interlocutors, the evidence that any US administration is willing to invest the necessary political capital to create a real momentum to this end remains doubtful. Moreover, the "realist" peace deals between Egypt, Jordan and the PLO on the one hand and Israel on the other were agreements between states rather than peoples. Democratic peace this was not, and while we should not be dismissive of the emergence of a popularly elected government in Egypt because of its avowedly Islamist hue, relations with Israel that have always been frosty are likely to get chillier still. In part this can only partly be explained by pan-Islamism and sympathy among Arabs for the conditions that most Palestinians endure in the West Bank and Gaza.

Indeed, the electoral success of Islamist parties in North Africa and Egypt has exposed the hollowness of successive claims by Israeli politicians—most famously Nathan Sharansky—that only with progress towards democratic governance across the region can any tangible peace process ever come to fruition. Failure by Israel to welcome the apparent reduction in the Arab democratic deficit is therefore seen as evidence enough that Israel continues to see the "Arab and Muslim world as a monolithic danger", and can only embrace a realist peace.[34] Moreover, without significant progress in talks with the Palestinians, the ability of Israel to engage, let alone build, tangible relationships with new political dispensations across the region will be nigh-on impossible. For many in Israel, preventing relations deteriorating further with Cairo and Amman in the current climate would be achievement enough.

Instead, in this era of uncertainty, most Israelis wish to cling to truths that are strategic in nature, date back to the aftermath of the October 1973 War and conform to a reshaping of the geopolitical landscape upon which hard core security concerns—and certainties—can act as a compass. Thus, analysis of indigenous factors behind the uprisings in

Syria, Bahrain and continued violence in Iraq is framed by a broader regional competition between Saudi Arabia and Iran, and where reference to Islamists and Islamism by Israeli spokespeople has become a catch-all epithet to explain threats to regional stability.[35] As one Israeli official was reported to have remarked, "When some people in the West see what's happening in Egypt, they see Europe 1989. We see it as Tehran 1979."[36]

No one should doubt that Israel's external security concerns are not real and enduring. To think otherwise would be churlish and, indeed, ignore the regional animosity towards the Jewish state that shapes a new emergent Arab nationalism, based on a popular sense of Arab–Islamic identity that 1) denies sectarian difference and 2) is shaped by a common agenda regarding core Arab issues. It remains, however very much a nationalism defined by what mass movements are against: sclerotic regimes, corruption, debilitating forms of patrimonial governance, the dominance of the security state and, externally, Israel's continued occupation, control and settlement of Palestinian lands. And while agreement on prescriptive measures to tackle the domestic malaise left by decades of autocratic rule remains elusive, on the issue of Palestine a consensus exists. As that veteran (and astute) Israeli observer of the Arab world, Zvi Barel, noted of protesters' demands in Egypt: if Jerusalem wants to have anything like a warm peace, it will have to pay the price in Palestinian coinage.[37] But it begs the question, is the present government (or indeed any government) able or willing to pay in this currency?

Conclusion

Golda Meir was once quoted as saying, "Israel is prepared to negotiate all issues with their Arab neighbours save one: the state of Israel is not an item to be negotiated." Adherence to this dictum has certainly stood the Jewish state in good stead in the aftermath of the October War. Backed by the United States, the great achievement of Israeli diplomacy was the fracturing of the Arab consensus over the absolute rejection of a sovereign Israeli nation in a predominantly Arab Muslim Middle East. The peace with Egypt underscored Israel's preference for such bilateral agreements, serving as it has done to disrupt any semblance of Arab unity beyond the rhetorical in response to a series of Israeli actions since the October 1973 War.

Equally, Washington's support, a support that until the demise of the Soviet Union was framed by the Cold War, remains conditioned by a belief that a strong Israel is more likely to be receptive to peace overtures that require territorial compromise; and certainly this underpinned the basis of the agreement reached between Cairo and Jerusalem in 1978. But the regional conditions that led to such peace deals are changing, nor least in the case of Egypt, where elites will have to be more responsive to popular sentiment; and where, for some, a conflation of Islamist and pan-Arab discourse will shape a new political arena across the Middle East.[38]

How this will play out in terms of future relations between Cairo and Jerusalem remains to be seen, but if intuitive knowledge of Egypt has been shaped by the images of Sadat and Mubarak as "allies", trust in the new Islamist dispensation with its obvious affiliation with the likes of Hamas in Gaza does not bode well. The lesson Israelis might quite naturally conclude is that a "realism"—perhaps devoid of formal peace agreements—remains the best guarantor for the future of the State of Israel. This is perhaps a logical position to take and even unavoidable. But Israel would do well to ensure that, amid such trepidation, a hand outstretched rather than a finger held aloof, remains visible to the Arab world, including the Palestinians. This might not be the most popular lesson Israel can draw from the October 1973 War, but perhaps it remains its most enduring.

NOTES

1. INTRODUCTION

1. See for example Richard B. Parker (ed.), *The Six-Day War: A Retrospective* (Gainesville: University of Florida Press, 1996); Michael B. Oren, *Six Days of War: June 1967 and the Making of the Modern Middle East* (Oxford: Oxford University Press, 2002); W. R. Lewis and Avi Shlaim (eds) *The 1967 Arab–Israeli War: Origins and Consequences* (Cambridge: Cambridge University Press, 2012).
2. Galia Golan, *Yom Kippur and After: The Soviet Union and the Middle East Crisis* (Cambridge: Cambridge University Press, 1977); V. Israelyan, *Inside the Kremlin During the Yom Kippur War* (Philadelphia: Pennsylvania University Press, 1995).
3. Henry Kissinger, *Years of Upheaval* (Boston: Little Brown, 1983), 560.

2. ASSESSING THE HISTORIOGRAPHY OF THE OCTOBER WAR

1. Otherwise known as the Yom Kippur War, Ramadan War, the 1973 War or Operation Badr.
2. Charles S. Liebman, "The Myth of Defeat: The Memory of the October War in Israeli Society", *Middle Eastern Studies* 29, 3 (1993), 399–418, 401.
3. *Ibid.*
4. *Ibid.*, 414.
5. Avi Shlaim, "Failures in National Intelligence Estimates: The Case of the October War", *World Politics* 28, 3 (1976), 348–80, 349.
6. Uri Bar-Joseph, "Main Trends in the Historiography of the October War: A Thirty-Year Perspective," *Journal of Israeli History* 24, 2 (2006), 251–66, 254.
7. Shlaim, "Failures in National Intelligence Estimates".
8. Richard K. Betts, *Surprise Attack: Lessons for Defense Planning* (Washington: Brookings Institution, 1982).

265

9. Nadav Safran, "Trial by Ordeal: The October War, October 1973," *International Security* 2, 2 (1977), 133–70, 167.

10. Betts, *Lessons for Defense Planning*, 69.

11. Elliot Cohen and John Gooch, *Military Misfortunes: The Anatomy of Failure in War* (New York: Vintage Books, 1991), 116.

12. *Ibid.*

13. Michael I. Handel, *Perception, Deception, and Surprise: The Case of the October War* (Jerusalem: Hebrew University of Jerusalem, 1976).

14. Uri Bar-Joseph, "Israel's 1973 Intelligence Failure," in P.R. Kumaraswamy (ed.), *Revisiting the October War* (London: Frank Cass, 2000), 11–35, 11–17.

15. *Ibid.*, 15–28.

16. Ahron Bregman, *Israel's Wars: A History Since 1947* (London: Routledge, 2000).

17. *Ibid.*, 113–20.

18. Janice Gross Stein, "Calculation, Miscalculation, and Conventional Deterrence II: The View from Jerusalem," in Robert Jervis, Richard Ned Lebow and Janice Gross Stein (eds), *Psychology and Deterrence* (Baltimore: Johns Hopkins University Press, 1985), 61.

19. *Ibid.*, 63–70.

20. *Ibid.*, 75.

21. *Ibid.*, 76.

22. *Ibid.*

23. Ephraim Kahana, "Early Warning Versus Concept: The Case of the October War 1973," *Intelligence and National Security* 17, 2 (2002), 81–104, 97.

24. Eli Zeira, *The October 73 War: Myth Against Reality* (Tel Aviv: Yedioth Ahronot, 1993). (Hebrew).

25. Israel Tal, *National Security: The Israeli Experience* (Westport: Praeger, 2000).

26. Bar-Joseph, "Main Trends in the Historiography of the October War".

27. Moshe Dayan, *Story of My Life* (London: Sphere, 1978), 601.

28. Golda Meir, *My Life: The Autobiography of Golda Meir* (London: Weidenfeld & Nicolson, 1976), 357.

29. *Ibid.*, 369.

30. Tal, *National Security*, 171–91.

31. Zeev Schiff, *October Earthquake: Yom Kippur 1973* (London: Transaction Publishers, 1974), 299.

32. *Ibid.*

33. *Ibid.*, 301–10.

34. Howard Morely Sachar, *A History of Israel: Vol. II, From the Aftermath of the October War* (New York: Oxford University Press, 1987), 4.

35. Bregman, *Israel's Wars*, 104.

36. *Ibid.*

37. Bar-Joseph, "Main Trends in the Historiography of the October War."

38. Barry Rubin, "US Policy and the October War," *MERIP Reports* 23 (1973), 3–12; "US Policy, January-October 1973," *Journal of Palestine Studies* 3, 2 (1974), 98–113.

39. Rubin, "US Policy, January-October 1973," 104.

40. *Ibid.*, 106.

41. Ray Maghroori, *October War: A Case Study in Crisis Decision-Making in American Foreign Policy* (Washington: University Press of America, 1981), 67.

42. Richard Nixon, *The Memoirs of Richard Nixon* (New York: Grosset & Dunlop, 1978); Henry Kissinger, *Years of Upheaval* (Boston: Little, Brown, 1982).

43. Boaz Vanetik and Zaki Shalom, "The White House Middle East Policy in 1973 as a Catalyst for the Outbreak of the October War," *Israel Studies* 16, 1 (2011), 53–78, 53.

44. *Ibid.*

45. *Ibid.*

46. Mordechai Gazit, "Egypt and Israel: Was There a Peace Opportunity Missed in 1971?" *Journal of Contemporary History* 32, 1 (1997), 97–115, 97.

47. *Ibid.*

48. Meir, *My Life*, 289–90.

49. Simcha Dinitz, "The October War: Diplomacy of War and Peace," in Kumaraswamy (ed.), *Revisiting the October War*, 104–5.

50. *Ibid.*, 105.

51. Edgar O'Ballance, *No Victor, No Vanquished: The October War* (San Rafael: Presidio Press, 1978), 329.

52. Peter Allen, *The October War* (New York: Scribner, 1982); Chaim Herzog, *The War of Atonement: The Inside Story of the October War* (London: Greenhill, 1998); Stuart Cohen, "Operational Limitations of Reserve Forces: The Lessons of the 1973 War," in Kumaraswamy (ed.), *Revisiting the October War*; Walter J. Boyne, *The October War and the Airlift that Saved Israel* (New York: St. Martin's, 2002).

53. Emmanuel Wald, *The Wald Report: The Decline of Israeli National Security Since 1967* (Boulder, Co: Westview Press, 1992).

54. *Ibid.*, 112.

55. *Ibid.*, 113.

56. *Ibid.*, 114.

57. Abraham Ben-Zvi, "Hindsight and Foresight: A Conceptual Framework for the Analysis of Surprise Attacks," *World Politics* 28, 3 (1976), 381–95; "Threat Perception and Surprise: In Search of the Intervening Variable," in Frank P. Harvey and Ben D. Mor (eds), *Conflict in World Politics: Advances in the Study of Crisis, War and Peace* (New York: St Martin's, 1998).

58. Ben Zvi, "Hindsight and Foresight," 387.

59. *Ibid.*

60. *Ibid.*, 395.

61. Handel, *Perception, Deception, and Surprise*; Handel, "The Yom Kippur and the Inevitability of Surprise," *International Studies Quarterly* 21, 3 (1977), 461–502.

62. Handel, "The October War and the Inevitability of Surprise," 469.

63. *Ibid.*

64. *Ibid.*, 470.

65. *Ibid.*, 477.

66. Shlaim, "Failures in National Intelligence Estimates," 349.

67. *Ibid.*, 366–75.

68. Alex Roberto Hybel, *The Logic of Surprise in International Conflict* (Lexington: Lexington Press, 1986).

69. Mohammed Heikal, *The Road to Ramadan* (New York: New York Times Books, 1975).

70. Saadel el Shazly, *The Crossing of Suez: The October War 1973* (London: Third World Centre for Research and Publishing, 1980).

71. Mohamed Abdel Ghani el-Gamasy, *The October War: Memoirs of Field Marshall el-Gamasy of Egypt* (New York: Columbia University Press, 1994).

72. Ibrahim Shihata, "The Territorial Question and the October War," *Journal of Palestine Studies* 4, 1 (1974), 43–54, 54.

73. Heikal, *The Road to Ramadan*, 14.

74. *Ibid.*, 15.

75. *Ibid.*, Foreword.

76. *Ibid.*, 260.

77. *Ibid.*

78. *Ibid.*, 41.

79. Shazly, *The Crossing of Suez*, 205.

80. Richard B. Parker, "Review: The October War: Memoirs of Field Marshal el-Gamasy of Egypt by Mohamed Abdel Ghani el-Gamasy, Gillian Potter," *Middle East Journal* 48, 3 (1994), 537–8, 538.

81. Uri Bar-Joseph, *The Watchman Fell Asleep: The Surprise of Yom Kippur and its Sources* (Albany: State University of New York Press, 2005), 235–51.

82. Bar-Joseph, "Main Trends in the Historiography of the October War," 251.

83. Liebman, "The Myth of Defeat," 412.

84. *Ibid.*, 415.

3. ISRAEL AND THE OCTOBER WAR

1. Charles Liebman, "The Myth of Defeat: The Memory of the Yom Kippur War in Israeli Society", *Middle Eastern Studies*, 29, 3 (1993), 399–418, 399, 413.

2. Idith Zertal and Akiva Eldar, *Lords of the Land: The War Over Israel's Settlements in the Occupied Territories, 1967–2007* (New York: Nation Books, 2007).

3. For a description of Israeli attitudes upon visiting the territories, see Tom Segev,

1967: Israel, the War and the Year that Transformed the Middle East (London: Little Brown, 2007), 424—431.

4. Gad Barzilai, *Wars, Internal Conflicts, and Political Order: A Jewish Democracy in the Middle East* (Albany: State University of New York Press, 1996), 84–87.

5. Avi Shlaim, *The Iron Wall: Israel and the Arab World* (London: Penguin, 2001), 251, 262.

6. Colin Shindler, *The Land Beyond Promise: Israel, Likud, and the Zionist Dream* (London: IB Tauris, 1995), 67.

7. Abba Eban, *Personal Witness: Israel Through My Eyes* (New York: Putnam's, 1992), 460.

8. Barzilai, *Wars, Internal Conflicts, and Political Order*, 93–4.

9. Gideon Rafael, *Destination Peace: Three Decades of Israeli Foreign Policy* (London: Weidenfeld & Nicolson, 1981), 209.

10. Elinor Burkett, *Golda Meir: The Iron Lady of the Middle East* (London: Gibson Square, 2008), 208.

11. Mordechai Gazit, *The Peace Process 1969–1973: Efforts and Contacts* (Jerusalem: Magnes Press, 1983), 17.

12. Golda Meir, *My Life* (London: Weidenfeld & Nicolson, 1975), 312.

13. Moshe Dayan, *Story of My Life* (New York: William Morrow & Co., 1976), 461.

14. Gershom Gorenberg, *The Accidental Empire: Israel and the Birth of the Settlements, 1967–1977* (New York: Times Books, 2006), 82–83; Zertal and Eldar, *Lords of the Land*, 8, 10–11, 13, 19–20; Shlomo Ben-Ami, *Scars of War, Wounds of Peace* (New York: Oxford University Press), 122–3.

15. Dayan, *Story of My Life*, 394.

16. Shlaim, *The Iron Wall*, 287.

17. Ben-Ami, *Scars of War, Wounds of Peace*, 130–1.

18. Eban, *Personal Witness*, 460–1.

19. Colin Shindler, *A History of Modern Israel* (Cambridge: Cambridge University Press, 2008), 136–7; Ben-Ami, *Scars of War, Wounds of Peace*, p. 123; Shlaim, *The Iron Wall*, 253–4.

20. Avi Raz, *The Bride and The Dowry: Israel, Jordan, and the Palestinians in the Aftermath of the June 1967 War* (New Haven: Yale University Press, 2012), 43–5;

21. Shlaim, *The Iron Wall*, 254, 259.

22. Benny Morris, *Righteous Victims: A History of the Zionist-Arab Conflict, 1881–1999* (New York: Alfred A. Knopf, 1999), 346.

23. Ben-Ami, *Scars of War, Wounds of Peace*, 128.

24. Raz, *The Bride and The Dowry*, 45–47; Ben-Ami, *The Bride and The Dowry*, 125.

25. Ben-Ami, *Scars of War, Wounds of Peace*, 129; Henry Kissinger, *Years of Upheaval* (London: Weidenfeld & Nicolson, 1982), 197–9.

26. Ahron Bregman, *Israel's Wars: A History Since 1947* (London: Routledge, 2002), 96–101; Burkett, *Golda Meir*, 257–8.

27. For an analysis of the Jarring mission, see Saadia Touval, *The Peace Brokers: Mediators in the Arab-Israeli Conflict, 1948–1979* (Princeton: Princeton University Press, 1982), 134–64.

28. The US had practically replaced the UN as the primary mediator in the Middle East, but American attention during this period was largely focused on China, Vietnam, and maintaining détente. Additionally, differences between the White House and the State Department meant that the latter's peace explorations did not have full executive support (William I. Zartman, "The Failure of Diplomacy" in Richard B. Parker [ed.], *The October War: A Retrospective* [Gainesville: University Press of Florida, 2001], 18–9, 29–30, 53–4).

29. Shlaim, *The Iron Wall*, 295–6.

30. Mordechai Gazit, *Israeli Diplomacy and the Quest for Peace* (London: Frank Cass, 2002), 93–7.

31. Zartman, "The Failure of Diplomacy", 60–1

32. Gazit, *Israeli Diplomacy*, 245.

33. Bregman, *Israel's Wars*, 81.

34. Eban, *Personal Witness*, 505. Sisco himself has said that he "never understood" Dayan's silence on the matter (Zartman, "The Failure of Diplomacy", 31).

35. Rafael, *Destination Peace*, 267.

36. Kissinger, *Years of Upheaval*, 215–6.

37. Simcha Dinitz, "The Yom Kippur War: Diplomacy of War and Peace" in P.R. Kumaraswamy (ed.), *Revisiting the Yom Kippur War* (London: Frank Cass, 2000), 105–106; Zartman, "The Failure of Diplomacy", 64–65; Gazit, *Israeli Diplomacy*, 107–8.

38. Bar-Joseph, "Last Chance to Avoid War: Sadat's Peace Initiative of February 1973 and its Failure", *Journal of Contemporary History*, 41, 3, 2006, 550; Rafael, *Destination Peace*, 280.

39. Kissinger, *Years of Upheaval*, 220–1.

40. Eban, *Personal Witness*, 517–8, 521–2.

41. *Ibid.*, 518; Chaim Herzog, *The War of Atonement: The Inside Story of the Yom Kippur War*, 1973 (London: Greenhill Books, 1998), 41; Bar-Joseph, *The Watchman*, 77.

42. Janice Gross Stein, "The Failures of Deterrence and Intelligence" in Parker (ed.), *The October War: A Retrospective*, 109.

43. Herzog, *The War of Atonement*, 41–2.

44. "Special Document: Israel: What Went Wrong on October 6?: The Partial Report of the Israeli Commission of Inquiry into the October War", *Journal of Palestine Studies*, 3, 4 (1974), 193.

45. *Ibid.*; Aryeh Shalev, *Israel's Intelligence Assessment Before the Yom Kippur War:*

Disentangling Deception and Distraction (Brighton: Sussex Academic Press, 2010), xiv, 227.

46. Stein, "The Failures of Deterrence and Intelligence", 105–6.
47. Israeli Commission of Inquiry, 200–202; Bar-Joseph, *The Watchman Fell Asleep: The Surprise of Yom Kippur and Its Sources* (Albany: State University of New York Press, 2005), 91–92, 113, 135; Herzog, *The War of Atonement*, 46–7.
48. Dayan, *Story of My Life*, 468–72.
49. Bar-Joseph, *The Watchman*, 83–6, 93–5, 122–9; Michael Brecher, *Decisions in Crisis: Israel 1967 and 1973* (Berkeley: University of California Press, 1980), 73–4.
50. Meir, *My Life*, 354–5.
51. Bar-Joseph, *The Watchman*, 160–1; Israeli Commission of Inquiry, 195
52. Bar-Joseph, *The Watchman*, 55–6.
53. Stein, "The Failures of Deterrence and Intelligence", 131.
54. Bar-Joseph, *The Watchman*, 190–9; Brecher, *Decisions in Crisis*, 184–90.
55. Meir, *My Life*, 358–9.
56. Herzog, *The War of Atonement*, 29, 49; Michael Brecher & Mordechai Raz, "Images and Behaviour: Israel's Yom Kippur Crisis 1973", *International Journal*, 32, 3, Summer 1977, 476.
57. Brecher, *Decisions in Crisis*, 62; Bar-Joseph, *The Watchman*, 76, 130–1, 237.
58. Meir, *My Life*, 357.
59. Shlaim, *The Iron Wall*, 288.
60. Meir, *My Life*, 358.
61. Dayan, *Story of My Life*, 460.
62. Dinitz, "The Yom Kippur War", 110–11.
63. Herzog, *The War of Atonement*, 277.
64. Bernard Reich, "Crisis Management" in Parker (ed.), *The October War: A Retrospective*, 211; Dinitz, "The Yom Kippur War", 117–18.
65. Bar-Joseph, *The Watchman*, 229–31.
66. Meir, *My Life*, 360–1.
67. Gabriel Sheffer, "From Crisis to Change: The Israeli Political Elites and the 1973 War", in Kumaraswamy (ed.), *Revisiting the Yom Kippur War*, 168.
68. Nadav Safran, "Trial by Ordeal: The Yom Kippur War, October 1973", *International Security*, 2, 2, Summer 1977, 149–50, 156–57. Though Safran notes that the airborne intervention "eased the pressure on Northern Command and allowed it slowly to regain hold of the situation", Bar-Joseph is highly critical of Dayan's decision, arguing that the attacks on Syrian anti-aircraft positions were not effective enough to warrant the change, and prevented the destruction of Egyptian air defences in the south, thus retaining the anti-aircraft threat on both fronts throughout most of the war (Bar-Joseph, *The Watchman*, 218–24).

69. Bregman, *Israel's Wars*, 133–41.

70. Herzog, *The War of Atonement*, 201–02; Brecher, *Decisions in Crisis*, 213.

71. Herzog, *The War of Atonement*, 41, 280–1.

72. Brecher, *Decisions in Crisis*, 214–5; Abba Eban, *An Autobiography* (London: Weidenfeld & Nicolson, 1978), 515.

73. Eban, *An Autobiography*, 528–30.

74. Kissinger, *Years of Upheaval*, 602.

75. Eban, *Personal Witness*, 538; Dinitz, "The Yom Kippur War", 119–20.

76. Reich, "Crisis Management".

77. Meir, *My Life*, 377–8.

78. Barzilai, *Wars, Internal Conflicts, and Political Order*, 111–19.

79. Meir, *My Life*, 364–5.

80. Barzilai, *Wars, Internal Conflicts, and Political Order*, 116.

81. Elias Shoufani, "Israeli Reactions to the War", *Journal of Palestine Studies*, 3, 2, Winter 1974, 61–2.

82. Jonathan Mendilow, *Ideology, Party Change, and Electoral Campaigns in Israel, 1965–2001* (Albany: State University of New York Press), 82; Yochanan Peres *et al.*, "Predicting and Explaining Voters' Behaviour in Israel", in Asher Arian (ed.), *The Elections in Israel—1973* (Jerusalem: Jerusalem Academic Press, 1975) 197; Shindler, *The Land Beyond Promise*, 76.

83. Arian (ed.), *The Elections in Israel—1973*.

84. Israeli Commission of Inquiry, 199–202.

85. *Ibid.*, 202–3.

86. Kissinger, *Years of Upheaval*, 563.

87. Herzog, *The War of Atonement*, 280–1, 41.

88. *Ibid.*, 206.

89. *Ibid.*, 196.

90. Israeli Commission of Inquiry, 207.

91. Herzog, *The War of Atonement*, 282.

92. Shlaim, *The Iron Wall*, 323.

93. Shoufani, "Israeli Reactions to the War", 59.

94. Barzilai, *Wars, Internal Conflicts, and Political Order*, 118–19.

95. Shindler, *The Land Beyond Promise*, 74–5; Benjamin Akzin, "The Likud", in Arian (ed.), *The Elections in Israel—1977*, 46; Mendilow, *Ideology, Party Change, and Electoral Campaigns in Israel*, 83.

96. Akzin, "The Likud", 46.

97. Shindler, *The Land Beyond Promise*, 77–80.

98. Yonathan Shapiro, "End of a Dominant Party System" in Arian (ed.), *The Elections in Israel—1977*; Mendilow, *Ideology, Party Change, and Electoral Campaigns in Israel*, 84.

99. Shindler, *The Land Beyond Promise*, 52–61.

100. Bar-Joseph, "Last Chance to Avoid War", 555.

101. Shindler, *The Land Beyond Promise*, 81.

102. Reuven Pedatzur, "The IDF—too big to assail", *Ha'aretz*, 3 March, 2013; Martin van Creveld, *Defending Israel: A Controversial Plan Towards Peace* (New York: Thomas Dunne Books, 2004).

4. THE OCTOBER WAR AND EGYPT'S MULTIPLE CROSSINGS

1. Yoram Meital, *Egypt's Struggle for Peace: Continuity and Change, 1967–1977* (Gainesville: University Press of Florida), 86–7.

2. Isma'il's words in Sa'ad al-Din al-Shazly, *The Crossing of Suez: The October War 1973* (London: Third World Center, 1980), 109.

3. For Sadat's words: *Ibid.*, 109.

4. Hafez Isma'il, *Amn Misr al-Qawmi fi 'Asr al-Tahadiyat* [Egypt's national security in the age of challenges] (Cairo: Markaz al-Ahram, 1987), 215; Henry Kissinger, *The White House Years* (Boston: Little, Brown, 1979), 1295, 1298–9.

5. For the full text of what was said in that meeting, see Musa Sabri, *Wath'iq Harb Uktubir* [October War Documents] (Cairo: al-Maktab al-Misri al-Hadith, 1974), 35–88.

6. For the back-channel exchange, see Isma'il, *Amn Misr al-Qawmi*, 247–61.

7. Patrick Seale, *Asad of Syria: The Struggle for the Middle East* (Berkeley: University of California Press, 1988), 197.

8. For the quotes, see 'Abd al-Ghani al-Jamasy, *Harb Uktubir 1973* [The October 1973 War] (Paris: al-Mansurat al-Sharqiyya, 1989), 263.

9. All the quotes in Shazly, *The Crossing of the Suez*, 30–31.

10. For the text of the two directives, see Anwar Sadat, *In Search of Identity: An Autobiography* (New York: Harper & Row, 1978), 326–8.

11. For the debate over Israeli intelligence failure, see: Uri Bar-Joseph, *The Watchman Fell Asleep: The Surprise of Yom Kippur and its Sources* (Albany: State University of New York Press, 2005).

12. All the quotes from Isma'il, *Amn Misr al-Qawmi*, 318–27.

13. Al-Shazly, *The Crossing of the Suez*, 164, 166.

14. Sadat's statement in the People's Council, 16 October 1973, in *Majmu'at Khutub w-Ahadith al-Ra'is Muhammad Anwar al-Sadat* [Arab Republic of Egypt, Sadat's speeches] (Cairo, 1970–81).

15. Isma'il, *Amn Misr al-Qawmi*, 351–2.

16. William Quandt, *Decade of Decisions: American Policy toward the Arab–Israeli Conflict, 1967–1976* (Berkeley: University of California Press, 1977), 197.

17. "Nixon Memo to the Congress," 24 April 1974, The Nixon Project, WHCF CO 76, Box 45.

18. Heikal, *'Ind muftaraq al-turuq* [At the Crossroads] (Beirut, 1983), 13–14. No

wonder, then, that Heikal entitled his most comprehensive book on the 1973 War *Uktubir 73: al-silah wa-'l-siyasa* [October 73: Arms and Politics] (Cairo, 1993), in which he examines the conduct of the war in the light of Sadat's personality and decisions. For similar contentions, see Imam, '*Ali Sabri Yatadhakkar* [The Remembrance of 'Ali Sabri] (Cairo, 1987), 96.

19. Al-Shazly, *The Crossing of the Suez*, 10.

20. Mohamed H. Heikal, *Autumn of Fury: The Assassination of Sadat* (London: Random House 1983), 281.

21. Shazly, for instance, wrote that Sadat had "thrown away the greatest army Egypt had ever assembled. He had thrown away the biggest airlift the Soviet Union had ever mounted. He had thrown away the greatest collaborative effort the Arabs had achieved in a generation." Al-Shazly, *The Crossing of the Suez*, 184. Fahmi asserted that "Egypt had not won the war in the sense of pushing the Israelis out of Sinai [...] but Egypt had scored a valuable political victory." Ismail Fahmy, *Negotiating for Peace in the Middle East* (London: Croom Helm, 1983), 33–4. Sayyid Ahmad perceived the war as a draw: there was no "decisive Arab victory any more than it was another decisive Israeli victory." Muhammad Sayyid Ahmad, *After the Guns Fall Silent: Peace or Armageddon in the Middle East* (London: Croom Helm, 1976), 15–19. Hamad also argued that victory had not been complete. Egypt had eventually found itself in a situation of grave strategic difficulty, caused, he thought, by the lack of a truly unified command in control of operations on both fronts. The existing so-called unified command structure had not functioned as such. Jamal Hamad, *Min Sina' ila al-Julan* [From Sinai to the Golan] (Cairo: al-Zahara, 1988), 537–8.

22. *Al-Siyasa al–Dawliyya* (October 1976), 248.

23. Hassan Nafi', *Misr wal-Sira' al-'Arabi al-Isra'ili* [Egypt and the Arab–Israeli Conflict] (Beirut, 1986), 50–92.

24. *Ibid.*, 86–114.

25. *Al-Ahram*, 14 December 1973.

26. *Ibid.*, 10 October 1973.

5. SYRIA AND THE OCTOBER WAR: THE MISSED OPPORTUNITY

1. See Dani Asher (ed.), *The Syrians on the Borders, the IDF Northern Command in the Yom Kippur War* (Tel Aviv: Ma'archot, 2008) (Hebrew), 21–44; (Lod: Zmora-Bitan Publishers, 2001) (in Hebrew), 417–18. See also Patrick Seale, *Asad of Syria, the Struggle for the Middle East* (London: I. B. Tauris, 1988), 211.

2. Seale, *Asad of Syria*, 195.

3. For more see Moshe Ma'oz, *Asad: The Sphinx of Damascus* (London: Weidenfeld & Nicolson, 1988); Eyal Zisser, *Asad's Legacy—Syria in Transition* (New York: New York University Press, 2000).

4. See Eyal Zisser, "June 1967: Israel's Capture of the Golan Heights," *Israel Studies*, 7, 1 (Spring 2002), 168–94.

5. See Mustafa Talas, *The Story of My Life* (Damascus: Dar Talas lil-Nashr, 1992), vol. III (Arabic), 697–754. See also Ze'ev Eytan, "The Syria Army," in Avner Yaniv, Moshe Ma'oz and Avi Kover (eds), *Syria and Israel's National Security* (Tel Aviv: Ma'archot, 1991), 155–170.

6. For more see Elie Podeh, *The Decline of Arab Unity, the Rise and Fall of the United Arab Republic* (Brighton: Sussex Academic Press, 1999); Zisser, "June 1967: Israel's Capture of the Golan Heights," 189–93.

7. See Mohamed Abdel Ghani el-Gamasy, *The October War* (Cairo: The American University in Cairo Press, 1993), 182–4; see Uri Bar-Joseph, *The Watchman Fell Asleep: The Surprise of Yom Kippur and its Sources* (Albany: State University of New York Press, 2005), 222–3. See also Talas, *The Story of My Life*, vol. III, 666–90; Seale, *Asad of Syria*, 185–201.

8. For 'Abd al-Halim Khaddam's version see *al-Safir* (Beirut), 17 February 2003.

9. See Anwar el-Sadat, *In Search of Identity* (New York: Harper & Row, 1978), 186–8.

10. See Seale, *Asad of Syria*, 192–4; el-Gamasy, *The October War*, 159–73, 182–4. See also Bar-Joseph, *The Watchman Fell Asleep, The Surprise of Yom Kippur and its Sources*, 222–3; Arieh Shalev, *Success and Failure in Alert, The Israeli Intelligence Assessments Towards the Yom-Kipur War* (Tel Aviv: Ma'arachot, 2006) (in Hebrew), 113–118.

11. Mohamed Hasanayn Heikal, *The Road to Ramadan* (New York: Ballantine, 1975), 20–3.

12. An interview by the author with Muhammad Basyuni (Tel Aviv, 13 January 1999).

13. An interview by the author with Patrick Seale (Tel Aviv, 13 June 1999). See also Seale, *Asad of Syria*, 194–6.

14. Seale, *Asad of Syria*, 197.

15. See Talas, *The Story of My Life*, vol. III, 697–754.

16. Seale, *Asad of Syria*, 197. See also Mustafa Talas, *The Story of My Life*, vol. III, 697–754.

17. See Seale, *Asad of Syria*, 198–9, 208.

18. See Seale, *Asad of Syria*, 199, 208–9. For Gamasy and Shazly's accounts on these meetings, see el-Gamasy, *The October War*, 182–6; Sa'ad al-Din al-Shazly, *The October War* (Beirut: Dar al-Nahar 1980) (in Arabic). See also Sa'ad al-Din al-Shazly, Al-shid 'ala al-'Asr, al-Jazira TV, 22 July 2009.

19. See Talas, *The Story of My Life*, vol. III, 697–892. See also Dani Asher (ed.), *The Syrians on the Borders*, 81–260; Seale, *Asad of Syria*, 211–15.

20. See Asher (ed.), *The Syrians on the Borders*, 81–116. See also Hanoch Bartov and David Elazar, *Dado: 48 Years and 20 more Days* (Tel Aviv: Ma'ariv, 1978)

(in Hebrew), vol. II, 9–142; Aviram Barkai, *On the Edge: the Story of Brigade no. 188 in the Yom Kippur War* (Tel Aviv: Ma'ariv, 2009) (in Hebrew).

21. See Talas, *The Story of My Life*, vol. III, 697–892; see also Seale, *Asad of Syria*, 211–15.

22. See Asher (ed.) *The Syrians on the Borders*, 181–260.

23. Seale, *Asad of Syria*, 219–20.

24. *Ibid.*

25. *Ibid.*, 219–20. See also Henry Kissinger, *Years of Upheaval* (Boston: Little, Brown, 1982), 779.

26. Anwar el-Sadat, *In Search of Identity* (New York: Harper & Row, 1978), 190–1.

27. See Seale, *Asad of Syria*,.218–19.

28. See Shimon Shamir, *Egypt under Sadat: the Search for a New Orientation* (Tel Aviv: Dvir, 1978) (in Hebrew).

29. See Faruq al-Shar', "Remarks on the October War" in *al-Safir* (Beirut), 17 February 2000. See also an interview given by Bashar al-Asad to *al-Hayat* (London), 7, 11 March 2000.

30. See Zisser, *Asad's Legacy*, 1–35; Eberhard Kienle, *Ba'th versus Ba'th: The Conflict between Syria and Iraq, 1968–1989* (London: I. B. Tauris, 1990). See also Eyal Zisser, "The 1982 Peace for Galilee War: Looking Back in Anger—Between an Option of a War and a War of No Option," in Mordechai Bar-on (ed.), *A Never Ending Conflict: A Guide to Israeli Military History* (London: Praeger, 2004), 193–210. See also Robert G. Rabil, *Embattled Neighbors, Syria, Israel and Lebanon* (Boulder, CO: Lynne Reiner Publishers, 2003).

31. See Eyal Zisser, "Syria and Israel—Between War and Peace," in Elie Podeh and Asher Kaufman (eds.), *Arab-Jewish Relations: From Conflict to Resolution?* (Brighton: Sussex Academic Press, 2006), 114–31. See also Hafez al-Asad's interview to *Newsweek*, 1 June 1974; Moshe Ma'oz, *Syria and Israel, From War to Peacemaking* (Oxford: Oxford University Press, 1995), 140–60 Seale, *Asad of Syria*, 241–61; Kenneth W. Stein, *Heroic Diplomacy: Sadat, Kissinger, Carter, Begin and the Quest for Arab–Israeli Peace* (New York: Routledge, 1999).

32. See "Abd al-Halim Khaddam" in *al-Safir* (Beirut), 17 February 2003.

6. US FOREIGN POLICY AND THE KISSINGER STRATAGEM

1. Richard Nixon, *RN: The Memoirs of Richard Nixon* (New York: Simon & Schuster, 1978), 937.

2. Alexander M. Haig with Charles McCarry, *Inner Circles: How America Changed the World: A Memoir* (New York: Warner Books, 1992), 409–10.

3. Robert Dallek, *Nixon and Kissinger: Partners in Power* (London: Penguin, 2007), 521–2.

4. See for example William B. Quandt, *Decade of Decisions: American Policy toward the Arab–Israeli Conflict, 1967–1976* (Berkeley: University of California Press, 1977); Salim Yaqub, "The Weight of Conquest: Henry Kissinger and the Arab–Israeli Conflict" in Fredrik Logevall and Andrew Preston (eds), *Nixon in the World: American Foreign Relations, 1969–1977* (New York: Oxford University Press, 2008), 227–48.

5. Asaf Siniver, *Nixon, Kissinger and U.S. Foreign Policy Making: The Machinery of Crisis* (New York: Cambridge University Press, 2008), 54; Jussi Hanhimaki, *The Flawed Architect: Henry Kissinger and American Foreign Policy* (New York: Oxford University Press, 2004), 188.

6. Henry Kissinger, *The White House Years* (London: Weidenfeld and Nicolson and M. Joseph, 1979), 1276–7.

7. See for example Mordechai Gazit, "Egypt and Israel—Was There a Peace Opportunity Missed in 1971?", *Journal of Contemporary History* 32, 1 (1997); 97–115; Gerschon Shafir, "The Miscarriage of Peace: Israel, Egypt, the United States, and the 'Jarring Plan' in the Early 1970s", *Israel Studies Forum* 21, 1 (2006), 3–26; Boaz Vanetik and Zaki Shalom, "The White House Middle East Policy in 1973 as a Catalyst for the Outbreak of the Yom Kippur War", *Israel Studies* 16, 1 (2011), 53–78.

8. Anwar Sadat, *In Search of Identity* (London: Collins, 1978), 228–31; Moshe Halfon, *From War to Peace: The Peace Course between Egypt and Israel, 1970–1979* (Tel Aviv: Hakibbutz Hameuchad, 2002), 16–17.

9. Interview with William Quandt, 26 August 2004, Charlottesville, VA.

10. Kissinger, *Years of Upheaval*, 227.

11. *Newsweek*, 9 April 1973, 10–11.

12. Memo from the NSC Staff, "Indications of Arab Intentions to Initiate Hostilities", May 1973. HAK Office Files, Box 135, Rabin/Kissinger (Dinitz) 1973 Jan-July (2 of 3), National Archives (College Park, MD), Nixon Presidential Materials Project (henceforth NPMP).

13. Memcon, Abba Eban, Simcha Dinitz, Avner Dan, Henry Kissinger, Harold Saunders, Peter Rodman, 12 May, 1973; Kissinger's office, the White House. Folder #4, Country Files—Middle East, HAK Office, Box 135, National Security Council Files (henceforth NSCF), NPMP.

14. Ephraim Kahana, "Early Warning Versus Concept: The Case of the Yom Kippur War, 1973", *Intelligence and National Security* 17, 2 (2002), 81–104; Uri Bar-Joseph, "Israel's 1973 Intelligence Failure", *Israel Affairs* 6, 1 (1999), 11–35; Uri Bar-Joseph, *The Watchman Fell Asleep: The Surprise of Yom Kippur and its Sources* (New York: State University of New York Press, 2005).

15. Memo, Quandt to Scowcroft, "Arab–Israeli Tensions", 6 October 1973. 1973 War (Middle East) 6 Oct. 1973 File No. 1, NSCF, NPMP.

16. Kissinger, *Years of Upheaval*, 458; Marvin and Bernard Kalb, *Kissinger* (Boston: Little Brown, 1974), 461–2; Quandt, *Decade of Decisions*, 170–1.

17. Bar-Joseph, *The Watchman Fell Asleep*, 225–6.

18. Memcon, Dinitz and Kissinger, 9 October, 1973, 8:20–8:40 a.m., the White House. RG 59, SN 70–73, Pol Isr-US, National Archives.

19. Memcon, Dinitz, Shalev, Kissinger, Scowcroft and Rodman. 9 October, 1973, 6:10–6:35 p.m., the White House. RG 59, SN 70–73, Pol Isr-US, National Archives.

20. After a stopover in Budapest, the first planes arrived in the Middle East on 9 and 10 October. When the war began the Kremlin estimated that the Arabs already had a significant qualitative advantage over Israel in weaponry, around 1.7 to 1. See Victor Israelyan, *Inside the Kremlin during the Yom Kippur War* (University Park: Pennsylvania State University Press, 1995), 58–60. Iraq supplied Syria with helicopters, fighter jets (with pilots) and tanks, while Egypt received jets and an infantry brigade from Algeria. Libya provided surface-to-air missiles, while Sudan contributed an infantry brigade. See Memcon, Dinitz, Gur, Kissinger and Scowcroft. 9 October, 1973, 8:20–8:40 a.m.; Memcon, "Military Briefing", 22 October 1973, 4:15 p.m.–4:57 p.m. RG 59, SN 70–73, POL 7 US/Kissinger, National Archives.

21. Memo, Quandt to Kissinger, "Middle East Issues", 9 October, 1973. Middle East War Memos & Misc. Oct. 6–Oct. 17, 1973, Box 664, NSCF, NPMP.

22. Memcon, Dinitz and Kissinger, 9 October 1973.

23. Mati Golan, *The Secret Conversations of Henry Kissinger: Step-by-Step Diplomacy in the Middle East* (New York: Quadrangle, 1976), 49.

24. Simcha Dinitz, "The Yom Kippur War: Diplomacy of War and Peace", *Israel Affairs*, 6:1 (1999), 113.

25. See for example Edward N. Luttwak and Walter Laqueur, "Kissinger and the Yom Kippur War", *Commentary*, 58 (September 1974), 33–40; Elmo R. Zumwalt, *On Watch: A Memoir* (Arlington, VA: Admiral Zumwalt & Associates, 1976), 433–5; Ted Szulc, *The Illusion of Peace: Foreign Policy in the Nixon Years* (New York: Viking, 1978), 735–8; Stephen E. Ambrose, *Nixon: Ruin and Recovery 1973–1990* (New York: Simon & Schuster, 1991), 234.

26. Interview with Quandt.

27. James Schlesinger, "The Airlift" in Richard Parker (ed.), *The October War: A Retrospective* (Gainesville, FL: University of Florida Press, 2001), 156–7; Richard N. Lebow and Janice G. Stein, *We All Lost the Cold War* (Princeton, NJ: Princeton University Press, 1994), 192.

28. Walter Isaacson, *Kissinger* (London: Faber and Faber, 1992), 521.

29. Kalb and Kalb, *Kissinger*, 475.

30. Nixon, *RN*, 927.

31. Kissinger, *Years of Upheaval*, 522.

32. "Soviet vs U.S. Supplies Delivered by Air to M.E." No date. Folder #3, MF, Box H-092, NSCIF, NPMP.

33. Memcon, "WSAG Principals: Middle East War", 17 October 1973, 4:00 p.m.

Folder #6, *WSAG Meetings*, Meeting Files, Box H-092, NSC Institutional Files, NPMP.

34. Cited in Yossi Melman and Dan Raviv, *Friends in Deed: Inside the U.S.–Israel Alliance* (New York: Hyperion, 1994), 163.

35. Golan, *The Secret Conversations of Henry Kissinger*, 51.

36. State Department Operations Center, Middle East Task Force, "Situation Report in the Middle East as of 06:00 Hours EDT, Oct. 19, 1973" (Situation Report #43), 19 October 1973, Middle East War, 19 Oct. 1973-File No. 14, Box 1173, NSCF, NPMP.

37. Nixon to Brezhnev (no title), 20 October, 1973. Dobrynin/Kissinger vol. 20 (October 12–November 27, 1973), Box 69, HAK Office Files, NPMP.

38. Kissinger, *Years of Upheaval*, 547, 548.

39. Hanhimaki, *The Flawed Architect*, 310–11; Lebow and Stein, *We All Lost the Cold War*, 211–15.

40. Kenneth Stein, *Heroic Diplomacy: Sadat, Kissinger, Carter, Begin, and the Quest for Arab–Israeli Peace* (New York: Routledge, 1999), 91.

41. *Ibid.*, 90.

42. Memcon, Meir, Gazit, Kissinger and Rodman, 22 October 1973, 1:35 p.m.–2:15 p.m. RG 59, SN 70–73, POL 7 US/Kissinger, National Archives.

43. *Ibid.*

44. Golan, *The Secret Conversations of Henry Kissinger*, 86.

45. Richard L. Garthoff, *Détente and Confrontation: American-Soviet Relations from Nixon to Reagan* (Washington, DC: The Brookings Institution, 1994, rev. edn), 87.

46. Anatoly Dobrynin, *In Confidence: Moscow's Ambassador to America's Six Cold War Presidents* (New York: Times Books, 1995), 293; Israelyan, *Inside the Kremlin during the Yom Kippur War*, 160.

47. Interview with Quandt.

48. Garthoff, *Détente and Confrontation*, 421–2.

49. Henry Kissinger, *Crisis: The Anatomy of Two Major Foreign Policy Crises* (New York: Simon & Schuster, 2003), 331–2, 343–4.

50. Kissinger, *Years of Upheaval*, 583.

51. Nixon, *RN*, 938.

52. Israelyan, *Inside the Kremlin during the Yom Kippur War*, 168. Israelyan served as the director of the Department of International Organisations in the Soviet Foreign Ministry during the war.

53. See Lebow and Stein, *We All Lost the Cold War*, 246–58; Hanhimaki, *The Flawed Architect*, 315.

54. Zumwalt, *On Watch*, 448; William Bundy, *A Tangled Web: The Making of Foreign Policy in the Nixon Administration* (New York: Hill and Wang, 1998), 444.

55. Kissinger, *Crisis*, 346, 347,

56. *Ibid.*, 347.
57. Garthoff, *Détente and Confrontation*, 425 (fn. 78).
58. Interview with Quandt.
59. Telecon, Scowcroft to Kissinger, 11 October 1973, 7.55pm. HAK Telcons, Box 22, File 10, 089, NPMP.
60. Kissinger, *Crisis*, 348; Haig, *Inner Circles*, 416. According to Kissinger, Sisco did not attend the meeting, while Haig's account does not mention Commander Howe.
61. Kissinger, *Crisis*, 350.
62. Garthoff, *Détente and Confrontation*, 427.
63. *Ibid.*, 353; Dowty, *Middle East Crisis*, 274.
64. Kissinger, *Crisis*, 351.
65. Dobrynin, *In Confidence*, 297.

7. THE SOVIET UNION AND THE OCTOBER WAR

1. For example, the Soviet chief of staff Ogarkov supported détente as a means of gaining technology beneficial for modernisation of the armed forces, but there were also some in the military who feared that détente would limit Soviet capabilities.
2. Yevgeny Primakov cites a *Time* interview early in 1972 in which Sadat said that he would ask the Soviet troops ("advisers") to leave once an interim agreement secured a partial Israeli withdrawal: Yevgeny Primakov, *Russia and the Arabs* (New York: Basic Books, 2009), 138.
3. In January Sadat chose the second half of May, August-September, October with the plan to begin apparent manoeuvres that would turn into a crossing of the Suez Canal in a limited war.
4. See numerous comments by Sadat and others in Galia Golan, *Yom Kippur and After* (Cambridge: Cambridge University Press,1977), 271–9. Sadat feared that Washington and Moscow were colluding on a peace deal that would not suit Arab interests, though he himself was involved in overtures to the United States. Former Soviet officials, for example, Primakov, *Russia and the Arabs*, 141, former KGB chief in Egypt Vasili Mitrokhin (Christopher Andrew and Vasili Mitrokhin, *The World Was Going Our Way: The KGB and the Battle for the Third World* [New York: Basic Books, 2005], 1545) and Vinogradov (V. M. Vinogradov, *Diplomatiia: Liudi i Sobitiia. Iz Zapisok Posla* [Moskva: Rospen, 1998], 238–45) have claimed there was Egyptian, US and even Israeli "collusion" regarding preparations for a limited war.
5. FRUS XXV, Doc. 73, 220, "Memorandum for the President's Files by the President's Assistant for National Security Affairs (Kissinger)," 23 June 23, 1973 (Brezhnev–Nixon meeting, San Clemente). Dobrynin concluded later that the

US seemed to think that Brezhnev's alarm was a tactical measure as part of nego-tiations. He said that Soviet alarm was genuine: "…Brezhnev had been specifi-cally instructed by the Politburo to draw the president's attention to the mounting threat of a new Arab–Israeli war," Anatoly Dobrynin, *In Confidence: Moscow's Ambassador to America's Six Cold War Presidents* (New York: Times Books, 1995), 283. The Soviets tended to over-estimate US influence on Israel and, therefore, Washington's ability to obtain Israeli concessions for a settlement.

6. For example, the July visit to Syria by Politburo member Kirilenko.

7. *Al Hawadess*, 16 August 1974. Preparation for the tentatively planned May offensive was noted with alarm by the Soviets in talks with the US (FRUS XXV, Doc. 56, 171, "Message from Soviet General Secretary Brezhnev to President Nixon," 13 May 1973).

8. FRUS XXV, Doc. 110, 317, "Transcript of Telephone Conversation Between the president's deputy assistant adviser for National Security Affairs (Scowcroft) and the Soviet ambassador (Dobrynin)", 6 October 1973, 290–1.

9. Victor Israelyan, *Inside the Kremlin During the October War* (University Park: Pennsylvania State University, 1995), 31–2, 53–6; Yevgeny Prylin, "Some Obser-vations (Memoires) About the Arab–Israeli War" (1973), unpublished memo-randum in Ned Lebow and Janice Stein, *We All Lost the Cold War* (Princeton, NJ: Princeton University Press, 1994), 184.

10. Heikal, "Ramadan," *Maariv*, 15 May 1973; *al Anwar* (Lebanon), 16 Novem-ber 1973.

11. Israel, whose position in Sinai was not favourable at the time, had agreed to this bid for a ceasefire in place.

12. *al Nida*, 17 April 1974; *al-Safir*, 16 April 1974 and Vinogradov in *Journal of Palestine Studies* 3, 4 (1974), 161–4; also Primakov, *Russia and the Arabs*, 149–150; Israelyan, *Inside the Kremlin During the October War*, 43–45 and Syrian analyst Murhaf Jouejati in Richard Parker (ed.), *The October War* (Gainesville, FL: University Press of Florida, 2001), 120. The successful Syrian offensive sud-denly stopped on the second day of the war, though the Syrians were later to complain that it was the Egyptians who had unexpectedly stopped. Egyptian army chief of staff Shazly later wrote that the Egyptians had two plans: the lim-ited one it in fact used, and the broader one conveyed to the Syrians in their pre-war meetings. Asad confirmed this in a 1983 conversation with Primakov (Primakov, *Russia and the Arabs*, 150–1).

13. FRUS XXV, Doc. 149, 432, "Message from Soviet Secretary General Brezhnev to President Nixon," Moscow, no date.

14. On 18 October Kosygin showed Sadat aerial photos of Israeli forces on the western bank.(Heikal, "Ramadan," *Maariv*, 23 May 1973, and Israelyan, *Inside the Kremlin During the October War*, 113).

15. Both Israelyan, *Inside the Kremlin During the October War*, 114 and Vinogra-

dov (*Journal of Palestine Studies*) revealed that Sadat's agreement came only after Kosygin's departure, though Sadat had told Kosygin that cease-fire talks could begin.

16. The Soviet position in all their ceasefire discussions; Kissinger maintained that reference to 242 would carry that meaning—which is the way Moscow presented it to the Arabs (for example, Moscow radio in Arabic, 22 October 1973).

17. *al-Anwar*, 30 October 1973 (Asad speech, 29 October 1973).

18. Riad el Rayyes and Dunia Nahas, *The October War* (Beirut: An Nahar Press, 1973), 95.

19. Boumedienne, in a trip to Moscow 14–15 October 1973, provided funds, as did Abu Dhabi. (Sadat interviews: DPA, 13 April 1974; MENA, 22 September and 8 October 1974.)

20. For other Soviet assistance by advisers on the ground, see Galia Golan, "The Soviet Union and the October War" in P. R. Kumaraswany (ed.), *Revisiting the October War* (London: Frank Cass, 2000), 126–52.

21. FRUS XXV, Doc. 121, 356, "Minutes of Washington Special Actions Group Meeting," 7 October 1972; Admiral Moorer, cited in D. O. Verrall, "The Soviet Navy in the Indian Ocean," unpublished paper, Halifax, 1974, 48.

22. *US News and World Report*, 24 December 1973, 27–8 (interview).

23. *Pravda*, 9 October 1973; *Krasnay zvezda*, 12 October 1973.

24. On Podgorny and others, Primakov, *Russia and the Arabs*, 133–41.

25. Israelyan, *Inside the Kremlin During the October War*, 91.

26. Qaddafi called the ceasefire resolution a "time bomb" (Tripoli radio, 22 October 1973).

27. FRUS XXV, Doc. 267, 734, "Message from Soviet Secretary General Brezhnev to President Nixon," Moscow, on date.

28. FRUS XXV, Doc.269, 737, "Memorandum for the Record," 24–25October, 1973, 10:30 p.m.—3:30 a.m.(meeting of National Security Council and Joint Chiefs of Staff).

29. *New York Times*, 26 October 1973.

30. Israelyan, *Inside the Kremlin During the October War*, 153–4.

31. Dobrynin, *In Confidence*, 295; Primakov, *Russia and the Arabs*, 157,

32. Interview with Israelyan in Lebow and Stein, *We All Lost the Cold War*, 238. Kulikov had reportedly sought earlier to authorise Egyptian use of Scud missiles but was over-ruled by Gromyko (E. D. Prylin, *Trudny i dolgii put' k miri* [Moskva: Rospen, 2002], 170–1). Two Scuds were fired on 22 October, but Israelyan explains that when the Egyptians pressured to be permitted to fire them just before the ceasefire was to go into effect, Vinogradov tried to contact Gromyko. Since Gromyko was not immediately available Grechko gave the go-ahead ("Go the hell ahead and fire it"). Israelyan, *Inside the Kremlin During the October War*, 144.

33. Primakov, *Russia and the Arabs*, 157.

34. In Lebow and Stein, *We All Lost the Cold War*, 237–8.

35. Primakov, *Russia and the Arabs*, 157; Dobynin, *In Confidence*, 295; Israelyan, *Inside the Kremlin During the October War*, 168.

36. Primakov, *Russia and the Arabs*, 157; Dobynin, *In Confidence*, 295. Both cite the same source: Gromyko's aide, Vasily Grubyakov; Israelyan, *Inside the Kremlin During the October War*, 168–9.

37. FRUS XXV, Doc. 269, 737–342, "Memorandum for the Record," 24–25 October 1973, 10:30 p.m. 3:30 a.m..

38. For example, *Pravda*, 8, 12 May 1974.

39. See Dobrynin's comments to Kissinger in their meeting prior to a visit by Gromyko to Washington (FRUS XXV, Doc. 157, 649, "Memorandum of Conversation," 1 February, 1974.

40. According to Vasili Mitrokhin (Andrew and Mitrokhin, *The World Was Going Our Way*, 2004).

41. While Kosygin was visiting in an effort to restrain Damascus, the Syrians invaded Lebanon, 1976.

42. Now in possession of aircraft carriers, longer-range aircraft and at-sea resupply capabilities, the Soviets were less dependent upon ground bases in the eastern Mediterranean.

43. See Galia Golan, "The Arab–Israeli Conflict in Soviet–US Relations" in Yaacov Ro'i', *The Limits to Power* (London: Croom Helm, 1979), 7–31, on progress at the global level versus collapse of détente in the Middle East.

44. Unable to understand the American system regarding the president's power (or powerlessness) vis-à-vis Congress, and also Watergate, the Soviets became increasingly suspicious of Washington's attitude to détente.

8. JORDAN'S WAR THAT NEVER WAS

1. Curtis R. Ryan, *Inter-Arab Alliances: Regime Security and Jordanian Foreign Policy* (Gainesville, FL: University Press of Florida, 2008); Avi Shlaim, *Lion of Jordan: The Life of King Hussein in War and Peace* (London: Penguin Books, 2007); Nigel Ashton, *King Hussein of Jordan: A Political Life* (New Haven and London: Yale University Press, 2008).

2. Foreign Relations of the United States, 1969–1976, Vol. 25, Arab-Israeli Crisis and War, 1973 (Washington: United States Government Printing Office, 2011) (hereafter FRUS).

3. David Rodman, 'Friendly Enemies: Israel and Jordan in the 1973 Yom Kippur War', *The Israel Journal of Foreign Affairs* 6, 1 (2012), 91–98.

4. Curtis Ryan, *Inter-Arab Alliances*, 74–7.

5. Eliyahu Kanovsky, *Economic Development of Jordan* (Tel Aviv: University Pub-

lishing Projects, 1976), 103–10; Laurie Brand, *Jordan's Inter-Arab Relations: The Political Economy of Alliance Making* (New York: Columbia University Press, 1994), 124; Warwick Knowles, *Jordan Since 1989: A Study in Political Economy* (London: I.B. Tauris, 2005), 32–41; Saunders to Kissinger, 5.4.1973, FRUS, 130–5.

6. Musa Braizat, *The Jordanian-Palestinian Relationship: The Bankruptcy of the Confederal Idea* (London: I.B. Tauris, 1998), 143–5; Philip Robins, *A History of Jordan* (Cambridge: Cambridge University Press, 2004), p. 136–8; Ashton, *King Hussein of Jordan*, 161–4.

7. Robins, *A History of Jordan*, 136.

8. Moshe Zak, *Hussein Makes Peace* (Ramat Gan: Bar Ilan University Press, 1996) [Hebrew], 151–64; Shlaim, *Lion of Jordan*, 346–52. For further details on Israel's secret talks with Jordan in 1972 see Kissinger to Nixon, undated, FRUS, 26–30.

9. Henry Kissinger, *Years of Upheaval* (Boston: Little Brown & Co, 1982), p. 219; Shlaim, *Lion of Jordan*, 344–5; Ashton, *King Hussein of Jordan*, 170–1. Apparently, Hussein even thought that Nasser "felt more responsibility for Jordan" than Sadat. See conversation between Hussein and Kissinger, 27.2.1973, FRUS, 89.

10. Kennedy to Kissinger, 2.1.1973, *Ibid.*, 1–2.

11. Amman to State, 22.1.1973, *Ibid.*, 6–7.

12. Saunders to Kissinger, 26.1.1973, Ibid., 12–19; State to Amman, 9.2.1973, *Ibid.*, 37–43; Tel Aviv to State, 13.2.1973, *Ibid.*, 48; conversation between Nixon and Kissinger, 21.2.1973, *Ibid.*, 55–9. Over the following months, Hussein himself became convinced that he should not be the first Arab leader to negotiate with Israel. See conversation between Eban, Idan, Kissinger and Saunders, 12.5.1973, *Ibid.*, 170; and Saunders to Kissinger, 30.8.1973, *Ibid.*, 254–7.

13. Conversation between Hussein and Kissinger, 27.2.1973, *Ibid.*, 91.

14. Saunders to Kissinger, 25.5.1973, Ibid., 192; and 30.8.1973, Ibid., 255. See also Moshe Zak, Hussein Makes Peace, 46–7, 163.

15. Kissinger to Nixon, undated, *Ibid.*, 26–8.

16. Saunders to Kissinger, 25.5.1973, *Ibid.*, 193.

17. Report on a message from Meir to Hussein, 12.6.1973, *Ibid.*, 242; Saunders to Kissinger, 30.8.1973, *Ibid.*, 254–7.

18. State to Amman, 9.2.1973, *Ibid.*, 39.

19. Conversation between Dinitz and Kissinger, 3.5.1973, *Ibid.*, 151–4; Saunders to Kissinger, 17.5.1973, *Ibid.*, 184–6.

20. Conversation between Dinitz and Kissinger, 3.5.1973, *Ibid.*, 152.

21. Hussein to Kissinger, 4.6.1973, *Ibid.*, 201.

22. Ashton, *King Hussein of Jordan*, 171.

23. Amman to State, 15.9.1973, FRUS 2011, 268.

24. Saunders and Quandt to Kissinger, 20.9.1973, *Ibid.*, 268–9.

25. Shlaim, *Lion of Jordan*, 359.

26. Ashton, *King Hussein of Jordan*, 171.

27. Shlaim, *Lion of Jordan*, 361.

28. See the report on the meeting on a website dedicated to Golda Meir, http://goldameir.org.il/archive/home/he/1/1253626834.html#a006 (accessed 15 April, 2012).

29. Ashton, *King Hussein of Jordan*, 172. On Salem's personal story, see Sa'd Abu Dayyeh, "The Iraqi Papers Reveal the Secrets of the Defection of the Iraqi Pilot to Jordan in 1960," al-Ghadd, 16 May 2008 [Arabic]. Accessed April 18, 2012. http://www.alghad.com/index.php/article/223826.html, and Jack O'Connell, King's Counsel (New York: W.W. Norton & company, 2011), 122–3.

30. Shlaim, *Lion of Jordan*, 360–4.

31. Ashton, *King Hussein of Jordan*, 171–3.

32. O'Connell, King's Counsel, 123.

33. Ashton, *King Hussein of Jordan*, 173.

34. Amnon Barzilai, 'Golda Meir's Nightmare', Ha'aretz, 3 October 2003 [Hebrew] http://www.haaretz.co.il/misc/1.914636 (Accessed April 18, 2012).

35. Memorandum to Kissinger, 30.9.1973, FRUS 2011, 278–9.

36. Syed A. El-Edroos, *The Hashemite Arab Army, 1908–1979: An Appreciation and Analysis of Military Operations* (Amman: the Jordan Armed Forces, 1980), 472–3.

37. An interview with Abu Daoud, al-Jazeerah, 11 September 1999, http://www.aljazeera.net/NR/exeres/C9C99F8F-AC8E-447D-A401-C8472C27AEE9 (accessed 15 April, 2012).

38. Ryan, *Inter-Arab Alliances*, 79.

39. Sami Khazendar, *Jordan and the Palestine Question: the Role of Islamic and Left Forces in Foreign Policy Making* (Ithaca: Ithaca Press, 1997), 22.

40. Saunders to Kissinger, 17.5.1973, FRUS 2011, 185.

41. el-Edroos, *The Hashemite Arab Army*, 430.

42. Assaf David, *In the Service of His Majesty? Civil-Military Relations in the Hashemite Kingdom of Jordan under the Reign of King Hussein and King Abdullah II* (unpublished PhD dissertation, Hebrew University of Jerusalem, 2011) [Hebrew], 136, 142, 171.

43. Amman to State, 7.1.1973, Ibid., 3; Saunders to Kissinger, 11.1.1973, Ibid., 3–4; Hussein to Kissinger, 4.6.1973, Ibid., 201.

44. el-Edroos, *The Hashemite Arab Army*, 472–5, 495–9.

45. Ashton, King Hussein of Jordan, 175.

46. Kissinger to Nixon, 6.2.1973, *Ibid.*, 35.

47. Miriam Joyce, *Anglo-American Support for Jordan: The Career of King Hussein* (Hampshire: Palgrave Macmillan, 2008), 120.

48. Kissinger to Nixon, 6.2.1973, *Ibid.*,31–6.

49. Hussein to Kissinger, 4.6.1973, *Ibid.*, 201.

50. Minutes of Washington Special Actions Group Meeting, 8.10.1973, Ibid., 381–8.

51. David, *In the Service of his Majesty*, 99–111, 123, 134–40.

52. Ryan, *Inter-Arab Alliances*, 75–7.

53. Shlaim, *Lion of Jordan*, 365.

54. Nahed Hattar, 'King Hussein: A Summary of a Unique Political Journey', *Studies in the Social History of Jordan* (Amman: Markaz al-Urdun al-Jadid, 2003) [Arabic], 628.

55. Ryan, *Inter-Arab Alliances*, 76.

56. Ashton, *King Hussein of Jordan*, 174.

57. Memorandum from Quandt and Donald Stukel to Kissinger, 8.10.1973, FRUS 2011, 367.

58. Amman to State, 8.10.1973, *Ibid.*, 376.

59. Memorandum to Kissinger, 8.10.1973, *Ibid.*, 375.

60. Amman to State, 8.10.1973, *Ibid.*, 374–6.

61. Amman to State, 9.10.1973, *Ibid.*, 400–01.

62. State to Amman, 9.10.1973, *Ibid.*, 403.

63. Tel Aviv to State, 9.10.19783, *Ibid.*, 405.

64. Tel Aviv and Amman to State, 9.10.1973, *Ibid.*, 405.

65. Amman to State, 9.10.1973, *Ibid.*, 404.

66. Quandt to Kissinger, 9.10.1973, *Ibid.*, 408–10.

67. Amman to State, 13.10.1973, *Ibid.*, 494.

68. Amman to State, 10.10.1973, *Ibid.*, 426–7.

69. Amman to State and CIA to National Security Council, 10.10.1973, *Ibid.*, 426.

70. Ashton, *King Hussein of Jordan*, 175.

71. Memorandum to Kissinger, 10.10.1973, *Ibid.*, 427.

72. Amman to State, 10.10.1973, *Ibid.*, 433.

73. Tel Aviv to State, 10.10.1973, *Ibid.*, 426.

74. The king was conveying a tacit message that he was repaying the Syrians with good for their evil. Personal communication with a Jordanian former military general, April 2012.

75. Amman to State, 10.10.1973, *Ibid.*, 433–4.

76. Amman to State, 10.10.1973, *Ibid.*, 434.

77. State to Amman, 10.10.1973, *Ibid.*, 434.

78. Amman to State, 11.10.1973, *Ibid.*, 436–437.

79. Amman to State, 11.10.1973, *Ibid.*, 439.

80. Amman to State, 11.10.1973, *Ibid.*, 439–40.

81. Ashton, *King Hussein of Jordan*, 175.

82. Amman to State, 11.10.1973, *Ibid.*

83. Amman to State, 12.10.1973, *Ibid.*, 453.

84. Amman to State, 11.10.1973, *Ibid.*, 440.

85. Memorandum to Kissinger, 11.10.1973, *Ibid.*, 443. Meir described the letter as "touching." See memorandum of conversation between Meir and Kissinger, 16.12.1973, *Ibid.*, 1105.

86. Ashton, *King Hussein of Jordan*, 175–6.

87. Henry Kissinger, *Crisis: The Anatomy of Two Major Foreign Policy Crises* (New York: Simon & Schuster, 2003), 189–90.

88. *Ibid.*, 190–2.

89. *Ibid.*, 194–5.

90. Telephone conversation between Nixon and Kissinger, 12.10.1973, *Ibid.*, 444–446.

91. Kissinger, *Years of Upheaval*, 506.

92. Amman to State, 12.10.1973, *Ibid.*, 453.

93. Amman to State, 13.10.1973, *Ibid.*, 480; Memorandum to Kissinger, 13.10.1973, *Ibid.*

94. Amman to State, 13.10.1973, *Ibid.*, 493.

95. Meir later disclosed that Israel cancelled a plan to shell the location of a meeting of all the Syrian generals after it had learned that the king might also be present. See memorandum of conversation between Israeli and American officials, 1.11.1973, *Ibid.*, 826–36, and memorandum of conversation between Meir and Kissinger, 16.12.1973, *Ibid.*, 1106.

96. Amman to State, 13.10.1973, *Ibid.*, 493–4.

97. Ashton, *King Hussein of Jordan*, 176.

98. State to Amman, 15.10.1973, *Ibid.*, 540–1.

99. Ashton, *King Hussein of Jordan*, 176.

100. State to Amman, 15.10.1973, *Ibid.*

101. State to Amman, 16.10.1973, *Ibid.*, 541.

102. Amman to State, 19.10.1973, *Ibid.*, 600–602. See also Kissinger's second letter to the king that day, *Ibid.*, 602.

103. Amman to State, 19.10.1973, *Ibid.*

104. Ashton, *King Hussein of Jordan*, 176.

105. State to Amman, 19.10.1973, *Ibid.*, 540–1.

106. el-Edroos, *The Hashemite Arab Army*, 524.

107. Minutes of Washington Special Actions Group Meeting, 19.10.1973, *Ibid.*, 606, 609.

108. Conversation between top Israeli officials and State officials, 22.10.1973, *Ibid.*, 605.

109. el-Edroos, *The Hashemite Arab Army*, 524.

110. Minutes of Washington Special Actions Group Meeting, 19.10.1973, *Ibid.*, 610.

111. el-Edroos, The Hashemite Arab Army, 524.
112. State to Amman, 21.10.1973, *Ibid.*, 644–5.
113. Amman to State, 21.10.1973, *Ibid.*, 645.
114. Scowcroft to Kissinger, 22.10.1973, *Ibid.*, 667.
115. Amman to State, 22.10.1973, *Ibid.*, 667–8.
116. Amman to State, 22.10.1973, *Ibid.*
117. State to Amman, 22.10.1973, *Ibid.*, 669.
118. Amman to State, 22.10.1973, *Ibid.*, 669–70.
119. Amman to State, 22.10.1973, *Ibid.*, 670.
120. Ashton, *King Hussein of Jordan*, 177.
121. Amman to State, 22.10.1973, *Ibid.*, 671.
122. State to Amman, 23.10.1973, *Ibid.*, 672.
123. Memorandum to Kissinger, 23.10.1973, *Ibid.*, 671.
124. Amman to State, 23.10.1973, *Ibid.*, 672.
125. Amman to State, 23.10.1973, *Ibid.*, 673.
126. Amman to State, 23.10.1973, *Ibid.*, 673.
127. Ashton, *King Hussein of Jordan*, 177–8.
128. el-Edroos, *The Hashemite Arab Army*, 525.

9. PALESTINIAN POLITICS IN TRANSITION

1. See, for example, Salah al-Din al-Bitar, "The Implications of the October War for the Arab World," *Journal of Palestine Studies* 3, 2 (1974), 34; Bonham G. Matthew, Michael J. Shapiro and Thomas L. Trumble, "The October War: Changes in Cognitive Orientation toward the Middle East Conflict," *International Studies Quarterly*, 23, 1 (1979), 8 and Ibrahim F. I. Shihata, "The Territorial Question and the October War," *Journal of Palestine Studies* 4, 1 (1974), 26.
2. Such a case is mentioned in Susan Silsby Boyle, *Betrayal of Palestine. The story of George Antonius* (Boulder, Colo.: Westview Press, 2001), xviii.
3. Philipp O. Amour, "Practical, Theoretical and Methodological Challenges of Field Research in the Middle East," *Historical Methods: A Journal of Quantitative and Interdisciplinary History* 45, 3 (2012), 143–9.
4. *Ibid.*
5. This chapter is based on my larger project entitled *The Birth of the Palestinian Cultural History*, that I conducted in the context of my unpublished PhD thesis Fribourg/Switzerland, 2010. This chapter was written during my postdoctoral affiliation at the University of Oxford, in the Department of Politics and International Relations (DPIR). It was funded by the Swiss National Science Foundation (SNSF), to which I am very grateful. I would like to thank Richard Caplan for his sponsorship and Alison Hunt, Jason Hussain and Janice French for their kind help.

6. The two most influential authors of the so called Nakba literature were Musa Alami, "The Lesson of Palestine," *Middle East Journal* 3, 4 (1949), 373–405 and Constantine Zurayk, *The Meaning of Disaster* (Beirut: Khayat's College Book Cooperative, 1956).

7. See for instance Nabil A. Badran, *Al-Ta'lim wal-Tahdith fil-Mujama' al-'Arabi al-Filastini (Education and Modernization in Palestinian Arab Society):* Part II: 1948–1967 (Beirut: Palestine research centre).

8. For more details see, for example, Leila El Khalidi, *The Art of Palestinian Embroidery* (London: Books, 1999) and Ahmad Qurei, Samed—*the productivity experience of the Palestinian revolution* [Arabic] (Beirut: Arab Institute for Research and Publishing, 2007).

9. The PLO is the focus of, among others, the following publications: Rex Brynen, *Sanctuary and Survival: The PLO in Lebanon* (Boulder, Colo.: Westview Press, 1990) and Jamal R. Nassar, *The Palestine Liberation Organization: From Armed Struggle to the Declaration of Independence* (New York: Praeger, 1991).

10. Philipp O. Amour, *The Birth of the Palestinian Cultural History* (Unpublished PhD thesis, University of Fribourg, 2010).

11. This typology is based on the actual politics and the orientation of the PLO, rather than upon its Pan-Arab Charta, which indeed recognised the military means as the sole way to liberate historical Palestine. I took the background of the founders and their first decisions into consideration in my typology. In other words, I focused more on their real politics and political orientation, not on their rhetoric. Orthodox social scientists and historians usually focus on the bibliography of Ahmad Al-Shukeiry, his speeches and the Pan-Arab Charta to extract the ideologies and philosophies of the PLO. By doing this, they rely on orthodox facts that were rarely questioned due to a number of factors; some of them were mentioned above.

12. Amour, *The Birth of the Palestinian Cultural History*.

13. Yousef Sayigh, *An Incomplete Autobiography* [Arabic] (Beirut, seen on 21 March 2007 before publication), Chapter 16, 2.

14. Many interviewees came across this information during my field research in the Middle East 2007–2009, for instance Munir Shafiq, interviews, Lebanon, Beirut, 15 March and 07 April 2007. The same point was made by Jaber Suleiman, interviews, Lebanon, Beirut, 26 March, 13 and 25 April, 06 June 2007 as well as 13 August 2008. The PLO became for similar reasons appealing for many Arab intellectuals and writers as well, see Mahmoud Darwish, *Memory for Forgetfulness* [Arabic] (Beirut: Arab Institute for Research and Publishing, 2007), 136.

15. See for instance Salah Khalaf (Abu Iyad) talking to Partick Seale, *Abu Nidal: A Gun For Hire. The Secret Life Of The World's Most Notorious Arab Terrorist* (New York: Random House, 1992), 68–9.

16. A shift is pointed out by Hisham Shurabi, "About the future of the [nature of the] Palestinian resistance." *Journal of Palestine Affairs*, 14 (1972), 9–25.

17. Mohammad Abu Maizar, interview held during my field research in Jordan, Amman, 24 September 2007.

18. Amour, *The Birth of the Palestinian Cultural History*.

19. Mohammad Abu Maizar, interview, Jordan, Amman, 24 September 2007.

20. Seale, *Abu Nidal*, 42.

21. According to Elias Shoufani, Yasir Arafat had asked the Palestine think tank to deliver an analysis in regard to the October War and its potential for the resolution of the Palestinian issue, interview during my field research in Syria, Damascus, 05 October 2007. The intensive engagement of the think tank within the debate around the October War was confirmed by Munir Shafiq, interview, Lebanon, Beirut, 07 April 2007.

22. The analysis and information here refer to Amour, *The Birth of the Palestinian Cultural History*. They are evident in the contemporary literature of the PLO journals and party magazines as well as in local publications.

23. Klofis Maqsoud, "The determinants of Palestinian the Palestinian decision process and their risk," *Journal of Palestine Affairs*, 28 (1973), 8–13.

24. See for instance Abu Iyad talking to Seale, *Abu Nidal*, 43 and see as well Mark Tessler, *A History of the Israeli-Palestinian Conflict* (Bloomington and Indianapolis: Indiana University Press, 1994), 481–3.

25. See for instance Abu Iyad talking to Seale, *Abu Nidal*, 43.

26. I had these thoughts as I read Bonham *et al.*, "The October War".

27. Amour, *The Birth of the Palestinian Cultural History*.

28. In regard to Jordan see Yezid Sayigh, *Armed Struggle and the Search for State. The Palestinian National Movement 1949–1993* (Oxford/New York: Oxford University Press, 1997), 344.

29. The material support is mentioned in Sayigh, *Armed Struggle*, 344–345. Mamdouh Nofel takes important notice of this in *Magdousheh: The Story of the War against the Refugee Camps in Lebanon* (Ramallah: Muwatin, 2006).

30. Mahmoud Shreih reported this, Beirut, Lebanon 02 and 06 and 11 April 2007.

31. Deep insights into this story can be read in Elias Shoufani, *Marthiat as-Safa: Autobiography* (Damascus: Dar al-Hasad, 2009).

32. The PLO leadership opposed any direct Palestinian involvement in the civil war in the beginning: Nabil Sha'th, interview during field research, Palestinian territories, Ramallah, 31 August 2007. The same position was confirmed by Munir Shafiq, interviews, Lebanon, Beirut, 15 March and 07 April 2007 and by Elias Shoufani, interview during field research, Syria, Damascus, 05 October 2007.

33. *Ibid.*, and Nayef Saada, interview during my field research, Lebanon, Beirut, 25 April 2007 and Jaber Suleiman, interview during my field research, 13 April 2007.

34. For examples one can refer to the aforementioned contemporary journals or the magazines and pamphlets of the related political parties and movements.

35. I received this information during interviews with previous employees at the PLO research centre and planning centre, for example: Anis Sayegh, interviews during my field research, Lebanon, Beirut, 17, 26 February and 06, 13, 28 March and 22 May and 19 June 2007 as well as 03 March 2009. Similar findings were reported by Issa Al-Shuaibi, interview during my field research, Jordan, Amman, September 2007.

36. This was reported in many interviews. For example by Subhi Taha, Interview during my field research, Jordan, Amman 17. und 18. September 2007.

37. Anis Sayegh, *Anis Sayegh 'n Anis Sayegh* [Arabic] (Beirut: Riad El-Rayyes Books S.A.R.L., 2006), 215–336. See as well related review Philipp O. Amour, "Anis Sayegh 'n Anis Sayegh," *British Journal of Middle Eastern Studies* 38, 3 (2011), 455–8.

38. Nabil Sha'th, interview during my field research, Palestinian territories, Ramallah, 31 August 2007.

39. Amour, *The Birth of the Palestinian Cultural History.*

10. FARAWAY CAUSES, IMMEDIATE EFFECTS: THE WAR
    AND EUROPEAN CONSEQUENCES

1. Geneviève Bibes, *L'Italie a-t-elle une politique étrangère?* (Paris: Centre d'Etudes des Relations Internationales, 1974).

2. Walter Laqueur, *Confrontation: The Middle East War and World Politics* (London: Abacus, 1974), 142–3.

3. Daniel Colard, "La Politique méditerranéenne et proche-orientale de G. Pompidou", *Politique étrangère* 43, 3 (1978), 283–96.

4. Philipe Simonnot, "The end of cheap oil," *Le Monde*, 25 October 1993.

5. Michel Jobert, *Mémoires d'avenir* (Paris: Bernard Grasset, 1974), 125.

6. Tom Little, "News Desk Notes," *Middle East International* (hereafter, *MEI*) 3 (December 1973), 26.

7. Edward Heath, *The Course of My Life: My Autobiography* (London: Hodder & Stoughton, 1998), 501–2.

8. Statement by European Community Foreign Ministers, 6 November 1973, reprinted in Yehuda Lukacs (ed.), *The Israeli–Palestinian Conflict: A Documentary Record, 1967–1990* (Cambridge, New York: Cambridge University Press, 1992), 14.

9. UN Security Council Resolution 338 of 22 October 1973 called for an immediate cease-fire, the "implementation" of UNSC Resolution 242 "in all its parts" and for "negotiations" to begin between the warring parties.

10. Statement by European Community Foreign Ministers, 6 November 1973.

11. P. E. L. Fellowes, "The Oil Weapon in Action," *MEI* 3 (December 1973), 8.
12. Memorandum on European Political Cooperation: Middle East Guarantees, 12 May 1975, British National Archives, Foreign & Commonwealth Office (hereafter, BNA/FCO) 30/3027.
13. Quoted in Haifaa A. Jawad, *Euro–Arab Relations: A Study in Collective Diplomacy* (Reading: Ithaca Press, 1992), 61.
14. George Lavy, *Germany and Israel: Moral Debt and National Interest* (London: Frank Cass, 1996), 164.
15. See Jan Deboutte and Alfred Van Staden, "High Politics in the Low Countries" in William Wallace and William E. Paterson (eds), *Foreign Policy Making in Western Europe: A Comparative Approach*, (Farnborough: Saxon House, 1978), 71.
16. See statement by Foreign Minister Eban in response to the EEC Declaration of 6 November, *Israel Documents* vol. 2 (Jerusalem: Ministry of Foreign Affairs), 1066–7.
17. *The Daily Telegraph*, 17 November 1973.
18. Heath, *The Course of My Life*, 501.
19. Kenneth Lewan, "West Germany Waits for the US," *MEI* 58 (April 1976), 10–11.
20. André Fontaine, "Une Derniére Chance pour les Neuf? Le Revelateur Petrolier," *Le Monde*, 7 November, 1973.
21. Declaration of the Arab Summit Conference at Algiers, 28 November 1973, *Israel Documents,* vol. 2, 1074–6.
22. *Al-Nahar*, 4 December 1973.
23. *The Economist*, 23 September 1972, 41.
24. Tom Little, "News Desk Notes," *MEI* 31 (January 1974), 25.
25. Daniel Yergin, *The Prize: The Epic Quest for Oil, Money and Power* (London, New York: Simon & Schuster, 1991), 627.
26. *Le Monde*, 25 December 1973.
27. See "An Open Letter from Europe to President Nixon," *Eurabia*, 14 May 1973.
28. Nadav Safran, "Engagement in the Middle East," *Foreign Affairs* 53, 1 (October 1974), 45.
29. Michel Jobert, *Les Américains* (Paris: Albin Michel, 1987), 164.
30. Jobert, *Mémoires d'avenir*, 126.
31. *The Times* (London), 2 November 1973.
32. *The Times* (London), 19 November 1973.
33. Communiqué of European Summit Meeting at Copenhagen, 14–15 December 1973, Washington DC: European Community Information Service, 20 December 1973.
34. *The Economist*, 26 January 1974, 36–7.
35. James O. Goldsborough, "France, the European Crisis and the Alliance," *Foreign Affairs* 52, 3 (April 1974), 539.

36. See interview with Christopher Mayhew, MP, *MEI* 35 (May 1974), 19–20.
37. Romano Prodi and Alberto Clô, "Europe," *Daedalus* 104, 4 (Fall 1975), 106.
38. European Parliament resolution on Community energy policy, 20 February 1975, reprinted in *Official Journal of the European Communities*, 60 (13 March 1975), 36.
39. Euro–Arab Dialogue Minutes, 17 and 22 December 1975, BNA/FCO 30/3045.
40. Document de Travail de la Présidence Dialogue Euro–Arabe, 18 February 1975, BNA/FCO 30/3023.
41. Joint Communiqué: Euro–Arab Dialogue, Cairo, 14 June 1975, BNA/FCO 30/3031.
42. *The Times* (London), 12 June 1975.
43. *The Financial Times*, 25 November 1975.
44. Minutes and Report of Euro–Arab Dialogue Meeting of Experts, Cairo, 11 June 1975, BNA/FCO 30/3030.
45. *Al Thawra*, 23 May 1975.
46. EAD: Meeting of Coordinating Group, Dublin, 22 January 1975, 3 February 1975, BNA/FCO 30/3022.
47. *Le Monde*, 29 November 1973.
48. See Arab League Summit Conference communiqué, Rabat, 29 October 1974, reprinted in Lukacs (ed.), *The Israeli–Palestinian Conflict*, 464.
49. *The Times* (London), 23 December 1969.
50. Richard H. Ullman, "After Rabat: Middle East Risks and American Roles," *Foreign Affairs* 53, 2 (January 1975), 284.
51. EAD: Meeting of Coordinating Group, Dublin, 22 January 1975, 3 February 1975, BNA/FCO 30/3022.
52. Minutes of Euro–Arab Dialogue, 17 December 1975, BNA/FCO 30/3045.
53. Memorandum on Euro–Arab Dialogue, 10 January 1975, BNA/FCO 30/3022.
54. Community briefing on Prime Minister Wilson and Foreign Minister Callaghan's meeting with President Ford and Dr Kissinger, 31 January 1974, BNA/FCO 30/3023.
55. West German briefing to ambassadors on Kissinger visit to Bonn, 19 February 1975, BNA/FCO 30/3023.
56. British Embassy, Washington, to Foreign Office, 1 July 1975, BNA/FCO 30/3032.
57. Minister of State memorandum on Euro–Arab Dialogue, 10 January 1975, BNA/FCO 30/3022.
58. Euro–Arab Dialogue: Ministers Meeting, Dublin, 13 February 1975, BNA/FCO 30/3023.
59. *Ibid.*
60. Joint Communiqué: Euro–Arab Dialogue, Cairo, 14 June 1975, BNA/FCO 30/3031.
61. Alan R. Taylor, "How to Bridge the Gap," *MEI* 67 (February 1977), 11–12.

62. *Le Monde*, 12 February 1977.

63. Statement on the Middle East by members of the EEC, 29 June 1977, *Israel Documents*, vol. 4, 19–20.

64. Statement on the Middle East by the Heads of Government of the EEC, London, 29 June 1978, *Israel Documents*, vol. 5, 442.

65. *Le Monde*, 19 September 1978.

66. Henry Kissinger, *Years of Renewal* (London: Weidenfeld & Nicolson, 1999), 367.

67. *The Financial Times*, 27 March 1979.

68. *The Financial Times*, 26 March 1979.

69. *MEI* 97 (13 April 1979), 2–3.

70. *Le Monde*, 31 March 1980.

71. Communiqué du Conseil des Ministres du 29 Mars 1979, reprinted in *France-Pays Arabes* (April-May 1979), 10.

72. See Fiorella Seiler, *"King of the Armed Ghetto": Israel in the West German National Press during Menachem Begin's First Government (1977–1981)* (Unpublished PhD dissertation, University of London, 2001), 100–80.

73. See speech by Mr Michael O'Kennedy, UN General Assembly, 34th Session, 25 September 1979, *Official Records of the UNGA* (New York: United Nations), 121.

74. Memorandum on Euro–Arab Dialogue prepared by European Integration Department, 17 December 1975, BNA/FCO 30/3045.

75. Jawad, *Euro–Arab Relations*, 159.

76. *MEI* 119 (29 February 1980), 4.

77. Livia Rokach, "No Progress in Euro–Arab Dialogue," *MEI* 120 (14 March 1980), 5.

78. *MEI* 122 (11 April 1980), 1.

79. John Palmer, "The EEC goes its own way," *MEI* 125 (23 May 1980), 2.

80. Robert Swann, "New Success for Palestinians in Europe", *MEI* 124 (9 May 1980), 3–4.

81. John Cooley, "The West's Ever Widening Rift over Palestine," *MEI* 126 (6 June 1980), 3.

82. *The New York Times*, 31 May 1980.

83. Palmer, "The EEC goes its own way", 2.

84. André Fontaine, "Transatlantic Doubts and Dreams," *Foreign Affairs* 59, 3 (1980), 589.

85. See the resolution of the heads of government and ministers of foreign affairs of the European Council (the Venice Declaration), 13 June 1980, reprinted in Lukacs (ed.), *The Israeli–Palestinian Conflict*, 17–19.

86. *The New York Times*, 21 May 1981.

87. Saleh A. Al-Mani, *The Euro–Arab Dialogue: A Study in Associative Diplomacy* (London: Palgrave Macmillan, 1983), 110.

88. Text of speech by Lord Carrington, House of Lords debate, 9 July 1980, vol. 411, col. 1187, http://hansard.millbanksystems.com/lords/1980/jul/09/africa-and-the-middle-east#column_1192.

89. Lord Carrington, "European Political Co-operation: America Should Welcome It." *International Affairs* 58, 1 (Winter 1981–2), 4.

90. Peter Alexander Rupert Carrington, *Reflect on Things Past: The Memoirs of Lord Carrington* (London: Collins, 1988), 340.

91. *MEI* 129 (19 July 1980), 5.

11. OIL AND THE OCTOBER WAR

1. It is important to emphasise that the production cutbacks and embargoes were undertaken by OAPEC, not OPEC (Organization of the Petroleum Exporting Countries). Calling the embargo "the OPEC embargo," as is common in both scholarly and popular studies, obscures the specific political circumstances that led to it.

2. Steven A. Schneider, *The Oil Price Revolution* (Baltimore, MD: Johns Hopkins University Press, 1983), 222; US Congress, Senate, Committee on Foreign Relations, Subcommittee on Multinational Corporations, *Multinational Oil Corporations and US Foreign Policy* (Washington, DC: US Government Printing Office, 1975 (hereafter *MNC Report*), 144. Standard Oil Company of California (SOCAL, later Chevron), Texaco, Exxon and Mobil jointly owned ARAMCO.

3. US Department of State, *Foreign Relations of the United States, 1969–1976*, vol. 36: *Energy Crisis, 1969–1974* (Washington, DC: US Government Printing Office, 2012), (hereafter *FRUS*, followed by volume and page numbers), 575; Schneider, *Oil Price Revolution*, 223; Francisco Parra, *Oil Politics: A Modern History of Petroleum* (London: I.B. Tauris, 2004), 176–8.

4. Mary Ann Tétreault, *The Organization of Arab Petroleum Exporting Countries: History, Policy, and Prospects* (Westport, CT: Greenwood Press, 1981), 46–50.

5. *FRUS 1969–76*, 36: 390–1, 446–52, 454–55, 468–9, 472–88, 499–501, 538–44; Nadan Safran, *Saudi Arabia: The Ceaseless Quest for Security* (Cambridge, MA: Harvard University Press, 1985), 151–5; Joseph Kéchichian, *Faysal: Saudi Arabia's King for All Seasons* (Gainesville, FL: University Press of Florida, 2008), 135–6; Bennett H. Wall, *Growth in a Changing Environment: A History of Standard Oil Company (New Jersey) and Exxon Corporation, 1950–1975* (New York: McGraw-Hill, 1988), 849–54; Mohammed Heikal, *The Road to Ramadan* (New York: Quadrangle/The New York Times Book Co., 1975), 268.

6. *FRUS, 1969–76*, 36: 575–6, 579–93; *MNC Report*, 144.

7. *FRUS 1969–76*, 35: 593–4: *MNC Report*, 144; Safran, *Saudi Arabia*, 156–60.

8. *FRUS*, 25: 545–56; Asaf Siniver, *Nixon, Kissinger, and U.S. Foreign Policy Making* (Cambridge: Cambridge University Press, 2008), 202.

9. Telegram 492 from Jedda to the Foreign Office, 16 October 1973, and Telegram 493 from Jedda to the Foreign Office, 16 October 1973, both in PREM 15/1765, United Kingdom National Archives (UKNA); Henry A. Kissinger, *Years of Upheaval* (Boston: Little, Brown, 1982), 872.

10. *FRUS 1969–76*, 36: 620–1; *MNC Report*, 144; Schneider, *Oil Price Revolution*, 226–7, 229.

11. Schneider, *Oil Price Revolution*, 229–30; Daniel Yergin, *The Prize: The Epic Quest for Oil, Money, and Power* (New York: Simon & Schuster, 1991), 606–7; Parra, *Oil Politics*, 180.

12. *FRUS 1969–76*, 25: 931; *FRUS 1969–76*, 36; 620–1, 626–7; Schneider, *Oil Price Revolution*, 227–8, 556, note 33, 667, note 43; Yergin, *Prize*, 607–8; Anthony Cave Brown, *Oil, God, and Gold: The Story of ARAMCO and the Saudi Kings* (Boston: Houghton Mifflin, 1999), 295; Rory Miller, *Inglorious Disarray: Europe, Israel, and the Palestinians since 1967* (London: Hurst & Co., 2011), 32–3.

13. Federal Energy Administration, *U.S. Oil Companies and the Arab Oil Embargo: The International Allocation of Constricted Supplies* (Washington, DC: US Government Printing Office, 1975 (hereafter *FEA Report*), 1–2 (The FEA prepared the report for the Senate Subcommittee on Multinational Corporations.); Yergin, *Prize*, 611; Cave-Brown, *ARAMCO*, 294–5; *MNC Report*, 145–6; Wall, *Exxon*, 863.

14. Yamani quoted in Schneider, *Oil Price Revolution*, 233.

15. *FEA Report*, 2; *FRUS 1969–76*, 36: 620–2; James Bamberg, *British Petroleum and Global Oil, 1950–1975: The Challenge of Nationalism* (Cambridge: Cambridge University Press, 2000), 479.

16. This figure includes natural gas liquids and other liquid hydrocarbons. US crude oil production peaked at 9.6 mbpd in 1970.

17. DeGolyer and MacNaughton, *Twentieth Century Petroleum Statistics 2005* (Dallas, 2005); *BP Statistical Review of World Energy*, 2012; Joel Darmstadter and Hans H. Landsberg, "The Economic Background" in Raymond Vernon (ed.), *The Oil Crisis* (New York: W.W. Norton & Co., 1976), 31–35; see also Schneider, *Oil Price Revolution*, 66–75; 230–1.

18. DeGolyer and MacNaughton, *20th Century Petroleum Statistics*; Darmstadter and Landsberg, "The Economic Background," 15–31; Schneider, *Oil Price Revolution*, 49–66, 520–2; *FRUS 1969–76*, 36: 620–5. By October 1973, however, US imports of Arab oil were about 2 mbpd and rising; CIA, "The Current State of the Arab Oil Embargo: Implications for Consumers," 24 October 1973, in CIA Freedom of Information Act Electronic Reading Room, "President Nixon and the Role of Intelligence in the 1973 Arab-Israeli War". Some studies calculated that Arab oil accounted for over 75 per cent of European oil consumption and over 50 percent of Japanese oil consumption; White House, "Oil Contingency Paper," 7 October 1973, *Ibid.*

19. *FRUS 1969–76*, 36: 730, 732–3; Keetie Sluyterman, *Keeping Competitive in Turbulent Markets, 1973–2007*, vol. 3 of *A History of Royal Dutch Shell* (Oxford: Oxford University Press, 2007), 27–9; Romano Prodi and Alberto Clô, "Europe" in Vernon (ed.), *The Oil Crisis*, 98.

20. *FRUS 1969–76*, 36: 622, 624–5.

21. Parra, *Oil Politics*, 180; for an appraisal of the oil situation in early December, see National Intelligence Estimate, NIE 1–1–73, "The World Oil Crisis: Economic and Political Ramifications for Producers and Consumers," 5 December 1973, *FRUS 1969–76*, 36: 735–52; Yergin, *Prize*, 616–17. There had been a brief disruption in shipments of oil to the Mediterranean in October due to the fighting.

22. See Tel. 196 to The Hague, 1 November 1973, in *Documents on British Policy Overseas*, Series 3, Vol. 4: *The Year of Europe: America, Europe and the Energy Crisis, 1972–1974* (hereafter *DBPO: Year of Europe*); Tel. 197 to The Hague, 1 November 1973; *Ibid.*

23. *FRUS 1969–76*, 36: 581, 645, 668, 745.

24. *FEA Report*, 4–5; *MNC Report*, 146–48; "Note on a Meeting Held at 10 Downing Street on 29 October 1973, "Subject: Oil Supplies," 31 October 1972, PREM 15/1840, UKNA; Record of a Meeting Held in the FCO, 7 November 1973, *DBPO: Year of Europe*; Davies to Prime Minister, "Oil Companies," 23 November 1973, PREM 15/1842, UKNA; Yergin, *Prize*, 620–22; and, in general, Robert Stobaugh, "The Oil Companies in the Crisis," in Vernon (ed.), *The Oil Crisis*, 179–202.

25. *FRUS 1969–76*, 36: 687–, 737–38; Schneider, *Oil Price Revolution*, 232–33; Yoshi Tsurumi, "Japan," in Vernon(ed.), *The Oil Crisis*, 123–23; Yergin, *Prize*, 628–29.

26. Report by the Joint Intelligence Committee, "The Main Effects of the Middle East War, 5 December 1973, *DBPO: Year of Europe*.

27. *FRUS 1969–76*, 36: 627–8, 675–8, 680–2, 735–6; Schneider, *Oil Price Revolution*, 231–2; Safran, *Saudi Arabia*, 156–9.

28. *FRUS 1969–76*, 36: 673–5; *FEA Report*, 3; Yergin, *Prize*, 617–18; Franklin Tugwell, *The Energy Crisis and the American Political Economy: Politics and Markets in the Management of Natural Resources* (Stanford: Stanford University Press, 1988), 102–05.

29. Discussion between the defence secretary and the US secretary of defense, 7 November 1973, *DBPO: Year of Europe*; Cromer to Douglas-Home, 15 November 1973, *DBPO: Year of Europe*; Ministry of Defence to the prime minister, "Middle East," 28 November 1973, PREM 15/1768, UKNA; Note by the Assessments Staff, Middle East: Possible Use of Force by the United States," 12 December 1973, PREM 15/1768, UKNA; *FRUS 1969–76*, 36: 691–2;

30. *FRUS 1969–76*, 36: 692; *FRUS 1969–76*, 25:1026–8; Kissinger, *Years of Upheaval*, 880.

31. *FRUS 1969–76*, 36: 693; Schneider, *Oil Price Revolution*, 232; Jeffrey Robinson, *Yamani: The Inside Story* (London: Simon & Schuster, 1988), 102.

32. Rachel Bronson, *Thicker Than Oil: America's Uneasy Partnership with Saudi Arabia* (New York: Oxford University Press, 2006), 106; Andrew Scott Cooper, *Oil Kings: How the U.S., Iran, and Saudi Arabia Changed the Balance of Power in the Middle East* (New York: Simon & Schuster, 2011), 129–30; Robinson, *Yamani*, 100–2; *FRUS 1969–76*, 25:875.

33. *FRUS 1969–76*, 36; 643.

34. *FRUS 1969–76*, 36: 643, 690–1; *FRUS 1969–76*, 25: 875.

35. "Note by the Assessments Staff, Middle East: Possible Use of Force by the United States," 12 December 1973, PREM 15/1768, UKNA; Hunt to the Prime Minister, "Middle East," 3 January 1974, PREM 115/2153, UKNA.

36. *FRUS 1969–76*, 36: 698, 706, 712, 717–18; *FRUS 1969–76*, 25: 1001; Schneider, *Oil Price Revolution*, 588, note 61; "Note by the Assessments Staff, Middle East: Possible Use of Force by the United States," 12 December 1973, PREM 15/1768, UKNA.

37. *FRUS 1969–76*, 36: 694, 799–800, 842–3; Cave-Brown, *ARAMCO*, 295–7; Bronson, *Thicker Than Oil*, 119–20; Naila Al-Sowayel, "An Historical Analysis of Saudi Arabia's Foreign Policy in Time of Crisis: The October War and the Arab Oil Embargo," (PhD Dissertation, Georgetown University, 1990), 129–30, 229–30.

38. *FRUS 1969–76*, 36: 725–8, 764; Schneider, *Oil Price Revolution*, 233–4.

39. *FRUS 1969–76*, 36: 762–4, 718–19, 731–5; Kissinger, *Years of Upheaval*, 896–97; Ian Skeet, *OPEC: Twenty-five Years of Prices and Politics* (New York: Cambridge University Press, 1988), 107; Fiona Venn, "International Cooperation versus National Self-Interest: The United States and Europe during the 1973–1974 Oil Crisis," in Kathleen Burk and Melvyn Stokes (eds), *The United States and the European Alliance since 1945* (Oxford: Berg, 1999), 78–86; Miller, *Inglorious Disarray*, 39–42.

40. *FRUS 1969–76*, 36: 774–6; Skeet, *OPEC*, 100–3; Parra, *Oil Politics*, 183–4; Cooper, *Oil Kings*, 143–6.

41. Kissinger, *Years of Upheaval*, 885–9; *FRUS 1969–76*, 36: 623; Cooper, *Oil Kings*, 149–50; Roham Alvandi, "Nixon, Kissinger, and the Shah: The Origins of Iranian Primacy in the Persian Gulf," *Diplomatic History* 36 (April 2012), 337–72.

42. Kissinger, *Years of Upheaval*, 889–90; Schneider, *Oil Price Revolution*, 237–8; *FEA Report*, 2.

43. *FRUS 1969–76*, 25: 1204–6; *FRUS 1969–76*, 36: 777–81, 793, 798–9

44. Kissinger, *Years of Upheaval*, 891–2; Schneider, *Oil Price Revolution*, 242.

45. *FRUS 1969–76*, 36: 795–7, 822–3, 840–4.

46. *FRUS 1969–76*, 36: 893–902; Kissinger, *Years of Upheaval*, 905–25; Ethan B.

Kapstein, *The Insecure Alliance: Energy Crises and Western Politics Since 1944* (New York: Oxford University Press, 1990), 171–5.

47. *FRUS 1969–76*, 36: 801–3, 808–21, 833–40, 933–4; Telecon, President Nixon/ Secretary Kissinger, 11 March 1974, Digital National Security Archive, Kissinger Telephone Conversations, KA 12113; Cooper, *Oil Kings*, 157–8; Safran, *Saudi Arabia*, 173–74; Schneider, *Oil Price Revolution*, 242–3.

48. Schneider, *Oil Price Revolution*, 244; *FEA Report*, 7; Yergin, *Prize*, 614; Skeet, *OPEC*, 100.

49. Schneider, *Oil Price Revolution*, 244; *FEA Report*, 8.

50. *FEA Report*, 8–9.

51. *FEA Report*, 9–10; Libya tried to plug this leak in the embargo in late December by cutting off shipments to the Caribbean.

52. *FEA Report*, 9; Prodi and Clô, "Europe," 101–3; Sluyterman, *Shell*, 27–30.

53. *FEA Report*, 6; Yergin, *Prize*, 621–2.

54. Schneider, *Oil Price Revolution*, 246–50; Yergin, *Prize*, 623–4; Bamberg, *BP*, 481–4.

55. Salim Yaqub, "The Weight of Conquest: Henry Kissinger and the Arab–Israeli Conflict" in Fredrik Logevall and Andrew Preston (eds), *Nixon in the World: American Foreign Relations, 1969–1977* (New York: Oxford University Press, 2008), 227–48.

56. Fiona Venn, *The Oil Crisis* (London: Longman, 2002), 145–72.

57. James E. Cronin, *The World the Cold War Made: Order, Chaos, and the Return of History* (London: Routledge, 1996), 178–96; Timothy Mitchell, *Carbon Democracy: Political Power in the Age of Oil* (London: Verso, 2011), 10–11; Thomas Borstelmann, *The 1970s: A New Global History from Civil Rights to Economic Inequality* (Princeton, NJ: Princeton University Press, 2012).

58. Giuliano Garavini, "Completing Decolonization: The 1973 'Oil Shock' and the Struggle for Economic Rights," *International History Review* 33 (September 2011), 473–87; Christopher Roy William Dietrich, *The Permanence of Power: Postcolonial Sovereignty, the Energy Crisis, and the Rise of American Neoliberal Diplomacy, 1967–1976* (PhD dissertation, University of Texas at Austin, 2012).

59. *FRUS 1969–1976*, 36: 980–4; Venn, *The Oil Crisis*, 173–200; Daniel J. Sargent, "The United States and Globalization in the 1970s" in Niall Ferguson, *et al* (eds), *The Shock of the Global: The 1970s in Perspective* (Cambridge, MA: Harvard University Press, 2010), 59; Dietrich, *Permanence of Power*, chapter 6.

60. Kenneth A. Rodman, *Sanctity vs. Sovereignty: The United States and the Nationalization of Natural Resource Investments* (New York: Columbia University Press, 1988), 245–69, 294–305; Bamberg, *BP*, 485–6; Sluyterman, *Shell*, 31–5; Brian Levy, "World Oil Marketing in Transition," *International Organization* 36 (Winter 1982), 113–33.

61. Skeet, *OPEC*, 240, 244; James A. Bill, *The Eagle and the Lion: The Tragedy of Iranian–American Relations* (New Haven: Yale University Press, 1988), 216–60; Mark J. Gasiorowski, *US Foreign Policy and the Shah: Building a Client State in Iran* (Ithaca NY: Cornell University Press 1991), 142–51, 187–222.

62. Richard Ned Lebow and Janice Gross Stein, *We All Lost the Cold War* (Princeton, NJ: Princeton University Press, 1994), 149–288; David S. Painter, *The Cold War: An International History* (London: Routledge, 1999), 77–80.

63. Marshall I. Goldman, *The Enigma of Soviet Petroleum: Half-Empty or Half-Full?* (London: HarperCollins, 1980), 85–111; Odd Arne Westad, "The Fall of Détente and the Turning Tides of History" in Odd Arne Westad, (ed.), *The Fall of Détente: Soviet–American Relations during the Carter Years* (Oslo: Scandinavian University Press, 1997), 3–33.

64. David S. Painter, "Oil and the American Century," *Journal of American History* 99 (June 2012), 35–38; Steven Hurst, *The United States and Iraq since 1979: Hegemony, Oil and War* (Edinburgh, 2009), 83–113; John S. Duffield, "Oil and the Decision to Invade Iraq," in Jane K. Cramer and A. Trevor Thrall (eds), *Why Did the United States Invade Iraq?* (London: Routledge, 2012) 145–66. (London, 2012). Percentages calculated from data in the *BP Statistical Review of World Energy, 2012*, using the total figure for the Middle East plus Algeria, Egypt, and Libya. On the current world oil situation, see Daniel Yergin, "How is Energy Remaking the World?' *Foreign Policy* 194 (July/August 2012), 60–61, 68.

12. ASHRAF MARWAN AND ISRAEL'S INTELLIGENCE FAILURE

1. Ahron Bregman, *Israel's Wars* (London: Routledge, 2000), 113.

2. Ahron Bregman, *A History of Israel* (London: Palgrave, 2002), 142–3; also *Yediot Ahronoth*, 19 September 2002 (in Hebrew). In fact, this was never one of his nicknames, but rather my invention to serve as a tool to hint at his real identity.

3. The above quotes appear in Halud el Gamal, an interview with Ahron Bregman, *Al Ahram al Arabi*, 300, 21 December 2002.

4. Transcript of Ahron Bregman & Ashraf Marwan first telephone conversation, 29 December 2002, in "The Bregman collection", Liddell Hart Archives (LHA), King's College London. Marwan felt that Egyptian journalists try to drive a wedge between us by squeezing from each of us provocative statements.

5. This is now deposited at the Liddell Hart Archives, King's College London, and is part of "The Bregman collection".

6. These are the messages: 1.52 p.m.: "Hello Hi, I am calling about your book if you could call me back in my mobile. Thank you." 2:51 p.m.: "Please, hallo can you call me about your book. Thank you." 3.11 p.m.: "Hello, Hi good afternoon. If you can call me I'm the subject of your book. Thanks you." The origi-

nal tape with these messages is at the LHA, King's College London, part of "The Bregman collection".

7. Transcript of Ahron Bregman and Ashraf Marwan telephone conversation, Tuesday 26 June 2007, around 4 p.m., "The Bregman collection", LHA, King's College London. The full recorded conversation (only Bregman can be heard) is also kept at the LHA, but is not open to the public.

8. The total sum of money transferred to Marwan over the years would reach $1,000,000, including a special bonus of $100,000 for Marwan's 5 October warning of war.

9. Nadav Zeevi, "The Betrayed", *Maariv*, 28 December 2007 (in Hebrew).

10. See Uri Bar-Joseph, *The Angel: Ashraf Marwan, the Mossad and the Yom Kippur War* (Or Yehuda: Kinneret, Zmora-Bitan, Dvir, 2011), 72–3 (in Hebrew). This book, which is a masterpiece, focuses on the life and work of Marwan with the Israelis.

11. Eli Zeira, *Myth versus Reality: The October 1973 War: Failures and Lessons* (Tel Aviv: Yediot Ahronoth Books, 2004), 155–6 (in Hebrew).

12. Arye Shalev, *Israel's Intelligence Assessment before the Yom Kippur War* (Eastbourne: Sussex Academic Press, 2010), 77, 125.

13. Arye Shalev, "The Intelligence Assessment towards War" in Moshe Shemesh & Zeev Drori (eds), *National Trauma: The Yom Kippur War thirty years on* [Ben Gurion Institute, Ben Gurion University, 2008], 110 (in Hebrew).

14. Moshe Dayan in conversation with Rami Tal, 22 November 1976, *Yediot Ahronoth*, 27 April 1997 (in Hebrew).

15. Zeira, *Myth versus Reality*, 161.

16. *Maariv*, 28 December 2007 (in Hebrew).

17. Ran Idelist, "Was this the head of Mossad?" *Yediot Ahronoth*, 24 September 1993 (in Hebrew); also Ronen Bergman and Gil Meltzer, *The Yom Kippur War: Moment of Truth* (Tel Aviv: Yediot Ahronoth Books, 2003), 41 (in Hebrew).

18. Bergman and Meltzer, *The Yom Kippur War*, 41.

19. Zeira, *Myths versus Reality*, 109–10, 159–63; in a meeting on 6 October at 5.45 the Defence Minister said that war would start "this evening", see Amnon Lorch, "The Surprise: The Head of AMAN's version", News1, 12 October 2001 (in Hebrew); also Bergman and Meltzer, *The Yom Kippur War*, 47.

20. Transcript of Ahron Bregman & Ashraf Marwan telephone conversation, 6 October 2006, in "The Bregman collection", LHA, King's College London.

21. Zvi Zamir, "The Last Spy", *Uvda*, a television documentary on Ashraf Marwan, 27 December 2007 (in Hebrew); Bar-Joseph, *The Angel*, 11.

22. Shlomo Gazit, "Death of an Agent", *Maariv*, 4 July 2007 (in Hebrew).

23. The reason why Sadat decided not to wait for the supply of weapons from the USSR before embarking on war against Israel is that he was tired of the continued Israeli occupation of his land, and the realisation that the USSR, given

her improved relationship with the US during the so called détente, would not provide him with the attack weapons requested.

24. Bar-Joseph, *The Angel*, 143–4.

25. Zeira, *Myths versus Reality*, 156. Bregman, *A History of Israel*, 144–5.

26. Anwar el Sadat, *In Search of Identity: An Autobiography* (New York: Harper & Row, 1977), 241.

27. Interview with Field Marshal Abdel Ghani el-Gamasy, Cairo, 24 February 1997, for the BBC series *The Fifty Years War*, LHA, King's College London.

28. Interview with Egyptian General Fuad Awidi, *Maariv*, 24 September 1993 (in Hebrew).

29. Zeira, *Myths versus Reality*, 123–4.

30. *Ibid.*, 126.

31. *Ibid.*, 162.

32. Ran Idelist, "Was this the head of Mossad?"

33. Bar-Joseph, *The Angel*, 195.

34. Bar-Joseph, *The Watchman Fell Asleep: The Surprise of Yom Kippur and its Sources* (Tel Aviv: Zmora Bitan, 2001), 146–50 (in Hebrew).

35. Bar-Joseph, *The Angel*, 11

36. General Saad el-Shazly, *The Crossing of the Suez* (London: Third World Centre for Research and Publishing, 1980), 151–2; Mohamed Heikal, *The Road to Ramadan* (New York: Ballantine, 1975), 22.

37. Summary of a meeting between Bregman & Marwan, 23 October 2003, in "The Bregman collection", LHA, King's College London.

38. Ahron Bregman in Yossi Melman, "Victim of the 'espionage game'", *Ha'aretz*, 27 May 2010.

39. Shlomo Gazit, "The trap of the top agent", *Malam* (a periodical of the Israeli Intelligence Community), 62, January 2012. See also Uri Bar-Joseph's response, *Malam*, 63, June 2012 (in Hebrew).

13. EVOLVING A DIPLOMATIC LEGACY FROM THE WAR: THE US, EGYPTIAN, AND ISRAELI TRIANGLE

1. For the Mufti, see Ghassan Kanafani, *The 1936–39 Revolt in Palestine* (New York: Committee for a Democratic Palestine, 1972 and London: Tricontinental Society, 1980). On Arafat, see Hani Shukrallah, *Al-Ahram Weekly*, 16–22 and 23–9, August 2001: Kenneth W. Stein, "Arafat's Legacy," *International Politik* (Transatlantic Edition), December 2004, http://ismi.emory.edu/home/assets/documents/stein-publications/website%20docs%202011–2004/arafatslegacy.pdf; and Yezid Sayigh, "Arafat and the Anatomy of a Revolt," *Survival* 43, 3 (Autumn 2001), 47 60.

2. For a comprehensive assessment of Sadat's personality and motives as character-

ised by the dozens of individuals who interacted with him, see Kenneth W. Stein, *Heroic Diplomacy: Sadat, Kissinger, Carter, Begin and the Quest for Arab-Israeli Peace* (Routledge, 1999), 1–18. See also Joseph Finklestone, *Anwar Sadat: Visionary Who Dared* (Frank Cass, 1996).

3. Nasser went to war in 1967 "to prove that he was a political giant and restore the awe and prestige that many of the Third World countries felt for him, but which had been in decline in recent months... Nasser triggered [the war]. He by his own unfortunate speeches created a political situation that he was unable to master." Interview remarks by Lucius Battle, US ambassador to Egypt, September 1963 to March 1967. When Battle returned from Cairo just prior to the 1967 war, President Lyndon Johnson sought his daily input on understanding Nasser and his motivations. From Battle's departure in March forwards, the US did not have an accredited ambassador in Cairo until after the October 1973 War. The designated US ambassador Richard Nolte knew little about Egypt, running an embassy, and was never accredited. Prior to and during the 1967 war, the US did not have an ambassador in Cairo. After the war, the US was represented by a US interest section located in the Indian embassy, first headed by the very savvy Donald Bergus. See Association for Diplomatic Studies and Training Foreign Affairs Oral History Project, *The Foreign Affairs Oral History Collection of the Association for Diplomatic Studies and Training*, 10 July 1991, http://memory.loc.gov/cgi-bin/query/r?ammem/mfdip:"field(DOCID+mfdip2004bat03); see also Michael Oren, *Six Days of War June 1967 and the Making of the Modern Middle East* (Oxford, 2002).

4. Remarks by Moshe Dayan, Israeli Defence Minister, *Jerusalem Post*, 23 November 1977.

5. Interview with Naftali Lavi, 8 July 1993; when Dayan was Defence Minister, Lavi was his press and media adviser.

6. Interview with Zbigniew Brzezinski, US National Security Adviser, 1977–1981, 30 October 1992, Washington, D.C.

7. Interview with Zaid Rifa'i, January 9, 1993, Amman, Jordan. Rifa'i was Jordan's Foreign Minister during and after the 1973 War.

8. Ken Stein, notes of a meeting between Jimmy Carter and Usamah al-Baz, 12 March 1990, Cairo. As Middle East Fellow of the Carter Center at the time, I took the trip notes at Carter's meetings with Middle Eastern policy-makers and leaders during our trips to the Middle East in March 1983, March 1987 and March 1990. These notes were deposited at the Carter Center in April 1990, with a set delivered to Carter personally. Carter never disputed that Sadat failed to support him on the matter of an Israeli settlement freeze, regardless of duration. In the 1970s and 1980s, al-Baz emerged as Sadat's and later Mubarak's most trusted political adviser on matters relating to the Arab world, Israel and the negotiating process. Al-Baz was part of the Egyptian delegation at the September 1978 Camp David talks.

9. Remarks by Anwar Sadat, Cairo Domestic Service, 11 February 1971, as quoted in *Foreign Broadcast Information Service, Daily Report—Middle East and North Africa*, 13 February 1971, D4.

10. Interview with Moshe Dayan by Rami Tal, 22 November 1976, *Yediot Aharanoth*, 27 April 1997; interviews with Naftali Lavi, 8 July 1993, Jerusalem, Israel and Yossi Ciechanover, 5 July 1993, Tel Aviv, Israel.

11. Interview with Gideon Rafael, 25 March 1992, Jerusalem, Israel. Rafael was director general of the Israeli foreign ministry.

12. Interview with Donald Bergus, head of the US interests section in Cairo, 67–1972, 24 January 1991. See Association for Diplomatic Studies and Training Foreign Affairs Oral History Project, *The Foreign Affairs Oral History Collection of the Association for Diplomatic Studies and Training*, http://memory.loc.gov/cgibin/query/S?ammem/mfdipbib:"field(AUTHOR+"od1(Bergus,+Donald+C+) Interview with Michael Sterner, Egyptian desk officer, Department of State, 1969–74, 13 May 1992. Memoranda of Conversations Henry Kissinger, National Security Adviser with Hafez Isma'il, Armonk, New York, 25–6 February 1973, National Archives, Washington, DC. Box 59, DSR, Kissinger, 1973–7 cat A; Memorandum of Conversation Henry Kissinger with Hafez Isma'il, 20 May, NA, 59, National Archives, Washington, DC, NPMP, NSCF, HAK, 135, 1973–7, 25, cat "C".

13. Text of Sadat's October War Anniversary Interview, 6 October 1977, Cairo Domestic Service, as quoted in *Foreign Broadcast Information Service, Daily Report—Middle East and North Africa Supplement*, 25 October 1977, 38.

14. Interview with Peter Rodman, 10 June 1992, Washington, DC; Mohamed Heikal, *Autumn of Fury: The Assassination of Sadat* (New York: Random House, 1983), 50–1.

15. Interview with Usamah al-Baz, 9 November 1992, Cairo, Egypt.

16. Interview with Zaid Rifa'i, 9 January 1993, Amman, Jordan.

17. Interview with Abd al-Halim Khaddam, 18 July 1993, Damascus, Syria. Khaddam was a very close confident of President Hafez al-Asad, at the time foreign minister and later vice-president of Syria.

18. Interview with Nabil al-Arabi, 26 February 1993, Atlanta, Georgia. Al-Arabi was in the Egyptian foreign ministry at the time of the 1973 War and would become a key adviser to Sadat and Mubarak and served Egypt in several significant diplomatic posts, including Arab League Secretary General.

19. Remarks by Joseph Sisco and Roy Atherton, United States Institute of Peace meeting, Washington, DC, 3 April 1991, 87–8. Both Sisco and Atherton served in the US State Department and were part of Kissinger's shuttle diplomacy team that negotiated the three disengagement agreements that followed the 1973 War. Atherton continued his service in the State Department during the Carter administration and was instrumental in narrowing substantive differences between Israel and Egypt prior to the 1978 Camp David negotiations.

20. Interview with Abdel el-Ghani al-Gamasy, 10 November 1992, Heliopolis, Egypt. El-Gamasy was the Egyptian chief of staff who planned the October War and later became Egyptian minister of defence.

21. Interview with Usamah al-Baz, 9 November 1992, Cairo, Egypt.

22. Interviews with Hermann F. Eilts, 11 April 1991, Boston, Massachusetts and Abdel el-Ghani el-Gamasy, 10 November 1992, Heliopolis, Egypt.

23. Interview with Hafez Isma'il, 7 January 1993, Cairo, Egypt. Isma'il was Sadat's national security adviser and later Cairo's ambassador to Moscow.

24. Interview with Hermann F. Eilts, 11 April 1991, Boston, Massachusetts. Eilts was US ambassador to Egypt from the end of the October War until 1979.

25. Interview with Omar Sirry, 5 January 1993, Cairo, Egypt.

26. Interview with Omar Sirry, 5 January 1993, Cairo, Egypt.

27. Interview with Ahmed Maher, an Egyptian foreign ministry official at the time, 29 July 1993, Washington, DC.

28. I am particularly grateful to General el-Gamasy and General Yariv for providing the opportunity to interview both of them at length, and in Yariv's case, reading his diary notes made at the Kilometer 101 talks directly into my tape recorder. El-Gamasy was no less candid in his recollection of the talks with Yariv. To my knowledge, and according to both of them, they did not meet again after their Kilometer 101 encounters.

29. Interview with Omar Sirry, 5 January 1993, Cairo, Egypt.

30. Interview with Abdel el-Ghani el-Gamasy, 10 November 1992, Heliopolis, Egypt.

31. Interview with Aharon Yariv, 26 March 1992, Ramat Aviv, Israel.

32. Interview with Abdel el-Ghani el-Gamasy, 10 November 1992, Heliopolis, Egypt.

33. Interview with Omar Sirry, 5 January 1993, Cairo, Egypt.

34. *Ibid.*; Mahmoud Riad, *The Struggle for Peace in the Middle East*, (London: Quartet Books, 1981), 256. Ismail Fahmy, *Negotiating for Peace in the Middle East* (Baltimore: Johns Hopkins University Press, 1983), 36.

35. Interviews with Harold Saunders, 12 May 1992, Washington, DC, and Peter Rodman, an adviser to Henry Kissinger, 10 June 1992, Washington, DC. Saunders and Rodman have almost identical recollections of this Kissinger pleading to Sadat.

36. Interviews with Harold Saunders, 12 May 1992, Washington, DC, and Hafez Isma'il, 7 January 1993, Cairo, Egypt.

37. Mohammed Heikal, *Autumn of Fury: The Assassination of Sadat*, (New York: Random House, 1983), 68.

38. Kissinger's enumeration of the six points was in a very different order and less explicit than one of the several Israeli drafts of the six points, see Henry Kissinger, *Years of Upheaval* (Boston: Little, Brown, 1982), 641; and Aharon Yariv,

"On the Way to the Israeli–Egyptian Peace at Kilometer 101," transcript of a lecture presented at the Dayan Center for Middle Eastern and African Studies at Tel Aviv University, 30 March 1992 (Tel Aviv: Dayan Center, 1992), 11–12. The six-point agreement was a consensus-made document in which Israelis, Egyptians and Americans participated in drafting.

39. Interviews with Aharon Yariv, 26 March 1992, Ramat Aviv, Israel, and Abdel el-Ghani el-Gamasy, 10 November 1992, Heliopolis, Egypt.

40. Aharon Yariv, "On the Way to the Israeli–Egyptian Peace at Kilometer 101", 14–16.

41. United States Department of State, Egyptian and Israeli Proposals on Disengagement, Meeting Summaries, "E29A," 19,22, 23 and 26 November 1997, 6 December 1973.

42. Aharon Yariv, "On the Way to the Israeli—Egyptian Peace at Kilometer 101" 14–6.

43. Remarks by Anwar Sadat, 28 November 1973, 18 April 1974, and 15 September 1975, as quoted in Raphael Israeli, *The Public Diary of President Sadat: The Road to Diplomacy, The Continuation of War by Other Means (November 1973–May 1975)*, Part Two (Leiden: E. J. Brill, 1979), 444, 474; and Raphael Israeli, *The Public Diary of President Sadat: The Road of Pragmatism (June 1975–October 1976)*, Part Three (Leiden: E. J. Brill, 1979), 1044.

44. Interview with Hermann F. Eilts, 11 April 1991, Boston, Massachusetts.

45. Henry Kissinger, *Years of Upheaval*, 751–2.

46. Interview with Simcha Dinitz, 20 March 1992, Jerusalem, Israel.

47. Interview with Abba Eban, 24 March 1992, Herzelia, Israel.

48. Interview with Hafez Isma'il, 7 January 1993, Cairo, Egypt.

49. Interview with Mordechai Gazit, 22 March 1992, Jerusalem, Israel.

50. Interviews with Hermann F. Eilts, 11 April 1991, Boston, Massachusetts; Hafez Isma'il, 7 January 1993, Cairo, Egypt; and Brian Urquhart, 28 February 1991, New York. Urquhart was a close aide to Secretary-General Kurt Waldheim during the period of the planning and convocation of the December 1973 Geneva Conference. See also Henry Kissinger, *Years of Upheaval*, 752.

51. Interview with Nicholas A. Veliotes, 7 September 1995, Washington, D.C.

52. Interview with Aharon Yariv, 26 March 1992, Ramat Aviv, Israel.

53. Interview with Joe Sisco, 27 February 1992, Washington, D.C.

54. Interview with Alouph Hareven, 2 August 1992, Jerusalem, Israel.

55. Interview with Hermann F. Eilts, 11 April 1991, Boston, Massachusetts.

56. Henry Kissinger, *Years of Upheaval*, 755.

57. Interview with Hafez Isma'il, 7 January 1993, Cairo, Egypt.

14. CLASHING NARRATIVES OF THE OCTOBER WAR: COLLECTIVE MEMORY AND GROUP PERSPECTIVE

1. Daniel Bar-Tal and Dikla Antebi, "Siege Mentality in Israel", *International Journal of Intercultural Relations* 16, (1992), 251–275; Victor D. Sanua, *War, Stress and Bereavement: a Report on Psychological and Social Services in Israel during the October War* (New York: Papercity College, 1975).

2. Amos Perlmutter, *The Military and Politics in Modern Times* (New Haven: Yale University Press,1977); Avraham Sela, "Civil Society, the Military, and National Security" in Gabriel Sheffer and Oren Barak (eds), *Militarism and the Israeli Society* (Bloomington: Indiana University Press, 2010).

3. Julian Schofield, *Militarization and War* (New York: Palgrave Macmillan, 2007); Ephraim Inbar, *Israel's National Security: Issues and Challenges since the October War* (London and New York: Routledge, 2008).

4. The expression is taken from the Book of Numbers (chapter 23: verse 9,), in which the Prophet Balaam foretells with remarkable prescience the future destiny of the Jewish people, predicting that "this is a people that shall dwell alone and shall not be reckoned among the nations."

5. Charles Liebman, "The Myth of Defeat: the memory of the October War in Israeli society", *Middle Eastern Studies* 29, 3 (1993), 399–418.

6. Ernest Renan, *Qu'est-ce qu'une nation?* (Sorbonne: lecture,1882); Johannes Gottfried Herder, *Treatise on the Origin of Language* (1772) and *Ideas for the Philosophy of History of Humanity* (1784–91); Martin Heidegger, *Time and Being* (1927).

7. Maurice Halbwachs, *La mémoire collective* (Paris: Presses Universitaires de France, 1950).

8. Benedict Anderson, *Imagined Communities: reflections on the origin and spread of nationalism* (London: Verso, 1991).

9. Maurice Halbwachs, *La mémoire collective*, 23.

10. An example is the thesis backed by Michael Oren, ex-Israeli ambassador, about the "primacy" of the 1967 War in "reshaping a completely new Middle East" (Michael Oren, *Six Days of War: June 1967 and the Making of the Modern Middle East* [New York: Presidio Press, 2002].)

11. Definition of "historical" and "metahistory" as reported in the Oxford Dictionary of Philosophy (Oxford: Oxford University Press, 2005).

12. "The October War, the oil weapon and the subsequent failure of nerves in the Western democracies raise perilous questions about the future." Moshe Davis, "Reflections on an Agenda for the Future", in Moshe Davis (ed.), *The October War. Israel and the Jewish People* (New York: Arno Press, 1974).

13. Fritz Stern, "The end of the postwar era", *Commentary* (1974), 27–35.

14. Raymond William Baker, *Egypt's Uncertain Revolution under Nasser and Sadat* (Cambridge, MA: Harvard University Press, 1978).

15. Wulf Kansteiner, "Finding Meaning in Memory: A Methodological Critique of Collective Memory Studies," *History and Theory* 41 (2002), 180.
16. Ella Shohat, *Israeli Cinema* (London: I. B. Tauris, 2010), 212.
17. Susan Hattis Rolef, "The domestic fallout of the October War", *Israel Affairs* 6, 1 (1999), 177.
18. Avihai Chiim, IDF spokesman, "38 years after October War: Israel still seeking security", last modified on 9 October 2011, http://www.idf.il/1283–13455-en/Dover.aspx.
19. From 1971 the demonstrations of the Black Panthers stormed the country and shook up society, advocating for the first time full equal rights (including economic rights) for the *Mizrahim*.
20. "Considering that they were exhausted, mourning their dead, and having difficulty in digesting recent events or comprehending the significance of them, the voters were merciful toward the Labor Party." Yitzhak Rabin, *The Rabin Memoirs* (Boston: Little, Brown, 1989), 236.
21. See Eyal Ben Ari and Edna Lomsky-Feder (eds), *The Military and Militarism in Israeli Society* (Albany: SUNY, 1999).
22. The opinion of the religious establishment was shared by many public figures who spread it to the wider public: a "testimonial" *par excellence* was former actor and TV star Uri Zohar, then turned religious or "come back with an answer", whose personal change from bold *Tsaber* to pious bearded Jew came to symbolise the parallel evolution of the country. See Dan Perry and Alfred Ironside, *Israel and the Quest for Permanence* (North Carolina: McFarland, 1999)
23. Exemplary of this paradigm was Motti Askhenazi's tent protest in front of the *Knesset* in February 1974. Lomsky-Feder pointed out how this logic "underlines the Peace Now movement, which began with the political organisation of reserve officers in spring 1978. Traumatic memories from the 1973 War were among the central motivations in setting it up, but its members' right to oppose government policy derived from their officership and from epitomising the warrior ethos." (Edna Losmky-Feder, "The discourse of psychology and the normalisation of war", in Sheffer and Barak (eds), *Militarism and Israeli Society*, 298.
24. Edna Lomsky-Feder, *As if there was no war: the perception of war in the life stories of Israeli men* (Jerusalem: 1998, Hebrew).
25. Totals of 231 IDF soldiers were captured by Egypt, sixty-two by Syria and two by Lebanon. "Archives of the Ministry of Foreign Affairs of Israel", last modified 26 January 2004, http://www.mfa.gov.il/mfa/mfaarchive/2000_2009/2004/1/background%20on%20israeli%20pows%20and%20mias.
26. "Dozens of Israeli prisoners parading humbled and handcuffed and blindfolded for the entire Arab world to see and rejoice at." These were images that had never been seen before by an Israeli public always used to what General. Bar-

Lev had called in 1967 "quick and elegant" victories. Shlomo Ben-Ami, *Scars of War, Wounds of Peace* (London: Weidenfeld & Nicolson, 2005), 147.

27. Arieh Segev, *Le Prisonnier du Kippour* (Paris: Ginglo Editeur, 2010).

28. *Ibid.*, 141. The lack of assistance upon their return to Israel and the suspicion that those prisoners might have revealed military secrets turned the memory of some ex-prisoners particularly bitter.

29. The *Mizrahi* "protest" differed from the content of the "Ashkenazi-led" protest movements set up in the aftermath of the war, such as *Dash, Ratz* and *Israel Shelanu*. The same gap could be traced between Segev's diary and that of Lieutenant Yagouri, another "prisoner" of the October War. See Asaf Yagouri, *Pagisha ba-Ruah: Roman* (Tel Aviv: Mahad, 1982).

30. *Mizrahi* Jews were discriminated against in the army too, and were, generally speaking, considered less brave than their Ashkenazi or *Sabra* comrades. Few were awarded a military medal of honour in the October War. The story of the Moroccan-born soldier Nathan Albaz, who, just drafted in the army, threw himself on a mine circulated around, more so as the heroic behaviour of a Sephardic Jew was uncustomary. Gal Reuven, *A Portrait of the Israeli Soldier* (Westport: Greenwood Press, 1986), 199.

31. "From 1967 on, Sapir deliberately set out to industrialise and develop Israel's economy by subsidising private investments…The policy rapidly degenerated into the 'system' ('*ha-Shitah*')." Bernard Avishai, *A New Israel: Democracy in Crisis, 1973–1988: Essays* (New York: Ticnor & Fields, 1990), 67.

32. *Ibid.*, 76.

33. "Too many Mapai functionaries wanted to make the new immigrants into stereotypical Israelis. Begin was content to allow them to remain Jews". Colin Schindler, *Israel, Likud and the Zionist Dream: power, politics, ideology from Begin to Nethanyau* (London: I.B. Tauris, 1995), 58.

34. Baruch Kimmerling, "Between hegemony and dormant Kulturkampf in Israel", *Israel Affairs*, 4/3–4 (1998), 49–72.

35. A good example of the Second Israel's backing of the Right is provided by Bernard Avishai, who illustrates how young Moroccan Jews had started backing the Likud in 1977 due to their nationalism, religiousness, extraneousness from Zionism and out of opposition to the Labor Party. Bernard Avishai, *A New Israel: Democracy in Crisis, 1973–1988: Essays*, 50.

36. Aharon Kellerman, *Society and Settlement* (New York: State University Press, 1993).

37. Inspired by the ideas of the "Revisionist movement" of Vladimir Jabotinsky, particularly regarding Greater Israel and its biblical boundaries.

38. In Hebrew, a reference is made to the aim of obtaining the "full" land of Israel, which is "the Movement for Greater Israel".

39. Rabbi Yehouda Amital, *Ha-ma'alot mi-m'amakim—The emergence from depths* (Jerusalem: Alon Shevut, 1977), 100.

40. A novel portraying the October War as viewed by the national–religious groups was published in 1999 by Haim Sabato, with the original title "Tium Kavanot" (in Hebrew, translated into English as "Adjusting Sights"), winner of the Prix Sapir in 2000. The focus of the story is the different experience of the war by religious soldiers, brutally wrenched from their *Yeshiva* studies. The story conveyed a main message: the firm belief that Orthodox Jews fought in the war as bravely as secular Jews but, in addition, abiding by their religious duties and keeping pure the moral fibre of the army and the Jewish people as a whole. The novel has been hailed as a great novelty, combining a "luminous literary technique with *Torah* values". Shira Leibowitz Schmidt and Jessica Setbon, "Double-Take: Haim Sabato's Books Make Waves on Israel's Cultural Scene", *Jewish Action* (Fall 5767/2006).

41. "The oath not to rebel against the Gentiles, for example, provided [Rabbi Schach] with a rationale for warning the Israeli government against engaging in adventurist military actions …Indeed, some formulations …include direct criticism of the two messianic approaches to the right and the left, portraying them as illegitimate deviations from the classical Jewish midway." Avier Ravitzky, *Messianism, Zionism and Jewish religious Radicalism* (Chicago: University of Chicago Press, 1996), 153–4. First edition printed in Hebrew as *Ketz ha-meguleh u-Medinat ha-Yehudim* (Tel Aviv: 'Am 'Oved, 1993).

42. "During the post-1973 settlements' boom and in subsequent years, the Israeli government established legal guidelines for approving settlements. …: the full Cabinet would need to approve the establishment of a new settlement; a settlement could be established only on 'state land'." Daniel Kurtzer, "Behind the settlements", *The American Interest* (2010).

43. The Council was composed of Mk Uri Avinery, Matti Peled, Ya'akov Arnon, Me'ir Pa'il, Yossi Amitai, Amos Kenan among others, all secular Jews, some of them politicians and other IDF reservists.

44. Bernard Avishai, *A New Israel: Democracy in Crisis, 1973–1988: Essays*, 47.

45. Edi Karni, "The Israeli Economy, 1973–1976: A Survey of Recent Developments and a Review of an Old Problem", *Economic Development and Cultural Change* 28, 1 (1979), 63–76.

46. Proceedings of the seminar on World Jewry and the October War, Davis (ed.), *The October War. Israel and the Jewish People*.

47. Daniel J. Elazar, "United States of America" in Davis (ed.), *The October War. Israel and the Jewish People*, 35.

48. Charles Liebman, "Israelis and the Jews" in *Dispersion and Unity* (Hebrew) 60, 6 (1972), 97.

49. This fact is refuted by Ephraim Karsh, who conversely claimed that "after 1973 there no longer existed the same desire in many circles to identify with Israel. …In the US, what had been termed the "Israelolatry" of the pre- and post-1967

years gradually diminished. While Israel still remains the centre of community life, little by little it began to share the spotlight with ...the institutionalized remembrance of the Holocaust." Ephraim Karsh, (ed.), "Israel: the first hundred years", *Israeli Society and Politics since 1948: problems of collective identity, vol. 3* (London: Frank Cass, 2002), 25.

50. *Midstream*, December 1973.
51. France, Italy and UK had not been harmed by the oil embargo. For more details on Western reactions to the oil embargo, see Robert J. Lieber, *Oil and the Middle East War: Europe in Energy Crisis* (Harvard: Cambridge Center for International Affairs, 1976).
52. On 6 November 1973, the Council of Ministers of the European Community passed a resolution urging Israel's return to the position held on 22 October (Point 3, *Bulletin Europe*, Brussels, December 1973). Six Arab foreign ministers in December 1973 attended the European summit in Copenhagen.
53. The Italian daily newspaper *Il Manifesto* offered a good example of the new anti-Semitic rhetoric: "The fate of the prisoners is becoming more and more the basic problem: Israel considers it unbearable that 400 of the members of the superior race be held as prisoners by filthy infidels." Editorial, *Il Manifesto*, 3 November 1973.
54. Adeed I. Dawisha, *Egypt in the Arab World: the Elements of Foreign Policy* (New York: Halsted, Wiley, 1976).
55. J. C. Moulton, "The 1973 October War: the Egyptian perspective"" (United States Air Force, 1977).
56. "No Westerner can fully understand the sense of peril we felt after 1967", declared a Lebanese intellectual. *Time Magazine*, 29 October 1973, 30.
57. Charles Liebman, "The Myth of Defeat", 399–418.
58. Mohammed Heikal, director of the daily *al-Ahram*, criticised publicly in his newspaper Sadat's US turn and the propaganda on the October War as a major Egyptian military victory, claiming instead it had been "nor victory, neither defeat". See Mohammed Heikal, *Road to Ramadan* (New York: Quadrangle, 1975).
59. Gihane Shahine, "From Suez to shanty town", *Al-Ahram Weekly*, 8–14 October 1988.
60. *Ibid.*
61. Baker, "Egypt's uncertain revolution", 158.
62. Dominic Coldwell, "Egypt's Autumn of Fury, the Construction of Opposition to the Egyptian–Israel Peace Process 1973–81" (Master of Philosophy, University of Oxford, 2003), 40.
63. *New Outlook*, 19 (1976), 73.
64. *al-Da'wa* (Cairo, September 1978).
65. "The Islamists argued that the Arab defeat of 1967 vindicated Qutb's arguments.

Launched under the banner of Arab socialism, the June War suggested that reliance on materialism alone could not be protected Egypt from Israeli encroachments." *al-Da'wa* (Cairo, September 1978).

66. Report on the 8th Conference of the Academy of Islamic Studies, 1977. See also Walid Mahmoud Abdelnasser, *The Islamic Movement in Egypt: Perceptions of International Relations, 1967–1981* (London: Kegan Paul International, 1994).

67. Coldwell, "Egypt's Autumn of Fury", 91.

68. Egyptian diplomat and former senior adviser to President Mubarak.

69. Avraham Hartman, "The view from Jerusalem" in Davis (ed.), *The October War*, 275.

70. Ze'ev Schiff, *October Earthquake* (New Jersey: Transaction Publisher, 1974), 311.

71. Chaim Herzog, *The War of Atonement* (Boston: Greenhill Books,1975).

72. *Ibid.*, 197.

73. Lomsky-Feder, "The discourse of psychology", 293.

15. GONE BUT NOT FORGOTTEN? THE OCCASIONAL LESSONS OF THE OCTOBER 1973 WAR

1. See E.H. Carr, *What is History?* (London: Penguin, 1990), 7–30.

2. Charles S. Liebman, "The Myth of Defeat: The Memory of the Yom Kippur War in Israeli Society", *Middle Eastern Studies* 29, 3 (1993), 413.

3. See Uri Bar-Joseph, *Hatzofeh Shenirdam: Hafta'at Yom Hakippurim Umekoroteha* [The Watchman Fell Asleep: The Surprise of Yom Kippur and its Sources] (Tel Aviv: Zmora Bitan, 2001), 532; Dani Asher, *Lishbor et HaKonceptzia* [Breaking the Concept] (Tel Aviv: Ma'arachot/Minstry of Defence Publishing), 400; Yossi Melman, "The Faithful Spy", *Ha'aretz* (in Hebrew), 17 December 2010. Memoirs of this time do of course exist from Egyptian and Syrian perspectives but they tend to be partial and not wholly objective in terms of their narrative, and accusation that can also be levelled at some Israeli accounts of the fighting. See for example Mohamed el-Gamasy, *The October War* (Cairo: American University of Cairo Press, 1993); Sa'ad el-Shazly, *The Crossing of the Suez* (San Francisco: American Mideast Research, 1989), 170–2.

4. Uri Bar-Joseph, "The Intelligence Chief who went Fishing in the Cold: How Maj. Gen. (res.) Eli Zeira Exposed the Identity of Israel's Best Source Ever", *Intelligence and National Security* 23, 2 (2008), 226–48. On the eve of war, UNIT 8200 deciphered a cable written by the Iraqi military attaché in Moscow to Baghdad, reporting that the Soviets believed that Syria and Egypt were about to launch a surprise attack. The distribution of the cable was delayed to the Israeli General Staff. In his testimony before the Agranat commission, Elazar claimed that had he received the cable sooner he would have definitely called up the reserves before

war broke out. See Amir Oren, "Yom Kippur as a case study: Intelligence and deterrence did not suffice", *Ha'aretz* (in English), 12 April 2013.

5. For the impact of the war on Anglo–American relations see Geraint Hughes, "Britain, the Transatlantic Alliance, and the Arab-Israeli war of 1973", *Journal of Cold War Studies* 10, 2 (2008), 3–40; Simon C. Smith, *Ending Empire in the Middle East: Britain, the United States and Post-war Decolonization* (London: Routledge, 2012), 147–58.

6. See Bertrand Russell, *A History of Western Philosophy* (London: Allen & Unwin, 1948), 592–601.

7. See Richard J. Aldrich, *GCHQ: The Uncensored Story of Britain's Most Secret Intelligence Agency* (London: HarperCollins, 2010), 297.

8. Samuel M. Katz, *Soldier Spies: Israeli Military Intelligence* (Novato, CA: Presido Press, 1994), 256–7.

9. Yigal Sheffy, "Our First Line of Defense: Intelligence and the Israeli National Security Perception" in Lars Christian Jenssen and Olav Riste (eds), *Intelligence in the Cold War: Organisation, Role and International Cooperation* (Oslo: Norwegian Institute for Defence Studies, 2001), 95.

10. Aharon Ze'evi-Farkash and Dov Tamari, *Eikh Neida? Mod'in, Mivtza'im, Mediniyut* [How Will We Know? Intelligence, Operations and State Politics] (Tel Aviv: Sifrei Aliyat Hagag/Yediot Books, 2011).

11. Uri Bar-Joseph, "Military Intelligence as the National Intelligence Estimator: The Case of Israel", *Armed Forces and Society* 36, 3 (2010), 512.

12. Ephraim Kahana, "Analysing Israel's Intelligence Failures", *International Journal of Intelligence and Counterintelligence* 18, 2(2005), 266–7.

13. Shlomo Brom, "The Steinetz Report: Israeli intelligence after Iraq", *Tel Aviv Notes* no. 103 (Jaffee Centre for Strategic Studies/University of Tel Aviv, 4 April 200), 1–2.

14. *Ibid.*, 2.

15. Aluf Benn, "Intelligence as moonlighting", *Ha'aretz* (in English), 1 April 2004.

16. Gideon Doron and Reuven Pedatzur, "Israeli Intelligence: Utility and Cost Effectiveness in Policy Formulation", *International Journal of Intelligence and Counterintelligence* 3, 3 (1989), 357–8.

17. Yair Evron, "Deterrence Experience in the Arab–Israeli Conflict" in Aharon Klieman and Ariel Levite (eds), *Deterrence in the Middle East: Where Theory and Practice Converge* (Boulder, CO: Westview Press, 1993), 107.

18. Emmanuel Sivan, "What the general is allowed", *Ha'aretz* (in English), 14 June 2004; Akiva Eldar, "Popular Misconceptions", *Ha'aretz* (in English), 11 June 2004. Former DMI Major General Amos Malka remained convinced that Arafat was caught by surprise by the outbreak of violence across the Occupied Territories following the failure of the Camp David accords to broker a deal between Israel and the Palestinians. By contrast his deputy, Amos Gilad who headed the

Research Division of AMAN, was adamant that there never was a Palestinian partner for peace.

19. Susan Hattis Rolef, "The Domestic Fallout of the Yom Kippur War", *Israel Affairs* 6, 1 (1999), 178.

20. Liebman, "The Myth of Defeat", 403.

21. Liebman, "The Myth of Defeat", 411.

22. Itamar Rabinovich, *The Lingering Conflict: Israel, the Arabs and the Middle East 1948–2011* (Washington, DC: Brookings Institute Press, 2011), 12.

23. Ahron Bregman and Jihan el-Thari, *The Fifty Years War: Israel and the Arabs* (London: Penguin/BBC Books, 1998), 108.

24. Yehezkel Dror, *Israeli Statecraft: National Security Challenges and Responses* (London: Routledge, 2011).

25. Eli Podeh, "Israel never wanted peace", *Ha'aretz* (in Hebrew) 16 December 2010

26. Amir Oren, "How Israeli and US leaders ignored the Arab drums of war in 1973", *Ha'aretz* (in English), 8 October 2011.

27. Quoted in Avi Kober, "Great Power Involvement and Israeli Battlefield Success in the Arab–Israeli Wars 1948–1982", *Journal of Cold War Studies* 8, 1 (2006), 42.

28. *Ibid.*, 42.

29. Meron Medzini, "Israel's evolving security concept", *Middle East Review of International Affairs* 14, 4 (2010), 91.

30. The policy of restraint in this instance actually had overwhelming public support. See Aharon Levan, *Israeli Strategy after Desert Storm* (London: Frank Cass, 1997), 5.

31. Medzini, "Israel's evolving security concept", 92.

32. Rabinovich, *The Lingering Conflict*, 27–54.

33. See Efaim Inbar, "Israeli Defense: The Arab Uprisings' Impact", *Middle East Quarterly* 19, 1 (Winter 2012), 41–2.

34. Zvi Bar'el, "Israel suffers from political alzheimer's disease", *Ha'aretz*, 8 January 2012. Other analysts go further, arguing that Israel's failure to take seriously the Arab peace initiative launched in Beirut in the spring of 2002 is part of a pattern by Israeli governments anxious not to upset a status quo that seems favourable to their interests. See Eli Podeh, "Israel never really wanted peace", *Ha'aretz* (in Hebrew), 16 December 2010.

35. Author's interview with Dr Ephraim Kam, deputy director, Institute for National Security Studies, Tel Aviv, 2 November 2011.

36. Daniel Byman, "Israels Pessimistic view of the Arab Spring", *The Washington Quarterly* 34, 3 (2011), 123.

37. Zvi Bar'el, "Israels take on Arab spring may undo peace with Egypt", *Ha'aretz* (in English) 30 November 2011.

38. Morten Valbjørn and André Bank, "The New Arab Cold War: rediscovering the Arab dimension of Middle East regional politics", *Review of International Studies* 38, (2012), 15.

INDEX

INDEX

Cohen, Elliot: 15

Cohen, Stuart: 'Operational Limitations of Reserve Forces: The Lessons of the 1973 War', 21

Colby, William: Director of CIA, 90, 175

Cold War: 4, 9, 13, 47, 173, 213, 259, 264; end of, 152; state system, 27

Cox, Archibald: Watergate Special Prosecutor, 85

Cromer, Lord (Rowland Baring): British Ambassador to USA, 182

Cuba: oil imports of, 192

Cuban Missile Crisis (1962): 96

Daoud, Abu: imprisonment of (1972), 123–4; Military Commander of Fatah, 123

Dayan, Moshe: 17–18, 31–2, 37, 39, 41, 43–5, 220; Israeli Defence Minister, 5, 16, 30, 200, 207–8, 212, 215, 235; memoirs of, 19, 25

Democratic Front for the Liberation of Palestine (DFLP): 146, 151–2

Democratic Republic of Vietnam (North Vietnam): 87–8

Denmark: 163; Copenhagen, 161, 163

détente: criticisms of, 192; decline of, 117; opposition to, 109, 117; Soviet use of, 4, 87, 94–5, 101–3, 105, 113–14, 117

al-Din, Ahmad Baha: 64

Dinitz, Simcha: 20, 93; Head of Private Office of Golda Meier, 35; Israeli Ambassador to USA, 40, 91, 129, 226

Dobynin, Anatoly: 95, 110, 113; Soviet Ambassador to USA, 90, 99

Doron, Gideon: 255

Douglas-Home, Alec: 158; British Foreign Secretary, 156

Eban, Abba: 32, 36, 42, 47, 226; Israeli Foreign Minister, 31, 89, 93, 158

el-Edroos, Ali: 123

Egypt: 1–4, 6–8, 11, 14, 25, 29–30, 33, 43, 61, 66, 71, 86, 99, 103, 105, 121, 137, 149, 168–9, 174, 196, 210, 223, 231, 242, 248, 250, 255, 262; Abu Rudeis, 244; Alexandria, 54–5, 72–3, 81–2, 204; Armed Forces Supreme Council, 50, 52; Burj al 'Arab, 72; Cairo, 5, 16, 50–5, 58–63, 65–6, 73–4, 79, 89, 95, 105, 108–9, 112, 122–3, 158, 164, 166, 169, 221–2, 244, 259–60, 262, 264; Coptic Christian population of, 245; Deversoir, 59–60; economy of, 49; Free Officers Movement, 244; Ismaïlia, 59; Kilometer 101, 219–23, 226, 228; military of, 5–6, 15, 41–2, 56–7, 59–62, 66, 74–5, 90–1, 94–6, 104, 110–12, 197, 199, 204, 206, 210, 212–13, 218–21, 225, 242; National Assembly, 77, 258; National Security Council, 55; navy of, 72, 221; 'Opening, the (al-intifah)', 62–3, 66; People's Council, 60; Presidential Information Bureau, 197–9; Ra's al-Tin, 72; Revolution (2011), 233, 245, 262; signatory of Camp David Accords (1978), 3; Sharm el-Sheikh, 32, 54, 58; Suez Canal, 5–6, 34–6, 38, 40, 49, 53–6, 59, 61–3, 65–6, 74, 80, 88–9, 95, 104, 106, 130, 199, 215, 217–18, 220, 222–4, 258

Egyptian-Israeli Peace Treaty (1979): 30, 66, 77, 99, 168, 233, 261;

319

INDEX

INDEX

Romania: 214

Rubin, Barry: 19

Ruckelshaus, William: resignation of (1973), 85; US Deputy Attorney General, 85

Russian Federation: 262

Ryan, Curtis: 119, 124

Sachar, Howard Morely: 18

Sadat, Anwar: 20, 49–50, 52–4, 58, 60–1, 63–5, 71–2, 74, 81–2, 86, 88, 96, 98–9, 104–5, 107, 109, 112, 114, 116, 125, 159, 205, 208, 210–11, 217, 220, 264; assassination of (1981), 245; defence policies of, 50–1, 56, 104; disbanding of New Wafd and NPUP, 245; expulsion of Soviet military advisers, 36; foreign policy of, 7, 18, 20, 34–5, 42, 55–6, 62–3, 77, 103, 110, 176, 201, 206, 213–15, 222, 243; issuing of Law of Shame (1980), 245; meeting in Cairo (1973), 122; meeting with King Faisal of Saudi Arabia (1973), 175, 201; memoirs of, 204; President of Egypt, 7, 250; role in Camp David Accords, 168; speech to National Assembly (1971), 88, 258; speech to People's Council, 60; visit to Jerusalem (1977), 82, 229, 240, 244

Sadek, Mohammed Ahmed: Egyptian War Minister, 15

Safran, Nadav: 'Trail by Ordeal: The October War, October 1973', 14

Said, Edward: 140

Salem, Abboud: defection to Jordan, 122

Sallam, Dr Beleid Abdul: Algerian Minister of Industry and Energy, 159

Saudi Arabia: 4, 55, 60, 128, 156, 158, 176–8, 185, 262–3; government of, 174; role in founding of OAPEC, 174; oil embargo against USA (1973–4), 177

Sauvagnargues, Jean: French Foreign Minister, 164; meeting with Mahmoud Riad (1974), 164

Sayigh, Anis: resignation of, 150

Scheel, Walter: West German Foreign Minister, 158

Schiff, Ze'ev: 18, 246

Schlesinger, James: 91, 183, 186; support for use of Military Aircraft Command, 92; US Defense Secretary, 90, 97, 111, 181–2

Schmidt, Helmut: West German Chancellor, 166, 169

Scowcroft, Brent: US Deputy National Security Adviser, 98

Seale, Patrick: 77–8; *Asad: The Struggle for the Middle East*, 69–70, 73–4, 80–1

Second World War (1939–45): 27, 161; Holocaust (Shoah), 247–8; Operation Barbarossa (1941), 22, 25, 27–8; Pearl Harbour Attack (1941), 22, 25, 27–8

Segev, Arieh: 236–7

Shafiq, Munir: 148, 150

Bin Shaker, Zeid: 125, 130; Chief of Staff of Jordanian Military, 123

Shakkur, Yusuf: Syrian Chief of Staff, 72

Shalev, Brigadier General Aryeh: 37, 252; criticised by Agranat National Committee of Inquiry, 44

Shalom, Zaki: 19

Shapiro, Michael J.: 46

Sharaf, Sami: Head of Presidential Information Bureau, 199

INDEX